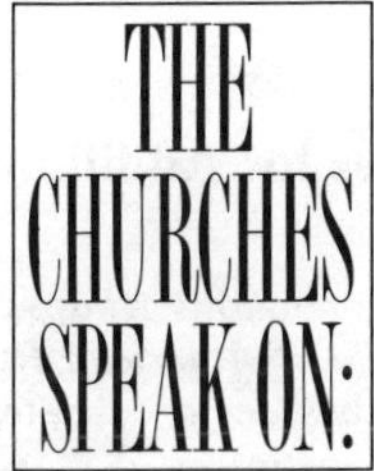

DATE			

Sources for Additional Research

For further information on the religious groups covered in this publication, consult J. Gordon Melton's *Encyclopedia of American Religions*, which contains information on approximately 1,600 churches, sects, cults, temples, societies, missions, and other North American religious organizations.

For additional information on the beliefs held by the religious groups covered in this publication consult the *Encyclopedia of American Religions: Religious Creeds*, a companion volume to the *Encyclopedia of American Religions*, which provides the creeds, confessions, statements of faith, and articles of religion of the groups covered.

To locate organizations concerned with the topics covered in this publication, consult the following terms in the Name and Keyword Index to Gale's *Encyclopedia of Associations*:

- Alternate Lifestyles
- Gay
- Gay/Lesbian
- Homophile
- Homosexual
- Lesbian
- Sexual Health

ISSN 1043-9609

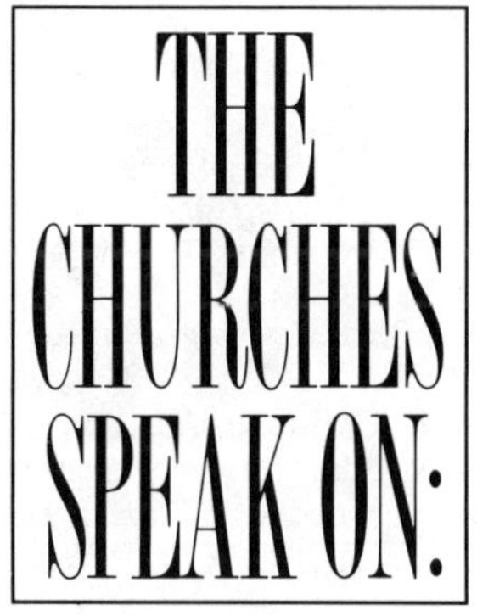

Homosexuality

Official Statements from Religious Bodies and Ecumenical Organizations

J. Gordon Melton

Gale Research Inc. • DETROIT • NEW YORK • LONDON

J. Gordon Melton

Gale Research Inc. Staff

Amy Lucas, *Senior Editor*

Bradley J. Morgan and Jill Ohorodnik, *Project Coordinators*

Aided by: Terri Kessler

Donald G. Dillaman, *Programming Consultant*

Victoria B. Cariappa, *Research Manager*
Jack Radike, *Research Supervisor*
Joseph Schroeder, *Editorial Associate*
Lisa Lantz, Philip Naud, and Dolores Perelli, *Editorial Assistants*

Mary Beth Trimper, *Production Manager*
Marilyn Jackman, *External Production Associate*

Arthur Chartow, *Art Director*
C. J. Jonik, *Keyliner*

Laura Bryant, *Production Supervisor*
Louise Gagné, *Internal Production Associate*
Yolanda Y. Latham, *Internal Production Assistant*

835 Penobscot Bldg.
Detroit, MI 48226-4094

ISBN 0-8103-7646-6
ISSN 1043-9609

Printed in the United States of America

Published simultaneously in the United Kingdom
by Gale Research International Limited
(An affiliated company of Gale Research Inc.)

Contents

Statements

Roman Catholic Church

Statements in this section are arranged chronologically by issuing date.

Protestant and Eastern Orthodox Churches

This section is arranged alphabetically by individual church, religious body, or ecumenical organization; the statements issued by each organization are presented chronologically within that organization.

Jewish Groups

Statements are presented chronologically.

Other Religious Bodies

This section is arranged alphabetically by individual church, religious body, or ecumenical organization; the statements issued by each organization are presented chronologically within that organization.

Preface

The Churches Speak is a quarterly series of monographs which systematically brings together the major official pronouncements of North American religious bodies and ecumenical organizations on the issues dominating today's headlines. Each monograph is devoted to a single topic and provides an overview of the topic itself, its historical background, and the full range of opinions found in the individual church statements. The statements themselves provide a unique and conveniently arranged survey of opinion on important contemporary issues, cutting across theological and denominational boundaries to influence the climate of social and political thought in our culture.

The formal statements issued by churches and other religious bodies are intended primarily to inform and guide their members, adherents, and supporters on the issue in question. These statements often attain additional importance, however, since they also exert influence on the actions of the religious agencies, clergy, and church administrators who initiate, direct, and regulate organizational programs. Church statements are also indirectly aimed at nonchurch members, in an attempt to alter public policy, mobilize public opinion, or advocate changes in legislation. And they can also become the focal point of intense controversy, functioning as the bulwark against which many people direct their dissent on a given issue. This controversy can become magnified within the issuing organization itself, when a significant minority of its members dissent from the positions taken by its hierarchies, judicatories, and boards of social concerns.

Focus is on Contemporary Topics From Major Religious Bodies

Each issue of *The Churches Speak* focuses on a single topic or a few closely related topics chosen for their high current public interest. Topics covered represent a wide range of vital social and political issues, such as AIDS, abortion, racism, the Middle East, euthanasia, capital punishment, and the ordination of women. Statements of major North American churches and religious organizations are included for each topic, providing comprehensive representation of the full range of opinions held on each topic.

The documents included in *The Churches Speak* were obtained through a mailing to all of the religious bodies in North America with more than 100,000 members. On any given issue, additional churches and religious organizations (including some outside of North America), and even some secular organizations known to have a special interest in the topic under consideration, were also solicited for their statements. Other statements have been identified in the files of the Institute for the Study of American Religion in Santa Barbara, California.

While most large churches and religious bodies make formal statements on important issues, it should be noted that many of the more than 1,500 denominations and religious organizations located in North America will not formulate any official statement or speak out on such issues. A number of religious bodies, including some of the largest denominations, do not make such statements as a matter of principle. Rather, they choose to leave actions and beliefs concerning social issues strictly up to individual effort and opinion.

Authentic Texts Used for All Statements

The statements presented in this series are in their authentic form, although obvious typographical errors have been corrected. The original wording, grammar, and punctuation of each statement remains intact. No attempt has been made to introduce foreign material or explanatory notes into the body of the statement's text.

Arrangement and Content

Each issue of *The Churches Speak* begins with an introductory essay which provides an overview of the topic itself and traces its recent historical manifestations. This essay also summarizes, compares, and contrasts the opinions found in the individual statements, allowing the user to place each one in the appropriate context. Each essay concludes with bibliographic citations to sources for further reading on the topic.

The statements presented in each monograph are arranged into four main sections based on broad religious families or traditions: The Roman Catholic Church (which represents the single largest religious body in the United States); Protestant and Eastern Orthodox Churches; Jewish Groups; and Other Religious Bodies.

Within the Roman Catholic Church section, statements are arranged chronologically by issuing date. The remaining sections are subarranged alphabetically by individual churches, religious bodies, or ecumenical organizations; the statements issued by each organization are presented chronologically within that organization.

Each of the four religious family sections is preceded by a note which provides background information on the family and analysis of its perspective on the issue in question. Individual statements contain the following elements:

Issuing organization. The name of the religious body or ecumenical organization issuing the statement.

Statement name. The actual or formal title of the statement. When no formal title is given, a descriptive title has been assigned.

Text of statement. The text of the statement is presented in its original form.

Notes. These appear in italic type following the text of each statement. When applicable, these remarks provide background information on the issuing organization's membership size and geographic distribution, and details about the circumstances under which the statement was made—including when it was passed, why it was passed, and whether or not it is binding on church members.

Index to Organizations, Statements, and Subjects Provided

To facilitate access to the material presented, each issue of *The Churches Speak* contains an Index to Organizations, Statements, and Subjects included in that issue. The index lists, in a single alphabetical sequence, the full titles of all the statements, the names of all religious bodies and ecumenical organizations mentioned in the statements' texts and notes, and specific subjects covered within the statements. Statement titles and organization names are also listed by important keywords that appear in their titles/names. Citations in the index refer to page numbers; page numbers rendered in boldface after an organization name indicate the location of that organization's statement(s) within the main text.

Sources of Additional Information

Additional information on many of the religious bodies covered in *The Churches Speak* can be found in the *Encyclopedia of American Religions.* The *Encyclopedia* provides details on approximately 1600 religious and spiritual groups in the United States and Canada, and is divided into two parts. The first part contains an essay covering the development of American religion, an essay providing a historical survey of religion in Canada, and historical essays grouped by general religious family. The second part contains directory sections listing individual churches and groups constituting the religious families discussed in the historical essays.

A companion volume, the *Encyclopedia of American Religions: Religious Creeds,* provides a comprehensive compilation of 464 religious creeds, confessions, statements of faith, summaries of belief, and articles of religion currently acknowledged by many of the churches or religious groups described in the *Encyclopedia of American Religions*. It also includes extensive notes on the history and textual variations of creeds, reflecting changing social, political, and doctrinal climates throughout the centuries. The material is arranged by major religious families, following, with minor variations, the approach used in the *Encyclopedia.*

Institute for the Study of American Religion

The Institute for the Study of American Religion was founded in 1969 for the purpose of researching and disseminating information about the numerous religious groups in the United States. More recently, the Institute's scope has been expanded to include religious groups in Canada, making it the only research facility of its kind to cover so broad a range of activity. After being located for many years in Evanston, Illinois, the Institute moved to Santa Barbara, California, in 1985. At that time, its collection of more than 25,000 books and its extensive files covering individual religious groups were donated to the Special Collections department of the library of the University of California—Santa Barbara. *The Churches Speak* has been compiled in part from the Institute's collection.

Suggestions Are Welcome

Users with particular questions about a religious group, suggested topics for coverage in or changes to *The Churches Speak,* or other information are invited to write to the Institute in care of its Director:

Dr. J. Gordon Melton
Institute for the Study of American Religion
Box 90709
Santa Barbara, CA 93190-0709

Introductory Essay:

The Churches' Ethical Dilemma with Homosexuality

In the decades since World War II, religious groups in the West have undergone a profound change in their position on homosexuality. This change has been related to the dramatic altering of the position of the homosexual community, which has become increasingly visible and accepted as an element of contemporary secular society. For some groups, the sheer visibility of the "gay" community has forced a reassertion of tradition sexual values which define homosexuality as an illegitimate sexual practice. For others, it has been a time of profound rethinking of the nature of human sexuality with a resultant emergence of a spectrum of opinion on homosexuality, from its complete acceptance as normal sexual behavior to be celebrated and pursued, to a staunch denial of homosexual practice coupled with programs for changing the homosexual's orientation. During the 1970s and 1980s, most church bodies (which had been silent on the issue) were forced to face homosexuality and take a public stand on the morality of specifically homosexual behavior, the presence of homosexuals in their membership, and the acceptability of homosexuals as candidates for ministry.

Kinsey and Wolfenden: The Early Reports

The issue of homosexuality cannot be separated from the complete rethinking of sexuality that has occurred during the twentieth century; however, certain events stand out as particularly important in forcing a reconsideration of homosexuality. The most important of these is the watershed "Kinsey" report on male sexuality published in 1948. The report, *Sexual Behavior of the Human Male* by Alfred Kinsey, A. C. Pomeroy, and C. E. Martin, placed two items on the rethinking homosexuality agenda. First, Kinsey and his colleagues discovered a much higher percentage of involvement in homosexual behavior than expected. Of the men questioned, four percent were exclusively homosexual, and an additional 10 percent were exclusively homosexual during a period of three or more years at some point in their adult life. But over one-third of the male population had had a significant homosexual encounter during their adult years. Secondly, the report highlighted the distinction that quickly became commonplace in considering the nature of homosexuality—the difference between homosexuality, the preference for sexual relationships with individuals of one's own gender, and homosexual behavior, the specific actions of a sexual nature performed with a person of one's own gender.

That is to say, there is a percentage of the population (at least five percent, but the exact figure is still a matter of dispute) that possesses a strong sexual attraction to people of the same sex. Some of these people actively and regularly pursue sexual contact, while for some sexual contact may vary from frequently to never (i.e., celibacy). In addition there are millions of men who are neither exclusively nor predominantly homosexual who have had homosexual encounters.

Out of the Kinsey report and other research in sexology has come an understanding of humans as being neither exclusively male nor female, neither exclusively heterosexual nor homosexual. Kinsey began to view humans as existing on a scale of masculine-feminine and heterosexual-homosexual. Contemporary psychology tends also to see each person as made up of both masculine and feminine aspects in varying proportions. Some females have a high masculine component while some males have a high female component. In this regard, while many men experience little or no homosexual urge in their personality, many others, if not the majority, have some, and a few have a predominant homosexual component. The same can be said of females.[1]

Second only to the Kinsey report is the *Wolfenden Report*, a report prepared by a committee of the British Parliament. The committee, originally suggested by the Moral Welfare Council of the Church of England and chaired by Sir John Wolfenden, produced a detailed study of both homosexuality and prostitution in England. In its consideration of the homosexual community, the widely publicized report, building on Kinsey and other studies of homosexuality, offered extensive recommendations concerning the decriminalization of homosexual activity. It concluded that "homosexual behavior between consenting adults in private should no longer be a criminal offense." Originally released in 1957, an American edition of the report was published in 1963 with a laudatory introduction by Dr. Karl Menninger. It quickly took its place beside the Kinsey report, and the two became the most quoted documents in the emergence of homosexuality in the last generation.

Organization of the Homosexual Community

The Kinsey report suggested to anyone who could count that the number of homosexuals in the United States numbered in the millions (from as few as five to as many as 15). That fact alone may have encouraged the second event that confronted the churches with the issue of homosexuality: the establishment of visible organizations to speak for the homosexual community and lobby for legal and other changes in the way society treats homosexuals. While prior to World War II there were several homosexual organizations, they were short lived and of little consequence. Among the first such organizations to form after the war was the Mattachine Society, formed in 1950 in Los Angeles. By 1952 there were 18 chapters in the greater Los Angeles metropolitan area, and it was joined by a second organization, One, Inc. The emergence of these two organizations and their spread to the East Coast came at the same time Senator Joseph McCarthy was conducting his hunt for communists. One focus of his attention was the movie industry, and along with accusations of suspected communist sympathy, he charged a number of individuals with homosexuality.

The Mattachine Society is generally credited with being the organization that conceived of homosexuals as a "minority group" in American society that should be treated as other minorities. This proved to be an important reconceptualization of the homosexual community and offered a way homosexuals could begin to demand their civil rights under the law. It would prove of immense significance once the civil rights movements for blacks and females experienced their successes in the 1960s and 1970s.

In San Francisco, California, in 1955, the first of the contemporary lesbian (female homosexual) organizations was formed, the Daughters of Bilitis. The eight founders seem to have been unaware of either the Mattachine Society or One, Inc., though they soon made contact with them and found some common cause.

The role of lesbians in the developing movement to recognize homosexuals is of vast importance on a number of levels, especially as they were able to become integrated in the women's movement. At the same time, in the fight for recognition of homosexuals in the churches, lesbians have remained largely invisible. While it is common in the homosexual community to distinguish male homosexuals and lesbians as two distinct if related phenomena, in the religious literature, that distinction is rare. The entire community (both male and female) has been treated simply as "the homosexuals," with little attempt to see them in their separate uniqueness.

The early homosexual organizations were relatively limited in their approach. Their programs centered upon assisting homosexuals with adjusting to the problems inherent in living in a hostile environment, trying to have laws against homosexuals revoked, and trying to counteract views of homosexuality as an illness. In effect, the older organizations attempted to create a safe space where homosexuals could quietly live without continual persecution by the larger society.

A new era for homosexuals began in the summer of 1969. In spite of a 1966 order which prohibited police from entrapping homosexuals in New York City, harassment of the local community continued. On the evening of June 27, 1969, such harassment led to a riot by angry patrons of the Stonewall Inn, a predominantly homosexual bar on Christopher Street in Greenwich Village. The confrontation with the police continued for four nights. This action, so unique in the history of the homosexual community, marked a turning point from the normally passive approach of the community. It led to the formation of the Gay Liberation Front in July 1969, and the emergence of the term "gay" in popular culture to describe the new assertive homosexual. With the successes of the civil rights movement in the South, gay people saw the chance not just to create some safe space but to move into the center of the culture. Over the next two years gay life emerged in all of the major metropolitan centers in the United States and spread to Canada and Europe.

Under the banner of "gay power" (a term derived from "black power"), homosexuals "came out of the closet" (i.e., publicly identified themselves as homosexuals) and began to create a gay subculture in the midst of a society which became increasingly tolerant (if not supportive) and accepting (if not approving). A major victory was scored in 1973 when the American Psychological Association declared that homosexuality was not an illness. The movement has encountered tremendous resistance but has settled in for the long fight to have its position in the culture secured in law and in the market place. In the process it has created a high profile for the "gay lifestyle," an openly gay existence with no apologies for the individual's homosexuality. Within the gay world, the homosexual's life is seen as merely one alternative lifestyle among many from which one could choose, with as much right to exist as any. Homosexuality, like skin color, is simply a fact of life for some people, and, as such, is morally neutral.

The Development of the Gay Church

Throughout the twentieth century, Christian churches have treated the phenomenon of homosexuality as quietly as possible. It was not simply a sin like other forms of sexual misbehavior, such as adultery or fornication. It was an abomination, a phenomenon so abhorred that it was only rarely called by name, but referred to by a number of polite circumlocutions. Within some churches, especially the Roman Catholic Church, the Church of England, and the Episcopal Church, a number of homosexuals were known to have found a home within the all-male communities of priests and brothers, a fact rarely acknowledged unless one was caught in an indiscretion. After World War II, however, that situation began to change. That time period saw the emergence of churches organized to serve the homosexual community and various ministries to homosexuals which were positioned along the broad spectrum of churchly responses to the newly visible gay community.

Possibly the first church organized primarily for homosexuals was formed in Atlanta, Georgia, in 1946. George Hyde, then a young minister in the independent Catholic movement, held the first services for approximately 85 people on Christmas Eve of that year in the Cotton Blossom Room, a gay cocktail room. The congregation took the name Eucharistic Catholic Church. In 1954, Hyde placed an announcement concerning the congregation in *One*, the magazine of the Mattachine Society. Among those who responded to the announcement was Michael F. Itkin. Hyde licensed Itkin as a minister for the congregation the following year and ordained him in 1957.

Hyde and Itkin would both become important figures in the gay church movement. Hyde, consecrated a bishop in 1959, took his following into the American Holy Orthodox Catholic Church and a few years later formed the Orthodox Catholic Church of America. The new denomination was not a gay church, but has continued a strong ministry to homosexuals over the years.

Michael Itkin became one of the more well-known gay activists during the 1970s and 1980s. He refused to follow Hyde into the American Holy Orthodox Catholic Church, an act he perceived to be a backing away from the commitment to homosexual church members. With his supporters he reorganized the congregation and formed the Primitive Catholic Church (Evangelical Catholic). He was consecrated a bishop in 1960 by Archbishop Christopher Maria Stanley, an independent bishop. Stanley traced his orders back to Ulric Vernon Herford, who had formed and led the Evangelical Catholic Communion, a small autonomous church in England. After several name changes, Itkin's body emerged as an American branch of the Evangelical Catholic Communion.

Over the years Itkin would write, speak, and demonstrate (occasionally in ways that embarrassed even his gay friends) for homosexual rights and work toward the development of an inclusive gay liturgy. After a period in the 1970s in which he renounced his episcopacy, he again assumed his leadership of an independent gay Catholic church called the Community of the Love of Christ (Evangelical Catholic). Itkin died of AIDS in 1989. During his last years he worked almost exclusively in San Francisco.

Several other openly gay churches formed over the years, but none became as significant to the homosexual community as the Universal Fellowship of Metropolitan Community Churches. The Metropolitan Community Church originated in the experience of Troy Perry, a Pentecostal minister who during the 1960s went through the experience of discovering and accepting his homosexuality. He recounted his story in his autobiography, *The Lord Is My Shepherd and He Knows I'm Gay* (1972). The early years of the church occurred just as the gay rights movement emerged, and the church quickly identified itself as a religious branch of the movement. The charismatic Perry soon drew not only a large congregation but other ministers from different denominations who had followed a similar pilgrimage. The church grew quickly and developed a well-trained leadership from among the mainline Protestant ministers who came into its ranks.

The Church Addresses the Homosexual Question

While church ethicists and biblical scholars had addressed the issue of homosexuality in books and articles throughout the century, the beginning of an open dialogue between church leaders and the homosexual community can be traced to the formation of the Council on Religion and the Homosexual in San Francisco in 1964. Methodist minister Ted McIlvenna, working with the Glide Urban Center, a private foundation with ties to the Glide Memorial (Methodist) Church, was confronted with the homosexuality of the people among whom he was called to minister. Becoming conscious of the lack of concern for homosexuals by most mainline Protestant churches, he called a meeting of leaders in the homosexual community and a group of ministers from the United Church of Christ, Episcopal, Methodist, and Lutheran churches. The gathering was held at a retreat center in Marin County, California. The three-day meeting led to the formation of the council, which was immediately faced with the problem of educating and sensitizing the several denominations to problems within the homosexual community.

The council moved to bring ministers from other denominations into the discussions. The local Episcopal diocese, then under the leadership of Bishop James A. Pike, responded with the formation of a diocesan Joint Committee on Homosexuality. The most substantive response came from the United Church of Christ, whose Council for Christian Social Action devoted the December 1976 issue of *Social Action*, the denominational magazine on social issues, to homosexuality and questions of civil liberties. The United Church of Christ would go on to become the Christian denomination most supportive of the homosexual community.

Meanwhile, the council set itself the task of promoting a continuing program of dialogue between the religious community and homosexuals. It promoted national meetings for discussion of theological and ethical issues arising from the homosexual experience. It also sent representatives to conferences on homosexuality and religion sponsored by other organizations. In 1966, the council extended its outreach to England through its participation in an international "Consultation on Church, Society, and the Homosexual," sponsored by a number of British and American denominations.

As the denominations took up the issues surrounding homosexuality in the 1970s, the council was superseded by a host of denominational organizations promoting the cause of homosexuals within each of the major denominations. Possibly the first of these denominational caucuses was Dignity, an organization of gay Roman Catholics and their supporters. Other similar organizations include Integrity (Episcopal), Affirmation (United Methodist), Presbyterians for Lesbian/Gay Concerns, United Church Coalition for Lesbian/Gay Concerns (United Church of Christ), Lutherans Concerned/North America, and Evangelicals Concerned (various conservative Evangelical denominations). These organizations took the lead in voicing the concerns of the homosexual community as the issue of homosexuality came to the fore during the last two decades. During the 1970s, they promoted a variety of legislation which they hoped would lead the churches to study and reexamine the question of homosexuality as it related to Christian faith, support civil rights for homosexuals, open congregations to the participation of homosexuals, and admit homosexuals to the ordained ministry.

During the 1970s the major North American and British churches diligently studied, deepened, and reevaluated their stance on homosexuality and homosexual behavior. They were aided in this regard by a number of books more or less sympathetic to the homosexual community. Among the most frequently cited were *Is Gay Good? Ethics, Theology, and Homosexuality*; *Loving Women/Loving Men: Gay Liberation and the Church*; *The Church and the Homosexual*; *Is the Homosexual My Neighbor?*; *Jonathan Loved David: Homosexuality in Biblical Times*; *Homosexuality and the Christian Faith: A Symposium*; and *Homosexuality and Ethics*. Throughout the decade of the 1970s, the question of homosexuality would become the hottest issue in the churches (and synagogues) of North America.

Biblical Approaches

Prior to 1970, both the Jewish community and the Christian churches had developed what could be termed a traditional consensus opinion of homosexuality. That opinion, universally hostile among both Jews and Christians, looked for its foundation in the Bible, which at first glance seems to offer a strong and straightforward condemnation of homosexual practice. However, the traditional stance against homosexuality was developed in a period prior to modern biblical criticism, which has suggested that many biblical passages can be more accurately understood in the light of modern critical scholarly approaches. It was possible that modern biblical scholarship had some reflections to offer on the several passages commonly cited as condemning homosexuality.

The most frequently cited biblical passage concerning homosexuality, of course, is the story of the town of Sodom which appears in Genesis 19:4–11. The story of Sodom (from which the term "sodomy" for anal intercourse is derived) relates the arrival of some strangers (in this case some angelic visitors traveling incognito) who take shelter for the evening in the home of a man named Lot. An angry crowd gathers in front of the house and demands that Lot produce the strangers that they might "know" them. "Know" is a term frequently used in the Hebrew to mean "to have sexual relations with." It would seem that such a knowing between the crowd (composed primarily of men) and the male strangers would have to be of a homosexual nature, and so it has been traditionally interpreted. In response, Lot proposes that he provide his daughters as substitutes. (Nothing happens, however, as the angels blind the crowd.)

Bolstering the standard interpretation of this passage are various passages elsewhere in the Bible that indicate the extreme sinfulness of the city, sinfulness which eventually led to its destruction. The prophet Ezekiel (16:50), for example, says that Sodom "committed abomination" before God. The Christian New Testament seems to say it in the most unmistakable terms. The Epistle of Jude (6–7) notes that the people of Sodom (and its sister city of Gomorrah) were fornicators who also went after "strange flesh." Thus, that Sodom was destroyed because of its sin, that its sin was deemed especially despicable, and that the sin of Sodom was believed to be homosexuality suggested to many commentators that homosexuality is an especially sinful act.

Within the Jewish Bible (i.e., the Christian Old Testament) two passages are frequently cited as condemnatory of homosexuality, both appearing in what is termed the "Holiness Code" in the Book of Leviticus. Leviticus 18:22, speaking to male Hebrews, says: "You shall not lie with mankind, as with womankind: it is an abomination" (the same word Ezekiel used to describe the sin of Sodom). Leviticus 20:13 reiterates the earlier admonition and adds a penalty, "if a man lie with mankind as with womankind, both of them have committed abomination; they shall surely be put to death; their blood shall be upon them." In Deuteronomy 23:17, homosexuality is mentioned in the condemnation of Canaanite sacred male prostitution.

In like measure, the Christian New Testament treats homosexual behavior, at least in passing. In Romans 1:26–27, the Apostle Paul reminds his readers of the fate of the Gentiles who knew God in their hearts but did not follow his will. God gave them up to dishonorable passion. Women gave up natural relations for unnatural ones, and men gave up natural relations (with women) and committed shameful acts with other men. In his First Epistle to the Corinthians (6:9–10) he warns that men who abuse themselves with other men shall not inherit the kingdom. Finally, the writer of the First Epistle of Timothy 1:9–10 (believed by many to be Paul or one of his students) also condemns those who abuse themselves with other men.

Both Jews and Christians who oppose homosexuality and homosexual behavior generally cite the above passages as their standard biblical authority for believing that homosexuality is simply sin, which, like other sins (such as murder, thievery, adultery, or idolatry) lies outside of accepted behavior for humans. The commission of such sins is a matter of choice in action and hence justly carries with it the condemnation of God and society. The reexamination of the key passages cited above, conducted in bits and pieces throughout the twentieth century, found an initial systematic treatment in Derrick Sherwin Bailey's landmark volume *Homosexuality and the Western Christian Tradition* (1955). Most reinterpretations of these passages draw heavily upon Bailey. Essential to Bailey's work and the biblical reconsiderations which have followed is the distinction between the person who is homosexual by nature and the person who on occasion commits homosexual acts even though s/he is primarily heterosexual by nature. Homosexuality as a condition of a person's psychic makeup is, argues Bailey (and most moral theologians since him), a morally neutral fact. Homosexuality may, however, find expression in specific actions, any of which may be subject to moral evaluation. Bailey offers as an initial possibility that the scripture may only condemn some homosexual actions, just as it condemns some heterosexual actions (for example, rape) while leaving others as morally acceptable.

In addition to the reworking of traditional interpretations of the biblical material, by the time the gay liberation movement emerged, ethicists had raised the issue of situational ethics. Situational, or contextual, ethics attempted to focus attention on those situations which seemed to demand actions in violation of legal norms. In its common presentation, situational ethics suggested that the demand to love other people occasionally presented ethically complex judgments in which the correct action (the loving action) would be opposite the legal regulation. The major motivation leading to the development of situational ethics seemed to be the need to offer guidance in new situations as yet open to moral clarification (for example, the control over life possible with new medical technology). The application of situational ethics to sexual questions dominated much of the public debate.

During the 1970s, professional counselors presented a strong case that a significant number of personal situations existed in which the traditional church rule of limiting sexual intercourse to marriage was not appropriate and that such extramarital sexual activity was acceptable. Again, public debate centered upon heterosexual, primarily premarital, sex, but the implications of the debate were by no means lost in the reconsideration of homosexual issues. In general, when arguing for the limitations of traditional sexual standards, religious leaders would appeal to the "pastoral" context, i.e., to situations encountered in personal contact with parishioners.

In his attempt to reinterpret the Sodom story, Bailey suggests that proper understanding hinges upon the different uses of the Hebrew verb translated "to know." In some places, such as the Adam and Eve story in the Book of Genesis, it obviously means sexual intercourse, i.e., to know in a most personal way. However, in many cases it has its more simple meaning "to have knowledge of." Bailey suggests that the men of Sodom were merely attempting to check the credentials of the visitors. Their actions constituted a violation of common laws of hospitality. Roman Catholic ethicist John J. McNeill largely follows Bailey's interpretation. Episcopalian Tom Horner argues that Bailey's exegesis fails because of the second use of the verb "to know" in relation to Lot's daughters, where it undoubtedly means sexual intercourse. He suggests, however, that the sin of Sodom was not homosexuality but rape. Horner's view is derived from Lot's offer of his daughters as an acceptable but heterosexual alternative. In Horner's view the Sodom story is parallel to another story in the nineteenth chapter of the Book of Judges. In this story men of the city of Gibeah demand the body of a stranger and are in turn given a concubine. In the Sodom story the attempted rape is stopped by the angels who blind the men in the crowd. In the Gibeah story, there is no angelic force present to stop the rape of the concubine.

The simple account of Sodom is complicated by the numerous mentions of it in other passages of the Bible, where Sodom becomes a symbol of God's wrath on sinful people. In the Christian New Testament, in both the Second Epistle of Peter and the Epistle of Jude, for example, Sodom is discussed following reference to the incident of Genesis 6:1-4 in which angels come to earth to have sexual relations with humans. The sin of Sodom is seen as desiring "strange flesh," that is, not homosexual relations, but seeking sexual relations with the nonhuman angels.

The passages in the Book of Leviticus, the most direct condemnation of homosexual practice, have proved the hardest to reinterpret. However, contemporary commentators have noted that the two passages occur in the larger context of the condemnation of Canaanite religion and that within that religion homosexuality was associated with idolatry, the worship of false gods. Writers such as McNeill suggest that what is really being condemned is not homosexuality per se, but Jewish association with the idolatrous practices of their non-Jewish neighbors.

The New Testament condemnation of homosexual activity by the Apostle Paul has also been given new understanding by placing it in the context both of Paul's general aversion to sex and the very open sexuality of ancient Corinth and Rome. Religious prostitution was quite widely practiced and it led in turn to widespread promiscuous behavior. Thus, it is again suggested that Paul did not intend to condemn homosexuality per se but participation in pagan religious sex (which he equated with idolatry) and sexual promiscuity (both heterosexual and homosexual varieties).

Out of the reinterpretation of the biblical passages in the light of modern historical and textual criticism has come a general perspective which suggests that the Bible does not condemn homosexuality, but like heterosexuality, simply attempts to regulate it. The Bible condemns homosexual rape, promiscuous homosexual activity, and the practice of homosexuality in a pagan religious context. On a more positive note, it is argued by many that the relationship of Jonathan and David recounted in the Books of Samuel was a homosexual relationship that went beyond simple male bonding.

Adding modern psychological insights into the reinterpretation of the Bible, it is noted that the Bible does not make the modern formal distinction between homosexuality as a condition dictating sexual preference and homosexual behavior. The Bible does not discuss the former, and it condemns only specific kinds of the latter, such as homosexual rape and prostitution. Modern commentators have suggested that an approved form of homosexual activity would be a long-term monogamous homosexual relationship analogous to heterosexual marriage. This position is assumed by the early report, *Towards a Quaker View of Sex* (1963), which states, "The Christian standard of chastity should not be measured by a physical act, but should be a standard of human relationship, applicable within marriage as well as outside it." Speaking more directly to the issue of homosexual relationships, the report observes:

> Further we see no reason why the physical nature of a sexual act should be the criterion by which the question whether or not it is moral should be decided. An act which expresses both affection between two individuals and gives pleasure to them both, does not seem to be sinful by reason alone of the fact that it is homosexual. The same criteria seem to apply whether the relationship is heterosexual or homosexual.

This position is most clearly affirmed in the pamphlet "Homosexuality: What the Bible Does and Does Not Say," published by the Universal Fellowship of Metropolitan Churches:

> Neither heterosexual love nor homosexual love is sinful in itself. Sex acts only become sinful when we act in lust or in abuse of another person, abandoning the ways of love. The relationship of two women or two men can be just as loving as a relationship between a woman and a man. Christ died for the sins of both homosexual and heterosexual. Therefore, Gays and Lesbians can come to the saving grace of Jesus Christ and yet still retain their identity and the rightful expression of their sexuality.

The Churches Respond

As the homosexual community began to organize in the 1950s, it became evident that many homosexuals were religious people, members of churches and synagogues. As a result, they faced a major dilemma in their lives by attempting to cope with their situation in light of the traditional Western religious condemnation of homosexuality. Among the people who discovered and/or acknowledged their homosexuality were religious professionals—Catholic priests, Protestant ministers, and Jewish rabbis. Thus, churches were presented with an immediate pastoral problem. However, the pastoral issue was placed on the back burner in the face of a more pressing issue, that of legal sanctions against homosexuals and the violation of the civil rights of homosexuals.

The first reactions to the plight of the homosexual came in the early 1950s when the Moral Welfare Council of the Church of England pressured the British Parliament to appoint a committee to investigate and recommend changes in laws concerning homosexuality. Parliament acted and the *Wolfenden Report* of 1957 led to the decriminalization of homosexuality in Great Britain. It was followed by the 1963 publication of *Toward a Quaker View of Sex*, with its even more radical acceptance of homosexuality and homosexual behavior. In the wake of the wide publicity given the Quaker document, the Council on Religion and the Homosexual was formed and was immediately plunged into the problems of the harassment of homosexuals by the police. On New Year's Day 1965, San Francisco police ignored an agreement to not interfere with a gay party at a rented downtown facility. They parked paddy wagons across the street from the gathering, photographed everyone entering the hall, and demanded to inspect the facility for violations of various city ordinances. Finally, after the police were denied entrance unless they showed a search warrant, several people, including the council's attorneys, were arrested. At a public press conference the next day, the council attacked the police and raised the question of persecution of an unpopular minority for the churches of North America and Europe. The work of the council was widely reported in Christian publications. The success of the council and others interested in forcing religious reconsideration of the homosexual's plight led to the August 1966 international conference in London attended by leaders of a number of North American and British churches. From that time forward, there was a renewed interest by denominations in questions raised by the presence of homosexuals.

Among the first churches to become concerned with homosexual issues was the United Church of Christ. In 1969 its Council on Christian Social Action adopted one of the first position statements on homosexuality in which it called for the decriminalization of homosexual activities between consenting adults. The same resolution also highlighted some of the issues on the relationship of homosexuality to the Christian faith and called for widespread discussion of these issues throughout the denomination. They were soon joined by the Unitarian Universalist Association, which also called for decriminalization in 1970.

By the early 1970s, one by one the major denominations were forced to speak out on the issue. In 1970, the general assembly of the United Presbyterian Church in the U.S.A., now a constituent part of the Presbyterian Church (U.S.A.), presented a lengthy report of its task force on "Sexuality and the Human Community." The report, which had been called for by the 1966 assembly, was presented amid much controversy. It called for a "pastoral" approach to sexual questions. Concerning homosexuality, it called into question many of the traditional biblical interpretations, especially the statements from Paul's epistles, and asked for more study in light of the possibility that the negative aspects of homosexual behavior (rape and promiscuity) should not determine the church's entire response to the issue.

The report of the task force was received by a divided assembly, which, after a lengthy and often acrimonious debate, narrowly accepted the report and authorized its publication as a study document for congregations. Immediately after that action, a further motion was also passed by a narrow margin mandating a statement in the foreword of the printed copies of the report which made it clear to the reader that the report was a study document and its acceptance by the general assembly should not be construed as an endorsement of its opinions.

The United Methodist Church, formed by a merger of the Methodist Church and the Evangelical United Brethren in 1968, dealt with homosexuality in only a perfunctory manner at its first general conference. Four years later the 1972 general conference produced a "pastoral" paragraph on the subject as part of a revised statement of its "Social Principles." The document encountered immediate and stiff reaction and occasioned the most heated debate of the two week gathering. By the end of the stormy session, the delegates had rejected the statement presented to them and significantly rewritten it. Their final text would withstand numerous attempts to alter it at future general conferences, and its basic perspective and wording have survived intact. The last two sentences read:

> Homosexuals no less than heterosexuals are persons of sacred worth, who need the ministry and guidance of the church in their struggles for human fulfillment, as well as the spiritual and emotional fellowship which enables reconciling relationships with God, with others, and with self. Further we insist that all persons are entitled to have their human and civil rights ensured, though we do not condone the practice of homosexuality and consider this practice to be incompatible with Christian teaching.

This position, which became the dominant position within liberal Protestantism, placed the church behind the struggle for civil liberties for homosexuals and welcomed homosexuals into the life of the church; however, it condemned homosexual behavior with the added implication that practicing homosexuals could not be ordained to the ministry. This implication was specifically legislated at future conferences.

America's largest religious body, and thus the church with the largest number of homosexual members, is the Roman Catholic Church. It did not move as quickly as some of the Protestant denominations to respond to the rethinking which ethicists such as McNeill, a Jesuit priest, were proposing. In the 1970s, however, it offered a series of decisive documents addressing homosexuality, the most important of which was issued from the church's headquarters in the Vatican City in 1975. The section on homosexuality of that "Declaration on Social Ethics" concluded that "...homosexual acts are intrinsically disordered and can in no case be approved."

The negative church statements on homosexuality in the early 1970s were viewed by many as hastily prepared preliminary statements. They were, thought many sympathetic to the homosexual cause, subject to further debate, study, clarification, and revision. They hoped for genuine change in the opinions of church leaders. Thus they welcomed the documents as a means to initiate discussion. Beginning in the mid-1970s and continuing through the 1980s, an intense debate (rivaled in strength only by the debate on abortion) emerged. Organizations composed of homosexuals and those sympathetic to their concerns were formed in every one of the larger Christian denominations and they perpetuated that debate. Out of it, the spectrum of opinion emerged.

Judaism and Homosexuality

Judaism has taken its place as part of the American religious establishment, and its leadership now regularly works in dialogue with Christian churches in developing approaches to social questions. Traditionally, the Jewish religious community shared with Christianity the abhorrence of homosexuality. Judaism ultimately derived its opinions from the same set of passages in the Jewish Bible (i.e., the Christian Old Testament) that were later cited by Christian authors. That opinion was strengthened by comments in the Talmudic writings (the gathered writings of ancient Jewish rabbinical leaders) and was included in the definitive codification of Jewish law made by Maimonides in the twelfth century.

Like Christian churches, the several Jewish rabbinical/congregational structures in America were faced with the challenges presented by the developing homosexual/gay community in the 1970s. In 1972, four Jewish males who had attended a service at the Metropolitan Community Church in Los Angeles decided to organize a synagogue in which gay Jews would feel at home. With the assistance of Troy Perry, the Metropolitan Community Temple was formed and sought and received assistance from the Southwest Council of the Union of American Hebrew Congregations (UAHC). Within a year, similar groups had emerged in San Francisco, California; Miami, Florida; Baltimore, Maryland; London, England; and Mexico City, Mexico. A similar congregation was soon formed in New York City. The very existence of these congregations, receiving at least some informal support form the UAHC (the Reform Jewish congregational organization), added new dimensions to debates which were growing over the role of women in the Reform Jewish community.

The debate within the Reform Jewish community centered upon the demands of both the biblical injunctions against homosexuality and the traditional rejection of homosexual behavior within the Jewish community. Given the treatment of Jewish law within the Reform community, were the scriptural story of Sodom and the injunctions in Leviticus applicable and did the weight of traditional Jewish opinion carry contemporary authority? Initially, a number of rabbis arose to defend the tradition. They noted the absence historically of homosexuality among Jews, even in the face of larger communities where it was openly practiced, and admitted some surprise in the early 1970s when significant numbers of gay Jews suddenly became undeniably visible. Gradually the opinion of the leadership in the Reform community shifted as the image of homosexuals as a minority within American society (not unlike the Jewish community itself) was accepted.

There was little positive response from Conservative and Orthodox Jews as the Reform debate continued throughout the 1970s and 1980s. The issue has been somewhat resolved through a series of resolutions in 1977, 1987, and 1989 in which the

UAHC successively supported civil rights for homosexuals, the inclusion of gay males and lesbians within the union's fellowship, and the ordination of gay rabbis. Currently, the original gay synagogue in Los Angeles, renamed Congregation Beth Chayim Chadashim ("the house of new life"), is headed by a lesbian rabbi.

The Development of a Consensus

By the end of the 1980s most of the major religious bodies in North America had reached a decisive opinion on the several basic issues raised by the homosexual community. As each church spoke a clear consensus of opinion shared by the Roman Catholic Church and most liberal Protestant church bodies emerged, with a smaller number of groups assuming a position to the right or left of that opinion.

Civil Rights for Homosexuals

The debate over homosexuality covered several specific issues. First and foremost was the issue of civil rights for homosexuals. That issue initially involved the decriminalization of homosexual practice between two consenting adults and ending police harassment of homosexual gathering places. However, as these two issues have been resolved, the debate has moved to discrimination in housing and jobs. Homosexuals have frequently been evicted from or denied access to apartments and/or fired or denied jobs because of their sexual orientation, a concern which has prompted special legislation to protect them. The most famous battle over such legislation came in 1977 in Dade County, Florida, where Evangelical Christians organized (with the help of singer Anita Bryant) to fight against homosexual rights. In addition, government jobs have been denied to homosexuals because of the threat of blackmail, and the Armed Forces have regularly discharged homosexuals discovered among the troops.

Overwhelmingly, the churches have followed the lead of the United Church of Christ and supported full civil rights for homosexuals. Dissenting from this opinion are some conservative Evangelical Protestant groups, most prominently the Southern Baptist Convention, the second largest religious body in America. The convention, which dealt with the issue in conjunction with the 1977 campaign in Florida, went on record as opposing attempts "to secure legal, social, and religious acceptance for homosexuality" and attempts to portray it as "normal behavior." In 1985, the convention again spoke in opposition to attempts "to pass public ordinances which, under the guise of human rights, has the effect of giving public approval to the homosexual lifestyle." The resolution attacked the idea of portraying the homosexual community as a minority analogous to ethnic minorities.

Accepting Homosexuality: Where the Churches Stand

Generally, at the same time they rendered their statement on civil rights for homosexuals, churches offered an opinion on homosexuality itself and the acceptance of homosexual persons in the membership and life of the churches' congregations. Again an overwhelming consensus appeared. Churches affirmed a traditional standard that limited sexual activity, specifically intercourse, to the bonds of heterosexual marriage. Hence, homosexual relations could not be approved. In this opinion the Roman Catholic Church, liberal Protestants, conservative Evangelicals, and both Conservative and Orthodox Jews were in agreement.

However, while there is an overwhelming agreement concerning the acceptability of homosexual behavior, a range of opinion is apparent on the issue of homosexuality itself. In general, Roman Catholicism and liberal Protestantism have accepted the distinction between homosexuality as a condition of human sexuality and homosexual behavior as actions which might flow either from a homosexual or bisexual orientation. As such, most ethicists related to these churches describe homosexuality as a morally neutral condition which some people at some point discover they possess quite apart from any conscious choice. Given the morally neutral nature of homosexuality, the churches have moved to fully accept homosexuals in their congregational life and have acted to dispel homophobia, the popular prejudice against homosexuals which had tended to view them as somewhat akin to lepers.

While most churches have accepted homosexuals (at least at the national level), most have also condemned homosexual acts and have suggested that under normal conditions, the only acceptable course of action is celibacy. This perspective is most clearly spelled out in the several Roman Catholic documents, but is implicit in most of the others as well.

On both sides of this issue there is dissent. On the conservative side, Evangelical Protestants condemn homosexuality as sin so strongly that self-identified homosexuals (whether practicing or not) are not welcome in the Christian community unless they repent of their sin. Most Evangelicals would view homosexuality as a serious sin embedded in a character trait which often needs extra effort to eradicate. Thus many Evangelicals support specific ministries which have been established to convert homosexuals and to assist them in reorienting their sexual preferences into a heterosexual mode. Among the more prominent of these ministries are Sexaholics Anonymous of Simi Valley, California; Exodus International of Minneapolis, Minnesota; Be Whole Ministries of Montgomery, Alabama; Homosexuals Anonymous of Reading, Pennsylvania; Love in Action of San Rafael, California; and Metanoia Ministries of Seattle, Washington. The perspective of the Evangelical community, in contradiction to Roman Catholics and liberal Protestants, is that all homosexuality can be changed into heterosexuality.

On the liberal side of the consensus, several groups have advocated the full acceptance of homosexuality and the practices which flow from it (especially stable, marriage-like homosexual relationships) as a fully acceptable alternative lifestyle. Of course, the Universal Fellowship of Metropolitan Community Churches and other gay denominations have adopted this position. Among more well-known American religious groups however, only the Unitarian Universalist Association and Reform Judaism also advocate such a position.

Among liberal Protestant groups, the United Church of Christ has come the closest to accepting homosexuality as an alternative lifestyle. However, among its many resolutions supportive of homosexuals as persons and declaring the moral neutrality of homosexuality, it has never accepted the viability of homosexual acts. As the church's synod stated in 1983, "A person's orientation is not a moral issue, but...sexual behavior does have moral significance." The church has many members and an active caucus that fully accept homosexual behavior, but it also has an active conservative caucus, the Biblical Witness Fellowship, which is just as staunchly in favor of the traditional view of homosexuality.

The Ordination of Homosexuals

Having resolved the issue of congregational membership and participation, those churches that were accepting of homosexuals as members were immediately faced with the issue of ordination of homosexuals to the priesthood and ministry. The issue was unequivocally placed before the churches in 1972 by the ordination of William R. Johnson, a homosexual, by the Golden Gate Association of the United Church of Christ. In general, issues of ordination are local affairs in the United Church of Christ, but Johnson's ordination raised the specter that more ordinations would follow. National officials felt the need to consider the problem. In 1973, the denomination's executive council called for further study of the question. The issue quickly became not homosexuality, considered a morally neutral state of existence, but whether or not the ministerial candidate was or intended to become a practicing homosexual. Homosexual behavior clearly stood outside of accepted moral standards limiting sexual relations to monogamous marriage. Hence, practicing homosexuals were not to be ordained, and Johnson failed to become the harbinger of the United Church's future.

Johnson's ordination also was seen by members of other groups as setting a possible trend in their denomination. Thus the consideration of the ordination question was addressed as a separate issue by the various churches and one by one they spoke against it. While the United Methodists had in essence legislated against it in 1972 by noting that homosexual practice was incompatible with Christian teaching, they later took a series of actions over a number of years that carefully defined their prohibitions concerning the ordination of practicing homosexuals. Not only could practicing homosexuals not be ordained, but ordained persons later discovered to be practicing homosexuals would have their ministerial status terminated.

Hope for homosexuals in the Episcopal Church was raised in 1975 when Bishop Paul Moore ordained Ellen Barrett, an avowed lesbian and student at the General Theological Seminary in New York, as a deacon, a step to the priesthood in that church. The ordination of Barrett, like the unauthorized ordination of the Episcopal women to the priesthood in 1976, forced the issue for the church's bishops and general convention. However, in this case it had opposite results. While the church moved to regularize women's ordination and authorize future ordinations, it moved to block the ordination of homosexuals, a position it has periodically reaffirmed, most recently in 1988.

As of 1990, the ordination issue seems dead in all of the major denominations. Only three major religious bodies have authorized it—the Universal Fellowship of Metropolitan Community Churches, the Unitarian Universalist Association, and Reform Judaism. A number of smaller, primarily gay denominations also ordain homosexuals, but these have not as a whole participated in the ongoing debates nationally.

In Conclusion

For the rest of the twentieth century, it would appear that little change in the present formal position of the churches on homosexuality is to be expected. Continued education on the issues is occurring in the mainline Protestant churches, and in the next generation there is the possibility of shifts of attitudes toward further acceptance of the homosexual community. In the meantime the various homosexual organizations within the several denominations have had to settle into a role of being support groups for those gay males and lesbians who have chosen to remain members of the mainline churches. Self-avowed homosexuals who have felt a call for the ministry will have to seek other avenues to exercise their gifts.

In the documents found in this issue of *The Churches Speak*, only passing reference will be found to the disease AIDS.[2] As a whole, the churches moved quickly to separate the question of the relation of homosexuals to the church from that of AIDS. In fact, the AIDS issue had no direct bearing on the churches' adoption of a position on homosexuality. However, in the long run, the AIDS issue may serve to alter church opinion due to the significant sympathy for the gay community which the epidemic has produced. On the other hand, that sympathy is partially countered by the fear of a deadly disease identified with homosexuals that the epidemic has instilled in some people.

Possibly the major long-term factor in the relationship of homosexuals to the church is decriminalization and growing recognition of the civil rights of homosexuals. This will place more and more homosexuals in visible positions in the work place and neighborhoods. As has been the case with various ethnic minorities, it will lead to informal acceptance by co-workers and neighbors who had previously never knowingly met a gay person. The growing social acceptance of gay people in secular society may be all that is necessary to influence future votes in those liberal denominations in which there is already significant support for gay people.

Endnotes

[1] This spectrum provides a place in the middle for people who have identified themselves as being bisexual, i.e., they feel strong emotional and sexual attraction to both genders, although one may predominate. Within the homosexual community, the difficulties encountered by bisexuals are often dealt with in association with homosexual concerns, but in the religious world, the issue of bisexuality has rarely been addressed.

[2] The churches' positions on homosexuality did have some relationship to their positions on AIDS. For more on this subject, see a previous volume in this series, *The Churches Speak on: AIDS* (Detroit: Gale Research Inc., 1989).

Selected Sources

Altman, Dennis. *The Homosexualization of America.* Boston: Beacon Press, 1982.

Bailey, D.S. *Homosexuality and the Western Christian Tradition.* New York: Longmans Green & Co., 1955.

Banks, John, and Martina Waltsch, eds. *Meeting Gay Friends: Essays by Members of Friends Homosexual Fellowship.* Manchester: Friends Homosexual Fellowship, 1982.

Batchelor, Edward, Jr., ed. *Homosexuality and Ethics.* New York: Pilgrim Press, 1980.

Bieber, Kenneth P., and Dale R. Bond. "Homosexuality and Ordination." *Engage/Social Action* 4 (February-March 1976): 6-11.

Chafin, Michael L. "On Being Homosexual and Christian." *Junction* 8 (Spring 1973): 24-28.

Chesebro, James W., ed. *Gayspeak: Gay Male & Lesbian Communication.* New York: Pilgrim Press, 1981.

Council on Religion and the Homosexual: 1964/1968. San Francisco: Council on Religion and the Homosexual, [1968].

Day, David. *Things They Never Told You in Sunday School: A Primer for the Christian Homosexual.* Austin, TX: Liberty Press, 1987.

Fletcher, Joseph. *Situation Ethics: The New Morality*. Philadelphia: Westminster Press, 1966.

Freehof, Soloman B. "A Responsum." *Central Conference of American Rabbis* XX (Summer 1973): 31–33.

Gearhart, Sally, and William R. Johnson. *Loving Women/Loving Men: Gay Liberation and the Church*. San Francisco: Glide Publications, 1974.

Hanigan, James P. *Homosexuality: The Test Case for Christian Sexual Ethics*. New York and Mahwah, NJ: Paulist Press, 1988.

Herman, Erwin L. "A Synagogue for Jewish Homosexuals?" *Central Conference of American Rabbis* XX (Summer 1973): 33–40.

Horner, Tom. *Jonathan Loved David: Homosexuality in Biblical Times*. Philadelphia: Westminster Press, 1978.

Human Sexuality: A Theological Perspective. A Report of the Commission on Theology and Church Relations of the Lutheran Church-Missouri Synod, as prepared by its Social Concerns Committee, September 1981. The Committee, 1981.

Humphreys, Laud. *Out of the Closets: The Sociology of Homosexual Liberation*. Englewood Cliffs, NJ: Prentice-Hall, 1972.

Hunter, John F. *The Gay Insider: USA*. New York: Stonehill Publishing Co., 1972.

Johns, Elizabeth, ed. "Civil Liberties and Homosexuality." *Social Action* XXXIV (December 1967).

Jones, H. Kimball. *Toward a Christian Understanding of the Homosexual*. New York: Association Press, 1966.

Kaufman, Gordon. *The Context of Decision: A Theological Analysis*. New York: Abingdon Press, 1961.

Lipton, Alan L. "A Congregation of Emotionally Ill?" *Central Conference of American Rabbis* XX (Summer 1973): 49–50.

Malinowsky, H. Robert. *International Directory of Gay and Lesbian Periodicals*. Phoenix: Oryx Press, 1987.

Marmor, Judd. "Pathologic or Normal?" *Central Conference of American Rabbis* XX (Summer 1973): 47–49.

McNeill, John H. *The Church and the Homosexual.* New York: Pocket Books, 1976.

Mickley, Richard R. *Christian Sexuality: A Reflection on Being a Christian and Sexual.* Los Angeles: Universal Fellowship Press, 1975.

More Light Ministry and Outreach in the Presbyterian Church (U.S.A.): Ministry With and Outreach To Lesbian and Gay People. 4th. ed., rev. New Brunswick, NJ: Presbyterians for Lesbian and Gay Concerns.

Oberholtzer, W. Dwight. *Is Gay Good? Ethics, Theology, and Homosexuality.* Philadelphia: Westminster Press, 1971.

Pennington, Sylvia. *But Lord, They're Gay: A Christian Pilgrimage.* Hawthorne, CA: Lambda Christian Fellowship, 1982.

Perry, Troy D., as told to Charles L. Lucas. *The Lord Is My Shepherd and He Knows I'm Gay.* Los Angeles: Nash, 1972. Reprinted in New York by Bantam, 1978.

Pittenger, Norman. *Time for Consent.* London: SCM Press, 1970.

Ragins, Sanford. "An Echo of the Pleas of Our Fathers." *Central Conference of American Rabbis* XX (Summer 1973): 41–47.

Scanzoni, Letha, and Virginia R. Mollenkott. *Is the Homosexual My Neighbor? Another Christian View.* San Francisco: Harper & Row, 1978.

Sexuality and the Human Community. Philadelphia: General Assembly of the United Presbyterian Church (U.S.A.), 1970.

Thielicke, Helmut. *The Ethics of Sex.* New York: Harper & Row, 1964.

Towards a Quaker View of Sex: An Essay by a Group of Friends. London: Friends Home Service Committee, 1963.

Twiss, Harold L., ed. *Homosexuality and the Christian Faith: A Symposium.* Valley Forge, PA: Judson Press, 1978.

Wolf, Deborah G. *The Lesbian Community.* Berkeley and Los Angeles: University of California Press, 1979.

Wolfenden Report: Report of the Committee on Homosexual Offenses and Prostitution. Authorized American Ed. New York: Stein and Day, 1963.

Wood, Robert W. *Christ and the Homosexual.* New York: Vantage Press, 1960.

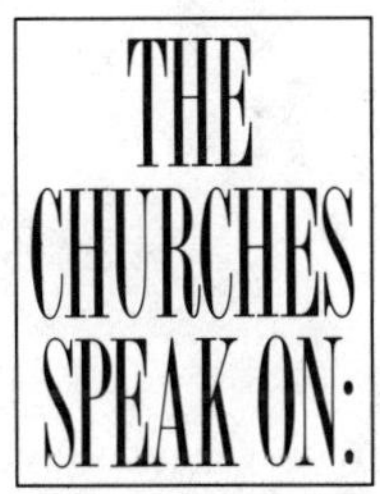

Homosexuality

Roman Catholic Church

As the gay rights movement burst upon the scene in both North America and Europe in the early 1970s, the Roman Catholic Church (the largest religious body in the West) was faced with thousands of ''gay and proud'' church members. Some of these homosexual Catholics turned to priests either for advice or to seek the church's sanction for their new open lifestyle. Thus, among the first questions which the episcopal leadership of the church was forced to confront concerned the response which priest-confessors (those who heard the confessions of church members) could give to those who ''confessed'' their awakening homosexual consciousness and resultant actions. The first significant document to appear in North America in response to the new gay life was a Guide to Confessors *distributed by the National Conference of Catholic Bishops.*

The traditional Roman Catholic approach to issues of sexuality and sexual behavior has assumed the priority and normalcy of the family unit. Under normal conditions, individuals should grow up and either marry or adopt a religious profession which necessitates an unmarried condition. In the former case, sexual activity is confined to marriage, and in the latter, the celibate life is normative. All deviations from those two life patterns are seen as questionable—disordered, abnormal, and/or sinful.

In the pastoral situation, the range of problems created by the process of ''coming out'' and accepting one's homosexual urges, however, presented a new complexity to the person genuinely concerned with assisting the homosexual in his/her dilemma. Gays were fearful, faced with an intense anxiety over the split between the reality of their lives and the negative teaching they had received about homosexuality. They were also perplexed about the new positive approach to homosexuality in the gay community so different from the disapproval of the church. Often the homosexual developed extremely low self-esteem, which became the major obstacle to resolving his problems.

In approaching the problem, the Roman Catholic Church moved between a kind openness and willingness to assist the homosexual with personal problems and a position that ultimately condemned any sexual activities of a homosexual nature. In some documents, the pastoral approach predominated and in some the doctrinal-moral element was primarily affirmed.

Throughout the 1970s and 1980s, the church presented a consistent front. The two most important documents were issued from the church's international headquarters in Rome by its Congregation for the Doctrine of the Faith in 1975 and 1986. The first document, the Declaration on Sexual Ethics, *covered a wide variety of sexual issues which grew out of the new sexual freedom of the 1960s. Its brief statement on homosexuality took a hard line toward homosexual behavior.*

In between 1975 and 1986, the church listened to various calls to revise its traditional approach to homosexuality, the most important of which was the "pro-homosexual" case being made by John J. McNeill, a Jesuit. That the church had already rejected McNeill's more radical position became evident in 1980. At that time the imprimi potest *(church's declaration that the book was free from doctrinal or moral error) was removed from McNeill's book, The* Church and the Homosexual, *and McNeill was ordered not to lecture or publish on the subject in the future. An end to the debate was signaled in 1986 by the re-affirmation of the church's traditional position. Symbolic of the church's decision that the debate was over was the movement of members of the American hierarchy against Dignity, the major organization of Roman Catholics advocating a positive view of homosexuality. Various dioceses had cooperated with Dignity in sponsoring a mass for homosexual church members. The discontinuation of that cooperative endeavor settled the question of homosexuality for the current generation.*

ROMAN CATHOLIC CHURCH—NATIONAL CONFERENCE OF CATHOLIC BISHOPS

PRINCIPLES TO GUIDE CONFESSORS IN QUESTIONS OF HOMOSEXUALITY (1973)

In increasing numbers Catholic homosexuals ask whether they can be involved in an overt homosexual relationship and receive regularly the Holy Eucharist. To reply to this question the confessor must seek some principles concerning sexuality which will guide him in the direction of homosexuals. He must also seek an understanding of the homosexual condition and the viable alternatives to living in an overt homosexual relationship. The term *homosexual* is understood to designate an adult person whose sexual inclinations are orientated predominantly toward persons of the same sex. While fully aware that individuals manifest a whole spectrum of sexual behavior, from extremely heterosexual to the opposite pole, our concern is with the individual whose attraction to his own sex has made him aware of a moral problem, namely, whether the genital expression of his inclinations is seriously sinful for him; and, if it is, what viable ways of living are open to him. (It is understood hereafter in this paper that the pronouns are intended to apply equally to male and female, except where the context makes it evident that only one sex is intended.)

The *objective* morality of sexual acts is based upon the teaching of the Church concerning Christian marriage: Genital sexual expression between a man and a woman should take place only in marriage. Apart from the intentions of the man and of the woman, sexual intercourse has a twofold meaning. It is an act of union with the beloved, and it is procreative. Neither meaning may be excluded, although for a variety of reasons, the procreative meaning may not be attained. By their nature homosexual acts exclude all possibility of procreation of life. They are therefore inordinate uses of the sexual faculty. It is assumed, moreover, that the only ordinate use of the sexual faculty must be oriented toward a person of the opposite sex. Sexual acts between members of the same sex are contrary not only to one of the purposes of the sexual faculty, namely, procreation, but also to the other principal purpose, which is to express mutual love between husband and wife. For these reasons homosexual acts are a grave transgression of the goals of human sexuality and of human personality, and are consequently contrary to the will of God.

The goals of human personality and sexuality demand that the exercise of the sexual faculty should take place within the family framework. The procreation and education of children is at least as important a goal in marriage as the expression of mutual love. But homosexual acts make the attainment of this goal impossible.

Homosexual acts are also a deviation from the normal attraction of man for woman, which leads to the foundation of the basic unit of society, the family. Two homosexuals cannot complement one another in the same way as male and female. Not surprisingly, lasting and fulfilling homosexual relationships are not found very often. Both Old and New Testament teaching confirms the heterosexual union of man and woman in procreation. Genesis' description is concerned with man and woman forming a new family. In Ephesians man and woman are compared with Christ and his Church. Whenever homosexual acts are mentioned, they are condemned. (See John F. Harvey, ''Homosexuality'', *NCE,* vol. 7, 116-119 at 118) Six references are found in Sacred Scripture, five to male and one to female: Lev. 18:2; 20:13 Rom. 1:27; I Cor. 6:9-10; I Tim. 1:9-10 (male); Rom. 1:26-27 (female).The clearest reference is Rom. 1:26-27: ''For this cause God has given them up to shameful lusts; for their women have exchanged natural intercourse for what is against nature, and in the same way men too, having given up natural intercourse with women, have burned in their lusts toward one another, men with men practicing that well known shamefulness and receiving in their own persons the fitting punishment of their perversity.'' (Kleist-Lilly translation).

That homosexual practices are a grave violation of the law of God is clear from the context in which St. Paul writes. Because the pagans had refused to worship the true God, God had given them up to practice of vices, including unnatural forms. God had withdrawn his grace from them in punishment for their idolatry. (Romans I:24-25)

The *subjective* morality of homosexual acts must be considered under two aspects, the origin of the tendency, and the manner in which the person controls it. Concerning the origin of the condition in a given person it can be said safely that man or woman does not will to become homosexual. At a certain point in life, the person discovers that he is homosexual and usually suffers a certain amount of trauma. Sometimes he is young enough to seek professional treatment to reorientate his sexual desires; sometimes he feels too old to benefit by such treatment, or cannot afford to pay for it. In every case he *discovers* an already existent condition.

Because a deeper knowledge of the possible causes of homosexuality may help both the counselor and the homosexual to understand the condition and to act with greater freedom it is of value to state briefly some of the prevalent theories concerning its origin. The term *possible* is used advisedly, inasmuch as the etiology of inversion demands further badly needed research. There is hardly a more difficult problem unless it is the conversion of developed homosexual tendencies into normal channels. Mindful of our ignorance, it is better to speak about factors which contribute to the genesis and growth of homosexuality rather than to speak about *causes* in the strict sense. With these reservations one may say that the theory which attributes homosexuality to psychogenic causes enjoys wide acceptance.

In a summary of research on heredity and hormonal factors Father Michael J. Buckley concludes that there is little available evidence that either factor contributes significantly to the formation of the homosexual. While some studies may suggest that homosexuality may run in families among brothers, as a genetic factor, other studies do not point in the same direction: ''Even if a high familial incidence could be demonstrated, a genetic conclusion would be vitiated in many cases by the identity among brothers of environmental conditions, which might also be the sole cause, or a contributory cause, of their homosexual condition.

''*The hormonal theory as a whole* affords little or no basis on which to construct moral principles, and it is beyond question that the general pattern of homosexuality is chiefly due to something other than hormonal imbalance.''

Recent studies focus more attention on the father than the mother in the development of the male homosexual, and more stress on the mother than the father in the growth of the female homosexual. Homosexual boys usually have too possessive mothers and too unconcerned fathers, and it is the unconcerned fathers with whom they fail to identify. Homosexual girls, on the other hand, usually have mothers who belittle the femininity of their daughters, and fathers who allow their wives to domineer over the family. In the development of both male and female homosexuals a weak father figure is typical—indeed in many cases a neglectful and alcoholic character. Very often repressed memories of sexual brutality of the father towards the mother shape the little girl's concept of men.

A neglected factor in the genesis of homosexuality is the pre-school boy's inability to form effective peer relationships. Perhaps of sickly disposition, and unduly sheltered from the other boys by mother, this youngster yearns to play with his peers, but is not allowed to do so. He sees other boys romping and playing and experiencing a kind of rough but warm relationship with companions. He feels left out. As a result of this feeling, he may never develop normal peer relationships, and eventually he will tend to seek physical fulfillment with peers whom he regards as more masculine. He will offer himself as a sexual object so as to be accepted and embraced by peers or other males. Basically, he has failed to identify with his own sex either in terms of father or of peers, and, consequently, he identifies with a female way of viewing reality.

Others hold that homosexuality represents arrested emotional development; for example, the adolescent who fails to get beyond a phase of homosexual attraction remains emotionally fixed at this level. The child who does not outgrow an earlier narcissistic stage may be capable of loving only a person as much like himself as possible, and very probably a person of the same sex. He may meet this person during adolescence. It seems that learning experience may precipitate a youngster into homosexual practices who otherwise might have passed through the adolescent phase without any overt acts. By "learning experience" is meant a form of seduction which induces the youth into seeking the same pleasure again.

The initiating factor may be unconscious fear of the opposite sex or lack of opportunity to contact such. In a broader sense, the future homosexual has "learned" from his or her early childhood *attitudes* towards the opposite sex which become the seed ground of adolescent seduction. While early childhood attitudes formed toward both parents and towards self do not make adolescent seduction inevitable, they certainly predispose the youngster towards inversion.

Other factors in the development of the homosexual person include; deprivatation of normal family life (for example, institutionalized children); anti-sexual puritanism, which regards woman as "untouchable." This idolization of woman may be a disguised fear of her. At any rate, such a person tends to regard actions with his own sex as innocent, or only slightly serious, thus forming a habit of homosexual practices out of which it is difficult to withdraw. Also, early unconscious seduction of child by parents in circumstances of extreme immodesty. Another factor is fear of inadequacy in fulfilling the role of male or female; a bad case of acne, deep shyness, the habit of stammering, may cause a boy to seek companionship and affection exclusively among his own sex. If the ordinary early adolescent seeks his own sex until he is sure of himself, all the more so will the very shy youth tend to find a refuge in the company of his own sex for a longer period of time with risk of homosexual seduction. Similar patterns are found among female inverts. Also, rigid, loveless family life: in his study of 106 homosexuals, Dr. Irving Bieber concluded that not one of them had a relationship with either parent that could "by any stretch of the imagination be called normal." Some see the origin of homosexuality in the child who perceives the lack of love between his or her parents.

From this summary of multiple factors involved in the *development* of the homosexual person it is clear that one cannot pinpoint precisely the *decisive* factors in the history of any homosexual. "Probably no single factor alone is present in all instances, and possibly no single factor is exclusively responsible in one individual, but to a greater or less extent many of the causes . . . are found as a thread of continuity in most instances of exclusive or overwhelming homosexual development."

Responsibility for controlling the homosexual tendency, however, is another matter,—indeed a complex question. Homosexuals vary in the *degree* of freedom which they possess in controlling their sexual desires. At one extreme are homosexuals who have as much control over their tendencies as normal heterosexuals; and at the other extreme are homosexuals who are as compulsive as alcoholics. Each homosexual has the obligation to control his tendency by every means within his power, particularly by psychological and spiritual counsel. A special word should be said about the compulsive homosexual. Compulsion may be described as a narrowing of consciousness concerned either with a fascination for some object or with obedience to an impulse regarded as intolerable unless accepted. In a broader sense, the term also includes a conviction, born of failure to control it, that a particular urge is irresistible. The compulsive nature of many homosexual acts may be surmised from the squalid circumstances, coupled with risk, in which many meetings take place. Reciprocal masturbation in a public washroom is hardly the sort of thing which would appeal to a normally free agent.

Since there are so many kinds and degrees of compulsion, it is practically impossible to say that an action was the result of a compulsive urge. Before one can say that an action was compulsive, one must know the whole person. Although the person may be regarded as a compulsive homosexual, he is not hopeless if he seeks professional help, which can help him either to live with the compulsion without giving voluntary consent to its movements, or to rid himself of it by therapy. It should be noted that heterosexuals also apparently have hopeless compulsions of various kinds, including self-abuse, alcoholism, drug addiction, and the like. In sexual compulsions, particularly, the real problem is not the strength of the sexual instinct, which usually is no stronger than in normal persons, but rather the individuals's inability to adjust to tensions within his personality.

In assessing the responsibility of the homosexual the confessor must avoid both harshness and permissiveness. It is difficult for the homosexual to remain chaste in his environment, and he may slip into sin for a variety of reasons, including loneliness and compulsive tendencies and the pull of homosexual companions. But, generally, he is responsible for his actions, and the worst thing that a confessor can say is that the homosexual is not responsible for his actions.

This does not mean that in most instances the homosexual has full freedom of will. Very often freedom is diminished, more in some situations than in others. One may speak of a weakened *voluntarium,* but at the same time one must be careful not to excuse the homosexual for past behavior. His or her responsibility is to discover ways of strengthening the power of the will through renewed vision and fresh motivation. It is the confessor's task to help the person work out an ascetical plan of life so that he or she realizes that one can draw motivation from any sources for leading a Christlike life. The person with homosexual tendency should be made aware that, despite the resolution to begin a new life, very probably there will be relapses because of long standing habit, but this must not be allowed to be an occasion for sterile self-pity.

PASTORAL APPROACHES: Since the teaching of the Catholic Church on sexuality does not permit homosexual acts, it is necessary to propose to individuals who have homosexual tendencies some alternatives, alternatives which will vary contingent upon the age and state of life of the person. The fact that there are so many degrees of homosexuality should also be noted. The first category may be called *temporary* homosexuals.

Temporary homosexuals: A teenage boy or girl or young adult confesses actions with members of his own sex. This may be only a passing experience, and it should be treated with prudence. The confessor must seek to know more to determine whether he is dealing with a person who is predominantly homosexual. He should encourage the young person to seek professional help and to return to the confessor for further guidance. The younger the person, the greater the chance that therapy can redirect his sexual inclinations. The confessor should encourage the person to form stable relationships with persons of both sexes. He should treat the person with this difficulty in the same way as he would help the heterosexual.

Some specific directives for the apparent adolescent homosexual. If prevention is better than cure, then counsellors should make extraordinary effort to help the adolescent (or even young adult) man or woman with apparently homosexual tendencies. Such a person must avoid obvious homosexual groups with their affectations of dress and speech; prowling in those areas of the city where sexual deviates congregate, usually in bars, conversations with strangers loitering in public lavatories, physical culture magazines and weight-lifting clubs; impassioned letters, while destroying all received; situations where immunity from adult observation is combined with a high degree of physical exposure (private swimming pools, summer camp cabins, dressing rooms for athletes). As these directives indicate, modesty is necessary in the individual's relationships with members of his own sex as well as the other. (See John F. Harvey, *Continuum,* "Morality and Pastoral Treatment of Homosexuality", 279-297 at 296.)

A similar approach is advisable with older persons who occasionally, particularly under the influence of liquor or drugs, lapse into homosexual acts.

While prisoners frequently submit to homosexual acts under terror, they are not entirely inculpable. Their culpability, however, is reduced significantly, and, once returned to society, the homosexual condition usually disappears. The confessor can help them best by seeking to remedy the total situation of the prison.

Apparent Permanent Homosexuality: The older person may come to argue with the confessor that the sole relationship in which he can find fulfilment is a homosexual one; or he may come to seek help to avoid the homosexual environment in which he finds himself regularly. If the person comes to argue the merits of faithful homosexual unions, he should be given time to express his feelings on the matter, but advised that only by lengthy discussion outside the confessional can the priest respond to his argument and to his need for direction.

The priest should do more than outline the arguments which we have indicated above; he should show the person that he can live chastely in the world by means of a plan of life, which will include personal meditative prayer, spiritual reading, reception of the sacraments, and some specific work of charity in the world. Two other elements which should be stressed are regular access to spiritual direction and the formation of a stable friendship with at least one person. One of the greatest difficulties for the homosexual is the formation of such a friendship.

Sometimes the individual seeks the confessor's help to break out of his homosexual environment. He does not need any persuasion concerning the morality of his way of living. He needs motivation to move out of a situation in which he has had a measure of human affection and support from others in the same condition as himself. While he should be encouraged to reintegrate himself into the heterosexual culture, he should seek to form stable friendships among both homosexuals and heterosexuals. On the surface, this may seem like placing the homosexual in "the proximate occasion of sin", but other elements in his plan of life, and spiritual direction, can temper this danger, which is justified, considering his need for deep human relationships, and the good which will come from them in the future. A homosexual can have an abiding relationship with another homosexual without genital sexual expression. Indeed the deeper need of any human is for friendship rather than genital expression, although this is usually an element in heterosexual relationships.

The confessor need not insist that the longtime homosexual seek psychiatric treatment, although it may be beneficial. Unfortunately, many homosexuals have a "hangup" about psychiatry, and will seek the aid of a clergyman instead. It is a mistake for the confessor to refuse to help such persons. When it is clear to the confessor that the person does not hope for any change in sexual orientation, the confessor should accept this fact and continue to provide an ascetical plan of life.

If a homosexual has progressed under the direction of a confessor, but in the effort to develop a stable relationship with a given person has *occasionally* fallen into a sin of impurity, he should be absolved and instructed to take measures to avoid the elements which lead to sin without breaking off a friendship which has helped him grow as a person. If the relationship, however, has reached a stage where the homosexual is not able to avoid overt actions, he should be admonished to break off the relationship.

The Married Homosexual: The first point to be determined by the confessor is whether the penitent is homosexual, bisexual, or basically heterosexual with occasional homosexual relapses. Usually, this cannot be determined immediately, and may call for professional counseling. If it is clear that the person has been homosexual for a long time, it would be better for the penitent to disclose this information to his wife, or vice versa, rather than to remain in a union which is doubtfully valid. The canonical aspects should be referred to the diocesan marriage tribunal, provided, of course, the penitent is willing to transfer the matter to the external forum. If, however, as is usually the case, the person has manifested capacity to be husband or wife, despite relapses into homosexual activities on certain occasions, and if the person wants to save his marriage, the confessor should encourage him to do so, provided the individual is willing to seek regular spiritual guidance and to make use of the various means already mentioned. Whether the husband or wife of such a person should be told by the person himself is a question which can be resolved by the ordinary rules of prudence. Where the person's behavior has the earmarks of compulsion, it is generally better that the spouse be told, and his or her help sought. In these circumstances secrecy itself increases the tension of the compulsive person.

The Seminarian, Religious, and Priest: In direction of seminarians who suspect this tendency in themselves the confessor should seek counsel from professional sources so as to distinguish between passing homosexual proclivities, known as "crushes", and a real homosexual orientation. If there is a real homosexual orientation, the individual should be advised to seek psychiatric help, because generally speaking, the person has other problems besides the homosexual condition, and the related question, whether this person should continue his studies for the priesthood, will have to be examined. While a confessor should have no hesitation in refusing absolution to a student who has regularly indulged in homosexual activity *unless he leaves the seminary,* there are other situations which are too complex for immediate solution. The teenager or young adult in the minor seminary who has failed seriously on one occasion in this regard should be guided differently from another individual who masturbates frequently with homosexual fantasy. It is very probable that the latter should leave the religious life or the priesthood, because the prognosis for a healthy religious or priestly life is poor. Homosexual fantasy leading to masturbation is symptomatic of deep seated problems. In the case of seminarians the basic question is whether the person will have such great difficulties in the practice of complete chastity that he will be constantly unhappy in the priesthood or in religious life. Doubts ought to be resolved in favour of the Church and really of the individual himself, because his departure very probably will avoid subsequent spiritual and emotional harm to himself and scandal to those who would be affected by his behavior in the future. In this area our hindsight can become foresight.

When it comes, however, to those already perpetually committed to religious life or the priesthood, the problem should be handled differently. As already mentioned, there are many different degrees of the homosexual condition. For the priest who *occasionally* slips into homosexual actions what is necessary is that he examine the KIND of occasion in which he is wont to fail. Oftentimes it is a combination of frustration and depression, need to escape, alcohol and cruising in the homosexual (gay) haunts. Just as the heterosexual priest under similar motivation may commit sins of unchastity, so the occasionally homosexual priest should be induced to see that in both cases persons tend to fall when they lose sight of their motives for the life to which they have committed themselves. Under guidance, then, the priest who slips only on occasion can learn to practice complete chastity.

Unfortunately, however, there are priests who are deeply steeped in a homosexual way of life and who usually do not make it a matter of confession, if they go at all. One reason why they do not mention homosexual activity is that they have convinced themselves that it is either not sinful for them, or not a serious sin. These individuals need a *complete spiritual rehabilitation* in which both psychologists and spiritual directors take part. The problem is both psychological and spiritual. An institute whose objective will be the rehabilitation of such priests and religious is in the process of formation. Meanwhile the confessor or spiritual director should encourage persons in this condition to pray and to hope that they can rise above their situation. Despite verbal rationalizations these priests really want to be chaste.

Lesbians: The confessor should become acquainted with some of the traits of the Lesbian. Female homosexuals differ from male in the depth of their attachments and in the relative permanency of their relationships. This means that the priest will encounter Lesbians who are living in a kind of faithful union more often than he will meet male homosexuals living together. Homosexual women have a better chance to express themselves, yet their relationship is less physical, and in some cases the physical action is very infrequent. Those who come for counsel are generally more receptive than male homosexuals to another point of view. She is more willing to admit the obviously emotional coloring in her attachments, to which she will cling, not so much in rebellion against moral principles, but rather from fear of the vacuum which she foresees as consequent upon her renunciation of the beloved. Finally, the social pressures to marry are greater in the life of the female homosexual. These differences have pastoral significance. First of all, female homosexuals do not feel the same need for physical expression as male. If they could maintain an intimate relationship with another woman without passionately physical expression, they would settle for it in order to avoid serious sin. Some Catholic women do maintain such a relationship. The emotional reward which they derive from such a relationship more than compensates for the lack of genital expression. Again, the Lesbian woman does not engage in rationalizations like the male. She seeks some form of intimate relationship, but has not been able to find it in heterosexual contacts. Now she prefers an intimate friendship with another woman. If she seeks it as a question of conscience she is willing to try to sublimate her sexual desires.

Many homosexual women did not accept this way of life until they had been engaged to marry or already married; many are able to engage in both heterosexual and homosexual relationships. On the whole, they are more fluid and open to the possibility of conversion into heterosexuality. Unfortunately, however, they are under greater social pressure to marry than their male counterparts. As in the case of the married male homosexual, a canonical cause for invalidity can be posed, but it is more difficult to prove.

The Overt Homosexual and the Reception of the Eucharist: One of the results of recent literature on the subject, coupled with the Gay Liberation movement, has been an increased demand by Catholic overt homosexuals that they be allowed to receive the Holy Eucharist. Usually the argument runs that homosexual actions are normal for them; and that just as the heterosexual person can enter into a faithful union with a person of the opposite sex in order to complete himself, so the homosexual should be allowed to form an analogous union with one of his own sex. He may have to go through a period of promiscuity before he arrives at such a stable relationship, but in this respect he is not significantly different from many heterosexuals who are involved in more than one passionate affair before marriage.

These concepts are championed by Catholic organizations composed of homosexuals and homophiles who are dedicated to helping the Catholic homosexual to develop a health respect for himself and to realize that his manner of sexual expression does not exclude him from full participation in the sacraments of the Church. Some Catholic homosexuals argue that as long as the person is trying to serve God and neighbor, the fact of his sexual deviation is of no major consequence. One looks to the fundamental way of living of the person, and not to the sexual aberrancies, which oftentimes the person himself does not see as abnormal.

To these relatively new arguments the confessor should respond with firmness, showing how erroneous is the idea that each person has the right to variety in sexual expression contingent upon his sexual orientation. The confessor, however, should provide the person with a viable alternative, however difficult the chaste life may be. Already mentioned are various elements in the plan of life which can be proposed to the homosexual. If possible, he should be encouraged to change his sexual orientation. He should seek to form at least one *stable* human relationship, if not more. He should not be surprised by periodic tensions and some relapses. He should sublimate repeatedly his sexual desires in the pursuit of service to God and neighbor. In short, the confessor helps him to live as a Christian in the world and in religion.

Notes: *The emergence of an open homosexual community, a substantial portion of whose members were Roman Catholic, led to many questions at the pastoral level concerning the compatibility of an active homosexual life and participation in the church. The crux of the issue for Roman Catholics was reception of the sacrament of the Holy Eucharist, and the nature of advice which priests should give to people who discuss their homosexual acts during confession. The church believes that, while homosexuals should be treated with understanding, the goal of pastoral care should be the cessation of homosexual acts, the removal of the person from an environment where homosexuality is promoted, and the development of a lifestyle without homosexual behavior.*

It is noteworthy that the question of homosexuality in the priesthood is raised. The priesthood, one example of an all-male subculture where sexual relations with members of the opposite sex is forbidden, has proven to be an option for some homosexual men. Subsequent studies have shown that a higher percentage of homosexuals are in the priesthood than in the general population.

ROMAN CATHOLIC CHURCH—SACRED CONGREGATION FOR THE DOCTRINE OF THE FAITH

DECLARATION ON CERTAIN QUESTIONS CONCERNING SEXUAL ETHICS (1975)

1. According to contemporary scientific research, the human person is so profoundly affected by sexuality that it must be considered as one of the factors which give to each individual's life the principal traits that distinguish it. In fact it is from sex that the human person receives the characteristics which, on the biological, psychological and spiritual levels, make that person a man or a woman, and thereby largely condition his or her progress towards maturity and insertion into society. Hence sexual matters, as is obvious to everyone, today constitute a theme frequently and openly dealt with in books, reviews, magazines and other means of social communication.

   In the present period, the corruption of morals has increased, and one of the most serious indications of this corruption is the unbridled exaltation of sex. Moreover, through the means of social communication and through public entertainment this corruption has reached the point of invading the field of education and of infecting the general mentality.

   In this context certain educators, teachers and moralists have been able to contribute to a better understanding and integration into life of the values proper to each of the sexes; on the other hand there are those who have put forward concepts and modes of behavior which are contrary to the true moral exigencies of the human person. Some members of the latter group have even gone so far as to favor a licentious hedonism.

   As a result, in the course of a few years, teachings, moral criteria and modes of living hitherto faithfully preserved have been very much unsettled, even among Christians. There are many people today who, being confronted with so many widespread opinions opposed to the teaching which they received from the Church, have come to wonder what they must still hold as true.

2. The Church cannot remain indifferent to this confusion of minds and relaxation of morals. It is a question, in fact, of a matter which is of the utmost importance both for the personal lives of Christians and for the social life of our time.[1]

   The Bishops are daily led to note the growing difficulties experienced by the faithful in obtaining knowledge of wholesome moral teaching, especially in sexual matters, and of the growing difficulties experienced by pastors in expounding this teaching effectively. The Bishops know that by their pastoral charge they are called upon to meet the needs of their faithful in this very serious matter, and important documents dealing with it have already been published by some of them or by Episcopal Conferences. Nevertheless, since the erroneous opinions and resulting deviations are continuing to spread everywhere, the Sacred Congregation for the Doctrine of the Faith, by virtue of its function in the universal Church[2] and by a mandate of the Supreme Pontiff, has judged it necessary to publish the present Declaration.

3. The people of our time are more and more convinced that the human person's dignity and vocation demand that they should discover, by the light of their own intelligence, the values innate in their nature, that they should ceaselessly develop these values and realize them in their lives, in order to achieve an ever greater development.

   In moral matters man cannot make value judgments according to his personal whim: "In the depths of his conscience, man detects a law which he does not impose on himself, but which holds him to obedience. . . . For man has in his heart a law written by God. To obey it is the very dignity of man; according to it he will be judged."[3]

   Moreover, through his revelation God has made known to us Christians his plan of salvation, and he has held up to us Christ, the Saviour and Sanctifier, in his teaching and example, as the supreme and immutable Law of life: "I am the light of the world; anyone who follows me will not be walking in the dark, he will have the light of life."[4]

   Therefore there can be no true promotion of man's dignity unless the essential order of his nature is respected. Of course, in the history of civilization many of the concrete conditions and needs of human life have changed and will continue to change. But all evolution of morals and every type of life must be kept within the limits imposed by the immutable principles based upon every human person's constitutive elements and essential relations—elements and relations which transcend historical contingency.

   These fundamental principles, which can be grasped by reason, are contained in "the divine law—eternal, objective and universal—whereby God orders, directs and governs the entire universe and all the ways of the human community, by a plan conceived in wisdom and love. Man has been made by God to participate in this law, with the result that, under the gentle disposition of divine Providence, he can come to perceive ever increasingly the unchanging truth."[5] This divine law is accessible to our minds.

4. Hence, those many people are in error who today assert that one can find neither in human nature nor in the revealed law any obsolete and immutable norm to serve for particular actions other than the one which expresses itself in the general law of charity and respect for human dignity. As a proof of their assertion they put forward the view that so-called norms of the natural law or precepts of Sacred Scripture are to be regarded only as given expressions of a form of particular culture at a certain moment of history.

   But in fact, divine Revelation and, in its own proper order, philosophical wisdom, emphasize the authentic exigencies of human nature. They thereby necessarily manifest the existence of immutable laws inscribed in the constitutive elements of human nature and which are revealed to be identical in all beings endowed with reason.

   Furthermore, Christ instituted his Church as "the pillar and bulwark of truth."[6] With the Holy Spirit's assistance, she ceaselessly preserves and transmits without error the truths of the moral order, and she authentically interprets not only the revealed positive law but "also . . . those principles of the moral order which have their origin in human nature itself"[7] and which concern man's full development and sanctification. Now in fact the Church throughout her history has always considered a certain number of precepts of the natural law as having an absolute and immutable value, and in their transgression she has seen a contradiction of the teaching and spirit of the Gospel.

5. Since sexual ethics concern certain fundamental values of human and Christian life, this general teaching equally applies to sexual ethics. In this domain there exist principles and norms which the Church has always unhesitatingly transmitted as part of her teaching, however much the opinions and morals of the world may have been opposed to them. These principles and norms in no way owe their original to a certain type of culture, but rather to knowledge of the divine law and of human nature. They therefore cannot be considered as having become out of date or doubtful under the pretext that a new cultural situation has arisen.

It is these principles which inspired the exhortations and directives given by the Second Vatican Council for an education and an organization of social life taking account of the equal dignity of man and woman while respecting their difference.[8]

Speaking of the "sexual nature of man and the human faculty of procreation," the Council noted that they "wonderfully exceed the dispositions of lower forms of life."[9] It then took particular care to expound the principles and criteria which concern human sexuality in marriage, and which are based upon the finality of the specific function of sexuality.

In this regard the Council declares that the moral goodness of the acts proper to conjugal life, acts which are ordered according to true human dignity, "does not depend solely on sincere intentions or on an evaluation of motives. It must be determined by objective standards. These, based on the nature of the human person and his acts preserve the full sense of mutual self-giving and human procreation in the context of true love."[10]

These final words briefly sum up the Council's teaching—more fully expounded in an earlier part of the same Constitution.[11]—on the finality of the sexual act and on the principal criterion of its morality: it is respect for its finality that ensures the moral goodness of this act.

This same principle, which the Church holds from divine Revelation and from her authentic interpretation of the natural law, is also the basis of her traditional doctrine, which states that the use of the sexual function has its true meaning and moral rectitude only in true marriage."[12]

6. It is not the purpose of the present Declaration to deal with all the abuses of the sexual faculty, nor with all the elements involved in the practice of chastity. Its object is rather to repeat the Church's doctrine on certain particular points, in view of the urgent need to oppose serious errors and widespread aberrant modes of behavior.

7. Today there are many who vindicate the right to sexual union before marriage, at least in those cases where a firm intention to marry and an affection which is already in some way conjugal in the psychology of the subjects require this completion, which they judge to be connatural. This is especially the case when the celebration of the marriage is impeded by circumstances or when this initiate relationship seems necessary in order for love to be preserved.

This opinion is contrary to Christian doctrine, which states that every genital act must be within the framework of marriage. However firm the intention of those who practice such premature sexual relations may be, the fact remains that these relations cannot ensure, in sincerity and fidelity, the interpersonal relationship between a man and a woman, nor especially can they protect this relationship from whims and caprices.

Now it is a stable union that Jesus willed, and he restored its original requirement, beginning with the sexual difference. "Have you not read that the creator from the beginning made them male and female and that he said: This is why a man must leave father and mother, and cling to his wife, and the two become one body? They are no longer two, therefore, but one body. So then, what God has united, man must not divide."[13] Saint Paul will be even more explicit when he shows that if unmarried people or widows cannot live chastely they have no other alternative than the stable union of marriage: ". . . it is better to marry than to be aflame with passion."[14] Through marriage, in fact, the love of married people is taken up into that love which Christ irrevocably has for the Church,[15] while dissolute sexual unions[16] defiles the temple of the Holy Spirit which the Christian has become. Sexual union therefore is only legitimate if a definitive community of life has been established between the man and the woman.

This is what the Church has always understood and taught,[17] and she finds a profound agreement with her doctrine in men's reflection and in the lessons of history.

Experience teaches us that love must find its safeguard in the stability of marriage, if sexual intercourse is truly to respond to the requirements of its own finality and to those of human dignity. These requirements call for a conjugal contract sanctioned and guaranteed by society—a contract which establishes a state of life of capital importance both for the exclusive union of the man and the woman and for the good of their family and of the human community. Most often, in fact, premarital relations exclude the possibility of children. What is represented to be conjugal love is not able, as it absolutely should be, to develop into paternal and maternal love. Or, if it does happen to do so, this will be to the detriment of the children, who will be deprived of the stable environment in which they ought to develop in order to find in it the way and the means of their insertion into society as a whole.

The consent given by people who wish to be united in marriage must therefore be manifested externally and in a manner which makes it valid in the eyes of society. As far as the faithful are concerned, their consent to the setting up of a community of conjugal life must be expressed according to the laws of the Church. It is a consent which makes their marriage a Sacrament of Christ.

8. At the present time there are those who, basing themselves on observations in the psychological order, have begun to judge indulgently, and even to excuse completely, homosexual relations between certain people. This they do in opposition to the constant teaching of the Magisterium and to the moral sense of the Christian people.

A distinction is drawn, and it seems with some reason, between homosexuals whose tendency comes from a false education, from a lack of normal sexual development, from habit, from bad example, or from other similar causes, and is transitory or at least not incurable, and homosexuals who are definitively such because of some kind of innate instinct or a pathological constitution judged to be incurable.

In regard to this second category of subjects, some people conclude that their tendency is so natural that it justifies in their case homosexual relations within a sincere communion of life and love analogous to marriage, in so far as such homosexuals feel incapable of enduring a solitary life.

In the pastoral field, these homosexuals must certainly be treated with understanding and sustained in the hope of overcoming their personal difficulties and their inability to fit into society. Their culpability will be judged with prudence. But no pastoral method can be employed which would give moral justification to these acts on the grounds that they would be consonant with the condition of such people. For according to the objective moral order, homosexual relations are acts which lack an essential and indispensable finality. In Sacred Scripture they are condemned as a serious depravity and even presented as the sad consequence of rejecting God.[18] This judgment of

Scripture does not of course permit us to conclude that all those who suffer from this anomaly are personally responsible for it, but it does attest to the fact that homosexual acts are intrinsically disordered and can in no case be approved.

9. The traditional Catholic doctrine that masturbation constitutes a grave moral disorder is often called into doubt or expressly denied today. It is that psychology and sociology show that it is a normal phenomenon of sexual development, especially among the young. It is stated that there is real and serious fault only in the measure that the subject deliberately indulges in solitary pleasure closed in on self (''ipsation''), because in this case the act would indeed be radically opposed to the loving communion between persons of different sex which some hold is what is principally sought in the use of the sexual faculty.

This opinion is contradictory to the teaching and pastoral practice of the Catholic Church. Whatever the force of certain arguments of a biological and philosophical nature, which have sometimes been used by theologians, in fact both the Magisterium of the Church—in the course of a constant tradition—and the moral sense of the faithful have declared without hesitation that masturbation is an intrinsically and seriously disordered act.[19]

The main reason is that, whatever the motive for acting in this way, the deliberate use of the sexual faculty outside normal conjugal relations essentially contradicts the finality of the faculty. For it lacks the sexual relationship called for by the moral order, namely the relationship which realizes the full sense of mutual self-giving and human procreation in the context of true love.[20] All deliberate exercise of sexuality must be reserved to this regular relationship. Even if it cannot be proved that Scripture condemns this sin by name, the tradition of the Church as rightly understood it to be condemned in the New Testament when the latter speaks of ''impurity,'' ''unchasteness'' and other vices contrary to chastity and continence.

Sociological surveys are able to show the frequency of this disorder according to the places, populations or circumstances studied. In this way facts are discovered, but facts do not constitute a criterion for judging the moral value of human acts[21] The frequency of the phenomenon in question is certainly to be linked with man's innate weakness following original sin; but it is also to be linked with the loss of a sense of God, with the corruption of morals engendered by the commercialization of vice, with the unrestrained licentiousness of so many public entertainments and publications, as well as with the neglect of modesty, which is the guardian of chastity.

On the subject of masturbation modern psychology provides much valid and useful information for formulating a more equitable judgment on moral responsibility and for orienting pastoral action. Psychology helps one to see how the immaturity of adolescence (which can sometimes persist after that age), psychological imbalance or habit can influence behavior, diminishing the deliberate character of the act and bringing about a situation whereby subjectively there may not always be serious fault. But in general, the absence of serious responsibility must not be presumed; this would be to misunderstand people's moral capacity.

In the pastoral ministry, in order to form an adequate judgment in concrete cases, the habitual behavior of people will be considered in its totality, not only with regard to the individual's practice of charity and of justice but also with regard to the individual's care in observing the particular precepts of chastity. In particular, one will have to examine whether the individual is using the necessary means, both natural and supernatural, which Christian asceticism from its long experience recommends for overcoming the passions and progressing in virtue.

10. The observance of the moral law in the field of sexuality and the practice of chastity have been considerably endangered, especially among less fervent Christians, by the

current tendency to minimize as far as possible, when not denying outright, the reality of grave sin, at least in people's actual lives.

There are those who go as far as to affirm that moral sin, which causes separation from God, only exists in the formal refusal directly opposed to God's call, or in that selfishness which completely and deliberately closes itself to the love of neighbor. They say that it is only then that there comes into play the fundamental option, that is to say the decision which totally commits the person and which is necessary if mortal sin is to exist; by this option the person, from the depths of the personality, takes up or ratifies a fundamental attitude towards God or people. On the contrary, so-called "peripheral" actions (which, it is said, usually do not involve decisive choice), do not go so far as to change the fundamental option, the less so since they often come, as is observed, from habit. Thus such actions can weaken the fundamental option, but not to such a degree as to change it completely. Now according to these authors, a change of the fundamental option towards God less easily comes about in the field of sexual activity, where a person generally does not transgress the moral order in a fully deliberate and responsible manner but rather under the influence of passion, weakness, immaturity, sometimes even through the illusion of thus showing love for someone else. To these causes there is often added the pressure of the social environment.

In reality, it is the fundamental option which in the last resort defines a person's moral disposition. But it can be completely changed by particular acts, especially when, as often happens, these have been prepared for by previous more superficial acts. Whatever the case, it is wrong to say that the particular acts are not enough to constitute mortal sin.

According to the Church's teaching, mortal sin, which is opposed to God, does not consist only in formal and direct resistance to the commandment of charity. It is equally to be found in this opposition to authentic love which is included in every deliberate transgression, in serious matters, of each of the moral laws.

Christ himself has indicated the double commandment of love as the basis of the moral life. But on this commandment depends "the whole Law, and the Prophets also.[22] "It therefore includes the other particular precepts. In fact, to the young man who asked, ". . . what good deed must I do to possess eternal life?" Jesus replied: ". . . . if you wish to enter into life, keep the commandments. . . You must not kill. You must not commit adultery. You must not steal. You must not bring false witness. Honor your father and mother, and: you must love your neighbor as yourself."[23]

A person therefore sins mortally not only when his action comes from direct contempt for love of God and neighbor, but also when he consciously and freely, for whatever reason, chooses something which is seriously disordered. For in this choice, as has been said above, there is already included contempt for the divine commandment: the person turns himself away from God and loess charity. Now according to Christian tradition and the Church's teaching, and as right reason also recognizes, the moral order of sexuality involves such high values of human life that every direct violation of this order is objectively serious.[24]

It is true that in sins of the sexual order, in view of their kind and their causes, it more easily happens that free consent is not fully given; that is a fact which calls for caution in all judgment as to the subject's responsibility. In this matter it is particularly opportune to recall the following words of Scripture: "Man looks at appearances but God looks at the heart."[25] However, although prudence is recommended in judgment the subjective seriousness of a particular sinful act, it in no way follows that one can hold the view that in the sexual field moral sins are not committed.

Pastors of souls must therefore exercise patience and goodness; but they are not allowed to render God's commandments null, nor to reduce unreasonably people's responsibility. "To diminish in no way the saving teaching of Christ constitutes to eminent form of charity for souls. But this must ever be accompanied by patience and goodness, such as the Lord himself gave example of in dealing with people. Having come not to condemn but to save, he was indeed intransigent with evil, but merciful towards individuals."[26]

11. As has been said above, the purpose of this Declaration is to draw the attention of the faithful in present-day circumstances to certain errors and modes of behavior which they must guard against. The virtue of chastity, however, is in no way confined solely to avoiding the faults already listed. It is aimed at attaining higher and more positive goals. It is a virtue which concerns the whole personality, as regards both interior and outward behavior.

Individuals should be endowed with this virtue according to their state in life: for some it will mean virginity or celibacy consecrated to God, which is an eminent way of giving oneself more easily to God alone with an undivided heart.[27] For others it will take the form determined by the moral law, according to whether they are married or single. But whatever the state of life, chastity is not simply an external state; it must make a person's heart pure in accordance with Christ's words: "You have learned how it was said; You must not commit adultery. But I say this to you: if a man looks at a woman lustfully, he has already committed adultery with her in his heart."[28]

Chastity is included in that continence which Saint Paul numbers among the gifts of the Holy Spirit, while he condemns sensuality as a vice particularly unworthy of the Christian and one which precludes entry into the kingdom of heaven.[29] What God wants is for all to be holy. He wants you to keep away from fornication, and each one of you to know how to use the body that belongs to him in a way that is holy and honorable, not giving way to selfish lust like the pagans who do not know God. He wants nobody at all ever to sin by taking advantage of a brother in these matters. . . . We have been called by God to be holy, not to be immoral. In other words, anyone who objects is not objecting to a human authority, but to God, who gives you his Holy Spirit."[30] "Among you there must not be even a mention of fornication or impurity in any of its forms, or promiscuity: this would hardly become the saints! For you can be quite certain that nobody who actually indulges in fornication or impurity or promiscuity—which is worshipping a false god—can inherit anything of the kingdom of God. Do not let anyone deceive you with empty arguments: it is for this loose living that God's anger comes down on those who rebel against him. Make sure that you are not included with them. You were darkness once, but now you are light in the Lord; be like children of life, for the effects of the light are seen in complete goodness and right living and truth."[31]

In addition, the Apostle points out the specifically Christian motive for practicing chastity when he condemns the sin of fornication not only in the measure that this action is injurious to one's neighbor or to the social order but because the fornicator offends against Christ who has redeemed him with his blood and of whom he is a member, and against the Holy Spirit of whom he is the temple. "You know, surely, that your bodies are members making up the body of Christ. . . . All the other sins are committed outside the body; but to fornicate is to sin against your own body. Your body, you know, is the temple of the Holy Spirit, who is in you since you received him from God. You are not your own property; you have been bought and paid for. That is why you should use your body for the glory of God."[32]

The more the faithful appreciate the value of chastity and its necessary role in their lives as men and women, the better they will understand, by a kind of spiritual instinct, its moral requirements and counsels. In the same way they will know better how to accept and carry out, in a spirit of docility to the Church's teaching, what an upright conscience dictates in concrete cases.

12. The Apostle Saint Paul describes in vivid terms the painful interior conflict of the person enslaved to sin: the conflict between "the laws of his mind" and the "law of sin in which dwells in his members" and which holds him captive.[33] But man can achieve liberation from his "body doomed to death" through the grace of Jesus Christ.[34] This grace is enjoyed by those who have been justified by it and whom "the law of the spirit of life in Christ Jesus has set free from the laws of sin and death."[35] It is for this reason that the Apostle adjures them: "That is why you must not let sin reign in your mortal bodies or command your obedience to bodily passions."[36]

This liberation, which fits one to serve God in newness of life, does not however suppress the concupiscence deriving from original sin, nor the promptings to evil in this world, which is "in the power of the evil one."[37] This is why the Apostle exhorts the faithful to overcome temptations by the power of God[38] and to "stand against the wiles of the devil[39] by faith, watchful prayer[40] and an austerity of life that brings the body into subjection to the Spirit.[41]

Living the Christian life by following in the footsteps of Christ requires that everyone should "deny himself and take up his cross daily,"[42] sustained by the hope of reward, for "if we have died with him, we shall also reign with him."[43]

In accordance with these pressing exhortations, the faithful of the present time, and indeed today more than ever, must use the means which have always been recommended by the Church for living a chaste life. These means are: discipline of the senses and the mind, watchfulness and prudence in avoiding the occasions of sin, the observance of modesty, moderation in recreation, wholesome pursuits, assiduous prayer and frequent reception of the Sacraments of Penance and the Eucharist. Young people especially should earnestly foster devotion to the Immaculate Mother of God, and take as examples the lives of the Saints and other faithful people, especially young ones, who excelled in the practice of chastity.

It is important in particular that everybody should have a high esteem for the virtue of chastity, its beauty and its power of attraction. This virtue increases the human person's dignity and enables him to love truly, disinterestedly, unselfishly and with respect for others.

13. It is up to the Bishops to instruct the faithful in the moral teaching concerning sexual morality, however great may be the difficulties in carrying out this work in the face of ideas and practices generally prevailing today. This traditional doctrine must be studied more deeply. It must be handed on in a way capable of properly enlightening the consciences of those confronted with new situations and it must be enriched with a discernment of all the elements that can truthfully and usefully be brought forword about the meaning and value of human sexuality. But the principles and norms of moral living reaffirmed in this Declaration must be faithfully held and taught. It will especially be necessary to bring the faithful to understand that the Church holds these principles not as old and inviolable superstitions, nor out of some Manichaean prejudice, as is often alleged, but rather because she knows with certainty that they are in complete harmony with the divine order of creation and with the spirit of Christ, and therefore also with human dignity.

It is likewise the Bishops' mission to see that a sound doctrine enlightened by faith and directed by the Magisterium of the Church is taught in Faculties of Theology and in Seminaries. Bishops must also ensure that confessors enlighten people's consciences and that catechetical instruction is given in perfect fidelity to Catholic doctrine.

It rests with Bishops, the priests and their collaborators to alert the faithful against the erroneous opinions often expressed in books, reviews and public meetings.

Parents, in the first place, and also teachers of the young must endeavor to lead their children and their pupils, by way of a complete education, to the psychological, emotional and moral maturity befitting their age. They will therefore prudently give them information suited to their age; and they will assiduously form their wills in accordance with Christian morals, not only by advice but above all by the example of their own lives, relying on God's help, which they will obtain in prayer. They will likewise protect the young from the many dangers of which they are quite unaware.

Artists, writers and all those who use the means of social communication should exercise their profession in accordance with their Christian faith and with a clear awareness of the enormous influence which they can have. They should remember that "the primacy of the objective moral order must be regarded as absolute by all,[44] and that it is wrong for them to give priority above it to any so-called aesthetic purpose, or to material advantage or to success. Whether it be a question of artistic or literary works, public entertainment or providing information, each individual in his or her own domain must show tact, discretion, moderation and a true sense of values. In this way, far from adding to the growing permissiveness of behavior, each individual will contribute towards controlling it and even towards making the moral climate of society more wholesome.

All lay people, for their part, by virtue of their rights and duties in the work of the apostolate, should endeavor to act in the same way.

Finally, it is necessary to remind everyone of the words of the Second Vatican Council: "This Holy Synod likewise affirms that children and young people have a right to be encouraged to weigh moral values with an upright conscience, and to embrace them by personal choice, to know and love God more adequately. Hence, it earnestly entreats all who exercise government over people or preside over the work of education to see that youth is never deprived of this sacred right."[45]

At the audience granted on November 7, 1975 to the undersigned Prefect of the Sacred Congregation for the Doctrine of the Faith, the Sovereign Pontiff by divine providence Pope Paul VI approved this Declaration "On Certain questions concerning sexual ethics," confirmed it and ordered its publication.

Given in Rome, at the Sacred Congregation for the Doctrine of Faith, on December 29, 1975.

FRANJO Card. SEPER
Prefect

fr. JÉRÔME Hamer, O.P.
Titular Archbishop of Lorium
Secretary

Endnotes

[1] Cf. Second Vatican Ecumenical Council, Constitution on the Church in the Modern World *Gaudium et Spes,* 47: AAS 58 (1966), p. 1067.

[2] Cf. Apostolic Constitution *Regimini Ecclesiae Universae,* 29 (August 15, 1967): AAS 59 (1967), p. 897.

[3] *Gaudium et Spes,* 16: AAS 58 (1966), p. 1037.

[4] Jn 8:12.

[5] Second Vatican Ecumenical Council, Declaration *Dignitatis Humanae,* 3: AAS 58 (1966) p. 931.

[6] 1 Tim 3:15.

[7] *Diginitatis Humanae,* 14: AAS 58 (1966), p. 940; cf. Piux XI, Encyclical Letter *Casti Connubii,* December 31, 1930: AAS 22 (1930), pp. 579-580; Pius XII, Allocution of November 2, 1954: AAS 46 (1954), pp. 671-672; John XXIII, Encyclical Letter *Mater*

et Magistra, May 15, 1961: AAS 53, (1961), p. 457; Paul VI, Encyclical Letter *Humanae Vitae,* 4, July 25, 1968: AAS 60 (1968), p. 483.

[8] Cf. Second Vatican Ecumenical Council, Declaration *Gravissimum Educationis,* 1, 8: AAS 58 (1966), pp. 729-730; 734-736. *Gaudium et Spes,* 29, 60, 67: AAS 58 (1966), pp. 1048-1049, 1080-1081, 1088-1089.

[9] *Gaudium et Spes,* 51: AAS 58 (1966), p. 1072.

[10] *Ibid.*; cf. also 49: loc. cit., pp. 1069-1072.

[11] *Ibid.* 49, 50: loc. cit., pp. 1069-1072.

[12] The present Declaration does not go into further detail regarding the norms of sexual life within marriage; these norms have been clearly taught in the Encyclical Letters *Cansti Connubii* and *Humanae Vitae*.

[13] Cf. Mt. 19:4-6.

[14] 1 Cor 7:9.

[15] Cf. Eph 5:25-32.

[16] Sexual intercourse outside marriage is formally condemned: 1 Cor 5:1; 6:9; 7:2; 10:8; Eph 5:5; 1 Tim 1:10; Heb 13:4; and with explicit reasons: 1 Cor 6:12-20.

[17] Cf. Innocient IV, Letter *Sub catholica professione,* March 6, 1254, DS 835; Pius II, *Propos. damn. in Ep. Cum sicut accepimus*, November 14, 1459, DS 1367;Decrees of the Holy Office, September 24, 1665, DS 2045; March 2, 1679, DS 2148. Pius XI, Encyclical Letter *Casti Connubii,* December 31, 1930: AAS 22 (1930) pp. 558-559.

[18] Rom 1:24-27: "That is why God left them to their filthy enjoyments and the practices with which they dishonor their own bodies, since they have given up divine truth for a lie and have worshipped and served creatures instead of the creator, who is blessed for ever. Amen! That is why God has abandoned them to degrading passions: why their women have turned from natural intercourse to unnatural practices and why their menfolk have given up natural intercourse to be consumed with passion for each other, men doing shameless things with men and getting an appropriate reward for their perversion." See also what Saint Paul says of *masculorum concubitores* in 1 Cor 6:10; 1 Tim 1:10.

[19] Cf. Leo IX, Letter *Ad splendidum nitentis,* in the year 1054: DS 687-688, Decree of the Holy Office, March 2, 1679: DS 2149; Pius XII, *Allocutio,* October 8, 1953: AAS 45 (1953), pp. 677-678; May 19, 1956: AAS 48 (1956), pp. 472-473.

[20] *Gaudium et Spes,* 51: AAS 58 (1966), p. 1072.

[21] ". . . if sociological surveys are useful for better discovering the thought patterns of the people of a particular place, the anxieties and needs of those to whom we proclaim the word of God, and also the opposition made to it by modern reasoning through the widespread notion that outside science there exists no legitimate form of knowledge, still the conclusions drawn from such surveys could not of themselves constitute a determining criterion of truth," Paul VI, Apostolic Exhortation *Quinque iam anni,* December 8, 1970, AAS 63 (1971,) p. 102.

[22] Mt 22:38, 40.

[23] Mt 19:16-19.

[24] Cf. note 17 and 19 above: Decree of the Holy Office, March 18, 1666, DS 2060; Paul VI, Encyclical Letter *Humanae Vitae,* 13,14: AAS 60 (1968,) p. 489-496.

[25] 1 Sam 16:7.

[26] Paul VI, Encyclical Letter *Humanae Vitae,* 29: AAS 60 (1968,) p. 501.

[27] Cf. 1 Cor 7:7, 34; Council of Trent, Session XXIV, can. 10: DS 1810; Second Vatican

Council, Constitution *Lumen Gentium,* 42, 43, 44: AAS 57 (1965), pp. 47-51; Synod of Bishops, *De Sacerdotio Ministeriali,* part II, 4, b: AAS 63 (1971), pp. 915-916.

[28] Mt 5:28.

[29] Cf. Gal 5:19-23; 1 Cor 6:9-11.

[30] 1 Thess 4:3-8; cf. Col 3:5-7; 1 Tim 1:10.

[31] Eph 5:3-8; cf. 4:18-19.

[32] 1 Cor 6:15, 18-20.

[33] Cf. Rom 7:23.

[34] Cf. Rom 7:24-25.

[35] Cf. Rom 8:2.

[36] Rom 6:12.

[37] 1 Jn 5:19.

[38] Cf. 1 Cor 10:13.

[39] Eph 6:11.

[40] Cf. Eph. 6:16, 18.

[41] Cf. 1 Cor 9:27.

[42] Lk 9:23.

[43] 2 Tim 2:11-12.

[44] Second Vatican Ecumenical Council, Decree *Inter Mirifica,* 6: AAS 56 (1964,) p. 147.

[45] *Gravissimum Educationis,* 1: AAS 58 (1966), p. 730.

Notes: *The noticeable change in public sexual mores around the world, of which homosexuality was but one aspect, prompted a series of statements concerning sexual behavior from the Roman Catholic Church. Among the earliest post-Vatican II statements was this communication on sexual ethics from the world headquarters of the church in Rome; it was issued by Franjo Cardinal Seper of the Sacred Congregation for the Doctrine of the Faith, one of the principal administrative offices of the church.*

The declaration briefly summarizes the church's position on a variety of topics having to do with sexual behavior. The bedrock of the Roman Catholic Church's stance is that "every genital act must be within the framework of marriage." Given that statement, its position on homosexuality is predictable. The declaration shows an awareness of the modern distinction between homosexual acts and the psychological tendency to be attracted to sexual partners of the same sex. However, it also rejects the relevance of the distinction, since it rejects homosexuality at every level. It also rejects any pastoral approaches which would imply a condoning of homosexuality.

This document clearly stated the opinion of the church and provided the base upon which later statements would be built.

ROMAN CATHOLIC CHURCH—ARCHBISHOP JOHN R. QUINN

A PASTORAL LETTER ON HOMOSEXUALITY (1980)

To the priests, deacons, religious and all the faithful of Christ in the Archdiocese of San Francisco: Grace and peace be yours from God our Father and from the Lord, Jesus Christ!

I. The Present-Day Situation

Vexing and serious questions arise with increasing frequency concerning the problem of homosexuality. While I cannot either treat or answer all possible questions on the subject, I feel it timely and important to offer some guidance and bring, I hope, some clarity to our understanding of the issue. It is with this purpose, then, that I write to you and commend to you the thoughts which follow in this pastoral letter.

A survey of the literature on the subject of homosexuality reveals that since 1974 especially there has been a growing public affirmation by individuals of their own homosexuality. At the same time pressures have been growing to remove prejudicial attitudes toward homosexual persons especially in regard to housing, hiring practices, teaching opportunities, etc. Still more there are growing pressures calling for recognition of the homosexual lifestyle as legitimate and worthy of societal, legal and ecclesiastical endorsement and approval.

In short, we are being besieged to move from a non-prejudicial attitude toward individuals to a point of view of total acceptance of homosexuality as a legitimate personal and public choice. Thus homosexuality is seen as a legitimate alternative to heterosexuality and the society is asked to support this position. Does this position warrant our agreement?

Several years ago, Jaroslav Pelikan attempted to crystallize the essence of the Catholic Church in the formula: identity plus universality. "By identity I mean that which distinguishes the church from the world—its message, its uniqueness, is particularity. By universality, on the other hand, I mean that which impels the church to embrace nothing less than all mankind in its vision and its appeal."

The general trend we are speaking of in regard to homosexuality reveals a determined bias toward the pole of universality, resulting in a distorted underemphasis on the pole of identity. Here it is well to recall Pope John Paul's reminder that the church must be a "sign of contradiction" to those elements of the world which threaten to distort, harm or destroy the authentic message of Christ.

And so as we move into the final decades marking 2,000 years since the birth of Christ, the church is keenly aware of a new and transforming consciousness of universality. But for the church this new consciousness stands within the perspective of a clear, certain and unambiguous Catholic identity which is embodied in the church's faith and witness to Jesus Christ.

Any effort, then, to deal with the question of homosexuality must have clearly in mind both poles of universality and identity and must be built on the recognition that the Gospel is not a dichotomy between love and truth, for God, who is love, is also proclaimed by the scriptures as truth, and Jesus said of himself, "I am the truth."

1. Statement of the Question.

There are several reasons why it is not easy to achieve a balanced and objective understanding of homosexuality. First of all, it is a highly charged emotional issue. Thus when certain mitigating factors at the subjective level are correctly pointed out, or when the human rights of homosexual individuals are defended, some wrongly conclude that this means an endorsement of homosexual activity.

In addition to the high emotions surrounding the issue, homosexuality in itself is enormously complex in its origins, its psychological vectors, medical ramifications, societal norms and in the application of valid moral principles to individual cases. Hence some of the aspects of the question do not admit of easy answers.

This does not at all say that the moral teaching of the church is unclear. It does say that it is necessary to recognize that we are dealing with an issue of considerable complexity in all dimensions.

Since not all persons who are homosexual engage in homosexual conduct, it is necessary at the outset to make the distinction between homosexual tendency and the acting out of homosexuality through specifically sexual encounters with persons of the same sex. It must also be pointed out that there is often a difference in understanding the language used in discussing homosexuality.

For instance, moral theologians tend to use the expression ''homosexual orientation'' to mean only the psychosexual attraction itself. On the other hand, legislative language often uses the expression ''homosexual orientation'' not merely for the psychosexual attraction, but also to include homosexual acts. For this reason the terminology used here is ''homosexual attraction'' or ''tendency.''

With this distinction in mind and respecting the contemporary data that in most cases the homosexual tendency has not been chosen, a working definition of homosexuality is a predominant, persistent and exclusive psychosexual attraction toward persons of the same sex; a homosexual person is one who feels sexual desire for a sexual for and a sexual responsiveness to persons of the same sex, and who seeks or would like to seek actual sexual fulfilment of this desire by sexual acts with a person of the same sex. This definition rightly emphasizes the distinction between the homosexual condition, attraction or tendency, and homosexual acts.

2. Context for Our Response

The major theme of Pope John Paul's first encyclical, *Redemptor Hominis,* is ''again and always man'' (n. 16). The whole encyclical is a powerful advocacy of respect and reverence for the dignity of the human person. Affirming that moral and spiritual progress is a necessity, the pope goes on to raise the question whether ''man, as man, is developing and progressing or is he regressing and being degraded in his humanity?'' (n. 15)

The encyclical thus indicates an awareness of the tensions we have already mentioned between identity and universality. The Holy Father acknowledges the need to understand every person, every system, every legitimate right (universality). But he clearly notes that this does not mean ''losing certitude about one's own faith or weakening the principles of morality'' (n. 6).

This strong sense of certitude—identity—is seen in the encyclical always in the context of love, a love that is greater than sin and weakness, and the futility of creation. ''It is stronger than death; it is a love always ready to raise up and forgive, always ready to go to meet the prodigal son, always looking for 'the revealing of the sons of God'. . . This revelation of love is also described as mercy; and in man's history this revelation of love and mercy has taken a form and a name: that of Jesus Christ'' (n. 9).

The pope thus calls us to draw near to Christ—with all our unrest, uncertainties, weaknesses and sinfulness. We must learn to ''appropriate and assimilate the whole of the reality of the incarnation and redemption'' (n. 10) in order to find authentic meaning. Moral identity, in other words, must be rooted in the person of Jesus Christ, and it is to this end that the church must fully dedicate herself (n. 13).

And so the church must always safeguard and proclaim the true calling and the true dignity of humanity by holding in reverence the ''transcendence of the human person'' (n. 13) immeasurably enhanced by the incarnation, death and resurrection of the Son of God, who became like us in all things but sin so that we might become one with him.

In responding to any moral question, then, we must keep a correct perspective concerning human dignity and transcendence.Our perspective derives from the Gospel and not from any ideology. The teaching of the faith and the Lord's supreme commandment of love rooted in truth must always underlie our analysis of this and every other moral question.

Recent Catholic teaching on the subject of homosexuality has approached the subject from the point of charity and the inherent dignity of the human person. In 1974 the bishops of the

United States issued a document titled *Principles to Guide Confessors in Questions of Homosexuality*. The document clearly reaffirms the objective gravity of homosexual acts.

At the same time it counsels sensitivity toward the individual homosexual person. The confessor, steering a course between harshness and permissiveness, should manifest great understanding, should give patient and loving encouragement to the individual in the often tedious and discouraging journey to grow in the image of Christ.

Similarly, in 1975 the Sacred Congregation for the Doctrine of the Faith issued a document titled *Declaration on Certain Questions Concerning Sexual Ethics*. This authentic document of the Holy See also reconfirms the objective wrongness of homosexual acts while drawing the important distinction between homosexual acts and a homosexual tendency or attraction.

Then in 1976 the American bishops wrote a lengthy pastoral letter touching on a variety of moral issues and bearing the title *To Live in Christ Jesus*. The teaching mentioned in the previous two documents is again stated.

In addition the pastoral letter adds the counsel that homosexual men and women should not suffer from prejudice on the basis of their sexual attraction. In fact, it states, the Christian community should provide a special degree of pastoral care and understanding for the special problems of the homosexual person.

Most recently the pope himself spoke about homosexuality to the bishops of the United States in Chicago Oct. 4, 1979. He said, "As men with the 'message of truth and the power of God' (2 Cor. 6:7), as authentic teachers of God's law and as compassionate pastors you also rightly stated 'Homosexual activity . . . as distinguished from homosexual orientation, is morally wrong.' In the clarity of this truth you exemplified the real charity of Christ; you did not betray those people who, because of homosexuality, are confronted with difficult moral problems, as would have happened if, in the name of understanding and compassion, or for any other reason, you had held out false hope to any brother or sister. Rather by your witness to the truth of humanity in God's plan, you effectively manifested fraternal love, upholding the true dignity, the true human dignity, of those who look to Christ's church for the guidance which comes from the light of God's word."

The recent teachings of the church therefore re-echo the clear teaching of the scriptures in declaring homosexual acts to be gravely evil and a disordered use of the sexual faculty. These same teachings also make clear the distinction between homosexual acts and homosexual orientation, and counsel sensitive and positive pastoral care in helping individual homosexual persons in their journey of discipleship.

The question then arises: What must be said to a subculture which advocates removing any distinction between homosexuality and heterosexuality? Given the fact that the authentic teaching of the church clearly affirms the objective gravity of homosexual acts, what must be said in light of the growing acceptance of homosexuality as a legitimate and alternative lifestyle?

3. The Real Problem

The term "homosexuality" is frequently used as if its meaning and connotations were self-evident. In fact, such is not the case. We have already noted how the term may apply either to a homosexual attraction or to homosexual conduct. In addition, we note that a fairly common view is that homosexuality represents an acquired condition that is both psychological and pathological. Yet many others do not accept homosexuality as pathological and view it as a variant form of sexual behavior. Some schools of thought hold that homosexuality is a purely physiological condition while others consider it only as a physiological predisposition.

These complexities in the data indicate the wide diversity of homosexual behaviors and only serve to increase the difficulty of arriving at a simple understanding of the problem. From a psychological point of view, homosexuality both in its origins and in its manifestations is a highly complex phenomenon and not always clearly understood even by experts.

Yet, it is because of developments in the fields of psychology and sociology that Catholic moral theology, guided by the distinction between sexual attraction and sexual behavior, is able to recognize more clearly factors which may in the case of individual conduct mitigate the gravity of such conduct on the subjective level.

But an additional problem arises for moral theology in a climate that increasingly encourages public revelation and proclamation of one's homosexual orientation. The emerging visibility of homosexuals and the militancy of the so-called "gay rights" movement only serve to heighten the problem. Still it is in light of this problem that the church must continue to uphold the human dignity and the human rights of every person, including homosexual persons.

On the one hand, then, homosexuality cannot be treated simply as the manifestation of a consciously chosen depravity. Homosexual persons cannot, merely because they are homosexual, be visited with harassment and contempt. The lynch-gang approach cannot be justified.

At the same time, however, opposition to homosexuality as a form of conduct, opposition to homosexuality as an acceptable lifestyle by the church or by society cannot be regarded as prejudice.

To agree that the persecution and harassment of homosexuals is incompatible with the Gospel is, therefore, not to say that the church and society should be neutral about homosexual activity. The church and society cannot and should not place the family which is and always will be the basic unit of society on a par with homosexual social units.

While we do not possess complete historical data on the subject, the fact is that in no culture has homosexuality been the dominant form of sexual expression and in Judaism and Christianity homosexual behavior has been clearly and consistently rejected as gravely contrary to the law of God.

II. Biblical Data

Unfortunately biblical scholars have published very little in recent years on the question of homosexuality in the Bible. As a result, a number of writers not trained in the discipline of biblical studies have attempted to address this question within the larger context of homosexuality as a pastoral problem. Most of these studies, regrettably, have not accurately interpreted the scriptural data and are therefore of little real value.

Before considering some individual scriptural texts it will be helpful to make a few general observations. First, the Bible is not merely a textbook of science or sociology. There is, of course, no question that the Bible contains ethical teachings concerning certain actions, but these are usually considered from a definite and well-defined point of view. For example, the Old Testament Israelite was commanded, "Thou shalt not kill." He would understand this as pertaining to the society within which he lived and would thus see no contradiction when he killed foreigners in taking over the promised land.

Consequently, the biblical writers did not necessarily see or experience all the aspects of a moral issue as we would comprehend it today. In other words, they did not necessarily ask the same questions about a given ethical or moral issue which we would ask today. Hence we cannot expect the scriptures of themselves to provide immediate answers to all of the moral problems that concern us.

Then, too, we must remember that while the scriptures hold a unique place in God's revelation to man, they are not self-interpreting. The true and authentic interpretation of the scriptures cannot be accomplished merely and exclusively by a recourse to exegetical and hermeneutical methodologies, as important as these are.

Ultimately the authentic interpretation of the scriptures lies with the living magisterium of the church, which has received from Christ the authority and the grace to determine the true meaning of the scriptures for the people of God. Hence all examination of the scriptures must be accompanied by recourse to the divine and living tradition of the magisterium of the church to which indeed the scriptures themselves bear witness.

With this in mind, it will be useful to take up several of the more important scriptural passages which deal with homosexuality.

1. The Old Testament

A. The Men of Sodom (Gn. 19:1-11; cfr. Jgs. 19:16-26)

A number of moral evils are involved in this episode. In both accounts a major sin is the refusal to show hospitality, which was a sacred obligation throughout the ancient Near East. But this is not the only sin involved. Despite the contentions of a few, there can be no doubt that the verb ''know'' in both texts refers to sexual intercourse.

Without any doubt the attempted rape serves to augment the evil of the incident. These texts, then, cannot be alleged either to approve of or to ignore the homosexual element of the incidents described.

B. David and Jonathan (1 Sm. 18-20; 2 Sm. 1:26)

In some ways, of course, it is not surprising that a Western reader would interpret the close friendship between David and Jonathan as a homosexual relationship. And if this view were correct it would be evidence for a tacit approval of such a relationship by the writers of the Old Testament.

But a closer study of the texts shows that the language used to describe their relationship is unmistakably drawn from the terminology of covenants between nations or individuals, such as the statement that ''Jonathan loved him (David) as his own soul'' (1 Sm. 18:1, 3). This is covenant terminology. It is not sexual.

The covenantal nature of their relationship is evident also from 1 Samuel 18:3: ''Then Jonathan made a covenant with David''; and from Chapter 20:8: ''Deal loyally with me (David), for you have brought me into a covenant with you—a covenant witnessed by the Lord''; also Verse 23: ''Behold the Lord is (a witness) between you and me forever.''

Nor is their kissing and weeping together any evidence of homosexuality (1 Sm. 20:41) since men in the Near East commonly express friendship more demonstratively than is allowed in our Western society.

Finally, there is David's extraordinary tribute to Jonathan: ''Your love for me was more wonderful than women's love'' (2 Sm. 1:26). Admittedly the language here is very strong, but does not necessarily refer to sexual love. The word for ''love'' in this passage is used elsewhere not only in a sexual sense but also of God's love for man and man's love for God.

And so here we probably have the typical ancient Near Eastern praise of men at the expense of women (v.g., cfr. Sir. 25:13-25). It also probably reflects David's own personal experience as a king. As a king his marriages were necessarily political and as a result, the love element may be assumed to be considerably less in them than the devotion shown him by his faithful friend, Jonathan.

C. Leviticus 18:12 and 20:13

These are the central Old Testament texts regarding homosexuality. They are found as part of the ''holiness code'' (Lv. 17-26) which is a collection of laws written down or rather edited probably during the Babylonian exile (587-538 B.C.).

All authorities acknowledge, however, that the basic content of these laws is considerably older. The two passages that deal with homosexuality are: ''You shall not lie with a male as with a woman; it is an abomination'' (Lv. 18:22); and ''If a man lies with a male as with a woman, both of them have committed an abomination'' (Lv. 20:13).

There is a widespread popular misconception that these texts prohibit homosexual activity because it is associated with pagan worship. Thus it would not be the homosexual aspect of the actions that is condemned, but rather the association with paganism. This view is definitely incorrect.

First of all, the verses in Chapters 18 and 20 which warn against imitating the practices of pagan neighbors date only from the time of exile. The laws themselves are considerably older. Hence later concerns cannot be read back into the laws themselves.

Second, Israel was not afraid of borrowing or imitating ideas in neighboring pagan cults. For instance, the Psalms are largely patterned on Canaanite religious poetry. Solomon's temple was built by Phoenician (i.e., Canaanite) architects and shows a number of striking influences of pagan cults. Some have tried to see in the term ''abomination'' which occurs in these two passages a specific reference to idolatrous practice. But the use of the term in the Old Testament is too broad to allow this narrow interpretation. (v.g., cfr. Prv. 11:1, 20; 12:22, etc.)

Finally, certain authors argue that these laws in Leviticus are of little or no relevance to the Christian today, being chiefly cultic and dietary in nature. It is, of course, true that most of the regulations here do concern such matters. But it is equally true that Leviticus contains ethical material as well. Note, for instance, that the ''second great commandment,'' ''Thou shalt love they neighbor as thyself'' is found between the two laws discussed here (19:18). One could hardly deny the ''relevance'' of this statement for the Christian.

2. The New Testament

The major New Testament statements on homosexuality come either from Paul or the ''deutero-Pauline'' letters (e.g., 1 Tm.). Before discussing specific texts we should say a word about Paul's attitude toward the law of the Old Testament. Some writers on the issue of homosexuality contend that Paul abrogated the law, by which they mean that the Old Testament ethical requirements were no longer in force. This is a fatuous and dangerously misleading position. Paul's point was that one who is baptized into Christ no longer acts from external motivation (the law), but from the inner guidance of the Holy Spirit.

Yet the results of such a teaching—i.e., how a person actually lived—would be what any Jew would recognize as a ''moral'' life, even from the Old Testament viewpoint. Thus the list of qualities Paul regards as essential to ''walking in the Spirit,''and their opposites (Gal. 5:16-24), is similar to lists of virtues and vices from both contemporary Jewish and pagan sources. Paul does not hesitate to condemn forcefully what is clearly called immoral behavior (v.g., 1 Cor. 5:1-5).

A. Romans 1:18-32

In this passage we are dealing with two things. First, the cause of homosexuality in pagan society and second, the moral judgment on homosexuality. In this passage, then, Paul reflects a common Jewish notion of his time, namely that certain vices particularly abhorrent to Jews were the result of or a punishment for idolatry. One of these vices is homosexual intercourse.

Note that Paul presents this as a perversion of the natural order of things. Of this there can be no doubt, since his whole point is that such ''perversity'' is the fitting punishment from God for those who refuse to worship him as the true God but pervert the order of nature by worshipping created things. Paul's condemnation of homosexual intercourse is clear in this passage. Yet the notion that this activity springs from idolatry is not entirely relevant to the situation today.

B. 1 Corinthians 6:9

Paul makes it abundantly clear to his Corinthian readers that freedom from the law does not mean license to practice immorality. His language is quite clear and quite strong. Two groups he lists here among others who will not "inherit the kingdom of God" and these are "catamites" and "sodomites" (vs. 9). The first word denotes the passive partner in an act of homosexual intercourse. The second (cfr. also 1 Tm. 1:10) literally means "those who lie (sexually) with males."

The claim that this was not one of the standard terms for homosexuals in the ancient world and that hence it would not have been understood by Paul's readers is completely groundless. The meaning of the word is self-evident in Greek.

Here too the popular misconception turns up that Paul's condemnation of homosexual activity simply represents a reaction to certain pagan rites current in Corinth. To maintain this view one would have to believe that Paul, an educated, pious Jew with rabbinical training, had never heard of the prohibition against homosexual intercourse in Leviticus, and that his repudiation of these practices was merely an ad hoc response to goings on in Corinth.

The absurdity of such a view is obvious. One should further note that the word Paul uses for "sodomite" in 1 Corinthians 6:9 closely reflects the terminology of Leviticus 20:13—more evidence that his view on homosexuality comes from his Old Testament background completed and expanded by the revelation made in Christ Jesus.

From the foregoing it is clear that the scriptures, both the Old and the New Testament, reject and condemn homosexual acts. The scriptures, it is true, do not explicitly deal with the question of homosexual attraction or with the issue of a homosexual lifestyle.

Nevertheless they do most clearly condemn an important element of that lifestyle, namely homosexual intercourse. Hence it is beyond dispute that there is a clear basis in scripture for the consistent rejection of a homosexual lifestyle as it exists in the moral teachings of the church including the most recent church teaching on the subject.

While it is clear that the scriptures condemn homosexual behavior, this does not imply any justification for exploitation of the homosexual or any injury to his or her dignity as a human person. Thus there is a clear difference between the acceptance of homosexual persons as worthy of respect and as having human rights, and approval of the homosexual lifestyle.

To make judgments from a Christian and cultural point of view about homosexual behavior is necessary since the church cannot be expected to deny its moral teaching and simply bless what is a contemporary cultural phenomenon.

The church certainly does not condemn those who discover within themselves a homosexual attraction or inclination and it must work to foster better care and guidance for those men and women whom society has often ostracized. The church must continue to work toward better education about homosexuality. It must tirelessly try to help homosexual men and women accept and live up to the moral teaching which the church has received from Christ.

But in no case can such acceptance or recognition of the homosexual person imply recognition of homosexual behavior as an acceptable lifestyle. The claim that homosexuality is simply a variant of normal sexual behavior and exists alongside heterosexuality as an equivalent expression of adult sexual maturation must be rejected. A normalization of homosexuality could only too easily foster and make more public homosexual behavior with the result of eroding the meaning of the family.

Both from the religious point of view as well as for the good of society itself, marriage and the family are realities that must be protected and strengthened. The family not only continues the human race, but it also glues it together. The family is the basic and living example of social cohesion.

Thus the Second Vatican Council affirmed, "All . . . who exercise influence over communities and social groups should work efficiently for the welfare of marriage and the family. Public authority should regard it as a sacred duty to recognize, protect and promote their authentic nature, to defend public morality and to foster the progress of home life.''

III. Moral and Ethical Considerations

The moral teaching of the church on the scriptures themselves, and consistent in all periods of history, holds that homosexual behavior is objectively immoral, a human disvalue, disordered. The teaching of the church recognizes the fact that homosexuality has generally not been chosen by a person, but rather that most homosexual persons gradually come to the realization that they are homosexual.

Thus thc church proposes various guidelines and pastoral approaches to assist and encourage the homosexual person's psychological and spiritual growth. (cf., v.g. *Principles to Guide Confessors in Questions of Homosexuality*, 1974)

The church recognizes the complexity of the question as it exists in the life of an individual person as well as the complexity of the question in the fields of the behavioral sciences. There must be sensitivity in treating the question. Homosexual persons must be helped and encouraged to strive for wholeness and personal integrity as indeed all other persons must be encouraged, homosexual or heterosexual.

Sexual intercourse cannot be legitimated merely by individual preference or on the basis of sociological surveys or because of mutual consent between two parties. Sexual intercourse is legitimate and morally good only between husband and wife. Thus while it is claimed that homosexuality in a few instances is more or less fulfilling for a limited number of individuals, the homosexual condition and homosexual behavior cannot be morally normative.

The church always remains the church of the eucharist and of the sacrament of penance. Every member of the church should pray daily, and many times daily, the prayer the Lord has taught us: ''Forgive us our trespasses as we forgive those who trespass against us.'' While the eucharist does manifest the community aspects of the church, ''it cannot be treated merely as an 'occasion' for manifesting this brotherhood'' (*Redemptor Hominis*, n. 20). More is required.

And so in this connection we must focus attention on the most recent encyclical letter of Pope John Paul II on the holy eucharist. He states: ''We cannot allow the life of our communities to lose the good quality of sensitivity of conscience. A sensitive conscience is guided solely by respect for Christ who, when he is received in the eucharist, should find in the heart of each of us a worthy abode. This question is linked not only with the practice of the sacrament of penance but also with a correct sense of responsibility for the whole deposit of moral teaching and for the precise distinction between good and evil'' (n. 11).

In order to receive the eucharist one must be in the state of grace, that is, in a living union with Christ characterized by the absence of grave sin. One must also be living in harmony with the moral and doctrinal teaching of the church.

Consequently, just as unmarried persons are not exempt from the moral teaching of the scriptures and of the church which has to do with sexual conduct, so homosexual persons are not exempt from this teaching either. Thus despite the difficulties, homosexual persons who wish to receive the eucharist must be honestly following the moral teaching of the church or at least sincerely striving to live up to that teaching.

This implies that like other Christians they must take advantage of the powerful graces that come from the reverent and frequent recourse to the sacrament of penance. In addition, of course, the natural aids they may need such as counseling, psychological help, etc., should and must be used where indicated and as needed.

In any case there is nothing to justify a departure from the church's normative pastoral and doctrinal teaching that one who has sinned gravely cannot approach the eucharist until he has been absolved from that sin in the sacrament of penance and this, of course, implies the firm amendment on the part of the penitent and his conscious intention to avoid that sin in the future.

Conclusion

Homosexual behavior cannot be viewed as an acceptable form of behavior morally or socially. At the same time persons who are homosexual must be treated with respect as human persons and they have a right to sound pastoral care.

It is the place of the church and her ministers to speak the whole moral teaching of the Gospel with clarity. The members of the church have the right to this even when the moral teaching is difficult. But the ministers of the church must present that moral teaching in a way that also encourages homosexual men and women to begin or continue the journey toward the fulfilment of the law of Christ.

On the other hand, when homosexual men and women claim that their way of life is a morally healthy one, insist on their intention to affirm and promote it publicly and ask that it be in some way approved by the church, they are clearly in contempt of the Christian conscience and in conflict with the teaching of the scriptures.

Indeed the church holds that there is no place for discrimination and prejudice against a person because of sexual attraction. But this does not mean that there is nothing wrong with homosexual conduct.

While homosexuality may constitute a unique problem and challenge for the homosexual man and woman, it is a mistake to isolate the homosexual person from the general body of disciples. All believers in Christ young and old, men and women, experience the weight of sin in their lives. All must experience the struggle with evil.

All must hear the voice of Christ enjoining his followers to enter on "the narrow way that leads to life," to "take up the cross each day and follow me." Christ chose the way of the cross. There is no other way for his followers. This is true of the homosexual as it is of all other Christians.

But in the eucharist and in the sacrament of penance supported by life of daily prayer and growing faith, every believer finds that what is judged impossible by the world is indeed possible. For as Jesus said, "All things are possible to him who believes."

Take to heart, then, the word of God which tells us:

"Get rid of all bitterness, a passion and anger, harsh words, slander and malice of every kind. In place of these, be kind to one another, compassionate and mutually forgiving just as God has forgiven you in Christ. . . There was a time when you were darkness, but now you are light in the Lord. Well, then, live as children of light. Light produces every kind of goodness and justice and truth" (Eph. 4:31-5:9).

Notes: *Archbishop Quinn presides over the San Francisco, California, archdiocese, which was the largest openly gay community in North America, if not the world. His pastoral letter is possible the most sensitive official document issued by the church on the subject of homosexuality and attempts to be as accepting of individual homosexuals as possible while upholding the official church's position. This lengthy, carefully worded document builds a rationale for its conclusion that, while the church wishes to accept the homosexual as a person of worth and dignitary, ". . . in no case can such acceptance or recognition of the homosexual person imply recognition of homosexual behavior as an acceptable lifestyle." He also adds that just as all people must be sincerely striving to follow the church's moral teaching on matters of sex to receive the eucharist (holy communion), homosexuals must also conform.*

ROMAN CATHOLIC CHURCH—CATHOLIC SOCIAL WELFARE COMMISSION

AN INTRODUCTION TO THE PASTORAL CARE OF HOMOSEXUAL PEOPLE (1981)

Human Relationships:

> "Man cannot live without love. He remains a being that is incomprehensible for himself; his life is senseless if love is not revealed to him, if he does not encounter love, if he does not experience it and make it his own, if he does not participate intimately in it".
>
> Pope John Paul II: Redemptor Hominis

Human love is supportive, enriching and healing; it produces harmony, unity and fulfilment. The very revealing of true love to another person is a purifying and wholesome experience.

A life without love is incomplete and disappointing. This deprivation, especially if it stems from childhood, is the origin of social misfits, either withdrawn and introspective or aggressive and disruptive.

It is within this setting that the pastor must encourage those who seek his guidance. But the pastor must unfold a further dimension which is not at first apparent. The love between people is very special, but its origins and its worth are to be found in God. God is the ultimate source of genuine love and when people experience love at the human level they are absorbing something of the divine love. In turn, a true love between people, originating as it does from God, will lead those loving people back to God. All human love is a reflection of the love in God which is the life of the Trinity. It is this divine dimension which not only ennobles human love but also reveals something of God's love for us.

Each person is made in "the image and likeness of God". The more we know and understand another person the more we should be able to recognise something of God in that other person. True personal relationships should develop this "seeing" of God in one another, and loving relationships within marriage or family or friendship should reveal this diving imprint more explicitly than casual acquaintance. Even within friendships or family there can be a differing degree of this revelation because human beings are different and they do not respond in exactly the same way to every other person.

All this means that attraction between people within the accepted settings of marriage, family and friendship is only possible, initially, because of God's love for us and because we are made for God. Love between human beings is all part of being gathered up into this divine love and the search for union with another person is essentially a search for that total union with God to which every person is invited. All human loving is a seeking after the One who is most lovable.

Our human loving is all part of longing for God and, in our human loving we are seeking out a point of contact between earth and heaven, between created and the Creator, between the many who are trying to love and the One who is total love. This search for a meeting point between the human and the divine is really a deep desire to lift the loved one up to the source of love, God. Or, looking at the loving relationship from a more human viewpoint, it is a longing for the completely loving God to enter and uplift humanity and this point of intersection of divine and human is the Incarnation and the sharing of the Incarnation with every person.

It is only when the pastor has presented this total meaning of interpersonal relationships that those seeking his guidance can understand the special forms which these relationships can take and appreciate their appropriate expression.

The special relationship between a woman and a man which we call *marriage* is an intensification of that general affection we must have for all who enjoy God's love and are made in His image. Ideally, the husband and wife focus their love more and more intensely on one another until there is that uninhibited giving of each other in the sexual union. This is more than a coming together of bodies. It is the union of minds and the complete trust of those who are prepared to surrender everything to one another. It is the culmination of a loving relationship and, at the same time, the growth point from which the man and woman move on to the deeper sharing of love which, like all love, has its origins in God. So this God-designed act is total and creative. It is exclusive, not in the negative sense of setting aside all love for other people, but it is exclusive in that such an intense and unique a gift of oneself could only be shared with one other person. This form of love expressed in this unique way must be total and irrevocable if it is to be true to all it claims to express.

Friendship like marriage is part of the overflow of God's love into his creation. The love between friends, like the love between wife and husband or between parents and children, find its source in God and, ideally, should be seeking to uplift people to experience and appreciate the divine love which enlivens all love.

Friendship implies a closeness; a coming together of similar tastes and outlook, a mutual attraction of spirit. Much has been written about the nobility of friendship and examples can be quoted form all history, including the lives of the saints. Friendship between persons of the same sex or different sexes is part of the normal inter-personal relationship within the human race.

Within this we can identify the *homosexual person* and it is important for the pastor to be sensitive to any special features which may be characteristic of the homosexual.

To be homosexual means that people of the same sex are more attractive than those of the opposite sex and this is a condition or disposition to be found in both women and men. To limit this attraction to physical and then just sexual attraction is a misleading generalisation and the term "homophilia" is sometimes preferred to "homosexuality" because close friendships between people of the same sex may be completely free of erotic or sexual behavior.

An important distinction must be made between the "pervert" and the "invert". This terminology is distasteful to some homosexual people but it does distinguish between the person who is predominantly heterosexual but indulges in homosexual activity (pervert) and the one who is predominantly homosexual (invert).

Homosexuality in the female (lesbianism) appears to differ from homosexuality in the male in that lesbians are less inclined to indulge in casual, impersonal homosexual activity. It seems that more lesbians marry than do male homosexuals and so the lesbian can become more involved in normal family life. Popular opinion and some research suggests that there are more male homosexuals than lesbians.

It is difficult if not impossible to determine the number of homosexuals in the general community. Reasonable estimates suggest that between 4 and 10% of the total population are exclusively homosexual. In terms of absolute numbers this cannot be dismissed as trivial. Many more pass through a homosexual phase in their lives and while such statistics are to be treated with reserve, they do indicate a sizeable proportion of the population.

The Wolfenden Report issued in 1957 concluded that homosexuality is not, despite the widely held belief to the contrary, peculiar to members of particular professions or social classes. The Wolfenden Report claims that the evidence presented to it showed that homosexuality existed in all callings and at all levels of society. It may be that while certain social classes or professions do not produce an unusual proportion of homosexual persons, it is reasonable to conclude that some social classes and professions are more prepared than other groups to accept them.

In this country in 1861 the death penalty was removed as a punishment for the convicted homosexual and in 1967 imprisonment was removed as a possible punishment for homosexual activity between consenting adults. Although the law has been modified there remains within our community some misunderstanding and hostility, sometimes hidden, towards the homosexual, a hostility which is frequently the result of grouping together all homosexuals as though they are stereotyped.

Social disapproval and rejection of the homosexual person simply because he or she has these tendencies is a distressing problem for the homosexual. Unfortunately, the misunderstanding frequently comes from "religious" people and ostracism of and discrimination against the homosexual can frequently result in many people who are practising Christians being unwilling to admit that they are homosexual. Some attack through ridicule and denunciation. Others withdraw from the company of homosexuals. Neither approach is helpful. A silent rejection, as though the subject is not to be discussed and not very "nice" is equally unhelpful. Society may be misunderstanding and even prejudging a large section of the community.

The following points may clarify some of the misunderstanding:

a. It is untrue to say that every homosexual is attracted to children and adolescents and wishes to have physical contact with them. There are, of course, heterosexuals with the same inclinations. In fact, it would seem that proportionately to their numbers in the population, the heterosexuals are more prone to child molestation than homosexuals.

b. It is inaccurate to claim that all male homosexuals are easily identifiable as effeminate or all female homosexuals as masculine.

c. It is misleading to say that homosexuals automatically recognize each other and form quasi secret societies.

d. It is untrue that homosexual persons are automatically unstable or promiscuous. They are, in fact, quite capable of forming good relationships which are lasting.

e. It is a generalisation to claim that homosexual people simply require will-power to correct their condition. There is no easy method of transition from the state of homosexuality to that of heterosexuality; as yet no consistent and reliable method of transference is known. The invert homosexual must not therefore be too readily blamed if he or she is hesitant about any attempt to adjust.

f. Homosexuality is often thought to be anti-family—a threat to the institution of the family itself. Some organisations do, in fact, threaten family life in the form in which we understand it today, but other homosexual organisations expressly aim to promote traditional, accepted standards. There is a danger of our identifying all homosexuals with radical and progressive pressure groups.

g. It is incorrect to claim that homosexuals have a high incidence of mental disorder. This is simply not borne out by research.

h. It is inaccurate to assert that homosexual persons are limited to certain social classes or professions. The evidence of the Wolfenden Report quoted above suggests otherwise.

The Causes of Homosexuality:

The pastor must appreciate the complexity of the debate on the causes of homosexuality. There are many causes and it is usually impossible to isolate any single one. Some people are unable to express themselves adequately when discussing this topic and this hesitancy is an added difficulty in the search for causes.

Biological explanations do not appear to command a general agreement although there are many biological theories. Heredity as a cause has never been proved convincingly. At best it is only a partial explanation of the homosexual condition.

In general terms the accepted possibilities are socio-psychological causes. Environment, upbringing and emotional relationships within the family, an over-dominant or possessive mother and a weak or absent father—all these and similar factors are accepted as possible explanations, but there is no agreed opinion. Seduction, especially at an early age, has been suggested as a possible cause. As far as can be ascertained seduction does not alter a sexual pattern but it may encourage and exaggerate an already existing sexual tendency. Most young people appear to pass through a phase when the homosexual tendency is dominant; but the emotional growth can be halted at this stage.

The pastor must be aware of these uncertainties associated with the state of homosexuality. The uncertainty about the causes leads to uncertainty about how to re-adjust the sexual tendencies. This in turn leads to a frustration and anxiety within the person who is homosexual and can add to his or her emotional distress. The pastor must also be aware of the variety of medical options, including hypnosis, aversion therapy and drugs, but it is not for the pastor or for this document to pass medical judgement on these matters.

The Christian Tradition:

Christian morality is primarily concerned with holiness of life. It is centred on worship and the personal union of the worshipper with God and with other people in Christ. The purposes of moral norms is to guide people towards God. Moral norms point out ways of living which impede union with God so that they may be avoided, and encourage ways of living which bring people nearer to God giving expression to the life of grace which the believer receives through Christ.

This must be the emphasis when discussing homosexuality; not just the imposing of a negative law. The support and guidance of the moral law is needed by everyone, whether they be homosexual or heterosexual but the moral law is not merely a negative imposition; it is a positive means of encouraging a way of life which leads to true fulfilment.

Homosexuality (or homophilia) as such is neither morally good nor bad. Homosexuality, like heterosexuality, is a state or condition. It is morally neutral and the invert homosexual, like the heterosexual, cannot be held responsible for his tendencies.

There can be no moral opprobrium attached to homophile friendships as such. As has been stressed, friendship in itself is good. A friendship can only be judged immoral if it were the occasion of immoral acts. Having made this distinction clear it is important that the moral teaching concerning homosexual acts be clarified even in a document emphasising pastoral care.

The traditional teaching of the Church on the morality of homosexual acts is repeated in the 1975 Declaration on 'Certain Questions concerning Sexual Ethics.' This was issued by the Sacred Congregation for the Doctrine of the Faith. There it said:

> "According to the objective moral order, homosexual relations are acts which lack an essential and indispensable finality."

With regard to homosexual acts, scripture and the on-going tradition of Christianity make it quite clear that these are immoral. Whatever pastoral judgement may conclude concerning personal responsibility in a particular case, it is clear that in the objective order homosexual acts may not be approved.

Christ emphasised love as the great commandment but this must be understood correctly. In advocating the law of charity as the supreme law, Christ did not set aside the traditional commandments but established love as the basis of all wholesome relationships including those expressly listed in the commandments. One of the tests of genuine love given by Christ was the keeping of the commandments and while he did not speak, as far as we know, about the specific problems of the homosexual, he did not reverse the Old Testament tradition. The teaching of the early Christians as expressed in the New Testament re-affirms that tradition. David Field in the "Homosexual Way" says:

> "Despite the very important modern distinction dividing inverts and perverts, it

> seems impossible to resist the conclusion that the new Testament puts a theological veto on all homosexual behaviour—however well motivated it may be.''

The constant tradition of the Church is that sexual intercourse is proper to the holy state of matrimony, in which it contributes to the sanctity of the married couple, being both an expression of covenant love and the origin of new members to the human race. The sexual union between husband and wife is the culmination of love, and, at the same time, leads to growth in love, all part of the growth towards God as the source and complete centre of love. The intimacy of married love is expressed in marital intercourse, which is fulfilling; a sign of true love which creative and maturing.

For people who are not married, whether they are homosexual or heterosexual, love and affection can be given some form of expression. But there is the need to be aware that perfectly legitimate expressions of affection can lead to genital activity which could be not only wrong, but destructive of a worthwhile and supportive relationship.

There has been an attempt to establish parity between a normal marriage and the on-going homosexual relationship. This is a false and unacceptable analogy. The pastor may distinguish between irresponsible, indiscriminate sexual activity and the permanent association between two homosexual persons, who feel incapable of enduring a solitary life devoid of sexual expression. This distinction may be borne in mind when offering pastoral advice and establishing the degree of responsibility, but the pastor will not be providing true and helpful advice if he gives the impression that the ''homosexual marriage'' is objectively moral.

Of course, pastoral care does not consist simply in the rigid and automatic application of objective moral norms. It considers the individual in his actual situation, with all his strengths and weaknesses. The decision of conscience, determining what should be done and what avoided, can only be made after prudent consideration of the real situation as well as the moral norm.

Section 8 of the Vatican Declaration states:

> ''no pastoral method can be employed which would give moral justification to these acts'' but it goes on to say ''homosexuals must certainly be treated with understanding. . . . and their culpability judged with prudence.''

The pastoral counselling of homophile persons cannot ignore the objective morality of homosexual genital acts, but it is important to interpret them, to understand the pattern of life in which they take place, to appreciate the personal meaning which these acts have for different people. Some would claim that, especially for the invert, the homosexual drive is almost irresistible. Degrees of decision are impossible to estimate accurately but the normal principles of diminished responsibility apply. If it is claimed that the homosexual is completely incapable of self-control, this may place homosexuality in the category of a serious disease—an opinion unacceptable to many, if not most, homosexual people.

There is some obligation on the homosexual person to seek guidance and, if possible, a re-adjustment of his or her condition, but it remains important pastorally to bear in mind that the homosexual condition is rarely, if ever, a matter of choice. Many homophiles find the loneliness of their lives a burden. They long for intimate partnerships as much as heterophiles, but cannot find it in marriage. It is this longing for intimacy which leads some to form stable union with each other. There will frequently be a physical genital expression in such unions. Objectively,this is morally unacceptable. The question is: Are some persons necessarily culpable? That judgement cannot be made in the abstract but in the concrete circumstances in which the acts take place. So the Vatican Declaration says:

> ''It is true that in sins of the sexual order, in view of their kind and their causes, it more easily happens that true consent is not fully given; this is a fact which calls for caution on all judgements as to the subject's responsibility. In this matter it is

particularly opportune to recall the words of Scripture: 'Man looks at appearances but God looks at the heart.' (1 Sam. 16:7).''

A specially delicate situation arises when homosexual persons are convinced that, although they accept that homosexual acts in themselves cannot be justified, it is found impossible in practice to lead a celibate life. They might then claim that the choice remains between a stable union, in which there is a necessary and inevitable physical relationship and an obviously distasteful promiscuous way of life. Such persons argue that in their particular case the stability of the union outweighs the disorder of the homosexual acts which take place within it. They would argue that the goodness or badness of an act can only be judged morally in practice when consideration has been given to intention and circumstances.

In assisting such people to apply their conscience to such a situation the accepted principles of morality must be used. While the objective norms are clear-cut the application of such norms may be complicated. As quoted above the Vatican Declaration states that ''no pastoral method can be employed which would give moral justification to these acts.'' Bearing this in mind pastors must be alive to the genuine guidance of moral theology and be prepared to apply it to the particular needs of the homosexual person.

Pastoral Guidelines:

In general terms the pastoral task might be considered as helping homosexual persons, or those who consider themselves to be homosexual persons, to understand and examine the meaning of their behaviour, sexual or otherwise, in the light of the love of God and the love of neighbour, together with the moral and pastoral teaching of Christianity. There are still many unanswered questions regarding the proper pastoral care of homosexuals. In the wake of research in the theological and social sciences and the experience of those already involved in pastoral care of homosexuals, the following guidelines could be offered:

1. The Church, in her pastoral effort is concerned first of all with people. How people are classified is secondary and is intended merely to be a help towards understanding people. Unfortunately, many classifications tend to have judgemental connotations. It is unfortunate that the term ''homosexual'' tends to classify people principally by their sexuality. The pastor and counsellor must see all people, irrespective of their sexuality, as children of God and destined for eternal life.

2. Before attempting to provide spiritual guidance or moral counselling to a homosexual person, pastors need to be aware of the homosexual condition itself. Homosexuality is commonly understood to imply only an erotic, sexual attraction of a person towards members of the same sex. It sometimes also means the absence of attraction to members of the opposite sex, even to the extent of positive disgust for sexual relationships with the opposite sex.

3. It is difficult to categorise people as simply heterosexual or homosexual. Empirical evidence suggests that sexual orientation in a limited number of individuals is totally exclusive. In those individuals in whom heterosexual disposition is dominant, there seems to exist a latent potentiality for homosexual interest of which the person may not be aware.

4. Before attempting to provide spiritual guidance or counselling for a homosexual person the pastor must be aware of his own limitations. Unconscious prejudice resulting from a biased, social tradition does injustice to the homosexual and renders effective counselling impossible. No real benefit can be expected unless the pastor clears away all traces of the misunderstandings that make real communication impossible.

5. One of the most important aspects of homosexuality is the awareness of being 'different' from the majority of people. This consciousness of being 'different,' of belonging to a minority, leaves the homosexual person suffering from the same problems as all minority groups with the added factor that their 'difference' is secret.

This leads to a deeper alienation. In a society that can see them as objects of cruel jokes and contempt, homosexuals commonly suffer from lack of self-esteem and a loneliness that heterosexuals find difficult, if not impossible, to comprehend. In ordinary mixed society, homosexuals feel like strangers. They are shunned and despised by people who may have an inaccurate or distorted knowledge of the homosexual person. Many homosexuals are reserved and even withdrawn, not anxious to draw attention to their difficulties. However, among both heterosexuals and homosexuals there are people who are exhibitionists—explicit and vulgar. In both categories these are a minority and the attention they attract is out of proportion to their numbers. Before 1967 the constant fear associated with homosexual acts was that of blackmail, but since the law has withdrawn the penalty for homosexual acts between consenting adults there have been explicit portrayals of the homosexual as ridiculous and bizarre. This means that the judgement of many people, including Christians, is based on a limited knowledge which is unaware of the deeper, distressing tensions which beset the person who is homosexual.

6. It is the role of the pastor to offer encouragement and support. Many good people who are homosexual are constantly struggling against the demands of their condition and they must not be allowed to despair. It is unworthy of a pastor to offer only superficial advice for such an intractable problem.

7. Pastors can be especially helpful in the 'coming out' process. This is the point at which the homosexual person admits openly to his or her homosexuality and it is frequently the first stage of being able to cope. The pastor seems to be an obvious person with whom to share these confidences and his own response must be sensitive and sympathetic. A clear re-affirmation of moral standards may be required but this must not be a blunt rejection based on prejudice and ignorance. Rejection can force homosexuals to rely exclusively on the companionship of fellow homosexuals where at least they will be met with the understanding which has been denied by the pastor.

8. Some would argue that societies specifically for homosexuals are the ideal setting for allowing people with the same tendencies to understand and cope with shared anxieties. It is difficult to assess the value of such associations. The pastor must advise against the homosexual society which has as its main purpose the introduction of, or a meeting with, people with at least the implied, if not explicit, purpose of encouraging homosexual activities. This form of group is quite unacceptable.

On the other hand, the existence of societies for homosexuals who are also Christians means that certain moral standards must be recognised. There are Christian groups explicitly formed for the encouragement of homosexuals to cope with their difficulties. The goodwill of these societies must not be automatically questioned, especially because their very existence may be due to the insensitivity of the general public. On the other hand, there are obvious dangers. Moral support may easily be turned to moral danger and the pastor must encourage the person who seeks his advice to face up to this real possibility. In addition, a society formed originally for the moral support of the homosexual might, even unwittingly, deepen an already existing problem. It might tend to relax standards rather than support efforts to cope with difficulties and homosexual activity may be nurtured rather than avoided.

However, the situation must be kept in proportion. A comparison with accepted social occasions might help to avoid exaggerated or prejudiced decisions. To condemn a social gathering simply because of possible moral dangers could lead to ridiculous restrictions. It could condemn a parish dance or a youth club. It would forbid the sharing of a flat. In fact, such an extreme attitude of mind would be so unreasonable that all social friendships could be under suspicion. This is an unhealthy attitude which destroys human relationships and frustrates that unity within the society which the pastor is supposed to be promoting.

9. Marriage has not proved to be a successful answer for most homosexuals. Marriage in these circumstances can be unfair to the partner and even extend the distress of the homosexual to the whole family. It may be marriage for the wrong reasons and, in any case, marriage must not be thought of as the only gateway to God and the only way to fulfilment.

10. Professional psychiatric treatment or psychological counselling is by no means the proven remedy for the homosexual condition. Very often it proves to be a frustrating experience that only heightens anxiety. Pastors and Counsellors may suggest psychological testing to determine whether a person is exclusively or predominantly homosexual, as opposed to a 'transitional' homosexual, who is passing through a temporary phase of psychological development. In the case of true homosexuals or 'inverts,' professional therapy may be helpful to assist them in accepting their condition positively, but therapy should never be suggested in a way that raises false expectations of a reverse or modification of the homosexual condition.

11. A positive help to the homosexual is the channelling of his energy into a variety of interests, but this sublimation must be positive and genuine. An artificial diversion is unconvincing.

12. However much is uncertain about the subject of homosexuality, it seems that the generic term does include three more specific and important categories;

    a. those who are well adjusted, stable people who have come to terms with their homosexuality, who never seek help and who are never in trouble with the law. These people are psychologically adjusted, sometimes even better, than the average heterosexual;

    b. those homosexuals who have psychological problems, eg. neurosis and alcoholism. This group has more in common with other neurotics than with other homosexuals;

    c. those homosexuals who have personality disorders which lead to deviant behaviour, eg. criminal offences. This group have more in common with other social deviants than with other homosexuals.

13. The Church has a serious responsibility to work towards the elimination of any injustices perpetrated on homosexuals by society. As a group that has suffered more than its share of oppression and contempt, the homosexual community has particular claim upon the concern of the Church. Homosexuals have a right to enlightened and effective pastoral care with pastoral ministers who are properly trained to meet their pastoral needs.

14. Homosexuals have the same need for the Sacraments as the heterosexual. They also have the same right to receive the Sacraments. In determining whether or not to administer Absolution or give Communion to a homosexual, a pastor must be guided by the general principles of fundamental theology that only a certain moral obligation may be imposed. An invincible doubt, whether of law or fact, permits one to follow a true and solidly "probable opinion" in favour of a more liberal interpretation.

15. Homosexuals may feel that nature in some way cheated them and produced tensions which are undeserved. The homosexual can be shattered on discovering that he or she has permanent tendencies through no personal fault which arouse antagonism, ridicule and rejection in society. The Christian task is to understand the homosexuals and restore respect for them as persons. They may well feel that the Church is demanding impossible standards. This challenge may lead to an abandonment of faith, but it also offers an added opportunity and resource. Truth is never reached by turning down the

clear directives of God and the Gospel. Such a course could only complicate the already existing confusion. God sets certain standards, but his power of sustaining is comprehensive. Christ emphasised his concern for those whom society has rejected. The many difficulties which the homosexual encounters ensures that the strength of God will be at hand. Christ asks that we take up our Cross and follow him and this may mean that the homosexual person is very near to true Christianity if he responds to this invitation.

The problem of the homosexual is part of a greater problem of the human incompleteness of a people who are on the way to God. Maturity comes when problems are acknowledged and faced. Only confusion arises when the problems are allowed to dictate or there is a pretence that they do not exist.

16. The pastor will help souls if he introduces them to an understanding of that love which is more comprehensive than sexuality. His role is to introduce people to Christian life in all its fullness. This does not mean instant serenity. There must be gradual purification and real growth in holiness. Every person with spiritual ambitions must cope with his personal limitations. These vary from person to person and are frequently complex and discouraging, but all people who, in spite of limitations and even failure, continue to struggle and grow in holiness of life deserve encouragement. Such people are very near to God.

Notes: *In September 1977, the National Conference of Catholic Priests asked the Roman Catholic bishops of England and Wales to prepare a document offering guidance on the question of homosexuality. The British church had long been among the most liberal in approaching the issue, and in 1981, the Catholic Social Welfare Commission of the United Kingdom issued its preliminary report. In the United States, the report was reprinted by New Ways Ministry, a Roman Catholic ministry to the homosexual community that praised the document. New Ways believed the document was a reaffirmation of the central moral teachings of the 1975* Declaration on Certain Questions Concerning Sexual Ethics *(see index) that also maintained an open mind towards new developments in moral theology, developments that offered alternatives in pastoral approaches to the gay community that were not evident in the 1975 document. This statement was also held to be superior to the 1973 statement* Principles to Guide Confessors in Questions of Homosexuality

This British document represents one part of the wide spectrum of opinion in the Roman Catholic Church. It is distinguished by its insistence upon a personalized approach to homosexual persons, an approach that emphasizes concern for the individual rather than universal laws concerning the performance of certain sexual actions. This statement also condemns society for stereotyping homosexuals and treating them with contempt. While agreeing with the 1975 statement in substance, it has much different tone than that earlier document, which referred to homosexuality as "a serious depravity." This statement raised hopes that the church might soften its position on homosexuality in the future.

ROMAN CATHOLIC CHURCH—BISHOPS OF MASSACHUSETTS

STATEMENT ON RIGHTS FOR HOMOSEXUALS (1984)

The rights of homosexuals, as well as heterosexuals, "should be limited whenever they come into conflict with the rights of others and the common good," the bishops of Massachusetts said in a statement on homosexual rights released May 31. The statement, issued by the Massachusetts Catholic Conference, specifically opposes a bill now before the Massachusetts General Court, or legislature, which seeks "the elimination of certain discrimination on the basis of sexual preference.'' The Bishops made a distinction between unjust discrimination, which they said all people must oppose, and the ''necessary limitations on our rights whenever . . . the common good is at stake.'' The bishops objected to the bill because it might be viewed as a step toward ''legal approval of the homosexual lifestyle.'' They also expressed concern that, should the bill become law, the church would be denied its ''hiring discretion.'' The church ''has the right and duty to establish certain standards of conduct for everyone she employs.'' The bishops stressed their ''disapproval of the unjust harassment of homosexuals,'' calling such behavior ''unconscionable,'' and urged ''proper respect for the rights of every citizen.'' The signers of the statement were Archbishop Bernard Law of Boston and Bishops Daniel Cronin of Fall River, Timothy Harrington of Worcester and Joseph Maguire of Springfield. The text of the statement follows.

At the present time there is a bill before the General Court of Massachusetts seeking ''the elimination of certain discrimination on the basis of sexual preference.''

During the past few months, the Massachusetts Catholic Conference has been asked to articulate its position on this issue. These requests have come not only from legislators who are seeking guidance from us on the church's stance, but also from concerned members of the Catholic community who feel that the lack of an official statement on this question implies a shift in our position concerning the morality of homosexual activity.

Conscious of our role as moral leaders in the community, we, the Roman Catholic bishops of Massachusetts, have decided to explain the position of the Catholic Church on this matter. We do so because the proposed bill has power to influence the lives of the youth as well as the adults of our commonwealth and because it has grave implications for the common good of our society.

First of all, some comments are in order on our church's stand on the question of homosexuality. Contemporary scholars make an important distinction between homosexual orientation (psycho-sexual attraction primarily directed toward members of the same sex) and homosexual activity (homogenital acts). Such orientation is regarded generally as morally neutral; it is viewed as a condition which, through no fault of the person involved, implies a lack of complete sexual integration. Homosexual activity, on the other hand, is seen as something objectively wrong inasmuch as it falls short of the ultimate norm of Christian morality in the area of genital expression, i.e., a relationship between male and female within the marital union. Whether or not homosexual activity is subjectively wrong (sinful) will, as in all human actions, depend on the presence of those elements of knowledge and freedom constituting the human act.

Second, some comments are also in order on the phenomenon known as discrimination. It must be remembered always that there is a necessary distinction, very often ignored, between unjust discrimination (the arbitrary limitation of human rights) and the necessary limitation placed on the exercise of human rights whenever such actions would interfere with the just rights of others and harm society. All people of good will must oppose unjust discrimination. However, there are times in our lives when each of us experiences the pain, discomfort and challenges of necessary limitations on our rights whenever there is a prudent judgment that the common good is at stake. For example, having a patient in an ambulance does not permit the driver of that vehicle to ignore pedestrians at a crowded intersection. Homosexuals, surely, possess all the rights proper to human beings but, as in the case of heterosexuals, these rights should be limited whenever they come into conflict with the rights of others and the common good.

As the Roman Catholic bishops of Massachusetts, we firmly oppose all forms of unjust discrimination whether against homosexuals or heterosexuals. We are of one mind and one heart with the sentiments expressed by the Catholic bishops of the United States in their pastoral letter on moral values ''To Live in Christ Jesus,'' issued in November 1976:

"Some persons find themselves through no fault of their own to have a homosexual orientation. Homosexuals, like everyone else, should not suffer from prejudice against their basic human rights. They have a right to respect, friendship and justice."

In reply to those who have requested our opinion of the bill presently before the legislature, we now wish to present some serious pastoral concerns which will place us among those members of the commonwealth who oppose its passage.

First, experience has shown that the passage of legislation of this type will be seen by many as a step toward legal approval of the homosexual lifestyle. Our concern in this regard is heightened by a common perception in our country that whatever is declared legal, by that very fact, becomes morally right. The tragic abortion experience of the past 10 years in the United States bears out the necessity for caution in these matters. Thus our failure to oppose this bill could give rise to the false impression that the Catholic Church accepts the homosexual lifestyle as a morally feasible option.

Second, the Catholic Church in her hiring practice is obliged to reflect her stance on the morality of sexual activity. She has the right and the duty to establish certain standards of conduct for everyone she employs. If the church favors this bill as it stands, it is quite possible that an improper interpretation of it may be advanced in the future denying hiring discretion whenever legitimate questions arise about the appearance, lifestyle and activity of certain homosexual employees.

In voicing our opposition to the passage of this bill, we must state publicly our disapproval of the unjust harassment of homosexuals by members of the heterosexual community. Such behavior is unconscionable and it must be stopped. However, we are of the opinion that this will be achieved only by a process of consciousness raising leading heterosexuals to proper respect for persons who happen to be homosexuals. What we need is education and a change of heart, not new and ill-advised legislation.

Such are our prayerful and heartfelt concerns about the passage of this bill. For the reasons stated above, we do not favor its approval by our legislature.

We do not deny that some members of our church have homosexual orientation. There is room in our church for everyone. Homosexuals, too, are our brothers and sisters in the Lord.

Our decision to stand in opposition to the passage of this bill must not be seen, therefore as indifference to the serious difficulties experienced by people who are homosexuals. Even though we take a firm moral stance on this issue and have many questions about the legitimacy of homosexual lifestyle, we urge proper respect for the rights of every citizen of the commonwealth. We will do all in our power to dispel the unfortunate myths and misunderstandings related to this issue. Finally, we stand in opposition to every form of harassment and unjust discrimination directed against homosexuals, and we respect them fully as fellow pilgrims on our earthly journey toward the kingdom of God.

Notes: *Civil and public rights for homosexuals were not specifically addressed in the Vatican statement of 1975. In 1984, a bill to eliminate discrimination against homosexual persons, one of many bills of similar bills introduced in state legislatures across the United States, was before the Massachusetts legislature. The bishops position, often difficult to explain to the laity of the church, rested in large part upon the idea of homosexuality as a condition of some people (just as some people were heterosexual). Homosexuality, as such is morally neutral. Both homosexuals and heterosexuals at times commit immoral acts, but that fact should not lead to discrimination against either.*

ROMAN CATHOLIC CHURCH—SACRED CONGREGATION FOR THE DOCTRINE OF THE FAITH

LETTER TO THE BISHOPS OF THE CATHOLIC CHURCH ON THE PASTORAL CARE OF HOMOSEXUAL PERSONS (1986)

1. The issue of homosexuality and the moral evaluation of homosexual acts have increasingly because a matter of public debate, even in Catholic circles. Since this debate often advances arguments and makes assertions inconsistent with the teaching of the Catholic Church, it is quite rightly a cause for concern to all engaged in pastoral ministry, and this Congregation has judged it to be of sufficiently grave and widespread importance to address to the Bishops of the Catholic Church this Letter on Pastoral Care of Homosexual Persons.

2. Naturally, an exhaustive treatment of this complex issue cannot be attempted here, but we will focus our reflection within the distinctive context of the Catholic moral perspective. It is a perspective which finds support in the more secure findings of the natural sciences, which have their own legitimate and proper methodology and field of inquiry.

   However, the Catholic moral viewpoint is founded on human reason illumined by faith and is consciously motivated by the desire to do the will of God our Father. The Church is thus in a position to learn from scientific discovery but also to transcend the horizons of science and to be confident that her more global vision does greater justice to the rich reality of the human person in his spiritual and physical dimensions, created by God and heir, by grace, to eternal life.

   It is within this context, then, that it can be clearly seen that the phenomenon of homosexuality, complex as it is, and with its many consequences for society and ecclesial life, is a proper focus for the Church's pastoral care. It thus requires of her ministers attentive study, active concern and honest, theologically well-balanced counsel.

3. Explicit treatment of the problem was given in this Congregation's "Declaration on Certain Questions Concerning Sexual Ethics" of December 29, 1975. That document stressed the duty of trying to understand the homosexual condition and noted that culpability for homosexual acts should only be judged with prudence. At the same time the Congregation took note of the distinction commonly drawn between the homosexual condition or tendency and individual homosexual actions. These were described as deprived of their essential and indispensable finality, as being "intrinsically disordered," and able in no case to be approved of (cf. n. 8, § 4).

   In the discussion which followed the publication of the Declaration, however, an overly benign interpretation was given to the homosexual condition itself, some going so far as to call it neutral, or even good. Although the particular inclination of the homosexual person is not a sin, it is a more or less strong tendency ordered toward an intrinsic moral evil; and thus the inclination itself must be seen as an objective disorder.

   Therefore special concern and pastoral attention should be directed toward those who have this condition, lest they be led to believe that the living out of this orientation in homosexual activity is a morally acceptable option. It is not.

4. An essential dimension of authentic pastoral care is the identification of causes of confusion regarding the Church's teaching. One is a new exegesis of Sacred Scripture which claims variously that Scripture has nothing to say on the subject of homosexuality, or that it somehow tacitly approves of it, or that all of its moral injunctions are so culture-bound that they are no longer applicable to contemporary life. These views are gravely erroneous and call for particular attention here.

5. It is quite true that the Biblical literature owes to the different epochs in which it was written a good deal of its varied patterns of thought and expression *(Dei Verbum 12)*. The Church today addresses the Gospel to a world which differs in many ways from ancient days. But the world in which the New Testament was written was already quite diverse from the situation in which the Sacred Scriptures of the Hebrew People had been written or compiled, for example.

   What should be noticed is that, in the presence of such remarkable diversity, there is nevertheless a clear consistency within the Scriptures themselves on the moral issue of homosexual behavior. The Church's doctrine regarding this issue is thus based, not on isolated phrases for facile theological argument, but on the solid foundation of a constant Biblical testimony. The community of faith today, in unbroken continuity with the Jewish and Christian communities within which the ancient Scriptures were written, continues to be nourished by those same Scriptures and by the Spirit of Truth whose Word they are. It is likewise essential to recognize that the Scriptures are not properly understood when they are interpreted in a way which contradicts the Church's living Tradition. To be correct, the interpretation of Scripture must be in substantial accord with that Tradition.

   The Vatican Council II in *Dei Verbum* 10, put it this way: "It is clear, therefore, that in the supremely wise arrangement of God, sacred Tradition, sacred Scripture, and the Magisterium of the Church are so connected and associated that one of them cannot stand without the others. Working together, each in its own way under the action of the one Holy Spirit, they all contribute effectively to the salvation of souls". In that spirit we wish to outline briefly the Biblical teaching here.

6. Providing a basic plan for understanding this entire discussion of homosexuality is the theology of creation we find in Genesis. God, by his infinite wisdom and love, brings into existence all of the reality as a reflection of his goodness. He fashions mankind, male and female, in his own image and likeness. Human beings, therefore, are nothing less than the work of God himself, and in the complementarity of the sexes, they are called to reflect the inner unity of the Creator. They do this in a striking way in their cooperation with him in the transmission of life by a mutual donation of the self to the other.

   In *Genesis 3,* we find that this truth about persons being an image of God has been obscured by original sin. There inevitably follows a loss of awareness of the covenantal character of the union these persons had with God and with each other. The human body retains its "spousal significance" but this is now clouded by sin. Thus, in *Genesis* 19:1-11, the deterioration due to sin continues in the story of the men of Sodom. There can be no doubt of the moral judgement made there against homosexual relations. In *Leviticus* 18:22 and 20:13, in the course of describing the conditions necessary for belonging to the Chosen People, the author excludes from the People of God those who behave in a homosexual fashion.

   Against the background of this exposition of theocratic law, an eschatological perspective is developed by St. Paul when, in *1 Cor.* 6:9, he proposes the same doctrine and lists those who behave in a homosexual fashion among those who shall not enter the Kingdom of God.

   In *Romans* 1:18-32, still building on the moral traditions of his forebears, but in the new context of the confrontation between Christianity and the pagan society of his day, Paul uses homosexual behaviour as an example of the blindness which has overcome humankind. Instead of the original harmony between Creator and creatures, the acute distortion of idolatry has led to all kinds of moral excess. Paul is at a loss to find a clearer example of this disharmony than homosexual relations. Finally, *1 Tim.* 1, in full continuity with the Biblical position, singles out those who spread wrong doctrine and in v. 10 explicitly names as sinners those who engage in homosexual acts.

7. The Church, obedient to the Lord who founded her and gave to her the sacramental life, celebrates the divine plan of the loving and live-giving union of men and women in the sacrament of marriage. It is only in the marital relationship that the use of the sexual faculty can be morally good. A person engaging in homosexual behaviour therefore acts immorally.

   To chose someone of the same sex for one's sexual activity is to annul the rich symbolism and meaning, not to mention the goals, of the Creator's sexual design. Homosexual activity is not a complementary union, able to transmit life; and so it thwarts the call to a life of that form of self-giving which the Gospel says is the essence of Christian living. This does not mean that homosexual persons are not often generous and giving of themselves; but when they engage in homosexual activity they confirm within themselves a disordered sexual inclination which is essentially self-indulgent.

   As in every moral disorder, homosexual activity prevents one's own fulfilment and happiness by acting contrary to the creative wisdom of God. The Church, in rejecting erroneous opinions regarding homosexuality, does not limit but rather defends personal freedom and dignity realistically and authentically understood.

8. Thus, the Church's teaching today is in organic continuity with the Scriptural perspective and with her own constant Tradition. Though today's world is in many ways quite new, the Christian community senses the profound and lasting bonds which join us to those generations who have gone before us, "marked with the sign of faith."

   Nevertheless, increasing numbers of people today, even within the Church, are bringing enormous pressure to bear on the Church to accept the homosexual condition as though it were not disordered and to condone homosexual activity. Those within the Church who argue in this fashion often have close ties with those with similar views outside it. These latter groups are guided by a vision opposed to the truth about the human person, which is fully disclosed in the mystery of Christ. They reflect, even if not entirely consciously, a materialistic ideology which denies the transcendent nature of the human person as well as the supernatural vocation of every individual.

   The Church's ministers must ensure that homosexual persons in their care will not be misled by this point of view, so profoundly opposed to the teaching of the Church. But the risk is great and there are many who seek to create confusion regarding the Church's position and then to use that confusion to their own advantage.

9. The movement within the Church, which takes the form of pressure groups of various names and sizes, attempts to give the impression that it represents all homosexual persons who are Catholics. As a matter of fact, its membership is by and large restricted to those who either ignore the teaching of the Church or seek somehow to undermine it. It brings together under the aegis of Catholicism homosexual persons who have no intention of abandoning their homosexual behaviour. One tactic used is to protest that any and all criticism of or reservations about homosexual people, their activity and lifestyle, are simply diverse forms of unjust discrimination.

   There is an effort in some countries to manipulate the Church by gaining the often well-intentioned support of her pastors with a view to changing civil-statutes and laws. This is done in order to conform to these pressure groups' concept that homosexuality is at least a completely harmless, if not an entirely good, thing. Even when the practice of homosexuality may seriously threaten the lives and well-being of a large number of people, its advocates remain undeterred and refuse to consider the magnitude of the risks involved.

   The Church can never be so callous. It is true that her clear position cannot be revised by pressure from civil legislation or the trend of the moment. But she is really concerned about the many who are not represented by the pro-homosexual movement and about those who may have been tempted to believe its deceitful propaganda. She is also aware that the view that homosexual activity is equivalent to, or as acceptable as, the sexual expression of conjugal love has a direct impact on society's understanding of the nature and rights of the family and puts them in jeopardy.

10. It is deplorable that homosexual persons have been and are the object of violent malice in speech or in action. Such treatment deserves condemnation from the Church's pastors wherever it occurs. It reveals a kind of disregard for others which endangers the most fundamental principles of a healthy society. The intrinsic dignity of each person must always be respected in word, in action and in law.

    But the proper reaction to crimes committed against homosexual persons should not be to claim that the homosexual condition is not disordered. When such a claim is made and when homosexual activity is consequently condoned, or when civil legislation is introduced to protect behaviour to which no one has any conceivable right, neither the Church nor society at large should be surprised when other distorted notions and practices gain ground, and irrational and violent reactions increase.

11. It has been argued that the homosexual orientation in certain cases is not the result of deliberate choice; and so the homosexual person would then have no choice but to behave in a homosexual fashion. Lacking freedom, such a person, even if engaged in homosexual activity would not be culpable.

    Here, the Church's wise moral tradition is necessary since it warns against generalizations in judging individual cases. In fact, circumstances may exist, or may have existed in the past, which would reduce or remove the culpability of the individual in a given instance, or other circumstances may increase it. What is at all costs to be avoided is the unfounded and demeaning assumption that the sexual behaviour of homosexual persons is always and totally compulsive and therefore inculpable. What is essential is that the fundamental liberty which characterizes the human person and gives him his dignity be recognized as belonging to the homosexual person as well. As in every conversion from evil, the abandonment of homosexual activity will require a profound collaboration of the individual with God's liberating grace.

12. What, then, are homosexual persons to do who seek to follow the Lord? Fundamentally, they are called to enact the will of God in their life by joining whatever sufferings and difficulties they experience in virtue of their condition to the sacrifice of the Lord's Cross. That Cross, for the believer, is a fruitful sacrifice since from that death come life and redemption. While any call to carry the cross or to understand a Christian's suffering in this way will predictably be met with bitter ridicule by some, it should be remembered that this is the way to eternal for *all* who follow Christ.

    It is, in effect, none other than the teaching of Paul the Apostle to the Galatians when he says that the Spirit produces in the lives of the faithful "love, joy, peace, patience, kindness, goodness, trustfulness, gentleness and self-control" (5:22) and further (v. 24), "You cannot belong to Christ unless you crucify all self-indulgent passions and desires".

    It is easily misunderstood, however, if it is merely seen as a pointless effort at self-denial. The Cross *is* denial of self, but in service to the will of God himself who makes life come from death and empowers those who trust in him to practise virtue in place of vice.

    To celebrate the Paschal Mystery, it is necessary to let that Mystery become imprinted in the fabric of daily life. To refuse to sacrifice one's own will in obedience to the will of the Lord is effectively to prevent salvation. Just as the Cross was central to the expression of God's redemptive love for us in Jesus, so the conformity of the self-denial of homosexual men and women with the sacrifice of the Lord will constitute for them a source of self-giving which will save them from a way of life which constantly threatens to destroy them.

Christians who are homosexual are called, as all of us are, to a chaste life. As they dedicate their lives to understanding the nature of God's personal call to them, they will be able to celebrate the Sacrament of Penance more faithfully and receive the Lord's grace so freely offered there in order to convert their lives more fully to his Way.

13. We recognize, of course, that in great measure the clear and successful communication of the Church's teaching to all the faithful, and to society at large, depends on the correct instruction and fidelity of her pastoral ministers. The Bishops have the particularly grave responsibility to see to it that their assistants in the ministry, above all the priests, are rightly informed and personally disposed to bring the teaching of the Church in its integrity to everyone.

    The characteristic concern and good will exhibited by many clergy and religious in their pastoral care for homosexual persons is admirable, and, we hope, will not diminish. Such devoted ministers should have the confidence that they are faithfully following the will of the Lord by encouraging the homosexual person to lead a chaste life and by affirming that person's God-given dignity and worth.

14. With this in mind, this Congregation wishes to ask the Bishop to be especially cautious of any programmes which may seek to pressure the Church to change her teaching, even while claiming not to do so. A careful examination of their public statements and the activities that promote reveals a studied ambiguity by which they attempt to mislead the pastors and the faithful. For example, they may present the teaching of the Magisterium, but only as if it were an optional source for the formation of one's conscience. Its specific authority is not recognized. Some of these groups will use the word "Catholic" to describe either the organization or its intended members, yet they do not defend and promote the teaching of the Magisterium; indeed, they even openly attack it. While their members may claim a desire to conform their lives to the teaching of Jesus, in fact they abandon the teaching of his Church. This contradictory action should not have the support of the Bishops in any way.

15. We encourage the Bishops, then, to provide pastoral care in full accord with the teaching of the Church for homosexual persons of their dioceses. No authentic pastoral programme will include organizations in which homosexual persons associate with each other without clearly stating that homosexual activity is immoral. A truly pastoral approach will appreciate the need for homosexual persons to avoid the near occasions of sin.

    We would heartily encourage programmes where these dangers are avoided. But we wish to make it clear that departure form the Church's teaching, or silence about it, in an effort to provide pastoral care, is neither caring nor pastoral. Only what is true can ultimately be pastoral. The neglect of the Church's position prevents homosexual men and women from receiving the care they need and deserve.

    An authentic pastoral programme will assist homosexual persons at all levels of the spiritual life: through the sacraments, and in particular through the frequent and sincere use of the sacrament of Reconciliation, through prayer, witness, counsel and individual care. In such a way, the entire Christian community can come to recognize its own call to assist its brothers and sisters, without deluding them or isolating them.

16. From this multi-faceted approach there are numerous advantages to be gained, not the least of which is the realization that a homosexual person, as every human being, deeply needs to be nourished at many different levels simultaneously.

    The human person, made in the image and likeness of God, can hardly be adequately described by a reductionist reference to his or her sexual orientation. Every one living on the fact of the earth has personal problems and difficulties, but challenges to growth, strengths, talents and gifts as well. Today, the Church provides a badly needed context for the care of the human person when she refuses to consider the person as a ''heterosexual'' or a ''homosexual'' and insists that every person has a fundamental identity: the creature of God, and by grace, his child and heir to eternal life.

17. In bringing this entire matter to the Bishop's attention, this Congregation wishes to support their efforts to assure that the teaching of the Lord and his Church on this important question be communicated fully to all the faithful.

In light of the points made above, they should decide for their own dioceses the extent to which an intervention on their part is indicated. In addition, should they consider it helpful, further coordinated action at the level of the National Bishops' Conference may be envisioned.

In a particular way, we would ask the Bishops to support, with the means at their disposal, the development of appropriate forms of pastoral care for homosexual persons. These would include the assistance of the psychological, sociological and medical sciences, in full accord with the teaching of the Church.

They are encouraged to call on the assistance of all Catholic theologians who, by teaching what the Church teaches, and by deepening their reflections on the true meaning of human sexuality and Christian marriage with the virtues it engenders, will make an important contribution in this particular area of pastoral care.

The Bishops are asked to exercise special care in the selection of pastoral ministers so that by their own high degree of spiritual and personal maturity and by their fidelity to the Magisterium, they may be of real service to homosexual persons, promoting their health and well-being in the fullest sense. Such ministers will reject theological opinions which dissent from the teaching of the Church and which, therefore, cannot be used as guidelines for pastoral care.

We encourage the Bishops to promote appropriate catechetical programmes based on the truth about human sexuality in its relationship to the family as taught by the Church. Such programmes should provide a good context within which to deal with the question of homosexuality.

This catechesis would also assist those families of homosexual persons to deal with this problem which affects them so deeply.

All support should be withdrawn from any organizations which seek to undermine the teaching of the Church, which are ambiguous about it, or which neglect it entirely. Such support, or even the semblance of support, can be gravely misinterpreted. Special attention should be given to the practice of scheduling religious services and to the use of Church buildings by these groups, including the facilities of Catholic schools and colleges. To some, such permission to use Church property may seem only just and charitable; but in reality it is contradictory to the purpose for which these institutions were founded, it is misleading and often scandalous.

In assessing proposed legislation, the Bishops should keep as their uppermost concern the responsibility to defend and promote family life.

18. The Lord Jesus promised, ''You shall know the truth and the truth shall set you free'' (*Jn* 8:32). Scripture bids us speak the truth in love (cf. *Eph* 4:15). The God who is at once truth and love calls the Church to minister to every man, woman and child with the pastoral solicitude of our compassionate Lord. It is in this spirit that we have addressed this Letter to the Bishops of the Church, with the hope that it will be of some help as they care for those whose suffering can only be intensified by error and lightened by truth.

During an audience granted to the undersigned Prefect, His Holiness, Pope John Paul II, approved this Letter, adopted in an ordinary session of the Congregation for the Doctrine of the Faith, and ordered it to be published.

Given at Rome, 1 October, 1986.

JOSEPH Cardinal RATZINGER
Prefect

ALBERTO BOVONE
Titular Archbishop of Caesarea in Numidia
Secretary

Notes: *In the eleven years following the issuance of its* Declaration on Certain Questions Concerning Sexual Ethics, *debate raged within the church on issues not specifically covered by the document. Some people hoped that as time passed more and more discoveries about homosexuality were made, the church would find an increased level of acceptance in its sacramental system for homosexuality and the "gay" lifestyle. In 1986 the Congregation for the Doctrine of the Faith, which was under the leadership of the very conservative Joseph Cardinal Ratzinger, issued a more definitive statement exclusively covering the issues related to homosexuals.*

Ratzinger specifically attacks the more liberal interpretations of the 1975 declaration and any notion that living as a homosexual is a morally acceptable option for Catholics. At the heart of the document is an attack upon attempts at biblical exegesis which downplay the admonitions against homosexuality in the Bible. Ratzinger concludes that the homosexual condition is one of objective disorder and that homosexual acts are not to be condoned. This document largely settled the issue of homosexuality in the church. In addition, it specifically condemned the role of organizations such as Dignity, a group which promotes homosexuality as an acceptable lifestyle and the compatibility of homosexuality and life within the Roman Catholic Church. As Ratzinger said, "No authentic pastoral programme will include organizations in which homosexual persons associate with each other without clearly stating that homosexual activity is immoral."

ROMAN CATHOLIC CHURCH—CARDINAL JOSEPH BERNARDIN

STATEMENT ON THE EVENING MASS AT ST. SEBASTIAN AND MINISTRY TO HOMOSEXUALS (1988)

For more than 17 years there has been a Sunday evening Mass at St. Sebastian Church that has served Catholics who are gay and lesbian. This Mass was begun by the parish itself as an outgrowth of the apostolate of the Legion of Mary among the members of the gay community. Subsequently, Dignity/Chicago assumed sponsorship for this Mass. Nonetheless, the Mass has always been considered by the pastor and parish council as an important part of the ministerial life of the parish. Moreover, as a regularly scheduled Mass, it has attracted some worshippers who are not members of the gay community.

Since its inception, the archdiocese has been aware of the Mass at St. Sebastian. The sponsorship/involvement of Dignity/Chicago has been monitored by the pastor of the parish. The archdiocese, however, never formally recognized the sponsorship of Dignity/Chicago because it saw an ambiguity in the position taken by Dignity with regard to church teaching on human sexuality. Its statement of purpose could be read either as being in conformity with church teaching or at variance with it. Last August, however, that ambiguity was eliminated when Dignity/National adopted a resolution which called for an "openness to discussion on the morality of homosexual acts." The context of this resolution clearly indicates that its intent is to change some fundamental teachings of the church on human sexuality as reaffirmed recently by the Congregation for the Doctrine of the Faith in its instruction "The Pastoral Care of Homosexual Persons."

In the near future I will present, in a series of columns in the Chicago Catholic, the church's teaching on human sexuality and in that context I will indicate why the position of Dignity is unacceptable.

I am very concerned that gay and lesbian Catholics receive the pastoral care of their church. That pastoral care involves in one way or another elements of acknowledgement, support and direction. This new development, however, has required that the status of Dignity/ Chicago's sponsorship of the Mass at St. Sebastian be reconsidered. It is my responsibility, as pastor of the church of Chicago, to make sure that the church's teaching on human sexuality is presented clearly and without any ambiguity. Moreover, it would be inappropriate to endorse an organization which officially advocates a position which is contrary to that of the church or to allow such an organization to assume a position of leadership in one of our parishes or agencies.

In order to resolve this dilemma in a way which will be doctrinally correct and pastorally sensitive, I have been meeting for over a year with the pastors of a number of parishes that have a significant number of gay and lesbian members. These pastors are already ministering in various ways to their gay and lesbian members. They are eager to develop this ministry, in collaboration with the archdiocese, in a way that will be both faithful to Catholic teaching and effective in their parishes.

The pastors and I have agreed on some basic principles upon which our ministry to the Catholic gay and lesbian community should be based:

1. The archdiocese strongly affirms the teaching of the church on the rights and dignity of all persons and the fact that these rights should be respected and protected.
2. The archdiocese condemns arbitrary discrimination and prejudice, violence and harassment against a person because of his or her sexual orientation.
3. The archdiocese fully supports the church's teaching on human sexuality, which rejects as immoral homosexual acts as distinguished from the person who is homosexual.
4. Accordingly, the archdiocese reaffirms its commitment to minister spiritually to its brothers and sisters who are homosexual. To that end, the archdiocese should pursue ways in which it can do this more effectively.
5. The archdiocese does not endorse any organization which assumes a position of advocacy against church teaching.

In the context of these principles, I wish now to address the matter of the Sunday evening Mass at St. Sebastian. The importance and significance of this Mass go beyond the question of "sponsorship" by Dignity/Chicago. The Mass is an important part of the parish's ministry and is supported by the parish pastoral council. The Mass has become a point of return to the life of the church for many persons, whether homosexual or not, whether members of Dignity or not. It has met a pastoral need that exists at St. Sebastian and other parishes. To cancel the Mass would be a serious pastoral mistake.

For this reason, I have decided that the archdiocese will assume responsibility for this Mass and have asked the pastors of neighboring parishes to collaborate with the pastor of St. Sebastian in this responsibility. They will have direct responsibility for the Sunday evening liturgy, celebrating Mass on a regular basis. This understanding does not preclude, however, their inviting other priests to preside and preach on occasion.

In the future the archdiocese, rather than Dignity/Chicago, will be the sponsor of the Mass. All of those who have been participating in the Mass are invited to continue. All who have been involved in the planning and celebration of the Sunday eucharist are invited to continue sharing their experience and talent. It will be the responsibility of the pastors to ensure that everything connected with the Mass and any events which might take place before or after the liturgy be in accord with church teaching and discipline.

Father John Flavin, as pastor of St. Sebastian and dean of the area, will serve as coordinator of this pastoral project. Periodically, I will review the situation with him and the other pastors. In addition, I will continue to dialogue with them and other interested people as to how we can extend further, as the authentic teaching of the church directs, our pastoral outreach to gay and lesbian Catholics throughout the archdiocese.

Notes: *A 1986 document by Cardinal Ratzinger clarifying the church's position on homosexuality had a variety of consequences through the church. Symbolic of the steps taken to bring practice into conformity with the new perception of the church's position, Cardinal Bernardin, archbishop of one of the most important archdiocese's in North America, moved against Dignity, the homosexual advocacy group within the Roman Catholic Church and took control of a mass which had previously been sponsored by Dignity at St. Sebastian Church. The mass had long been a focus of pro-homosexual support. Bernardin had previously tried to work with Dignity, but reacted sharply to a clarification in their pro-homosexual position, which he perceived as opposed to the church's position.*

Protestant and Eastern Orthodox Churches

Over half of the religiously affiliated individuals in North America identify with one of the many Protestant or Eastern Orthodox denominations. Within these bodies there exists widely divergent Christian theologies and opinions on social issues. On the issue of homosexual activity, the great majority of churches also place a high value on the family unit as a normative social unit and commonly believe that sexual activity should be limited to heterosexual relations between a couple in a monogamous marriage.

Challenged in the 1960s and 1970s to reconsider their traditional rejection of homosexuality, the churches conducted a variety of seminars and other activities. Not only did these activities educate a generation of church leaders on the complex problems of the homosexual life, but they also led to a consensus of opinion which reaches across theological divisions between liberal and conservative Protestant and Orthodox churches. No traditional Protestant or Orthodox church found sufficient rationale in all it had learned to adopt a position which would allow it to sanction homosexual relations. As a result, none have been willing to accept practicing homosexuals as a candidate for ordination to the ministry or priesthood.

The rejection of homosexual behavior and homosexual ministerial candidates by the Protestant and Orthodox churches has led in several instances to the establishment of new churches which operate out of a Western theological perspective but have altered their approach to homosexuality. These churches not only view homosexuality as a natural (if minority) way some people are created, but believe that homosexual relationships can be part of an acceptable (if alternative) lifestyle. The major new denomination to adopt such a perspective is the Universal Fellowship of Metropolitan Community Churches.

ASSEMBLIES OF GOD

STATEMENT ON HOMOSEXUALITY (1979)

Homosexual behavior, whether male or female, is one area which reflects an alarming erosion of national moral standards. Unprecedented boldness is being manifested in the demands homosexuals are making. Others who deny involvement in this aberration have nevertheless become champions of these people.

One reason why Christians are deeply concerned about this problem is that a nation's tolerance or intolerance of homosexuality is one indication of the nation's spiritual condition. When Israel drifted away from God, it tolerated various evils, including sodomy (1 Kings 14:24). When Israel returned to God, homosexuality was not tolerated (1 Kings 15:12).

The Assemblies of God believes all faith and conduct must be evaluated on the basis of Scripture. Since the Bible speaks to the issue of homosexuality, it must be considered the authoritative rule by which a position is established.

Homosexuality is Sin

Human reason sometimes considers homosexuality to be a psychological problem, a physical condition, or the deliberate choice of an alternate life-style. Scripture considers it sin against God and man. The church's concern about this problem is not a matter of discrimination against a minority group. This is a moral issue. The Bible makes this very clear.

1. *Homosexuality is sin because it is contrary to the principles of sexuality which God established in the beginning.*

   When God created man, "in the image of God created he him; male and female created he them" (Genesis 1:27). After God had created the man, He indicated it is not good for man to live alone (Genesis 2:18). It is for this reason that God created a companion suitable for man (Genesis 2:18). It should be noted that man's loneliness was not remedied by the creation of another man, but by the creation of woman.

   When God brought the woman to him, Adam said, "This is now bone of my bones, and flesh of my flesh: she shall be called Woman, because she was taken out of Man." The Scripture then states: "Therefore shall a man leave his father and his mother, and shall cleave unto his wife: and they shall be one flesh" (Genesis 2:23, 24).

   In the creation of mankind God established principles of sexuality by which the human race was to develop. Psychologically this relationship was sound. Physically the relationship was natural. Sociologically it established the ideal family unit. The Biblical concept is that human sexuality ideally is a heterosexual, monogamous relationship.

   When people choose to be homosexuals, they reject God's principles of sexuality. Their aberrant sexual behavior results in sin against the nature of sexuality which God established (Romans 1:27). And they establish a social unit contrary to the divine instruction of the man leaving father and mother and cleaving "unto his wife: and they shall be one flesh" (Genesis 2:24).

   In His discussion with the Pharisees Jesus reiterated the principle of sexuality which God established in the beginning (Matthew 19:4-9). He pointed out that the only approved lifestyle apart from heterosexual marriage was celibacy for the kingdom of heaven's sake (Matthew 19:10-12).

2. *Homosexuality is sin because the Bible refers to it as evil.*

   When God called Israel to be His nation in a distinctive sense, He miraculously provided for its deliverance from Egyptian bondage. But God did more. He provided a code by which His people were to guide every aspect of conduct. Among the laws relating to morals, specific reference was made to homosexuality.

   In Leviticus 18:22 God commanded: "Thou shalt not lie with mankind, as with womankind: it is abomination." Then in Leviticus 20:13, the commandment is reinforced with severe penalty for violations. The record states: "If a man also lie with mankind, as he lieth with a woman, both of them have committed an abomination; they shall surely be put to death, their blood shall be upon them.

   This prohibition is reiterated in other portions of the Bible.

   In Romans 1:21-27 Paul recorded the results which followed in the lives of those who rejected God and worshipped and served the creature more than the Creator. They dishonored their bodies between themselves. They changed the natural use of sex into that which is against nature. They were filled with all unrighteousness, fornication, wickedness, covetousness, maliciousness. They were without natural affection, implacable, and unmerciful.

In Paul's day the city of Corinth was notorious for immorality. It was not only the crossroads of commerce, but of vice and immorality as well. Because the church was being established in this city, it was important that people understood how God perceived immorality of every kind.

The record is very explicit. Paul wrote: "Know ye not that the unrighteous shall not inherit the kingdom of God?" Then he continued: "Be not deceived: neither fornicators, nor idolaters, nor adulterers, nor effeminate, nor abusers of themselves with mankind . . . shall inherit the kingdom of God" (1 Corinthians 6:9,10). C.K. Barrett in *The First Epistle to the Corinthians* indicates that the word translated "effeminate" refers to catamites, while the word translated "abusers of themselves with mankind" refers to sodomites. These two expressions thus refer to both the passive and active partners in male homosexual relations.

In his letter to Timothy, Paul wrote that the Law was made "for the lawless and disobedient, for the ungodly, and for sinners, for unholy and profane, for murderers of fathers and murderers of mothers, for manslayers, for whoremongers, for them that defile themselves with mankind [homosexuals] . . ." (1 Timothy 1:9, 10). These people are identified as ungodly in contrast to those who are described as being righteous.

Scripture consistently identifies homosexuality as sin.

3. *Homosexuality is sin which comes under divine judgment.*

The ancient city of Sodom has become a synonym for homosexuality. While other evils existed in this community, sodomy was prominent. The homosexuals of Sodom were so depraved that they threatened to abuse visitors to their community. The historical record indicates they became violent and tried to break down the door of the house in which Lot entertained his guests. Only divine intervention spared Lot and his household from their evil intentions.

These people became so depraved it was necessary for God to destroy the cities of Sodom and Gomorrah (Genesis 19:4-11, 24, 25). The severity of judgment on these cities was of such intensity that it is used as an illustration of divine judgment both by Peter (2 Peter 2:6) and Jude (Jude 7).

Homosexuals Can Be Saved

While scripture makes it clear homosexuality is sin and will come under the judgment of God, it also indicates homosexuals can be saved. Homosexuality is a moral problem, and only God can help the sinner. Nothing is impossible with God.

In the church at Corinth were former homosexuals who had been delivered from the power of sin by the grace of God. In 1 Corinthians 6:9 Paul listed homosexuals among those who cannot inherit the kingdom of God. Then in verse 11 he wrote: "And such were some of you." This is in the past tense. They had been homosexuals, but they had also been delivered from this sin by the power of God.

Scripture makes it clear that the efficacy of the Atonement is unlimited for those who accept it. There is no stain of sin so dark that it cannot be removed. John the Baptist announced: "Behold the Lamb of God, which taketh away the sin of the world" (John 1:29).

Paul wrote: "For He [God] hath made him to be sin for us, who knew no sin; that we might be made the righteousness of God in him" (2 Corinthians 5:21).

John wrote: ''If we confess our sins, he is faithful and just to forgive us our sins, and to cleanse us from all unrighteousness' (1 John 1:9).

Through the regenerating power of the Holy Spirit, people, regardless of the nature of their sin, can be made new creatures in Christ Jesus (2 Corinthians 5:17).

God's plan of salvation is the same for all. The homosexual who wants to be delivered from the penalty and power of sin must come to God in the same way other sinners come to God.

The act of turning to God for salvation includes both repentance and faith. There must be an acceptance of Jesus as Lord and Saviour. While these aspects of conversion may be simultaneous rather than in sequence, Scripture makes it clear they are both involved.

Jesus, in His instruction to the disciples prior to His ascension, indicated that repentance and remission of sins should be preached (Luke 24:47). Since repentance represents a change of mind in which there is a turning from sin, the person coming to God must recognize the sinfulness of sin. This includes not only the sin of Christ-rejection, but other attitudes and conduct contrary to the teaching of God's Word.

Like the Philippian jailer who asked what he must do to be saved, those desiring salvation must believe in the Lord Jesus Christ (Acts 16:30, 31)—believe that He can save from the power as well as the penalty of sin. Obedient faith, like repentance, is a condition of salvation.

Christian Attitude Toward Homosexuals

Christians are not only concerned with what the Bible teaches about homosexuality, but also what the attitude of Christians should be toward those involved in this practice. Some sins seem more reprehensible than others because they not only affect the pervert but often involve recruitment as well. For this reason Christians must be sure their attitudes toward homosexuals are in harmony with the teaching of Scripture. They must on the one hand avoid the sentimental credulity which results in tolerance of this behavior. On the other hand they must not overlook opportunities to help those who want to live according to God's Word.

Caution must be exercised as opportunities for witnessing develop. Believers must trust the Holy Spirit to guide them in distinguishing between those who honestly want God's salvation and those who may be recruiting sympathizers for homosexuality as an alternate life-style.

Scripture warns believers: ''Let no man deceive you with vain words: for because of these things [immorality described in verse 5] cometh the wrath of God upon the children of disobedience'' (Ephesians 5:6). It continues to warn that Christians are not to be partakers with them or have fellowship in ''the unfruitful works of darkness, but rather reprove them'' (Ephesians 5:7, 11).

The Church cannot condone what God condemns.

If homosexuals reject God's offer of salvation, Scripture places them outside the bounds of God's kingdom along with others who reject Jesus Christ. For this reason they cannot be accepted into the fellowship of the Church.

However, when those involved in homosexual perversion are really looking for salvation through Christ, Christians should do all they can to help. As the love of God is shed abroad in the believer's heart, this love will be manifested to all. Like God, the believer can love the sinner while at the same time hating the sin.

In other words, believers must be true to God and His Word in helping homosexuals recognize the sinfulness of their ways. They should testify to the transforming power of God and the fulfilling life there is in a right relationship with Him. They should pray for them and do all that is possible to help those who want the blessings of God's mercy and grace.

They will then have the satisfaction of knowing ''that he which converteth the sinner from the error of his way shall save a soul from death, and shall hide a multitude of sins'' (James 5:20).

Notes: *The Assemblies of God, one of the largest of the Pentecostal denominations, follows a conservative, traditional view of homosexuality and homosexual behavior as sin. Homosexuality is sinful to the extent that if the homosexual does not turn from its practice, s/he has placed him/herself outside of the kingdom of God.*

ASSOCIATION OF FREE LUTHERAN CONGREGATIONS

RESOLUTION ON ABORTION AND HOMOSEXUALITY (1978)

BE IT FURTHER RESOLVED, That we offer the hand of Christian love to those homosexuals who wish to be helped by God's power: We have love for the sinner but hate the sin.

BE IT RESOLVED, That we support and pray for government, and law enforcement agencies in their effort to control terrorists, ''. . . that we may lead a quiet and peaceable life in all godliness and honesty.'' (I Tim. 2:2)

BE IT RESOLVED, That we continue to oppose the sins of abortion and homosexuality and that our position upon those two subjects be as follows:

INASMUCH as the government of the beloved United States has allowed the use of abortions as a means of birth control, AND WHEREAS the indiscriminate taking of a human life, including that of a human fetus, is against our understanding of the Word of God,

BE IT RESOLVED, That the Annual Conference of the AFLC stands opposed to abortion as a means of birth control.

BE IT FURTHER RESOLVED, That each congregation and individual within the AFLC is encouraged to protest in writing to their respective legislative officials.

WHEREAS, Due to the increased moral decay of our society, specifically regarding the gay rights movement, we heartily support those who on the basis of the Bible oppose homosexuality.

Notes: *This very conservative Lutheran body tied the practice of abortion and the rise of homosexuality to the moral decay in society.*

CHRISTIAN CHURCH (DISCIPLES OF CHRIST)

RESOLUTION CONCERNING CHRISTIAN MORALITY (1979)

Substitute Resolution Concerning Christian Morality (1979)

WHEREAS, the divine will for creation is that God's eternal power and deity be revealed in all the things that have been made (Rom 1:20); and the divine will for humanity is that all persons, created in God's own image, love and serve God by their worship, obedience, love and care for one another, and daily life.

WHEREAS, Christians are called to ''be perfect as your heavenly Father is perfect'' (Matt. 5:48); to lead lives ''worthy of the calling to which you have been called'' (Eph. 4:1) to give attention to whatever is true, honorable, just, pure, lovely, and gracious (Phil 4:8); and

WHEREAS, the witness of law and gospel, prophets and apostles, saints and scholars, condemns idolatry, injustice, and immorality, and all sins against God, against creation, against our own selves, and testifies to the steadfast love and mercy of God who "sent the Son into the world, not to condemn the world, but that the world might be saved through Him" (John 3:17): and

WHEREAS, many individuals, as well as the culture as a whole, are experiencing confusion concerning the goals of life and principles to guide behavior; as well as the breaking down of patterns, structures; and disciplines that have previously guided them in all aspects of life;

THEREFORE, BE IT RESOLVED, that the General Assembly of the Christian Church, meeting in St. Louis, Missouri, October 26-31, 1979, declare anew its allegiance to Jesus' summary of the law, that we love God with all our heart, soul, mind, and strength; and that we love our neighbor as ourself (Mk 12:30-31); and

BE IT FURTHER RESOLVED, that this Assembly call upon the members of the Christian Church (Disciples of Christ) to reaffirm this allegiance to the divine will in their prayers, their thinking about morality and ethics, their personal behavior, their public actions, and the activities and teachings of their congregations; and

BE IT FURTHER RESOLVED, that this Assembly encourage the regions and other units and organizations of the Christian Church (Disciples of Christ) to strengthen the processes that will enable this church to contribute to the current search for ways of life that are faithful to God's will, ethically sound, and personally fulfilling.

Notes: *On several occasions, strongly worded resolutions condemning homosexuality and homosexuals have been considered by the General Assembly of the Disciples of Christ. One such resolution was submitted in 1979. In response to the original resolution, this one, advocating a general stance against "idolatry, injustice, and immorality" and without direct reference to homosexuality, was passed. Opponents of this resolution thought it sidestepped the issue.*

CHRISTIAN IDENTITY CHURCH

DOCTRINAL STATEMENT OF BELIEFS (UNDATED)

We believe men and women should conduct themselves according to the role of their gender in the traditional Christian sense that God intended. Homosexuality is an abomination before God and should be punished by death (Lev. 18:22, 20:13; Rom. 1:24-28, 32; I Cor. 6:9).

Notes: *The Christian Identity Church is better known for its stance on racial issues, believing that the white race is chosen by God. As a conservative Bible-oriented organization, however, the church also takes literally the passages in both the Old and New Testaments condemning homosexuality.*

CHRISTIAN REFORMED CHURCH IN NORTH AMERICA

STATEMENT ON HOMOSEXUALITY (1973)

The Synod of 1970 observed that homosexuality "is a growing problem in today's society" and decided to appoint a committee "to study the problem of homosexuality and to delineate the church's position on this matter" (Acts of Synod, 1970, p. 12). This committee submitted its report to the Synod of 1973. Synod decided to "submit the Study

Report re Homosexuality (Part 1) to our churches as providing a background study for our understanding of the problem of homosexuality and the formulation of a Christian position'' (Acts of Synod, 1973, p. 51). Synod then adopted the following eleven statements of pastoral advice together with an ''introductory note.''

Decision of 1973

For a proper reading and understanding of the pastoral advice it is imperative to observe the following definitions:

> A ''homosexual'' is a person who has erotic attractions for members of the same sex. Such a person may or may not actually engage in homosexualism. ''It must be pointed out that there are people who have strong erotic attractions for members of the same sex who nevertheless never engage in homosexual acts for various reasons, such as, for example, their religious convictions. They are homosexuals, that is they are constitutionally (by either biological or psychological conditions or both) predisposed to homosexuality but do not engage in homosexualism.''
>
> ''Homosexuality'' is a condition of personal identity in which the person is sexually oriented toward persons of the same sex.
>
> ''Homosexualism'' is explicit (overt) homosexual practice.

Decision of 1973

That synod serve the churches with the following statements of pastoral advice:

1. Homosexuality (male and female) is a condition of disordered sexuality which reflects the brokenness of our sinful world and for which the homosexual may himself bear only a minimal responsibility.
2. The homosexual may not, on the sole ground of his sexual disorder be denied community acceptance, and if he is a Christian he is to be wholeheartedly received by the Church as a person for whom Christ died.
3. Homosexualism—as explicit homosexual practice—must be condemned as incompatible with obedience to the will of God as revealed in Holy Scripture.
4. The church must exercise the same patient understanding of and compassion for the homosexual in his sins as for all other sinners. The gospel of God's grace in Christ is to be proclaimed to him as the basis of his forgiveness, the power of his renewal, and the source of his strength to lead a sanctified life. As all Christians in their weaknesses, the homosexual must be admonished and encouraged not to allow himself to be defeated by lapses in chastity, but rather, to repent and thereafter to depend in fervent prayer upon the means of grace for power to withstand temptation.
5. In order to live a life of chastity in obedience to God's will the homosexual needs the loving support and encouragement of the church. The church should therefore so include him in its fellowship that he is not tempted by rejection and loneliness to seek companionship in a ''gay world'' whose godless lifestyle is alien to a Christian.
6. Homosexuals, especially in their earlier years, should be encouraged to seek such help as may effect their sexual reorientation and the church should do everything in its power to help the homosexual overcome his disorder. Members of the churches should understand that many homosexuals, who might otherwise seek therapeutic aid, are deterred from doing so by the fear of detection and consequent ostracism. Christian acceptance and support can in all such cases be a means toward healing and wholeness. On the other hand, to those who are not healed and who must accept the limitations of their homosexuality, the church must minister in the same spirit as when it ministers to all who are not married.

7. Christians who are homosexual in their orientation are like all Christians called to discipleship and to the employment of their gifts in the cause of the kingdom. They should recognize that their sexuality is subordinate to their obligation to live in wholehearted surrender to Christ.

   By the same token, churches should recognize that their homosexual members are fellow-servants of Christ who are to be given opportunity to render within the offices and structures of the congregation the same service that is expected from heterosexuals. The homosexual member must not be supposed to have less the gift of self-control in the face of sexual temptation than does the heterosexual. The relationship of love and trust within the congregation should be such that in instances where a member's sexual propensity does create a problem, the problem can be dealt with in the same way as are problems caused by the limitations and disorders of any other member.

8. It is the duty of pastors to be informed about the condition of homosexuality and the particular problems of the homosexual in order that the pastor may minister to his need and to the need of others, such as parents, who may be intimately involved in the problems of homosexuality. The pastor is also in a position to instruct his congregation in appropriate ways about homosexuality and to alert members and office holders to the responsibility they bear toward homosexuals in the fellowship. He can encourage an understanding of and compassion for persons who live with this sexual disorder, and dispel the prejudices under which they suffer.

9. The church should promote good marriages, and healthy family life in which the relations between husband and wife and between parents and children are such that the psychological causes that may contribute to sexual inversion are reduced to a minimum. Parents should be encouraged to seek Christian counsel and help when they see signs of disordered sexual maturation in their children.

10. Institutions and agencies associated with the church that are in a position to contribute to the alleviation of the problem of homosexuality are encouraged to do so by assisting ministers to become better informed, by offering counseling services to the homosexual and his family, and by generally creating a Christian attitude in the churches as well as in society as a whole.

11. The church should speak the Word of God prophetically to a society and culture which glorifies sexuality and sexual gratification. It should foster a wholesome appreciation of sex and expose and condemn the idolatrous sexualism and the current celebration of homosexualism promoted in literature, the theatre, films, television, advertisements and the like.

References: Acts of Synod, 1970, p. 12.
Acts of Synod, 1973, p. 51.

Notes: *While this resolution is clearly opposed to homosexuality and condemns homosexual practice, it is relatively open and accepting. It begins by noting that the homosexual is a victim of the fall of the world and, thus, has minimal responsibility of his/her condition. It also calls upon the church to provide support and understanding, and to accept homosexuals into membership and leadership positions (without making reference to the ordained ministry) in the church.*

CHURCH OF ENGLAND

EXCERPTS FROM THE WOLFENDEN REPORT (1957)

Chapter III

Homosexuality

17. We are concerned, in this part of our inquiry, with homosexual offenses. Any lengthy or detailed study of the nature or origins of homosexuality would, in our view, have fallen outside our terms of reference, even if we had felt ourselves qualified to embark upon it. Nevertheless, since we are concerned also with the treatment of those who have been convicted of homosexual offenses we have found it necessary to acquaint ourselves with at least the elements of the subject in general, and the following paragraphs set out some of the points and problems which have been raised in our discussions. We owe much to the evidence of our medical witnesses and, in the interpretation and assessment of that evidence, to our own medical colleagues, to whom the nonmedical members of the Committee are greatly indebted.

18. It is important to make a clear distinction between "homosexual offenses" and "homosexuality." The former are enumerated . . . below. For the latter, we are content to rely on the dictionary definition that homosexuality is a sexual propensity for persons of one's own sex. Homosexuality, then, is a state or condition, and as such does not, and cannot, come within the purview of the criminal law.

19. This definition of homosexuality involves the adoption of some criteria for its recognition. As in other psychological fields, an inference that the propensity exists may be derived from either subjective or objective data, that is, either from what is felt or from what is done by the persons concerned. Either method may lead to fallacious results. In the first place, introspection is neither exhaustive nor infallible; an individual may quite genuinely not be aware of either the existence or the strength of his motivations and propensities, and there is a natural reluctance to acknowledge, even to oneself, a preference which is socially condemned, or to admit to acts that are illegal and liable to a heavy penalty. Rationalization and self-deception can be carried to great lengths, and in certain circumstances lying is also to be expected. Secondly, some of those whose main sexual propensity is for persons of the opposite sex indulge, for a variety of reasons, in homosexual acts. It is known, for example, that some men who are placed in special circumstances that prohibit contact with the opposite sex (for instance, in prisoner-of-war camps or prisons) indulge in homosexual acts, though they revert to heterosexual behavior when opportunity affords; and it is clear from our evidence that some men who are not predominantly homosexual lend themselves to homosexual practices for financial or other gain. Conversely, many homosexual persons have heterosexual intercourse with or without homosexual fantasies. Furthermore, a homosexual tendency may not be manifested exclusively, or even at all, in sexual fields of behavior, as we explain . . . below.

20. There is the further problem how widely the description "homosexual" should be applied. According to the psycho-analytic school, a homosexual component (sometimes conscious, often not) exists in everybody; and if this is correct, homosexuality in this sense is universal. Without going so far as to accept this view *in toto*, it is possible to realize that the issue of latent homosexuality, which we discuss more fully . . . below, is relevant to any assessment of the frequency of occurrence of the condition of homosexuality. However, for the purposes of the main body of our report, and in connection with our recommendations, we are strictly speaking concerned only with those who, for whatever reason, commit homosexual offenses.

21. In spite of difficulties such as those we have mentioned in the preceding paragraphs, there is a general measure of agreement on two propositions: (i) that there exists in

certain persons a homosexual propensity which varies quantitatively in different individuals and can also vary quantitatively in the same individual at different epochs of life; (ii) that this propensity can affect behavior in a number of ways, some of which are not obviously sexual; although exactly how much and in what ways may be matters for disagreement and dispute.

22. The first of these propositions means that homosexuality as a propensity is not an "all or none" condition, and this view has been abundantly confirmed by the evidence submitted to us. All gradations can exist from apparently exclusive homosexuality without any conscious capacity for arousal by heterosexual stimuli to apparently exclusive heterosexuality, though in the latter case there may be transient and minor homosexual inclinations, for instance in adolescence. According to the psychoanalytic school, all individuals pass through a homosexual phase. Be this as it may, we would agree that a transient homosexual phase in development is very common and should usually cause neither surprise nor concern.

It is interesting that the late Dr. Kinsey, in his study entitled "The Sexual Behavior of the Human Male," formulated this homosexual-heterosexual continuum on a 7-point scale, with a rating of 6 for sexual arousal and activity with other males only, 3 for arousals and acts equally with either sex, 0 for exclusive heterosexuality, and intermediate ratings accordingly. The recognition of the existence of this continuum is, in our opinion, important for two reasons. First, it leads to the conclusion that homosexuals cannot reasonably be regarded as quite separate from the rest of mankind. Secondly, as will be discussed later, it has some relevance in connection with claims made for the success of various forms of treatment.

23. As regards the second proposition, we have already pointed out that a distinction should be drawn between the condition of homosexuality (which relates to the direction of sexual preference) and the acts or behavior resulting from this preference. It is possible to draw a further distinction between behavior which is overtly sexual and behavior, not overtly sexual, from which a latent homosexuality can be inferred.

It must not be thought that the existence of the homosexual propensity necessarily leads to homosexual behavior of an overtly sexual kind. Even where it does, this behavior does not necessarily amount to homosexual offense; for instance, solitary masturbation with homosexual fantasies is probably the most common homosexual act, many persons, though they are aware of the existence within themselves of the propensity, and though they may be conscious of sexual arousal in the presence of homosexual stimuli, successfully control their urges towards overtly homosexual acts with others, either because of their ethical standards or from fear of social or penal consequences, so that their homosexual condition never manifests itself in overtly sexual behavior. There are others who, though aware of the existence within themselves of the propensity, are helped by a happy family life, a satisfying vocation, or a well-balanced social life to live happily without any urge to indulge in homosexual acts. Our evidence suggests however that complete continence in the homosexual is relatively uncommon—as, indeed, it is in the heterosexual—and that even where the individual is by disposition continent, self-control may break down temporarily under the influence of factors like alcohol, emotional distress or mental or physical disorder or disease.

24. Moreover, it is clear that homosexuals differ from one another in the extent to which they are aware of the existence within themselves of the propensity. Some are, indeed, quite unaware of it, and where this is so the homosexuality is technically described as latent, its existence being inferred from the individual's behavior in spheres not obviously sexual. Although there is room for dispute as to the extent and variety of behavior of this kind which may legitimately be included in the making of this inference, there is general agreement that the existence of a latent homosexuality is an inference validly to be drawn in certain cases. Sometimes, for example, a doctor can infer a homosexual component which accounts for the condition of a patient who has

consulted him because of some symptom, discomfort or difficulty, though the patient himself is completely unaware of the existence within himself of any homosexual inclinations. There are other cases in which the existence of a latent homosexuality may be inferred from an individual's outlook or judgment; for instance, a persistent and indignant preoccupation with the subject of homosexuality has been taken to suggest in some cases the existence of repressed homosexuality. Thirdly, among those who work with notable success in occupations which call for service to others, there are some in whom a latent homosexuality provides the motivation for activities of the greatest value to society. Examples of this are to be found among teachers, clergy, nurses and those who are interested in youth movements and the care of the aged.

25. We believe that there would be a wide measure of agreement on the general account of homosexuality and its manifestations that we have given above. On the other hand, the general position which we have tried to summarize permits the drawings of many different inferences, not all of them in our opinion justified. Especially is this so in connection with the concept of "disease." There is a tendency, noticeably increasing in strength over recent years, to label homosexuality as a "disease" or "illness." This may be no more than a particular manifestation of a general tendency discernible in modern society by which, as one leading sociologist puts it, "the concept of illness expands continually at the expense of the concept of moral failure."[1] There are two important practical consequences which are often thought to follow from regarding homosexuality as an illness. The first is that those in whom the condition exists are sick persons and should therefore be regarded as medical problems and consequently as primarily a medical responsibility. The second is that sickness implies irresponsibility, or at least diminished responsibility. Hence it becomes important in this connection to examine the criteria of "disease," and also to examine the claim that these consequences follow.

26. We are informed that there is no legal definition of "disease" or "disease of the mind"; that there is no precise medical definition of disease which covers all its varieties; that health and ill health are relative terms which merge into each other, the "abnormal" being often a matter of degree or of what is accepted as the permissible range of normal variation; and that doctors are often called upon to deal not only with recognizable diseases, but also with problems of attitude and with anomalies of character and instinct.

The traditional view seems to be that for a condition to be recognized as a disease, three criteria must be satisfied, namely (i) the presence of abnormal symptoms, which are caused by (ii) a demonstrable pathological condition, in turn caused by (iii) some factor called "the cause," each link in this causal chain being understood as something necessarily antecedent to the next. An example would be the invasion of the body by diphtheria bacilli, leading to pathological changes, leading to the symptoms of diphtheria.

While we have found this traditional view a convenient basis for our consideration of the question whether or not homosexuality is a disease, it must be recognized that the three criteria, as formulated above, are oversimplified, and that each needs some modification. Moreover, there are conditions now recognized as diseases though they do not satisfy all three criteria. Our evidence suggests, however, that homosexuality does not satisfy any of them unless the terms in which they are defined are expanded beyond what could reasonably be regarded as legitimate.

27. In relation, first, to the presence of abnormal symptoms, it is nowadays recognized that many people behave in an unusual, extraordinary or socially unacceptable way, but it seems to us that it would be rash to assume that unorthodox or aberrant behavior is necessarily symptomatic of disease if it is the only symptom that can be demonstrated. To make this assumption would be to underestimate the very wide range of "normal" human behavior, and abundant evidence is available that what is socially acceptable or

ethically permissible has varied and still varies considerably in different cultures. From the medical standpoint, the existence of significant abnormality can seldom be diagnosed from the mere exhibition of unusual behavior, be this criminal or not, the diagnosis depending on the presence of associated symptoms. Further, a particular form of behavior, taken by itself, can seem to be within the range of the normal but may nevertheless be symptomatic of abnormality, the abnormality consisting in (i) the intensity and duration of the symptoms, (ii) their combination together, and (iii) the circumstances in which they arise. Certain mental diseases, for example, can be diagnosed by the mere association of symptoms to form a recognized psychiatric syndrome, an example of this being schizophrenia, which has no known or generally accepted physical pathology. On the criterion of symptoms, however, homosexuality cannot legitimately be regarded as a disease, because in many cases it is the only symptom and is compatible with full mental health in other respects. In some cases, associated psychiatric abnormalities do occur, and it seems to us that if, as has been suggested, they occur with greater frequency in the homosexual, this may be because they are products of the strain and conflict brought about by the homosexual condition and not because they are causal factors. It has been suggested to us that associated psychiatric abnormalities are less prominent, or even absent, in countries where the homosexual is regarded with more tolerance.

28. As regards the second criterion, namely, the presence of a demonstrable pathological condition, some, though not all, cases of mental illness are accompanied by a demonstrable physical pathology. We have heard no convincing evidence that this has yet been demonstrated in relation to homosexuality. Biochemical and endocrine studies so far carried out in this field have, it appears, proved negative, and investigations of body build and the like have also so far proved inconclusive. We are aware that studies carried out on sets of twins suggest that certain genes lay down a potentiality which will lead to homosexuality in the person who possesses them, but even if this were established (and the results of these studies have not commanded universal acceptance), a genetic predisposition would not necessarily amount to a pathological condition, since it may be no more than a natural biological variation comparable with variations in stature, hair pigmentation, handedness and so on.

In the absence of a physical pathology, psychopathological theories have been constructed to explain the symptoms of various forms of abnormal behavior or mental illness. These theories range from rather primitive formulations like a repressed complex or a mental "abscess" to elaborate systems. They are theoretical constructions to explain observed facts, not the facts themselves, and similar theories have been constructed to explain "normal" behavior. These theoretical constructions differ from school to school. The alleged psychopathological causes adduced for homosexuality have, however, also been found to occur in others besides the homosexual.

29. As regards the third criterion, that is, the "cause," there is never a single cause for normal behavior, abnormal behavior or mental illness. The causes are always multiple. Even the invasion of the body by diphtheria bacilli does not of itself lead to the disease of diphtheria, as is shown by the existence of "carriers" of live diphtheria bacilli. To speak, as some do, of some single factor such as seduction in youth as the "cause" of homosexuality is unrealistic unless other factors are taken into account. Besides genetic predisposition, a number of such factors have been suggested, for instance, unbalanced family relationships, faulty sex education, or lack of opportunity for heterosexual contacts in youth. In the present state of our knowledge, none of these can be held to bear a specific causal relationship to any recognized psychopathology or physical pathology; and to assert a direct and specific causal relationship between these factors and the homosexual condition is to ignore the fact that they have all, including seduction, been observed to occur in persons who become entirely heterosexual in their disposition.

30. Besides the notion of homosexuality as a disease, there have been alternative hypotheses offered by others of our expert witnesses. Some have preferred to regard it as a state of arrested development. Some, particularly among the biologists, regard it as simply a natural deviation. Others, again regard it as a universal potentiality which can develop in response to a variety of factors.

We do not consider ourselves qualified to pronounce on controversial and scientific problems of this kind, but we feel bound to say that the evidence put before us has not established to our satisfaction the proposition that homosexuality is a disease. Medical witnesses have, however, stressed the point, and it is an important one, that in some cases homosexual offenses do occur as symptoms in the course of recognized mental or physical illness, for example, senile dementia. We have the impression, too, that those whose homosexual offenses stem from some mental illness or defect behave in a way which increases their chances of being caught.

31. Even if it could be established that homosexuality were a disease, it is clear that many individuals, however their state is reached, present social rather than medical problems and must be dealt with by social, including penological, methods. This is especially relevant when the claim that homosexuality is an illness is taken to imply that its treatment should be a medical responsibility. Much more important than the academic question whether homosexuality is a disease is the practical question whether a doctor should carry out any part or all of the treatment. Psychiatrists deal regularly with problems of personality which are not regarded as diseases, and conversely the treatment of cases of recognized psychiatric illness may not be strictly medical but may best be carried out by non-medical supervision or environmental change. Examples would be certain cases of senile dementia or chronic schizophrenia which can best be managed at home. In fact, the treatment of behavior disorders, even when medically supervised, is rarely confined to psychotherapy or to treatment of a strictly medical kind. This is not to deny that expert advice should be sought in very many homosexual cases. We shall have something more to say on these matters in connection with the treatment of offenders.

32. The claim that homosexuality is an illness carries the further implication that the suffer cannot help it and therefore carries a diminished responsibility for his actions. Even if it were accepted that homosexuality could properly be described as a "disease," we should not accept this corollary. There are no *prima facie* grounds for supposing that because a particular person's sexual propensity happens to lie in the direction of persons of his or her own sex it is any less controllable than that of those whose propensity is for persons of the opposite sex. We are informed that patients in mental hospitals, with few exceptions, show clearly by their behavior that they can and do exercise a high degree of responsibility and self-control; for example, only a small minority need to be kept in locked wards. The existence of varying degrees of self-control is a matter of daily experience—the extent to which coughing can be controlled is an example—and the capacity for self-control can vary with the personality structure or with temporary physical or emotional conditions. The question which is important for us here is whether the individual suffers from a condition which causes diminished responsibility. This is a different question from the question whether he was responsible in the past for the causes or origins of his present condition. That is an interesting inquiry and may be of relevance in other connections; but our concern is with the behavior which flows from the individual's present condition and with the extent to which he is responsible for that behavior, whatever may have been the causes of the condition from which it springs. Just as expert opinion can give valuable assistance in deciding on the appropriate ways of dealing with a convicted person, so can it help in assessing the additional factors that may affect his present responsibility.

33. Some psychiatrists have made the point that homosexual behavior in some cases may be "compulsive," that is, irresistible, but there seems to be no good reason to suppose

that at least in the majority of cases homosexual acts are any more or any less resistible than heterosexual acts, and other evidence would be required to sustain such a view in any individual case. Even if immunity from penal sanctions on such grounds were claimed or granted, nevertheless preventive measures would have to be taken for the sake of society at large, in much the same way as it is necessary to withhold a driving license from a person who is subject to epileptic fits. This is particularly true of the offender who is a very bad risk for recurrence, but is not certifiable either as insane or as a mental defective.

34. When questions of treatment or disposal of offenders are being considered, the assessment of prognosis is very important, and expert advice may need to be sought on such questions as whether the factors that in the view of the doctors lead to diminished control, that is, diminished "responsibility," are capable of modification, or what environmental changes should be advocated or ordered to reduce the chances of a recurrence. Thus it is just as reasonable for a doctor to recommend that a paedophiliac should give up schoolmastering as it would be to recommend to another patient never to return to a hot climate.

35. Some writers on the subject, and some of our witnesses, have drawn a distinction between the "invert" and the "pervert." We have not found this distinction very useful. It suggests that it is possible to distinguish between two men who commit the same offense, the one as the result of his constitution, the other from a perverse and deliberate choice, with the further suggestion that the former is in some sense less culpable than the latter. To make this distinction as a matter of definition it seems to prejudice a very difficult question.

Similarly, we have avoided the use of the terms "natural" and "unnatural" in relation to sexual behavior, for they depend for their force upon certain explicit theological or philosophical interpretations, and without these interpretations their use imports an approving or a condemnatory note into a discussion where dispassionate thought and statement should not be hindered by adherence to particular preconceptions.

36. Homosexuality is not, in spite of widely held belief to the contrary, peculiar to members of particular professions or social classes; nor, as is sometimes supposed, is it peculiar to the *intelligentsia*. Our evidence shows that it exists among all callings and at all levels of society; and that among homosexuals will be found not only those possessing a high degree of intelligence, but also the dullest oafs.

Some homosexuals, it is true, choose to follow occupations which afford opportunities for contact with those of their own sex, and it is not unnatural that those who feel themselves to be "misfits" in society should gravitate towards occupations offering an atmosphere of tolerance or understanding, with the result that some occupations may appear to attract more homosexuals than do others. Again, the arrest of a prominent national or local figure has greater news value than the arrest of (say) a laborer for a similar offense, and in consequence the Press naturally finds room for a report of the one where it might not find room for a report of the other. Factors such as these may well account to some extent for the prevalent misconceptions....

Chapter VII

Preventive Measures and Research

213. Our terms of reference are confined, strictly speaking, to the criminal law and the treatment of persons convicted of offenses against that law. The law is, however, concerned with the prevention of crime no less than with its detection and punishment, and we have felt that it would not be proper to conclude our inquiry without giving some consideration to possible preventive measures.

214. Clearly, one of the most effective ways of reducing crime would be to eliminate its causes, if these could be identified and dealt with. Most homosexual behavior is no doubt due to the existence of the homosexual propensity, in a greater or less degree, in one or both of the participants. As we have said earlier, various hypotheses have been put before us about the nature and origins of this propensity. But there is still a great deal of work to be done before any of the proffered explanations can be regarded as established, or any inferences from them accepted as wholly reliable. We have no doubt that properly coordinated research into the etiology of homosexuality would have profitable results.

215. Secondly, there is much to be learnt about the various methods of treatment, their suitability to various kinds of patients, their varying chances of success, and the criteria by which that success is to be judged. Whether or not it is possible to establish the nature or origins of homosexuality, it is evident that psychiatric treatment has beneficial results in some cases. As we have said elsewhere, this treatment does not always involve psychotherapy, neither does it necessarily lead to any discernible change in the direction of sexual preference. But reliable information showing what type of person was likely to benefit, and in what way, from a particular form of treatment, would clearly be of great value as a preventive measure.

216. We therefore recommend that the appropriate body or bodies be invited to propose a program of research into the etiology of homosexuality and the effects of various forms of treatment. The actual carrying out of such research would necessarily be in the hands of those directly concerned with the treatment of the homosexual, since it is only from observations carried out over long periods by doctors treating individual cases that results can be established. These should include both prison doctors and psychiatrists working outside the prisons. The organization of the research suggests the establishment, on the pattern familiar to the Medical Research Council, of a research unit which would include, for example, psychiatrists, geneticists, endocrinologists, psychologists, criminologists and statisticians. This unit could well be based on some establishment (for example, a University Department) experienced in socio-medical research and having access to prisons, psychiatric clinics and other centers where homosexuals are undergoing treatment. We hope that such work will form part of a wider study of forensic psychiatry, not confined to homosexuality, for which this country has fewer facilities than some others. Research of this kind would also increase the two-way flow between the prison medical service and outside psychiatrists, which, as we have said earlier, we consider to be desirable.

217. Researches of the kind we have proposed will necessarily take a long time. We have, however, had suggested to us several other measures which might be taken to diminish the incidence of homosexual offenses. Some of them are general and wide in their application, such as the desirability of a healthy home background; medical guidance of parents and children; sensible education in matters of sex, not only for children but for teachers, youth leaders and those who advise students. Particularly, it is urged that medical students should be given more information about homosexuality in their courses, and that clergy and probation officers should be better equipped to deal with the problems about which they are often consulted.

218. The Press might do much towards the education of public opinion, by ensuring that reports of court cases concerning homosexual offenses were treated in the same way as that in which matrimonial cases have been treated for some years past; for there is little doubt that the influence of detailed reports of such cases is considerable and almost wholly bad. We have incidentally, encountered several cases in which men have got into touch with homosexual offenders whose convictions were reported in the Press, with the result that further homosexual offenses were committed.

219. It has been suggested, especially, that more care should be taken by those responsible for the appointment of teachers, youth leaders and others in similar positions of trust, to ensure that men known to be, or suspected of being, of homosexual tendencies, should be debarred from such employment. In regard to teachers, we are aware, and approve, of the steps taken by the Ministry of Education and the Scottish Education Department to ensure that men guilty of homosexual offenses are not allowed to continue in the teaching profession. But it appears that headmasters of private schools are sometimes lax in taking up references in respect of teachers whom they propose to employ, and it occasionally happens that a teacher who has been dismissed, or asked to resign, from one post because of misconduct with boys under his charge subsequently finds employment in another school, where his misconduct is repeated. As far as youth organizations are concerned, these vary so much in their nature and structure that it is not possible to devise watertight measures. But we hope that the Criminal Record Office would be ready to supply, to responsible officers of the Headquarters of recognized youth organizations, information about the convictions of persons who seek positions of trust in those organizations.

220. On a point of detail, it has been put to us that the number of lavatory offenses would be substantially reduced if all public lavatories were well lighted; but the facts do not seem to support this suggestion, since some of the lavatories at which most of the offenses take place are particularly well lit. Our own opinion is that if uniformed police officers in the course of their duties on the beat keep a vigilant eye on public lavatories, that is more likely to discourage potential offenders than anything else. We have been informed that in some places in Scotland there are in force bylaws making it an offense to stay for more than a certain time in a public lavatory; and it is for consideration whether the wider adoption of some similar bylaw might further discourage the improper use of such places.

221. The preventive measures we have mentioned above are not, in our view, such as to call for legislation, but we put them forward for consideration by the appropriate bodies.

Recommendations

355. The following is a summary of our Recommendations:—

(a) Homosexual Offences

We recommend:—

i. That homosexual behavior between consenting adults in private be no longer a criminal offense. . . .

ii. That questions relating to "consent" and "in private" be decided by the same criteria as apply in the case of heterosexual acts between adults. . . .

iii. That the age of "adulthood" for the purposes of the proposed change in the law be fixed at twenty-one. . . .

*iv. That no proceedings be taken in respect of any homosexual act (other than an indecent assault) committed in private by a person under twenty-one, except by the Director of Public Prosecutions or with the sanction of the Attorney-General. . . .**

v. That the law relating to living on the earnings of prostitution be applied to the earnings of male, as well as female, prostitution. . . .

vi. That the law be amended, if necessary, so as to make it explicit that the term "brothel" includes premises used for homosexual practices. . . .

vii. That there be introduced revised maximum penalties in respect of buggery, gross indecency and indecent assaults. . . .

viii. *That buggery be reclassified as a misdemeanor. . . .**

ix. *That except for some grave reason, proceedings be not instituted in respect of homosexual offenses incidentally revealed in the course of investigating allegations of blackmail. . . .*

x. *That Section 29 (3) of the Larceny Act, 1916, be extended so as to apply to all homosexual offenses. . . .**

xi. *That the offense of gross indecency between male persons be made triable summarily with the consent of the accused. . . .**

xii. *That male persons charged with importuning for immoral purposes be entitled to claim trial by jury. . . .**

xiii. *That except for indecent assaults, the prosecution of any homosexual offense more than twelve months old be barred by statute. . . .*

xiv. *That subject to any necessary special safeguards, managers and headmasters of approved schools be allowed the same measure of discretion in dealing with homosexual behavior between inmates as that enjoyed by those responsible for the management of any other educational establishment. . . .*

xv. *That the organization, establishment and conditions of service of the prison medical service be reviewed. . . .*

xvi. *That a court by which a person under twenty-one is found guilty of a homosexual offense be required to obtain and consider a psychiatric report before passing sentence. . . .*

xvii. *That prisoners desirous of having estrogen treatment be permitted to do so if the prison medical officer considers that this would be beneficial.*

xviii. *That research be instituted into the etiology of homosexuality and the effects of various forms of treatment.*

Endnote

*These Recommendations have application only in relation to England and Wales.

Notes: *In 1954, at the urging of the Church of England's Moral Welfare Council, the British Parliament appointed a Committee of Homosexual Offenses. The committee, under the chairmanship of Sir John Wolfenden, reported in 1957. The widely-heralded report had a direct effect in decriminalizing homosexual activities in Great Britain and also became one of the most important documents in forcing the reconsideration of the issue of homosexuality by the Christian churches of the entire Western world.*

This report was among the first to make a clear distinction (derived largely from the Kinsey report) between homosexuality as the preference for sexual partners of one's own sex and homosexual acts. It also restated Kinsey's assumption of a spectrum of homosexual behavior reported in the general population. In the end, the report questioned the popular understanding of homosexuality as a disease. It made recommendations for regulating some homosexual offenses (such as enticing minors into homosexual contact) and it recommended the complete decriminalization of homosexual behavior between consenting adults. While it might seem conservative by current standards, the gradual acceptance of its recommendations set the stage for the debates in the 1980s.

The Wolfenden Report *is a lengthy document (over 1000 pages). The text printed above excerpts the most important paragraphs from that portion of it directly concerned with homosexuality.*

CHURCH OF ENGLAND

RESOLUTION ON HUMAN SEXUALITY (1987)

This Synod affirms that the biblical and traditional teaching on chastity and fidelity in personal relationships is a response to and expression of God's love for each of us, and in particular affirms:

1. that sexual intercourse is an act of total commitment which belongs properly within a permanent marriage relationship;
2. that fornication and adultery are sins against this ideal, and are to be met by a call to repentance and the exercise of compassion;
3. that homosexual acts also fall short of this ideal, and are likewise to be met by a call to repentance and the exercise of compassion;
4. that all Christians are called to be exemplary in all spheres of morality, including sexual morality, and that holiness of life is particularly required for Christian leaders.

Notes: *In 1987, the General Synod of the Church of England issued a brief statement that summarized its current stand on sexuality. In relation to homosexuality, it saw homosexual acts as sinful and acts from which participants need to repent. While not addressing the issue directly (the ordination of homosexuals), it did note that Christian leaders need bearers of an especially high standard of sexual morality.*

CHURCH OF ENGLAND

HOMOSEXUALITY AND A PASTORAL CHURCH (1988)

1. The Church of England has gained a reputation over the centuries for being an exceptionally pastoral church. That reputation is seriously endangered at the moment by its attitude to one particular group of people: to those who are homosexual.
2. This pamphlet is a plea for the pastoral care of the homosexual.
3. Ten years ago, the Church of England issued a Report: *Homosexual Relations: A Contribution to Discussion* (CIO Publishing 1979). Its Preface was signed in July 1978 by the Bishop of Gloucester. A year later, the present Bishop of London, then Bishop of Truro and Chairman of the General Synod Board for Social Responsibility, signed its Foreword. The time that had elapsed is significant: for it signified the division at the heart of the Church, and not least at the heart of the Board for Social Responsibility. The Bishop wrote:

   > 'We do believe *that the Report and the attached critical comments can make an important contribution to the process of forming the mind of the Church. We therefore envisage a period during which widespread discussion takes place on the issues* raised in this document. . . .'
   >
   > (p.i. para. 3. lines 8/12).

4. A debate in the General Synod of the Church of England took place—significantly, nearly two years after the publishing of the Report in February 1981; but the '*widespread* discussion' did not—in spite of the motion being carried. 'That this Synod commends this Report for discussion in the Diocesan and Deanery Synods, especially with regard to social implications and pastoral support and care.' Indeed, the Report itself, which was bound to be at the heart of any discussion, quickly sold out, and at this moment is still out of print, in spite of requests for its re-publication.

5. The 1978 Lambeth Conference had spoken of 'the need for deep and dispassionate study of the question. . . .' In 1975, the Roman Catholic Church had issued a 'Declaration on Certain Questions concerning Sexual Ethics' which dealt *inter alia* with Homosexuality, and in 1979 a report on Human Sexuality, which included a section on homosexuality, was presented to the Methodist Conference. The British Council of Churches at that time also published a report *God's 'Yes' to Sexuality,* (Fontana 1981).

6. Part of the purpose of this pamphlet is to encourage 'The Discussion That Never Was' to take place—and for it to be widespread.

7. It has to be admitted that when it was published, the Report *Homosexual Relationships* satisfied very few. Many homosexual men and women disliked it; so did many who were heterosexual. That did not necessarily mean it was 'bad'—in the sense that the Working Party had done its work badly. Rather, it meant, as the then Bishop of Truro stated in his Foreword, that

   'diverse attitudes to homosexuality exist within the Board reflecting a similar diversity within the Church of England, which therefore makes it impossible to contemplate a definitive statement at the moment.'

   That was true 10 years ago, hence the importance of 'widespread discussion'; but it is certainly as true now as it was then—which is not surprising, in view of the absence of *widespread discussion.*

8. On such a subject as homosexual relationships, feelings, of course, run high. It is certainly a test of a Church whether it can handle discussion of such a subject. Perhaps the fact that there has been no widespread discussion, and that the Report was allowed to go out of print, means that the Church of England *cannot* handle such a discussion. If that were so it would be sad and serious, for on such a discussion depends the pastoral care of those who are homosexual, and, it may be said, the health of the whole state of the Church; for it is not only those who are homosexual who need to discuss homosexuality; and it is not only homosexuality which has to be discussed, but sexuality; and not to be able to discuss sexuality is not to be able to discuss who we are: the identity of each one of us.

9. So far, no mention has been made of the notorious debate on Sexuality Morality which took place in the General Synod of the Church of England in November 1987. This is in no way to ignore that debate or to imply that it was insignificant. On the contrary, it was of tragic significance, not least because it took place without widespread discussion in the Church at large which should have followed the publication of *Homosexual Relationships.* In his Foreword, the then Bishop of Truro had written:

   'We do not think that the Church of England is yet ready to declare its mind on the subject of homosexuality';

   and then, 10 years later, with little further study or discussion, there was the Synod declaring its mind—and individual bishops, priests and laity declaring theirs. The November '87 Synod debate had blown up like a storm at sea. The metaphor is not inapt (though there is evidence that the storm has been most carefully 'brewed'). It caught most of the Church of England unprepared—bishops, clergy and laity. While the storm lasted there was considerable panic on board, and all sorts of things were said and done in haste. The ship of the Church of England eventually limped into port—with some of the crew missing and some valuables cast overboard.

10. Again: it is the purpose of this pamphlet—in spite of the November '87 motion and the amendment (also amended) which was carried in Synod—indeed, because of it—to encourage that discussion in the Church to take place which should have preceded such a debate in Synod.

11. For any discussion of integrity to take place on a subject like homosexual relationships, it has first to be presented with integrity. The Working Party under the Bishop of Gloucester was a tribute to the resources of the Church of England. Its composition was in itself a work of pastoral care for the subject.

    It consisted of:

    The Rt. Revd. John Yates, Bishop of Gloucester (Chairman)

    The Revd. Canon R. Askew. Principal of Salisbury and Wells Theological College (now Dean of King's College, London)

    The Revd. Canon P.R. Baelz, Canon of Christ Church and Regius Professor of Moral and Pastoral Theology in the University of Oxford (now Dean of Durham)

    The Revd. C.R. Bryant, Society of St. John the Evangelist (now deceased)

    The Revd. Canon P.E. Coleman, Director of Ordination Training in the Diocese of Bristol and Canon Residentiary of Bristol Cathedral (now Suffragan Bishop of Crediton)

    Dr. M.J. Courtenay, General Practitioner and Chief Medical Adviser to the Advisory Council for the Church's Ministry (now retired)

    Mrs. J. Davies, Lecturer in Personal Relationships, Inner London Education Authority (now Advisory Teacher in the ILEA Religious Education Inspector's Team, with responsibility for Personal Relationships and children with special needs)

    The Revd. M. Day, Member of the Anglican Chaplaincy to the Universities in London, (now also Priest-in-Charge of St. George's, Bloomsbury)

    J.D. McClean, Professor of Law at the University of Sheffield.

    B.G. Mitchell, Nolloth Professor of the Philosophy of the Christian Religion and Fellow of Oriel College, Oxford

    Miss J. Pelham, Principal Medical Social Worker, Booth Hall Children's Hospital, Manchester (now Social Worker, The Child Development Centre, Reedley Hall, Nr. Burnley, Lancs.)

    The Revd. Canon J.R. Porter, Professor of Theology at the University of Exeter

    The Revd. D. Wainwright, Deputy Secretary to the Board for Social Responsibility (Secretary) (now Secretary to the Oxford Board for Social Responsibility)

12. The Working Party met over a period of 4 years and on 27 occasions. It is of very considerable significance that its Report was *unanimous*. However, the Board itself which had set up the Working Party was, as we have said, 'deeply divided' by the Report and published the Report with 'a statement of the main criticisms within the Board'.

13. Such a division of opinion is nothing to be ashamed of. It may be embarrassing or confusing to those who think that on such an important subject as sexuality there are, or should be, unchanging 'Yes' and 'No' answers.

14. What should be shaming is that such a unanimous Report, from a Working Party of such undeniable authority, should virtually have been pigeon-holed.

15. Again: the purpose of this pamphlet must be to encourage discussion and to indicate some of the areas which must inevitably be involved in the discussion. The then Bishop of Truro wrote, for instance, in his Foreword:

    > *'The question of homosexuality raises questions to do with the authority of Scripture and the Church's tradition.'*

    This is undoubtedly true; but it raises, of course, more than these two questions. In fact, the earlier chapters of *Homosexual Relationships* reflect the Working Party's understanding of

i. the social

ii. the medical, and

iii. the biblical material related to the subject.

The remaining chapters grapple with

iv. the theological

v. the ethical

vi. the legal, and

vii. the pastoral problems.

which evidence submitted to the Working Party raised. And with these problems we have only begun.

16. Let us therefore make some random reflections on *Homosexual Relationships*—after 10 years—to attempt to provoke and stimulate the necessary discussion. In such a modest pamphlet, a full treatment of the subject is, of course, out of the question. (It is devoutly to be wished that *Homosexuality Relationships* will be re-published, and be available to assist discussion.)

17. First: a word more about the significance of the division between the *then* Church of England Board for Social Responsibility and the Working Party. It is obvious that the divisions were deep and genuine and that those divisions have not diminished. This must surely mean that it is of huge importance that we do not simply shout what we already believe at one another across the divide, but attempt to listen, to understand, and to grow together. That was the point of a period of wide discussion.

(On the subject of Nuclear Disarmament, for instance, on which there is probably as much emotional involvement, the Scottish Churches 'pack' has been a model for what could, and surely should, be produced on the subject of homosexuality.)

Unless we do not budge an inch from where we now stand, we may well find such a learning process 'disturbing'. Indeed, unless we now know *all,* we must expect literally to be disturbed. This pamphlet and the discussion it seeks to promote ought therefore to be disturbing.

18. *Homosexual Relationships* boldly states: 'We know very little about the majority of homosexual men and women.' This statement—after more than four years work—is important, for it means that dogmatic statements are particularly dangerous without *further* learning and education.

19. It is worth underlining the point which the Working Party makes in its Preface that 'no adequate consideration of homosexuality can be divorced from a consideration of human sexuality as a whole.' Of course, having said this, the Report necessarily concentrated on homosexual relationships. But the point needs emphasis for a series of reasons: e.g.

i. As the Report says:

> *'For many people sexual preference is not a matter of stark alternatives, but is to be found somewhere on a continuum between an exclusive preference for sexual relationships with one's own sex and an equally exclusive preference for sexual relationships with the opposite sex.'*

ii. The number of married men and women who admit to strong homosexual attraction.

iii. The uncertainty about the range of people's sexual feelings and the extent to which they may change during any individual's lifetime. Kinsey estimated 4% of white American males as exclusively homosexual *throughout* their lives after adolescence, 8% were exclusively homosexual for at least 3 years between the ages of 16 and 55.

iv. Any comparing and contrasting of homosexual and heterosexual relationships will need to consider the point and purpose of sexual relationship.

20. *Homosexual Relationships* begins with 'The Social Setting of Homosexuality.' It describes our times, 'in which people's interest in sexuality is not only intense but also explicit and overt' and the 'popular assumption that more or less everybody is sexually active. It is widely assumed, for example, that any two people living together will inevitably engage in genital activity.'

'Too often' the Report continues 'the deeper questions about the nature of human relationships, including friendship, are swept aside by this overriding interest.' The point is well made. Any priest who, over a period of 40 years, has been preparing people for marriage, will know well that at the beginning of that period it was assumed that the persons to be married had not been living together and engaging in genital activity; now the opposite assumption can most often be made—and the Church has remained virtually silent on this remarkable change in so short a time, largely pretending the change has not occurred and providing little significant guidance to 'the deeper questions.'

21. It was in this period, in 1957, that the Wolfenden Committee issued its Report. In 1952 the Church of England Moral Welfare Council had initiated a study programme on 'the problems of homosexuality' which undoubtedly influenced the Government in appointing the Wolfenden Committee. The Church Assembly approved the recommendations concerning the change in the law. In 1958 the Homosexual Law Reform Society was formed, with the support of some senior churchmen, including Dr. Robert Mortimer, then Bishop of Exeter. The Sexual Offences Act was passed in 1967. During this time a large number of 'homophile' organisations appeared which have sought to educate the general public on the subject of homosexuality and to support and counsel those who are homosexual. The best known specifically Christian homophile organisation is the Gay Christian Movement (GCM), which has changed its name since the publication of *Homosexual Relationships* to LGCM: Lesbian and Gay Christian Movement.

22. At this juncture it should be clearly stated that female homosexuality—lesbianism—many would maintain, has different origins, and different characteristics from male homosexuality and must not simply be subsumed under a discussion of homosexuality expressed in male terms. (Homosexual acts between women are not subject to legal restriction).

23. In fact, a whole homosexual culture has emerged in recent years. The fortnightly publication of *Gay News* was the clearest expression of that culture; another was the emergence of homosexual clubs and the overt use by the homosexual community of particular public houses as meeting places.

24. *Homosexual Relationships* pointed out that not all organisations active in this area are homophile. The Nationwide Festival of Light, for instance, consistently expressed its vigorous opposition to the acceptance of homosexual behaviour as a morally acceptable means of sexual expression.

25. What cannot be doubted is that if there has been some growth in tolerance of homosexuals there has also been as strong a growth of hostility, with outbreaks from

time to time of 'queer bashing.' (The 1987 debate in Synod undoubtedly served to increase the hostility to homosexual clergy). Alongside homophile activity, that is to say, there has also been 'homophobic' activity. Anyone who approaches the subject of homosexuality with a view to education and learning may therefore expect to encounter hostility in some quarters. It will be for them in due course to evaluate that hostility—to see "whether it be of God or of men."

26. It is since *Homosexual Relationships* was published that AIDS has begun to hit Britain. Although the major route for the spread of AIDS in Africa has been heterosexual contact, in the USA and Great Britain it has been through drug addicts and homosexuals. This latter fact has undoubtedly caused a very considerable increase in homophobia in recent years in Great Britain.

27. It may be thought curious that we have been able to proceed thus far with the argument of the pamphlet without defining the adjective 'homosexual.' This has been of set purpose. There is much to be said for seeing a term in its setting and waiting till definition is demanded. We have now reached that point, because, for instance, some of the homophobia and hostility to homosexual men and women is said to be related to the fact that the homosexual condition is 'unnatural.'

28. It is easy to define homosexuality as 'a preference for sexual relations with one's own sex.' But

    a. that preference is not always exclusive

    b. it would appear to belong to most people for some part of their life

    c. the evidence is that there is more than one cause for such a preference

    d. there is still a great deal of uncertainty about the origins of such a preference;

    so that it may be more accurate to speak of 'homosexualities'—plural: preference for sexual relations with one's own sex which may stem from different originating causes in different people.

29. The word 'unnatural' is notoriously difficult to handle, and in relation to homosexuality is particularly difficult. Some people, for instance, mean that homosexuality is 'unnatural' because it is against nature as summarised in, say, the opening chapters of Genesis: others, because it seems to them, in more general Biblical terms, against the purpose of God in creaction as revealed in the Bible—though they will usually also quote particular passage of scripture. Others may quote, for instance, the *Letter to the Bishops of the Catholic Church on the Pastoral Care of Homosexuals* (1986):

    > *'According to the objective moral order, homosexual relations are acts which lack an essential and indispensable finality.'*

    Yet other Christians, who read the Bible with sincerity, prayer and integrity, do not see it condemning homosexuality as a *condition,* though few would deny that particular acts are condemned in the Bible as immoral and sinful.

30. What will be clear is the painful problem a homosexual man or woman may well have in accepting his or her homosexuality. And to such a person the Board for Social Responsibility—in its Preface to *Homosexual Relationships* in 1979—confesses:

    > *'We do not think the Church of England is yet ready to declare its mind on the subject of homosexuality.'*

    Such social—and pastoral—responsibility! (Perhaps there is only one thing more irresponsible than 'not being ready'—and that is for a Synod suddenly to declare its condemnation of homosexual genital acts—as it did in the November 1987 Synod—*without* widespread discussion of and further profound reflection on *Homosexual Relationships,* which had stated the Church of England is not 'yet ready.'

31. No less painful a problem for the homosexual man or woman is whether his or her homosexuality shall be made public—though often the confusion of homosexual men and women who have married—and those who are bisexual—is as painful, and in particular need of the Church's pastoral care and understanding.

32. The second section of *Homosexual Relationships* considered homosexuality in its 'medical dimension'—a rather curious term to have employed. It stated clearly that:

> *'in the present state of medical science the causes of homosexuality are unknown . . . the medical evidence is inconclusive.'*

Such a careful statement is worth weighing. Professor John Bowker has written more recently (*Aids and Christian Action, July 1987):*

> *'Does a homosexual predisposition lie within nature, in the sense that it precedes the choice or learning experience of some individuals? It is becoming increasingly clear, through the work of biogenetic structuralism, or through such careful analysis as that of Bell, Weinberg and Hammersmith (*Sexual Preference*) that the answer is, yes, it is natural for many people. It is natural (in nature) in the sense that they are prepared for those behaviours, in the same way that heterosexual interaction and "triggering" in the brain are initiated from the genes that build the proteins the structures and chemicals that prepare us for those behaviours.'*

Later, (p. 11) Professor Bowker says:

> *'It is certainly becoming increasingly clear that as the majority of people are literally "turned on" in the limbic system in a heterosexual interaction, so some are "turned on" in a homosexual interaction (though this will only be true for some, not all homosexuals). In that sense, homosexual disposition precedes some individuals: it is not a consequence of learning, or of defects in infant experience, or whatever. In that sense, it is natural (in nature), accepting that all nature, in a Christian perspective, is in a condition of fallen disorder. Nevertheless, in that context it is obvious that a homosexual couple can be as much a means of grace to each other and to others, as can a heterosexual couple.'*

33. *Homosexual Relationships* stated:

> *'at present, medical science can give only a very incomplete account of the formation of sexual orientation. What we do know suggests that people have the responsibility for deciding whether or not to express their orientation in sexual acts, though the very strong nature of the sexual drive must be reckoned with.'*

That final concessive clause is of *very considerable importance*.

34. *Homosexual Relationships* undoubtedly moved towards the acceptance of homosexuality as a 'given fact'—though the Working Party did not give to homosexual partnership equality with heterosexual partnership; but what the Report lacked—and it is difficult to see how that lack might have been supplied without fresh research—was a full and accurate study of the way of life of homosexual men and women: e.g.

> How long do most homosexual partnerships last?
>
> What are the primary causes of their breakdown?
>
> How many homosexual men and women want homosexual partnerships that are lasting and deep?
>
> What are the pressures that drive so many homosexual men to pursue clandestine relationships and impersonal encounters in, for instance, public lavatories?

Only with such knowledge can several of the important pastoral questions be answered:

What are they contending with?

How can they be helped and supported—embraced and affirmed by individuals and by the community?

What would assist homosexual relationships to be deep and lasting?

How can the relationships between homosexuals best be enhanced and celebrated?

Again, it must be emphasised that such a study should not simply be of those who *publicly* declare their homosexuality.

35. *Homosexual Relationships* was concerned to proclaim that sexual relationships between human beings are rooted in biological existence; but much of its 'medical' concern was also with the psycho-sexual. No one could read the Report without being made aware of the need for a close partnership between pastoral theology and pastoral psychology.

36. *Homosexual Relationships* was one of the first Church reports to escape that degree of condescension which has so often characterised Church statements on Homosexuality. *Homosexual Relationships* did not always seem to be suggesting that homosexual men and women are desperately sinful—by their very existence—in a way that heterosexuals are not.

37. The third section of *Homosexual Relationships* concerned the Biblical evidence. This is clearly not the place for a full scale study of that evidence; and there is a sense in which *Homosexual Relationships* raised an even more important question than what the Bible says directly about homosexuality, and did it explicitly in several sentences and paragraphs: e.g.

> *'. . . the question cannot be settled by reference simply to biblical texts that deal directly with homosexuality. These have to be considered in the light of the underlying message of the Bible, especially the New Testament, and in assessing and interpreting this, we need to take account of knowledge not available to biblical writers, and moral intuitions formed in the Christian tradition. Thus the bearing of the biblical material on how we should think and act in our present situation has also to be evaluated in the light of those other theological, philosophical, medical and social insights which are discussed in other chapters of this Report . . .'*
>
> *'. . . the issue is how far specific biblical statements on moral and ethical behaviour and attitudes provide . . . timeless principles and patterns of morality.'*
>
> *'. . . We live in a society which is in many ways very different from anything to be found in the Bible and we are often able to see a degree of relativity in biblical attitudes and standards, in a way that was not possible to previous generations, in the light of historical, anthropological, sociological and psychological knowledge which was not available to them. In other words, even when we can be confident that our text of the Bible is fixed and constant, the Church's understanding and use of it, and hence the attitudes and actions which derive from this, are not.'*
>
> *'It is important to bear in mind how many moral and ethical precepts which in the Bible are presented as the direct commands of God have been re-interpreted in the course of Christian history and even in some cases abandoned as guides or standards for the conduct of individual and social life. One might instance the doctrines of the "holy war". . . .',*

and, we might add, of usury.

38. The fourth section of *Homosexual Relationships* contained an important paragraph which a pastorally responsible church cannot simply ignore. It stated:

> *'We are, however, bound to conclude that neither of the traditional approaches, in the form in which they have generally been presented, provides us with an understanding of sexuality that is adequate to the task of forming a Christian judgment about homosexuality. The appeal to Scripture, if it is to be illuminating, must look to the biblical treatment of the central themes of human love and marriage rather than to the occasional and somewhat peripheral texts that mention homosexuality itself: and the appeal to nature must be made in a broader context than the merely biological.'*

39. Later in this fourth section, the Working Party declared:

> *'Sex may have precisely the same effect in expressing and confirming a loving relationship between persons of the same sex as it does between married couples, and also the same symbolic character. It is true that Christian tradition has consistently taught otherwise, but this, it is argued, is one of those instances which must occur from time to time in the history of the Church, when later and more profound reflection upon certain central doctrines leads to the abandonment of more peripheral judgments which are seen to have been erroneous or of merely temporary validity.'*

Again; it is a pastoral failure—not only to homosexual men and women, but to their parents and to the pastors of congregations—for the Church of England, having through its Board for Social Responsibility responsibly set up its Working Party and having gained from it a unanimous Report, and having secured from the Synod a mandate for its discussion in Diocesan and Deanery Synods, to fail to see that mandate carried out.

40. The Working Party recognised that for some

> *'the celebration of homosexual love as an alternative and authentic development of the living Christian tradition which ought to be accepted as such by the Church today would involve the repudiation of too much that is characteristic, and rightly characteristic of Christian teaching about sex'*

but went on to say

> *'To declare that homosexuals may not in any circumstances give physical expression to their erotic love is unduly to circumscribe the area of responsible choice, to lay on individuals a burden too heavy for some to bear, and, by restricting the options open to them, to hinder their search for an appropriate way of life. In the light of some of the evidence we have received we do not think it possible to deny that there are circumstances in which individuals may justifiably choose to enter into a homosexual relationship with the hope of enjoying a companionship and physical expression of sexual love similar to that which is to be found in marriage.'*

These are not the words of some radical group of homosexuals, but of bishops, a dean, a monk noted for his work on spirituality for today, Christian professors of theology and philosophy, and so on. Again, the pastoral irresponsibility of debating the Report in Synod and then in the Dioceses virtually passing it by on the other side, is considerable. Indeed, here, surely, is serious dereliction of pastoral duty.

41. The word 'tradition' is used frequently in *Homosexual Relationships*—by the then Bishop of Truro in his Foreword and the Bishop of Gloucester in his Preface—and in the body of the Report. Yet where Sexual Ethics are concerned the evidence for variation and change over the centuries is very considerable e.g. in regard to the centrality of procreation. There is also much in the Christian 'tradition' on sexuality—

spoken, written and done—which is, frankly, best repented of rather than simply forgotten—and this concerns not simply minor aberration.

42. The final section of *Homosexual Relationships* concerns Social Implications and Pastoral Care. It is a sensitive and caring chapter; but its conclusions are not all that different form the conclusion of the November 1987 debate in General Synod. *Homosexual Relationships* states:

> '*We have already come to the conclusion that the only sexual union to which the Church can give public recognition in the lives of her members is marriage. A homosexual priest who has 'come out' and openly acknowledges that he is living in a sexual union with another man should not expect the Church to accept him on the same conditions as if he were married. What then should a priest in this situation do? We recognise that he might be absolutely clear in his own conscience about the relationship and that he and others might think it a matter of regret that the Church has no way of accepting it or validating it. . . . In the end we came to the conclusion that a priest in this position ought to offer his resignation to the bishop of the diocese so that he as the minister bearing responsibility for the Church in the locality could with the pastoral care appropriate to his office decide whether it should be accepted or not. We realize that the obligation to offer his resignation would be a moral one. It would not be enforceable. . . .*'

43. This is a disappointing conclusion after the earlier assertion that

> '*to declare that homosexuals may not in any circumstances give physical expression to their erotic love is unduly to circumscribe the area of responsible choice. . . .*'

It is clearly pragmatic: an attempt to wrestle with the realities of a situation in which down-to-earth decisions have to be taken and in which all cannot win. It is a world away from Mr. Higton's Private Member's Motion on Sexual Morality which was the basis of the untimely Synod Debate of November 1987.

44. But it is a grave matter of Social Responsibility—which should also involve other Boards of the Church e.g. the Board of Education and ACCM. The Church of England, if it is a pastoral church, dare not leave the situation where the November Synod Debate left it.

45. We have already suggested some of the people who may get hurt if the situation is left. There are others. There is no denying that not a few priests, particularly those who minister in inner cities—in areas where married men and women with families have sometimes found the conditions of ministry too stressful—are homosexual priests who have felt no call to celibacy but have felt called to a homosexual partnership for the mutual society, help, and comfort, that the one ought to have of the other, both in prosperity and adversity, indeed, in order that the natural instincts and affections—natural, as they believe, to them—and implanted by God, should be hallowed and directed aright.' And there are ordinands who will no longer seek ordination if such a partnership, to which they believe themselves called, is forbidden. (The 1988 ACCM statistics concerning ordination candidates give grounds for believing this may already be having its effect.)

46. It may be that in this situation it is Truth which stands to suffer most. If the conclusions of a Working Party such as that which unanimously signed *Homosexual Relationships* are ignored, it is Truth which may suffer. But Truth is not simply the concern of intellectuals: it is of pastoral concern, and must be the concern of any Church which lays claim to be exceptionally pastoral.

47. It was Christ the Pastor whose words the author of the Fourth Gospel records:

> '*I have many things to say unto you but you cannot bear them now. . . .*'

It may be that the truth which lies behind so many homosexual relationships of depth and discipline is part of the Truth which is too much to be borne by the Church *now;* but that can only be a cause for contrition, confession and, in due course, amendment.

48. And may it not be that a Church which *fails* to envisage and encourage for homosexual men and women the same kind of embodied partnerships of pure, controlled, directed passion—as it does for heterosexual men and women—is in fact guilty of assisting, indeed provoking, just those casual relationships which it deplores and the dire effects of which are so tragically manifest in our generation.

49. It is often suggested that any plea for a fundamental revision of the Christian view of sexuality—including homosexuality—is a departure from 'Catholic' tradition, and will be ecumenically devisive. Since *Homosexual Relationships* was published, the work of the Roman Catholic psychiatrist Dr. Jack Dominian has been notable in this field and gives the lie to the suggestion. It is impossible to summarise Dr. Dominian's work in a paragraph; but it may be of value to quote at length a review of Dr. Dominian's *Sexual Integrity* by Anthony Clare, Professor of Psychological Medicine at St. Bartholomew's Hospital, London, in *The Tablet 17.9.88*:

> "*. . . the need for a fundamental revision of the Christian view of sexuality, which he fervently argues, would exist and did exist long before the appearance of the AIDS virus, and Jack Dominian was one of those who most passionately called for it.*
>
> *The elements of this new sexuality are straightforward enough to identify. Christianity must emerge as the champion of loving sex instead of being seen as insisting on a fundamental link between procreation and sex, while millions of Christians as well as non-Christians clearly believe that morality as well as medicine has moved on. Basing the moral law on the equivalence of animal and human behaviour through the common pathway of biology, is, Dominian forcefully argues, fundamentally wrong and, by endorsing such a reductionist view, the Church misses a crucial opportunity to establish sexuality between men and women as a personal encounter which has to be judged by authentic human attributes.*
>
> *"The assessment of sexuality on the basis of depositing sperm in the vagina is a crude and totally unsatisfactory criterion of evaluation," is his characteristically robust way of saying just that. Within such a view, he examines such sexual behaviour as homosexuality, masturbation, premarital intercourse, infidelity, promiscuity and contraception. Given his insistence on the link between love and sexuality, his disappointment with the emphases of the current AIDS campaigns in the mass media is understandable.*
>
> *He laments the implicit assumption that people, young people especially, are going to have sex and therefore what we need to do is help them have it more safely and hygienically. Why has the opportunity been missed of emphasising the value of sex linked with personal love? Why has the chance not been taken to illustrate the hazards of indiscriminate, impersonal sexuality and the human value of a sexuality which contains within it authentic personal commitment? Why have chastity and sexual restraint been undersold?*
>
> *Implicit in his own answer to this question is a powerful indictment of the present Catholic position on sex. . . . Dominian believes that the Church, meaning the whole organism, the Church as a* koinonia, *a communion, can, should and will review its teaching and his book is a passionate statement of this conviction. . . .*'

50. The Lambeth Conference of 1988 passed the following three resolutions:

The Conference:

1. reaffirms the Statement of Lambeth Conference of 1978 on homosexuality recognizing the continuing need in the next decade for 'deep and dispassionate study of the question of homosexuality, which would take seriously both the teaching of Scripture and the results of scientific and medical research.'
2. urges such study and reflection to take account of biological, genetic and psychological research being undertaken by other agencies, and the socio/cultural factors that lead to the different attitudes in the Provinces of our Communion.
3. calls each Province to reassess, in the light of such study and because of our concern for human rights, its care for and attitude towards persons of homosexual orientation.

The point of this pamphlet is to urge that in the Provinces of the Church of England, these resolutions should be more than the mere words they were after the 1981 Synod.

51. In the summer of 1986 the House of Bishops asked the Board for Social Responsibility to advise them further on questions concerning homosexuality and Lesbianism. A Working Party was set up, which has not yet reported to the House of Bishops. (Each Diocesan bishop must bear some personal responsibility for the fact if there has been no discussion of *Homosexual Relationships* in his particular Diocesan and Deanery Synods). It is important—and urgent—that their Report, which will, of course, at first be confidential to the House of Bishops, should be made public without delay, to assist the widespread discussion for which this pamphlet pleads. Only with such widespread discussion can the Church of England validly claim to be a pastoral church in respect of those who are homosexual.

MICHAELMAS DAY 1988

Notes: *The Church of England has proven itself a leader in thoughtful reflection on matters of Christian ethical concern. In 1978, it published a report entitled* Homosexual Relations: Contribution to Discussion, *which led to a decade of debate within the Church of England and within other prominent Protestant churches as well.*

In 1988, Eric James (chaplain to Queen Elizabeth) authored this new study of homosexuality. Created after an observation that, in spite of debates in the general synod of the church, a widespread discussion on the subject had never occurred, the study summarizes the major points of the earlier report and calls for a new discussion on the issue. The study refrains from drawing any conclusions that might hinder such future discussions.

CHURCH OF GOD (ANDERSON, INDIANA)

STAND AGAINST HOMOSEXUALITY (1979)

Since the world is invaded by sex perversion in the form of homosexuality, we, the Church of God Reformation Movement, do hereby express our conviction concerning the issue:

WHEREAS we in the Church of God, being an evangelical people, committed to biblical holiness, give high regard to scriptural injunctions against homosexuality, we are also a redemptive body and seek to express love, compassion, and a chaste relationship in Christ for everyone;

BE IT RESOLVED that the General Assembly of the Church of God go on record as affirming our conviction that biblically we believe homosexuality is sin. We hereby stand firmly opposed to the licensing, ordination, or approving of persons in leadership actively involved in this life-style;

BE IT FURTHER RESOLVED that we stand opposed to any instruction in our church-sponsored institutions or the use of curriculum material which accepts homosexuality as either normal, desirable, or Christian.

Notes: *The Church of God, which has a holiness background, has always held strict* *standards concerning sexual behavior. When it decided to directly address the issues of homosexuality, the church took an expected stance and strongly opposed it.*

CHURCH OF THE BRETHREN

HUMAN SEXUALITY FROM A CHRISTIAN PERSPECTIVE (1983)

I. Position of the Church

Sexuality is elemental in human beings. It encompasses all that we are when we say "I am female" or "I am male." Physical attributes, including genitals, are an integral part of our sexual identity; however, sexuality is not just physical. It includes all thinking, feeling, acting and interacting that is derived from our maleness and femaleness.

This sexuality enriches human relationships in ways that are basic to God's own nature (Gen. 1:27). Furthermore, it offers human beings partnership with God in holy creation and re-creation (Gen. 1:28).

In their enjoyment of these privileges concomitant with sexuality, God's people are to be responsible. The church identifies love and covenant as two guidelines for sexual responsibility. Furthermore, the church holds the teaching that sexual intercourse, which can be the most intimate expression of sexuality and the most bonding of human relationships, belongs within heterosexual marriage.

The church maintains an attitude of openness and willingness to evaluate specific issues related to sexuality. Moreover, the church recognizes that highly personal issues are best resolved in the confidentiality of a private setting with pastor, counselor, or family rather than in the open debate of conferences and council meetings. Seeking the guidance of Scripture, the Holy Spirit, and responsible contemporary research, the church continues to study and search for the mind of Christ in dealing with the complexities of responsible sexuality.

II. Biblical Perspective

The significance of sexuality is evident in scripture. In the Genesis 1 account of creation, sexuality is one of the first human attributes to be identified: Male and female God created them (Gen. 1:27). Other distinguishing characteristics—race, stature, intelligence—are omitted. The lifting up of sexuality in this concise account of human origin suggests how basic sexual identity is.

In Genesis 2, sexuality is associated with companionship and completeness. The first reference to humans in this chapter is neither masculine nor feminine. The Hebrew word *adham* (verse 7), translated "man" in English, is a collective noun, undifferentiated by gender. In this state, *adham* was lonely. Then another type of human was made from *adham*. Only then is one human called *ish*, a masculine noun meaning "man," and the other is called *ishshah*, a feminine noun meaning "woman." *Adham's* problem of loneliness was remedied by the separation of humankind into two sexes and by the intimacy they experienced together. This creation of *ish* and *ishshah* and the ensuing companionship culminates the Genesis 2 account of creation.

As revealed in Genesis 3, this dual sexuality can exacerbate the discordant, testing, rebellious nature of man and woman. Adam and Eve allowed themselves to be seduced by the serpent and its offer of forbidden fruit. The freedom they exerted in choosing evil rather than good resulted in their separation from each other and from God. Immediately they "knew" they were naked and they were ashamed. They were thrust into a world of conflict with all of creation, even with each other (Gen. 3:6-24.)

Human experience substantiates and vitalizes these biblical revelations about sexuality. We rejoice in God's creation of two sexes, *ish* and *ishshah*. Despite "the fall" and the conflict we experience, we do not prefer an absence of sexuality. Brokenness can be healed.

By God's grace we discover anew that femaleness and maleness enrich and complete our personhood.

Yet while sexuality is an important component of our being, it is not paramount. Paul urged his readers to keep perspective. He emphasis was on the new life in Christ, not on sexuality. He wrote: ". . . there is neither male nor female, for you are all one in Christ Jesus" (Gal. 3:28). Our oneness in Christ supersedes the old human distinctions and inequalities including race, economic status, and sex. Paul gave enough attention elsewhere to sexuality to make it clear that he did not ignore this subject. Yet, sexuality was not his foremost concern.

Likewise, sexuality was not central for Jesus. Although Jesus briefly addressed a few issues related to sexuality—adultery, marriage, divorce and celibacy—these were not the emphases in his teaching. When asked to identify the greatest commandment, he named two: "Love God and love neighbor" (Mark 12:28-30). For Jesus, love was primary in all human relationships; sexuality was secondary.

Our society is preoccupied with sexuality. The repression of sex in earlier generations has been replaced now by an obsession with sex. One result is that increasing numbers of people expect too much of sexual intercourse. Performance is stressed over relationship, resulting in personal frustration and interpersonal strain. Christian values are ignored. Sex rather than God becomes the center of life.

Even the church loses perspective, although in a different way. To prepare and to consider a denominational statement on human sexuality creates anxiety. Such statements are called "monumental" by some and "the most controversial issues the church has faced in a generation" by others. If these appraisals are true, the church has overreacted. Alarmists fail to remember that generations come and generations go, but the Lord remains forever (Psa. 90:1-2). Sexual misuses and abuses are serious sins; however, they are not the only sins. There is no reason to become tense and condemnatory about sexual abuses out of proportion with numerous other sins that are equally serious. For the sake of the world, for the unity of the church, and for the benefit of our personal health, this is a timely moment in history to keep sexuality in perspective.

III. Biblical Guidelines for Sexual Morality

In order for sexual experiences to be complete and appropriate in God's sight, persons need to make choices based upon counsel of the Scriptures and also of the church. Two key biblical words relating to the morality of sexual experiences are love and covenant.

A. Love

The English word love has two antecedents in the Greek language, *eros* and *agapé,* which are crucial to the understanding of sexual morality.[1,2] *Eros* is the love that grows out of one's own need to love and to be loved. It is the love that fulfills one's dreams and desires. It is the impulse toward life, union, creativity, and productivity. It is the self-actualizing drive affirmed in Genesis 1 where God created male and female and told them to be fruitful and multiply. It is the satisfying union affirmed in Genesis 2: "The two shall become one flesh."

Sexual attraction is a dynamic of *eros* but *eros* is more than the mere sensation of physical pleasure. A preoccupation with techniques in our society strips *eros* of its tenderness and delight. The human body—its sensations, its beauty, its capability—is not to be disparaged. The whole body is a marvellously designed gift from God. It is to be enjoyed and utilized. But the body is not to be separated from the soul. Lovemaking is most fulfilling when it is a comfort to the body and the soul. This blending of physical pleasure and spiritual intimacy is *eros* at its best.

The Song of Songs affirms romantic love emphatically and delightfully. It is the unashamed, sensual, joyful poetry of two youthful lovers. The poem romantically describes the lips, eyes and hair of the lovers. The man tells the woman he loves her because her love is sweet (4:10-11). He desires her because he finds her beauty attractive. She loves him because his body and his speech are desirable (5:11-16). They love each other because each brings to the other a gladness and a fullness of life. Very early, the book was viewed as an allegory by the Jews as Yahweh's love for Israel, and by the Christians as Christ's love for the church. This interpretation influence the book's acceptance into the canon and has inspired Christian thought through the centuries. Still, the book itself contains no clue that it is meant to be understood allegorically. We must also be ready to read it as it stands: an appropriate celebration of the *eros* that leads to and finds its consummation within marriage. The Song of Songs affirms the *eros* that is a valued aspect of the human nature God created.

Agapé is an equally significant dimension of love. *Agapé* is unrestrained compassion for another. It is selfless giving. It is a generous responsiveness to another's needs beyond any gain for oneself. It is the love of 1 Corinthians 13 that is patient and kind, not jealous or boastful, nor arrogant or rude, does not insist on its own way, is not irritable or resentful, does not rejoice in the wrong but rejoices in the right (13:4-6.) The ultimate expression of *agapé* is to lay down one's life for the sake of another (John 15:13). The prototype of *agapé* is Jesus' giving his life on the cross.

Eros is of the order of creation, a God-given gift to our human nature. *Agapé*, on the other hand, is of the order of redeeming grace, the gift of the covenanting God to covenanting people. Even so, *eros* and *agapé* are gifts of God and part of his plan for humanity. Neither is to be despised. Indeed, it is only when romantic love is constituted of both that it can be said, "Lo, it is very good."

B. Covenant

Christians need more than love to guide them in decision-making. Love is nebulous. Moreover, we are susceptible to self-deception, particularly in moments of sexual excitement and desire. At such times the claim of love is to be tested by actual commitment that gives content to the declaration of love. Such commitment disciplines, protects, and nurtures loves relationships. Christians need covenant as well as love to guide them.

Covenants abound in biblical history, shaping relationships and undergirding community. These covenants take many forms. Some are written; many are spoken. Some are unilateral promises without obligations upon the recipient; others are conditional with specified terms. Some covenants are between equals; others are between a superior and a subordinate.

Since no single model exists, it is difficult to describe biblical covenants precisely. Characteristics present in some are absent in others, but despite these variations, several elements of biblical covenants can be identified.

Biblical covenants were generally *public*. They were not private agreements isolated from community. Even God's covenants with Noah, Abraham, and Moses were not merely individualistic. They were major covenants affecting and including the whole community for many generations. To acknowledge these communal ties, the covenants were generally confirmed by formal acts—a sign, a ritual, a recognizable verbal formula—visible or audible to the community. The rainbow was a sign of God's covenant with Noah (Gen. 9:12.) Circumcision was a sign of God's promise to Abraham (Gen. 17). The "blood of the covenant," splashed over the altar and over the people, signified God's covenant with Moses (Exod. 24:5-8.) In the New Testament, the bread and the cup symbolize the new covenant (1 Cor. 11:23-26). These tokens and rituals are continuing witnesses to the community of the covenants that are the foundation of the people's life together.

Biblical covenants are *pious,* reflecting Israel's sense that covenants are grounded in God. Sometimes God initiates the covenant as a primary participant. Other times God is only indirectly involved. For example, people make covenants between themselves but seal them with an oath. The oath implies religious sanction. Thus, being faithful to God implies being faithful to the covenant.

Biblical covenants are *permanent*. Sometimes this expectation of permanence is challenged by changing circumstances and bitter disappointments, yet the promise is not withdrawn. For example, the Davidic covenant that the throne of Israel would remain forever in the line of David's descent did not collapse with the Exile (586-538 B.C). Instead there emerged new hope for a future king who would be the son of David. Furthermore, when terms of the covenant are violated, broken relationships and misery result. In such circumstances the old covenant may be dissolved by God and a new beginning offered (Jer. 31:31-34.) Despite these vicissitudes in covenantal relationships, the common understanding is that covenants last forever.[3]

Finally, biblical covenants often presuppose *pilgrimage*. Abraham, Moses, and David were adventurers. God's covenants with these men pointed beyond their present realms of living to a destination—to a nation, a land and a kingdom not yet fully reached. Jesus and his disciples were travelers. Initially, Jesus beckoned them to a journey, "Follow me. . . ." Later, he commissioned them to another journey, "Go into the world. . . ." He promised them, ". . . I am with you always . . ." (Mark 1:17, Matt. 28:19-20). His promise was a covenant: He said he would be with them in their journeys. Such covenants have unfolding qualities. They foster adventure, newness, and surprise.

Pilgrims accept a code of conduct for their journey. Sometimes the code is specific and direct about behaviorial expectations (the Holiness Code in Leviticus 17-26, the Deuteronomic Code, or Zacchaeus' promise to Jesus in Luke 19:8). Covenants set limits. Yet the spirit of the covenant is to nourish relationships, not regiment them. Covenants, unlike contracts, offer fidelity that exceeds specification: "You will be my people; I will be your God" (Jer. 31:3b, Hosea 2:23).

The influence of covenants upon sexual behavior and relationships within Israel is evident. Unlike much contemporary, popular literature, the Bible is not primarily a story about lovers and their disconnected affairs. Rather, it is an account of families and marriages and continuing loyalties. To be sure, there are many lapses in covenantal faithfulness. This reality does not diminish the significance of covenant in the life of Israelites; rather it underscores their need for a new covenant that incorporates not only law and judgement but also grace and renewal.

C. The Church's Guidance

In contemporary life we are often hesitant to make covenants. There are many reasons for that hesitancy. We make hasty, unwise commitments and find ourselves entangled in painful relationships. We say, "Never again." We are motivated by self-interest, convenience, and momentary pleasure at the expense of long-range rewards. We resist the responsibility of long-term commitment. We want to be autonomous, with little obligation to the community. For all these reasons we may resist making covenants, choosing instead agreements that are tentative.

The result is that in contemporary life we lack the sense of belongings and the covenantal structure that helps a relationship endure through periods when emotion is not a sufficient bond. We lack a sense of being part of a purpose and a people that extends far beyond our individual lives. It is time for the church to speak assertively of covenant, of belonging and loyalty.

To apply biblical covenant to sexuality in the modern world does not require the church to formulate a comprehensive code to cover all eventualities and contingencies. Ours is a complex and changing world. Differing family patterns, changing male and female roles, effective contraceptives, overpopulation, and the science dealing with human sexual behavior are among the phenomena that represent new dilemmas and choices profoundly affecting sexual relationships.

In addressing these realities the church must avoid undercutting individual discretion, eliminating personal responsibility for growth, and stifling the work of the Spirit among us. Yet within the covenant community, there is need for general guidelines, Bible study and frank conversation.

In a society in which people are purported to "have sex more but enjoy it less," the time has come to reconsider the importance of both love and covenant. There are no easy answers about how to apply love and covenant to some of the real-life situations in which people find themselves. Is the church willing to struggle with these issues even when answers are not always clear? The struggle will be unsettling and difficult, but the outcome may enhance morality, not diminish it, and contribute to a fuller, more human life for all persons.

IV. Implications for Human Sexuality

Much research on the subject of human sexuality is being done by physical and social scientists. For the church, however, scriptural guidance and biblical scholarship must be brought to bear upon that scientific information in order to come to an adequate understanding of the implications of human sexuality for our day.

Some specific concerns related to human sexuality have been dealt with in recent Annual Conferences: birth control,[4] pornography,[5] male and female roles,[6] abortion,[7] marriage,[8] artificial insemination,[9] and divorce.[10] It would be repetitious to dwell again on these issues.

Major issues that have not been dealt with by recent Annual Conferences include (1) sexuality for single persons, (2) homosexuality, and (3) marital fidelity. Sexuality for single persons is an area of rapidly changing mores in our society. Homosexuality is discussed now more openly than ever before in modern history. The difficulties of maintaining marital fidelity are compounded by current social stresses and continuing silence within the church on sexuality.

A. *Single Persons and Sexuality*

More than one-third of the adults in our society are single—unmarried, divorced, or widowed. Our biblical faith affirms singleness as a meaningful lifestyle. The lifestyles and teachings of both Jesus and Paul are models of singleness. Jesus placed singleness on a par with marriage (Matt. 19:12). Paul felt that in terms of an undivided allegiance to Christ, being single had some advantages (1 Cor. 7:1-9,24-40).

Fullness of life for single persons depends upon certain conditions. Family is important but may exist in different forms in different times and places. However, the endurance of the family reflects the need of people, whether married or unmarried, for a primary relationship in which personhood is fostered, loneliness is diminished, and closeness and belonging are experienced. Jesus cherished his family of faith as much as his biological family (Matt. 10:35-37; 12:49). His example should spur the church toward being a spiritual family to one another in the fellowship.

Furthermore, every adult needs significant friends of the opposite sex. Jesus had female friends. His friendship with Mary, sister of Martha and Lazarus, was especially close. It was a friendship not just of chores, convenience and function, but also of warm conversation and closeness (Luke 10:38-42). Priscilla (Acts 18:2, 18; 1 Cor. 16:19; Rom. 16:3) and Phoebe (Rom. 16:1-2) were especially important to Paul in his work. St. Francis of Assisi had a very close female companion, Sister Clara, whose friendship was invaluable especially in his later years. These are all helpful models of a nurturing friendship between persons of opposite sex, a friendship not involving sexual union. Such intimacy is an affirmation of maleness and femaleness and addresses basic human needs for wholeness of personhood among single people.

1. Biblical Insights.

Although the Scriptures do not deal extensively with the sexual behavior of single persons, some boundaries are established. In the Old Testament, certain types of premarital sexual activity are punishable (Deut. 22:13-21, 23-29). In the New Testament, Paul teaches that union with a prostitute is immoral because that act inseparably joins two persons (1 Cor. 6:12-20). Paul also specifically addresses the unmarried and the windowed who find it difficult to control sexual passion (1 Cor. 7:2, 9, 36-38.) Paul advocates marriage for such persons, implying that sexual intercourse is to be practiced within marriage.

2. The Church's Response.

The requirement of celibacy for singles is a thorny issue that the church faces. Our current social circumstances heighten the difficulties. Physical maturation has accelerated three years in one generation. A girl now reaches puberty at 11 or 12 years of age and a boy at 13 or 14 years. Moreover, the median age at first marriage is later than ever before: 23 years for men and 21 years for women. The 10-year span between sexual maturity and marriage creates a difficult situation in which to preserve chastity, a situation different from the biblical era.

Premarital sexual relationships, especially among teenagers, are creating many problems in our society. Sexually active adolescents experience conflict in determining their values. Emotional and psychological development is impaired, at times irreversibly. Suicide is sometimes a factor. Teenage pregnancy, venereal disease and permanent sterilization are occurring in epidemic proportions. Often these problems are the inevitable result of a society that is seductive and permissive, and promotes freedom and pleasure above responsibility and long-term satisfactions. This society and all too often a negligent church have failed to provide moral support to those many youth who do have values and seek to live by them.

The teen years should be used to mature socially and emotionally, to learn the skills of communication and problem-solving, and to express sexual identity in nongenital ways. These experiences contribute to the maturity that is necessary in order to learn what love really is, to find a compatible partner, and to establish a covenant that is sound and lasting. The church believes that these principles are still valid in our time.

The engagement period should be a time for the couple to share about families, dreams, goals, habits, likes, dislikes, past experiences. It is the time to develop common interests and good communication patterns. Christian persons in dating relationships should resist the strong desire for full sexual expression and the pressures of the media and culture for sexual exploitation.

Also in contemporary society there are rapidly increasing numbers of previously married single adults. A higher divorce rate, an extended life expectancy, and the preponderance of women over men in the middle and upper age brackets are among the factors leading to this increase. Many of these persons have experienced sexual intercourse within marriage, but such experience is no longer available to them. Some of the problems that exist in our contemporary world when singleness is a matter of circumstances rather than choice did not exist in such proportions in the biblical world. It is incumbent on our society and the church to acknowledge these problems and to seek solutions.

The church counteracts the cultural emphasis on sexual self-indulgence by teaching the benefits of self-discipline and the positive aspects of a life of commitment and fidelity. In a time of casual lovemaking and pleasure seeking, covenants provide structure that sustains us in the fluctuating joys and pains of authentic relationships. Ongoing loyalties give continuity to our lives. The marks of covenant include mutual respect, public vows, lifetime accountability, and religious sanction. The church teaches that sexual intercourse belongs within the bonds of such love and covenant.

The church as a covenant community encourages single people, as well as married people, to speak of their needs and concerns including sexuality. In the continuing interchange of ideas and feelings, the church seeks to be more evangelical and caring than condemnatory.

B. Homosexual Persons and Sexuality

The Church of the Brethren never has dealt officially with the issue of homosexuality. The time is here to examine openly this matter that profoundly affects the lives of millions of homosexual people and their families.

1. Misunderstandings About Homosexuality.

Misunderstandings and unnecessary fears about homosexuality abound. Contrary to popular opinion, most homosexuals are not flagrantly promiscuous and do not engage in offensive public behavior. Male homosexuals are not identifiably "feminine" and lesbians are not characteristically "masculine." Teachers with homosexual orientation are often suspected of influencing pupils towards homosexual behavior but most sexual offenses reported between teacher and pupil are heterosexual in nature. For most practicing homosexuals, sexual activity is a proportionate part of their lives. Most of the time they engage in pursuits common to all.

2. Causes of Homosexuality.

The causes of homosexuality are not definitely known. Is it inborn or learned? No one has the definitive answer. What is known is that people do not simply decide to become homosexual; it is more complex than that.

Some recent research suggests that the predisposition for homosexuality may be genetic. Other research suggests that certain types of family pathology produce a higher incidence of homosexuality. However, such research has not been sufficiently extensive or scientific to be conclusive. It is generally agreed that the homosexual orientation usually is formed early in life. From 5 to 10 per cent of the population is said to be primarily homosexual in orientation.[11]

A significant percentage of people have occasional homosexual interests and/or experience but are not exclusively homosexual. Perhaps the majority of people are somewhere on the continuum between exclusive homosexuality and exclusive heterosexuality.

3. Biblical Insights.

The Bible refers directly to homosexual conduct seven times. Genesis 18-19 and Judges 19 are narratives. Leviticus 18:22 and 20:13 are prohibitions in the Holiness Code. Romans 1:26ff, 1 Corinthians 6:9-10, and 1 Timothy 1:10 are excerpts from epistles.

Genesis 18-19

The attempted homosexual assault by a mob of men is mentioned in the story about the decadence and subsequent destruction of the city of Sodom. Such offensive behavior was not the only sin of this wicked city. Isaiah, Ezekiel, and Jesus point to Sodom's self-indulgence, arrogance, inhospitality, and indifference to the poor. Thus, in its own later interpretations of the episode at Sodom, the Bible does not dwell on homosexual sins of the city in the way that more recent interpreters do. Nevertheless, sexual misconduct, particularly assault, is an important element in the story about Sodom's sin and destruction (2 Pet. 2:4-14, Jude 7).

Judges 19

The Judges 19:22-26 account of an incident at Gibeah is strikingly similar to the Genesis 19:4-8 account of the mistreatment of guests at Lot's house in Sodom. Since the stories are so similar, what one decides about the meaning of one passage would apply also to the other.

Leviticus 18:22; 20:13

Leviticus denounces male homosexual acts decisively in two almost identical texts. However, some difficulty arises in interpreting these verses because of their context. The Leviticus proscriptions against homosexual acts are intermingled with statutes that forbid the planting of two kinds of seed in one field, wearing garments made of two kinds of material, and trimming the edges of a man's beard (Lev. 19:9, 27). Another statute mandates executing children who curse their parents (Lev. 20:9). The church does not enforce all laws from this section of Leviticus (i.e., the Holiness Code, chapters 17-26). Some interpreters inquire: "Upon what basis does the church select one law for enforcement, but ignore other laws?" The key is to examine the overarching principles of the total Bible. Does the rest of scripture, particularly the New Testament, reaffirm the laws from the Holiness Code that denounce male homosexual acts? To that question we now direct our attention.

Romans 1:26-27

The first chapter of Romans states that both lesbianism (the only mention of female homosexuality in the Bible) and male homosexuality are manifestations of the corruption that arises from idolatry (Rom. 1:23-27.) The lust and unnaturalness of the homosexuality described in this passage are examples of how distorted life becomes when people worship and serve created things rather than the Creator (Rom. 1:25.)

The persons described in this chapter "gave up natural relations for unnatural" (verses 26-27.) This phrase connotes that homosexual behavior is the willful acts of persons who had previously engaged in heterosexual relations. Not all homosexuality can be described this way. Some persons never experienced what Paul calls "natural relations" because their orientation (genetic or conditioned) is homosexual. This circumstance opens the question: Does Paul consider all kinds of homosexuality idolatrous, or does he mean to denounce only those kinds of homosexual behavior described in this passage? The one thing that is clear in this passage is that Paul considers the behavior of those who exchange heterosexual for homosexual relations to be "unnatural" and sinful.

1 Corinthians 6:9-11, 1 Timothy 1:9-11

1 Corinthians and 1 Timothy list a series of sins of which are condemned. Both of these lists include the Greek word *arsenokoitia* which is a form of sexual immorality. But, *arsenokoitia* is an obscure word. A comparison of English versions reveals that *arsenokoitia* is variously translated to mean heterosexual male prostitution, or sodomy, or cultic homosexuality, or all forms of homosexual activity. Apparently, there are overtones of lust and cultic prostitution. Again the question arises in the minds of some whether Paul in naming *arsenokoitia* means to denounce *all* forms of homosexual behavior.

In summary, seven passages forcefully denounce a variety of homosexual behavior: rape, adultery, cultic prostitution, and lust. These scriptures do not deal explicitly with some contemporary questions about various forms of homosexuality, about homosexuality as an orientation, about the onset of homosexuality prior to the age of moral accountability, and about genetic and/or environmental predispositions.

While the seven direct references in the Old and New Testaments are often isolated as the focal point of an interpretation of the biblical teaching homosexuality, these texts are best understood within the larger framework from which the Bible approaches sexuality in general. This overarching framework, identified in the opening sections of this paper, upholds heterosexuality as the reflection of God's image (Gen. 1:27) and as the culmination of creation (Gen. 2:18-25). It is in union with a sexual opposite that male and female find fulfillment as persons and identify as a family. While some modern distinctions about homosexuality are missing in the Scriptures, homosexual behavior is considered contrary to heterosexual norm that runs throughout scripture.

Jesus reinforced the unified biblical view of human sexuality. He upheld the sanctity of heterosexual marriage, reciting from scripture God's original intention in creation: "Have you not read that He who made them from the beginning made them male and female, and said, 'For this reason a man shall leave his father and mother and be joined to his wife, and the two shall become one'? So they are no longer two but one" (Matt. 19:4-5). Thus, Jesus affirms that heterosexual marriage is the pattern for sexual union God intended from the beginning.

This biblical affirmation of heterosexuality does not automatically exclude every other choice of sexual expression or nonexpression. Although Jesus is clear about the biblical norm, he is not categorical. In the same passage in which he upholds the sanctity of marriage (Matt. 19:3-12), he acknowledges, "not every one can receive this precept, only those to whom it is given." He then identifies some persons for whom heterosexual union is not possible: some because of factors of birth; others because of what has been done to them; and still others because they choose not to marry for the sake of the kingdom. Thus Jesus does not prescribe heterosexual marriage for every person.

4. The Church's Response.

The Church of the Brethren upholds the biblical declaration that heterosexuality is the intention of God for creation. Nature, in the very functional compatibility of male and female genitalia, confirms that this biblical revelation that males and females are meant for each other. This intimate genital contact between two persons of opposite sexes is not just a physical union; it also embodies the interlocking of persons. This intimate companionship is heterosexuality at its fullest. It is the context for the formation of family.

Some persons, for reasons not fully understood, experience a romantic attraction for persons of the same sex. Some of these persons claim Christ as Lord and are actively involved in the life of the church. They need the active support and love of the church as they struggle with God's plan for their lives.

In ministry to homosexual persons, the church must guard against oversimplifying Christian morality. Instead the church should endeavor with Christian love and with gentle evangelistic skill to offer redemptive help. Proof texts, condemnation, and a sense of guilt will not empower change. Rejection isolates homosexual persons from the church. It frequently results in a preoccupation with an intensification of the very inclinations their accusers deplore. The power of the Gospel incorporates an acceptance of persons who seek forgiveness for their sins and who strive to be disciples of Jesus Christ. It is this non-accusatory acceptance that sets people free from guilt, depression and fear. When we are saved it is not because we are without sin but because our sins are not held against us by God's grace. We are made whole through God's righteousness, not ours (Rom. 3:21-4:5).

In relating to homosexual persons, the church should become informed about such lifestyle options as the following:

Celibacy, refraining from sexual activities, is one alternative that homosexuals and bisexuals choose. The scriptural teaching on celibacy for heterosexuals provides a model for this lifestyle. Celibacy ought to be voluntary and not a requirement (1 Tim. 4:1-3). Those for whom celibacy is a gift and a special calling (Matt. 19:11-12; Cor. 7:6-7) are to be honored and supported.

Conversion to a heterosexual orientation is another option. For many homosexual persons, however, this choice is extraordinarily difficult and complex. For some it is impossible. The church must seek to create a climate for hope, for praise of God, for renewed effort, for claiming and exploring the heterosexual dimensions of being. Thus the Good News is shared with homosexual persons who seek to convert to heterosexuality. Yet not all are set totally free from homosexual feelings and urges. For some, impulses diminish, mindsets change, the grip of homosexuality is broken, and affectional and physical attraction to the opposite sex can begin.

Covenantal Relationships between homosexual persons is an additional lifestyle option but, in the church's search for a Christian understanding of human sexuality, this alternative is not acceptable.

There are special ways in which the church can extend Christ-life comfort and grace to homosexual and bisexual persons. These include:

—welcoming all inquirers who confess Jesus Christ as Lord and Savior into the fellowship of the church. This welcome and the resources of the church are made available by the grace of God who calls us as repentant sinners to be partakers of the faith. Some guidelines for the church's response and for discipleship have been delineated;

—intensifying efforts to understand how genetic makeup and childhood experiences have influenced the development of sexual orientation and behavior;

—challenging openly the widespread fear, hatred, and harassment of homosexual persons;

—engaging in open, forthright conversations with homosexuals. When we stop alienating one another and instead venture toward understanding, some fears disappear and interpersonal relationships become more honest;

—advocating the right of homosexuals to jobs, housing and legal justice;

—stating clearly that all antisocial, sexually promiscuous acts are contrary to Christian morality;

—giving strong support to persons who seek to be faithful to their heterosexual marriage covenant, but for whom this is difficult because of struggles with homosexuality.

Fortunate are persons who learn not to be afraid of their feelings and thoughts and can accept these components of their sexuality within disciplined bounds. Discovering that God has good use for these dimensions of our lives helps to defuse unacceptable impulses. We all, whether homosexual or heterosexual, have desires and drives that need to be channelled appropriately to avoid sin and to centre our sexuality in right relationships.

Endnotes

[1] Barclay, William, *Letters to Galatians and Ephesians.* Philadelphia: Westminster Press, 1954; p. 54. In addition to *eros* and *agapé*, there are two additional Greek words for love: *philia* which refers to the warm but nonromantic love we feel for those close to us and *storge* which refers especially to the love between parents and children.

[2] Nygren, Anders, *Agapé and Eros.* Philadelphia: Westminster Press, 1953. The separation between the words *eros* and *Agapé*, *eros* having to do with love involving the needs of self and *agapé* having to do with love involving the needs of other persons, has been in vogue since the publication of this book. It is not clear that this neat, sharp distinction can in fact be sustained either in the New Testament or in Hellenistic literature. However, the perspective commonly called *eros* is definitely in the biblical tradition even if the word is not.

[3] Roop, Eugene, "Two Become One Become Two," *Brethren Life and Thought,* Vol. XXI, No. 3, Summer 1976; pp. 133-137. An analysis of the expectation of permanence with covenants and yet the possibility of new covenants.

[4] *Minutes of the Annual Conference, 1955-64,* "Family Planning and Population Growth," (1964), p. 328.

[5] *Minutes of the Annual Conference, 1965-69,* "Theological Basis of Personal Ethics," (1966), p. 118.

[6] *Minutes of the Annual Conference, 1975-79,* "Equality for Women in the Church of the Brethren," (1977), p. 340.

[7] *Minutes of the Annual Conference, 1970-74,* "Abortion," (1972), p. 227.

[8] *Minutes of the Annual Conference, 1955-64,* "Divorce and Remarriage," (1964), p. 320, and *Minutes of the Annual Conference, 1975-79,* "Marriage and Divorce," (1977), p. 300.

[9] *Minutes of the Annual Conference, 1955-64,* "Family Planning and Population Growth," (1974), p. 328.

[10] *Minutes of the Annual Conference, 1955-64,* "Divorce and Remarriage," (1964), p. 320 and *Minutes of the Annual Conference, 1975-1979,* "Marriage and Divorce," (1977), p. 298.

[11] Kinsey, Alfred C.; Pomeroy, Wardell B.; Martin, Clyde E.; and Gebhard, Paul H., *Sexual Behavior in the Human Male and Sexual Behavior in the Human Female.* Philadelphia: W.B. Saunders Company, 1948 and 1953.

Notes: *Within the context of a full exposition on the role of sexuality in human life, the Church of the Brethren explored the issue of homosexuality. While adopting a pastoral stance toward homosexuals and noting that Jesus did not categorically reject homosexual relationship, the church finds the continued practice of homosexuality (even in a single conventional relationship) as unacceptable.*

Even with its refusal to condone homosexuality activity, the church goes as far as it can in denouncing homophobia, advocating civil rights for homosexuals, and accepting homosexual persons as people of worth.

CHURCH OF THE NAZARENE

STATEMENT ON HOMOSEXUALITY (1985)

We recognize the depth of the perversion that leads to homosexual acts, but affirm the biblical position that such acts are sinful and subject to the wrath of God. We believe the grace of God sufficient to overcome the practice of homosexuality [1 Corinthians 6:9-11]. We deplore any action or statement that would seem to imply compatibility between Christian morality and the practice of homosexuality. We urge clear preaching and teaching concerning Bible standards of sex morality (Genesis 1:27; 19:1-25, Leviticus 20:13; Romans 1:26-27; 1 Corinthians 6:9-11; 1 Timothy 1:8-10.]

Notes: *This statement from the 1985* Manual *of the Church of the Nazarene follows closely the pattern of the conservative Protestant position.*

EPISCOPAL CHURCH

STATEMENT ON HOMOSEXUALITY (1979)

WE—BISHOPS IN THE CHURCH OF GOD WHO ASSOCIATE OURSELVES WITH THIS STATEMENT—affirm our belief that Holy Matrimony between a man and a woman as a covenanted, exclusive, and [by God's help) a permanent relationship is the predominant and usual mode of sexual expression, blessed by God, for Christian people particularly and for humankind generally. To this state the vast majority of persons have clearly been called.

We also affirm the sacrificial sign of celibacy, for the small minority genuinely called to that state, as a valid and valuable witness to a broken and selfish world of the virtues and spiritual power of Christian self denial in the service of others.

Nothing in what follows is intended to deny or to weaken either the vocation to Christian marriage or to Christian celibacy, and nothing, especially, intended to weaken or demean, or deny the centrality of, the institution of the Christian family.

However, there is a minority of persons who have clearly not been called to the married state, or given the graces for it—whether they realize this before, or painfully and often tragically discover it afterwards—and who are incapable in the very nature of their formed personalities of conforming to the predominant mode of behavior. Why this is so is a mystery known only to God; even the researchers of modern science have been unable to provide an adequate answer for it. Nor is there convincing evidence that these people, of homosexual orientation, have been given the very special and extraordinary grace the Church has always seen to be necessary for the healthy expression of Christian celibacy.

We who associate ourselves with this statement are deeply conscious of, and grateful for, the profoundly valuable ministries of ordained persons, known to us to be homosexual, formerly and presently engaged in the service of this Church. Not all of these persons have necessarily been celibate; and in the relationships of many of them, maintained in the face of social hostility and against great odds, we have seen a redeeming quality which in its way and according to its mode is no less a sign to the world of God's love than is the more usual sign of Christian marriage. From such relationship we cannot believe God to be absent.

Furthermore, even in cases where an ideally stable relationship has not, or has not yet, been achieved, we are conscious of ordained homosexual persons who are wrestling responsibly, and in the fear of God, with the Christian implications of their sexuality, and who seek to be responsible, caring and non-exploitive people even in the occasionally more transient relationships which the hostility of our society towards homosexual persons—with its concomitants of furtiveness and clandestinity—makes inevitable.

We believe that the action of this House, which declares that "it is not appropriate for this Church to ordain a practicing homosexual or any person who is engaged in heterosexual relations outside of marriage," while it has the specious appearance at first glance of reaffirming and upholding time honored verities, carries with it a cruel denial of the sexual beings of homosexual persons—against whom, given the title of this resolution, it is principally aimed. It also carries with, in implied logic, a repudiation of those ministries, by homosexual persons and to homosexual persons, already being exercised in our midst; and it invites, furthermore, the prospect of retroactive reprisals against ordained homosexual persons, with consequences of untold harm to the Church and its people, whether homosexual or heterosexual.

This action also speaks a word of condemning judgement against countless laypersons of homosexual orientation who are rendered by its implications second-class citizens in the Church of their baptism, fit to receive all other sacraments but the grace of Holy Order—unless, in a sacrifice not asked of heterosexual persons generally, they abandon all hope of finding human fulfilment, under God, in a sexual and supportive relationship. This action, thus, makes a mockery of the vow and commitment which the Church has made to them in that sacrament of baptism, to "do all in (its) power to support these persons in their life in Christ"—all of these persons, without exception—and calls into question the vows of us all to "strive for justice and peace among all people, and respect the dignity of every human being."

Furthermore, speaking for the future, if these recommendations were to be carried out as this House seems to intend, they would fatally restrict our traditional freedom and duty as Bishops in the Church of God—with the concurrence of our Standing Committees, Ministry Commission, and the like—to determine the fitness and calling of individual persons to Holy Orders—with each case being decided, not on the basis of the individual's belonging to a particular category or class of excluded persons, but on the basis of his or her individual merits as a whole human being, and in the light of the particular circumstances obtaining in this case.

We have no intention of ordaining irresponsible persons, or persons whose manner of life is such as to cause grave scandal or hurt to other Christians; but we do not believe that either homosexual orientation as such, nor the responsible and self-giving use of such a mode of sexuality, constitutes such a scandal in and of itself.

Our position is based, consistent with our Anglican tradition—which values the gifts of reason and welcomes truth from *whatever* source—on the insights of what we understand to be the best and most representative current findings of modern science and psychology on this subject. But even more, our position is based, ultimately, on the total witness of Holy Scripture. For we are persuaded that modern exegesis and interpretation of the Scriptures—in the light of the original languages and our enhanced understanding of the cultural context of the particular passages which relate, or seem to relate, to the subject of homosexuality—gives no certain basis for a total or absolute condemnation either of homosexual persons or of homosexual activities in all cases. Holy Scripture indeed condemns homosexual excesses and exploitation, but it no less condemns heterosexual excesses and exploitation as well; and as the cure for the latter is a more responsible and less selfish expression of heterosexuality, so the cure for the former is a more responsible and less selfish expression of homosexuality, not a conversion from one to the other. On the other hand, the total witness of Holy Scripture is to a gracious God of justice, mercy, and love. It is on that witness we take our stand, and it is to that God we make our appeal.

Taking note, therefore, that this action of the House is recommendatory and not prescriptive, we give notice as we are answerable before Almighty God that we cannot accept these recommendations or implement them in our Dioceses insofar as they relate or give unqualified expression to Recommendation 3. To do so would be to abrogate our responsibilities of apostolic leadership and prophetic witness to the flock of Christ, committed to our charge; and it would involve a repudiation of our ordination vows as Bishops, in the words of the new Prayer Book, *boldly [to] proclaim and interpret the Gospel of Christ, enlightening the minds and stirring up the conscience of (our) people, and to encourage and support all baptized people in their gifts and ministries . . . and to celebrate with them the sacraments of our redemption,* or in the words of the old, *to be to the flock of Christ a shepherd, not a wolf.* Our appeal is to conscience, and to God. Amen.

Signatories to the above message in 1979 were as follows:

Robert M. Anderson, Minnesota
Charles E. Bennison, Western Michigan
Edmond Browning, Hawaii
John Burgess, ret. (Massachusetts)
Otis Charles, Utah
David C. Cochran, Alaska
Ned Cole, Central New York
William A. Dimmick, Northern Michigan
Wesley Frensdorff, Nevada
John M. Krumm, Southern Ohio
H. Coleman McGehee, Michigan
Paul Moore, Jr., New York
J. Brooke Moseley, Delaware
C. Kilmer Myers, California
Lyman C. Olgilby, Pennsylvania
Frederick W. Putnam, Suffragan, Oklahoma
Francisco Reus-Froylan, Puerto Rico
William B. Spofford, Eastern Oregon
Richard M. Trelease, Jr., Rio Grande
John T. Walker, Washington

Bishops Signing Statement in 1988

John Shelby Spong, Newark
Otis Charles, (resigned)
John M. Krumm, Southern Ohio (retired)
Thomas K. Ray, Northern Michigan
C. Shannon Mallory, El Camino Real
Hebert D. Edmundson, Assistant, Central Florida
Douglas E. Theuner, New Hampshire
Paul Moore, Jr., New York
Donald P. Hart, Hawaii
Walter D. Dennis, New York

Quintin E. Primo,Jr., Chicago
Herbert A. Donovan, Jr., Arkansas
Lylan C. Ogilby, Pennsylvania (retired)
John-Charles, SSF, Polynesia (retired)-collegial
Daniel L. Swenson, Vermont
Frederick H. Borsch, Los Angeles
Philip A. Smith, New Hampshire (retired)
William G. Burrill, Rochester
Donald J.Davis, Northwestern Pennsylvania
Robert M. Anderson, Minnesota
A. Theodore Eastman, Maryland
Charles J. Child, Jr., Atlanta
Stewart C. Zabriskie, Nevada
Orris G. Walker, Jr., Long Island
John T. Walker, Washington
Frank T. Griswold, Chicago
Frederick W. Putnam, Navajoland (retired)
George N. Hunt, Rhode Island
William G. Black, Southern Ohio
David E. Richards, (resigned)

Notes: *In one of its earlier statements on homosexuality, a number of bishops of the Episcopal Church issued this statement of recommendation concerning homosexuality and the ministry. It suggested that, in light of modern exegesis of scripture, that no absolute denouncement of homosexuality or homosexual activities, even among ordained ministers, could be made. These particular bishops also opposed action by the House of Bishops, which declared that the church could not ordain practicing homosexuals. In 1988, this statement was adopted and signed by an additional number of bishops, though they were still in the minority.*

EPISCOPAL CHURCH

REPORT OF THE TASK FORCE ON CHANGING PATTERNS OF SEXUALITY AND FAMILY LIFE (1987)

Introduction

Following the mandate of the Diocesan Convention on January, 1985, the Task Force on changing Patterns of Sexuality and Family Life has been meeting for study and discussion, focusing its attention on three groups of persons representative of some of the changing patterns of sexuality and family life: 1) young people who choose to live together without being married; 2) older persons who choose not to marry or who may be divorced or widowed; 3) homosexual couples. All three kinds of relationships are widely represented in the Diocese Newark, and it has been recognized that the Church's understanding of and ministry among the people involved has not been adequate.

The aim of the Task Force has not been original social scientific research. Members of the Task Force have engaged in Biblical, theological, historical, sociological and psychological study, and in extensive discussion of the issues raised. The intent of the Task Force has been two-fold: to prepare a document that would help the clergy and laity of the diocese to think about the issues, and to suggest broad guidelines for the Church's pastoral response to persons in the three groups and to those not in those groups but who are concerned about the issues raised.

The process of study and discussion engaged the members at the deepest levels of their self-understanding as human beings and as Christians. We sometimes found ourselves confused, angry, hurt, uncertain. The subject brought up basic fears and prejudices which members had to struggle with corporately and privately. We became more deeply aware of our own fallibility and of our need for each other's response, correction and support. Each member is a distinct person with her or his own distinct experience and viewpoint; complete uniformity was neither sought nor attained.

But the Task Force became and remains convinced that such a process of search and person-to-person engagement is essential for the Church to respond to the social, cultural and personal realities involved in the changing patterns of sexuality and family life. Appropriate response to these issues requires the willingness to confront within ourselves some of our most deeply formed impulses and assumptions, and some of our traditions's most firmly embedded attitudes. This can only occur in a context of conversation with others whose experience and viewpoints enable our own to be transformed.

We understand the Church to be a community in search, not a community in perfection. As a community in search, the Church must recognize the needs among its members, among all Christians, indeed among all persons, for loving support, for mutual trust, and for growth through learning from each other. As one contemporary writer has put it ". . . as such a *community* the Church is of prime significance in making love a reality in human life—incarnating the Incarnate Love. . . . These images affirm not only intimacy and mutuality but also inclusiveness; there are implications for a diversity of sexual patterns within a congregation. Different sexual lifestyles being lived out with integrity and in Christianly humanizing ways need not simply be tolerated—they can be positively supported. The 'family of God' can ill afford to make the nuclear family its sole model." (James Nelson, *Embodiment*. Minneapolis: Augsberg Publishing House, 1978, p. 260.]

This report crystallizes the Task Force's perspective on these issues. It does not summarize each discussion, nor does it present all the research and data that informed these discussions. The report is offered to the Diocese of Newark to stimulate our corporate thinking and discussion. The Task Force's major recommendation is that discussion continue on an intentional, Diocese-wide basis. This and other recommendations are offered in the final section.

I. The Cultural Situation

The social and cultural changes that have occurred in American society over the past half-century are increasingly being reflected in the changing attitudes of members of the Anglican communion regarding some of the basic moral values and assumptions which have long been taken for granted. Profound changes have occurred in our understanding and practices in areas involving sexuality and family life. Traditionally, the Church has provided, virtually unchallenged, direction and guidance on these matters that deeply affect the individual, the family unit and the community at large. Today, the Church is no longer the single arbiter in these matters, which were once thought to be within its sacred province. Some of the factors that have led to the diminution of this status are:

1. Secularization of American society as it moved from a predominately rural background at the turn of the century to today's predominately urban setting. This has produced new and competing centers of values and morality.
2. Social, economic and geographical mobility that has individually and collectively loosened structures traditionally provided by the community, church and family. These structures tended to channel and constrict values, choices, and behavior in the areas involving sexuality, marriage and family life.
3. Advances of technology, which have provided means of disease control and birth control, which have effectively separated the act of sexual intercourse from procreation.
4. Reduction of the age at which puberty begins. This confronts children with issues of sexuality earlier than in the past.

5. Adolescent dating without chaperonage. This removes a powerful external structure of control of sexual behavior.

6. Many in contemporary culture begin and establish a career at a later age than formerly. Marriage also tends to occur later. These two developments combined with convenient methods of birth control, the earlier onset of puberty and the absence of chaperonage, significantly lengthens the period when sexuality will be expressed outside of marriage.

7. The gradual, but perceptible changes in attitude regarding what constitutes a ''complete'' human being: the human body and sex are no longer considered something to be ashamed of, and these physical realities as well as intellect and spiritually constitute essential elements in the development of a complete human being.

8. The decline of exclusive male economic hegemony, which has resulted in a realignment of the male/female relationships in society.

9. The existence of a better educated society, which does not depend upon authorities to determine ''what is right'' on issues such as nuclear war or power plants, abortion, birth control, poverty, environment, etc.

10. The intensifying clash between the claims of traditional authority as demanded by the family, church and society and the aims of twentieth century men and women to seek their own fulfilment in ways that were not necessarily acceptable in the past. This is, of course, an ancient tension; it gains its particular contemporary character in American society from the dissolution of the degree of ethical consensus as the society has become increasingly pluralistic.

    The Church needs to think clearly about these social, cultural and ethical realities. It must order its teachings and corporate life so as to guide and sustain all persons whose lives are touched by these realities. The challenges that these realities pose to our beliefs and practices must be examined and responded to.

    As indicated in the introduction, this report is intended to contribute to the Church's understanding of these issues, and to offer perspective on and suggestions for the Church's response.

II. Biblical and Theological Considerations

A. Tradition and Interpretation

The Judeo-Christian tradition is a tradition precisely because, in every historical and social circumstance, the thinking faithful have brought to bear their best interpretation of the current realities in correlation with their interpretation of the tradition as they have inherited it. Thus, truth in the Judeo-Christian tradition is a dynamic process to be discerned and formulated rather than a static structure to be received.

The Bible is misunderstood and misused when approached as a book of moral prescriptions directly applicable to all moral dilemmas. Rather, the Bible is the record of the response to the word of God addressed to Israel and to the Church throughout centuries of changing social, historical and cultural conditions. The Faithful responded within the realities of their particular situation, guided by the direction of previous revelation, but not captive to it.

The text must always be understood in context: first in the historical context of the particular Biblical situation and then in our own particular social and historical context. The word of God addresses us through scripture. It is not freeze-dried in prepackaged moral prescriptions, but is actively calling for faithful response within the realities of our particular time. Any particular prescription in scripture, any teaching of the law, must be evaluated according to the overarching direction of the Bible's witness to God, culminating in the grace of Christ.

B. The Centrality of Christ and the Realm of God

The central point of reference for the thinking Christian is the life, ministry, death, and resurrection of Jesus Christ. The history of interpretations of the meaning of that event begins in scripture itself and continues into our immediate present. The central fact about Jesus's life and teaching is that he manifested in his relationships, acts, and words, the imminent and future Kingdom of God, which will be referred to as the Realm of God.

The Realm of God as presented by Jesus in his relationships and in his parables is characterized by loving action on behalf of all men and women including especially the poor, the sick, the weak, the oppressed and the despised, the outcast, and those on the margins of life. The Realm of God presents us with both the fulfilment and the transcendence of the inherited law. The Realm of God presents us with an overturning—even a reversal—of the structures by which humans attempt to establish their own righteousness, which inevitably oppresses or exploits, or marginalizes others.

The challenge to the Church to respond creatively to changing patterns of sexuality and family life in America must be seen as an instance of the Holy Spirit leading us to respond to the blessing and claim of the Realm of God foreshadowed and made continually present by the life of Christ Jesus. In his death Jesus exemplifies sacrificial love that is faithful to his vision of the Realm of God. In the resurrection we know God's ultimate faithfulness and sovereignty.

It is in response to this central example and teaching of Jesus regarding the Realm of God that we attempt to discern what should be the Church's response to changing patterns of sexuality and family life. We discover in the actions and parables of Jesus that the Realm of God manifests grace unfettered by legalistic obligation to tradition and "the law". When the choice is between observance of the law or active, inclusive love, Jesus embodies and teaches love. It is in the light of this fundamental principle of God's active reconciling love that any religious law or dogma, social or economic arrangement is to be assessed.

C. The Realm of God and Human Social Structures

The specific instances of changing patterns of sexuality and family life that this Task Force addresses do not occur in a cultural vacuum but in the cultural turmoil marked by the ten developments noted in the opening sections of this document. Not one of these developments is morally unambiguous. All of them are marked—as has been every development of social history—by the human propensity for self-deception and self-aggrandizement at the expense of others, which Christians call "sin."

Jesus's radical claim is that in his person the Realm of God confronts us, in every age, with our bondage to sin. Included in sin's manifestations are the social norms and arrangements by which we conventionally order our lives. In parable after parable Jesus presents us with the need to see historical relativity, the need to examine the arbitrariness and the maintenance of power by traditional structures. The Church itself and the authority of its traditional teachings is subject to judgement by the ongoing activity of the Realm of God.

Judged by the grace of God starkly presented by the parables, Jesus's preaching and his actions show us that response to Realm of God requires us to be ready to perceive and modify those structures in our society that hurt and alienate others rather than heal and extend love to those in circumstances different from our own.

With this consciousness we hear the challenges to our conventional attitudes and practices regarding sexuality and the family and try to discern how these challenges should influence our understanding of our traditional values and our response to new realities. We engage in this process knowing (and discovering anew) that all our thoughts are laced with our desire for self-justification, our need for self-aggrandizement, and the willingness to hurt those whom we see as opposing us. Sin is our human condition; it permeates all our institutions, all our traditions, and all our relationships, so it has always been for humankind; so it has always been in the Church.

D. Historical Relativity

Recalling our sinful condition causes us to look critically both at the Church's conventions and at the demands for change put forward by various groups in our culture. The relativizing impact of the Realm of God enables us to see more clearly what Biblical and historical research discloses: that beliefs and practices surrounding marriage and sexuality have varied according to time, culture and necessity. We tend for sacralize the familiar and project into the past our current practices and beliefs and the rationales supporting them.

Such is the case with our assumptions about marriage. We tend to project into early Biblical times a twentieth century model of monogamous self-chosen marriage when clearly, at various periods in the Old Testament records, polygamy was assumed (at least for the wealthy). Even into the Middle Ages a marriage was an economic event, perhaps an alliance, between two families or clans.

Marriage was not given the status of a sacrament by the Church until 1439. And not until 1563 did the Church require the presence of a priest at the event. And even then marriage functioned to solemnize an agreement which had been entered into more for reasons of procreation, the channeling of sexuality, and economic benefit to the families than as a means for preexisting love between the two persons to develop and flourish, as we expect of present-day marriage.

In the Bible and in our own Western heritage, sexuality outside of marriage has been proscribed for women—not men. When women were found adulterous, the violation was of property rights rather than of sexual morality as we tend to conceive it, because women were viewed as property of fathers, and then of their husbands.

Homosexual behavior was condemned because it was part of pagan religious practices from which Israel sought always to differentiate itself. Biblical scholarship maintains that in the story of Sodom and Gomorrah, Lot's concern was not with the homosexual nature of the implied rape of his guests, but with such behavior as a violation of rules of hospitality. Homosexuality as a fundamental human orientation is not addressed in scripture; and Jesus himself was entirely silent on the subject.

E. Revised Understanding of the Person

A major change in perspective is occurring in religious thinking regarding sexuality and the body. Greek philosophical and agnostic thought had great influence on the early development of Christianity. Since that time the Church has tended to teach that the body is a dangerous vessel, subject to temptation and sin which temporarily houses the superior soul of spirit. Whereas the Greeks regarded the mind or spirit as able to reach its triumph only by freeing itself from the corrupting captivity of the physical body, the Hebrew knew no such separation. In Hebraic thought one does not *have* a body, one *is* a body. What we today refer to as body, mind, and spirit were—in Hebraic thought—dimensions of an indivisible unity.

The contemporary more Hebraic understanding of the person runs counter to the traditional dualistic teaching of the Church, which has tended either to try to ignore the fact that humans are embodied selves, or has looked at the physical, sexual body as the root of sin. The contemporary attitude views sexuality as more than genital sex having as its purpose procreation, physical pleasure and release of tension. Sexuality includes sex, but it is a more comprehensive concept.

Sexuality is not simply a matter of behavior. Our sexuality goes to the heart of our identity as persons. Our self-understanding, our experience of ourselves as male or female, our ways of experiencing and relating to others, are all reflective of our being as sexual persons.

We do not have *bodies,* we *are* bodies, and the doctrine of the Incarnation reminds us that God comes to us and we know God in the flesh. We come to know God through our experience of other embodied selves. Thus our sexual identity and behavior are means for our experience and knowledge of God. This theological perspective means that issues of homosexuality, divorce, and sexual relations between unmarried persons involve not only matters of ethics but have to do with how persons know and experience God.

It is our conclusion that by suppressing our sexuality and by condemning all sex which occurs outside of traditional marriage, the Church has thereby obstructed a vitally important means for persons to know and celebrate their relatedness to God. The teachings of the Church have tended to make us embarrassed about rather than grateful for our bodies. As means of communion with other persons our bodies sacramentally become means of communion with God.

III. Ethical Essentials

From the perspective of Jesus's teaching regarding the Realm of God, all heterosexual and homosexual relationships are subject to the same criteria of ethical assessment—the degree to which the persons and relationships reflect mutuality, love and justice. The Task Force does not in any way advocate or condone promiscuous behavior which by its very definition exploits the other for one's own aggrandizement. The commitment to mutuality, love and justice which marks our ideal picture of heterosexual unions is also the ideal for homosexuals unions. Those who would say homosexuality by its very nature precludes such commitment must face the fact that such unions do in fact occur, have occurred and will continue to occur. The Church must decide how to respond to such unions.

It is becoming clear that many persons—single, divorced, or widowed—may not seek long-term unions, while some commit themselves to such unions without being formally married. The overriding issue is not the formality of the social/legal arrangement, or even a scriptural formula, but the quality of the relationship in terms of our understanding of the ethical and moral direction pointed to by Jesus in the symbol of the Realm of God.

The challenge to the Church is to discern and support the marks of the Realm of God in all these relationships. The Church should be that community above all which is marked by its inclusion of persons who are seeking to grow in their capacity for love and justice in their relationships and in their relation to their world-neighbors. The Church should actively work against those social and economic arrangements which militate against the establishment of such relationships.

IV. Marriage and Alternate Forms of Relationship

Our nation has been described as a ''highly nuptial'' civilization. This means that for whatever reasons many Americans see marriage as a vehicle for happiness and satisfaction. Life-long marriage offers the possibility of profound intimacy, mutuality, personal development, and self-fulfilment throughout the years of the life cycle. On the other hand, of course, a marriage can be marked with the sin of self-centredness and exploitation of the other, and by the estrangements of male from female, weaker from stronger.

Ideally, marriage can be a context in which children can develop their identities by drawing on both male and female ways of being a person. It can therefore provide a uniquely rich context for the formation of children into adults who cherish and intend the qualities of the Realm of God—love and justice—in the context of ongoing relationships marked by sacrifice, forgiveness, joy, and reconciliation. It can also give to parents the opportunity to mature and develop their own capacities for caring generativity.

The Church must continue to sustain persons in the fulfilment of traditional marriage relationships both for the well-being of the marriage partners and because such marriage provides the most stable institution that we have known for the nurturing and protection of children. But the Church must also recognize that fully intended marriage vows are fraught with risks. Belief that deeper knowledge each of each in marriage will enable the original intentions of love and devotion is not always fulfilled. Persons living through the dissolution of marriage need especially at that time the support of an understanding and inclusive community. Such is true obviously also for divorced persons, whether living singly or in new relationships.

One of the Church's present deficiencies is its exclusionary posture toward those who have "failed" in the conventional arrangement of marriage and family and the conventional understanding (and avoidance) of sexuality has blinded us to present reality. The Church needs actively to include separating and divorced individuals and single parents.

The Church must take seriously that Jesus's teaching and manifesting of the Realm of God were concerned not with the formal arrangements of our lives but with our responsiveness to the vision of the Realm of God. Admittedly, this confronts all of us with a relativization of all personal, social and economic arrangements by which we live. We cannot live without structure in our relationships; but these structures are subject to continual correction by the image of the Realm of God. If the Church is to err it must err on the side of inclusiveness rather than exclusiveness.

Marriage has served as a stabilizing force in American society, channeling sexuality in socially acceptable directions, providing a structure for the procreation and nurturing of children, and enabling enduring companionship between a man and a woman by defining the legal and spiritual responsibilities of the married couple. Although marriage has taken many forms in human society, it has been a central, constant building block of human society in all cultures. The power of sexuality both to attract persons, and satisfy persons, and to disrupt the social order has been recognized in the practices, mythologies, and laws of all cultures.

Marriage has bound the family, clan, and tribe to customs and traditions which insure survival and identification of a people as a people. The church must consider the consequences of calling into question institutional relationships which have permitted the Church to flourish and survive. However, our contemporary consciousness of racial, sexual, and economic domination and exploitation has raised our culture's consciousness about some of the oppressive, repressive and exploitative dimensions of marriage and family arrangements. This heightened sensitivity, combined with a cultural ethos that favors self-fulfilment over the dutiful but self-abnegating adherence to conventional marriage and family arrangements has caused many to deny that life-long monogamous, heterosexual marriage is the sole legitimate structure for the satisfaction of our human need for sexuality and intimacy.

There are those who think that even though the forms have been enormously diverse, the pervasive human tendency to union with an individual of the opposite sex in a committed relationship and the universal presence of family structure in some form evidences something fundamental about the nature of the created human order itself. Biologically, this has been the only option for the perpetuation of the human race as we know it. While other arrangements may be appropriate to the given nature of particular individuals, monogamous, life-long marriage and family organization ought not to be thereby relativized as simply one option among others.

Given the Church's traditional view of the exclusive primacy of marriage and the nuclear family and the (relative) opprobrium with which the Church has viewed other options, the Church must learn how to continue to affirm the conventional without denigrating alternative sexual and family arrangements. Again, the criteria are the quality of the relationships and their potential for developing persons responsive to the Realm of God. The Church must find ways genuinely to affirm persons as they faithfully and responsibly choose and live out other modes of relationship.

We live after the Fall. The metaphor of the Realm of God reinforces the realization of brokenness and finitude in all our human arrangements and relationships. We sin daily in our self-deception, self-centredness, self-justification, and readiness to exploit and oppress others for our own material and emotional self-aggrandizement. And this is clearly seen in our readiness to interpret scripture and tradition to reinforce what we perceive as our own best interests so that we appear righteous and those who differ from us appear unrighteous.

The dynamic process of God's incarnational truth has brought us to a time in history when the critical consciousness made possible by modern forms of knowledge—including Biblical scholarship—enables us to see the Realm of God as a present reality relativizing all human knowledge and social arrangements. We are therefore suspicious of the invocation of tradition even while we believe that in God's ongoing creation not all relational arrangements are equally aligned with a caring God's purposes for humankind.

Those who believe that the heterosexual family unit headed by monogamous heterosexual partners offers the best possibility for the development of children who will become confident, loving, compassionate and creative adults must acknowledge the historical fallibility of the family in accomplishing such results. All sexual and family arrangements must be judged by the same criteria suggested by the metaphor of the Realm of God.

Ultimately, do couples (of whatever orientation) and families of (whatever constitution) exist for the sake of their own self-fulfilment? The Gospel does not support such an individualistic possibility. Nor does it support promiscuous behavior, which by its very nature uses the other person simply for one's self-aggrandizement, whether mere sexual release, as compensation for feelings of inadequacy or to express hostility. Theologically, patterns of sexual and family arrangements are to be judged according to the degree to which they reflect and contribute to the realization of the Realm of God. Since this is a dynamic not a static reality, continual diversity, exploration, experimentation, and discernment will mark the life of the faithful Church.

In the absence of set rules, great demands are thus placed on clergy and others who counsel persons regarding these issues. We believe that at the level of congregational life, the Church ought not focus its concern on this or that particular pattern. The Church's focus ought to be on persons as they seek to understand and order their lives and relationships. All relationships and arrangements are to be assessed in terms of their capacity to manifest marks of the Realm of God: healing, reconciliation, compassion, mutuality, concern for others both within and beyond one's immediate circle of intimacy.

V. Considerations Regarding the Three Alternate Patterns

As indicated in the Introduction, the Task Force decided to address specifically the Church's response to young adults who choose to live together unmarried, adults who never married or who are "post-marriage," due to divorce or the death of their spouse, and homosexual couples. We do not address the subject of adolescent sexuality, although we agree on the need for more thorough-going education of adolescents within the Church regarding sexuality and relationships.

We believe that certain questions of context are appropriate whenever persons consider beginning a sexual relationship: a) Will the relationship strengthen the pair for greater discipleship in the wider context? Will they be better enabled to love others? Will their relationship be a beneficial influence on those around them? b) Will the needs and values of others in the larger context be recognized and respected, especially the needs of their own children (if any), their parents, and their parish community? Since an ongoing sexual relationship between two persons occurs within a network of relationships to parents, children (perhaps adult children), colleagues, and fellow parishioners, such a relationship needs to be conducted with sensitivity to the possible emotional and relational effects on these other persons. c) what is the couple's intention regarding the procreation and/or raising of children?

Regarding the relationship itself, the following considerations are appropriate: a) The relationship should be life-enhancing for both partners and exploitative of neither. b) The relationship should be grounded in sexual fidelity and not involve promiscuity. c) The relationship should be founded on love and valued for the strengthening, joy, support and benefit of the couple and those to whom they are related.

A. *Young Adults*

One of the issues facing the Church in our time comes under the broad category of what used to be called ''pre-marital sex''. The issue for the Church to which attention is given in the following discussion is specifically defined as that of young adults of the opposite sex living together and in a sexual relationship without ecclesiastical or civil ceremony. (Of course, many young adults, for economic and social reasons share housing without having a sexual relationship. We do not address these relationships in what follows.)

From an historical perspective, such relationships are not unfamiliar to our culture. For many years common-law marriage had legal validity for purposes of property and inheritance settlements. Attitudes concerning careers, emotional and sexual commitments and intimacy, marital economics, and experiences (either through observation or background) all contribute to decisions concerning the form of relationship a man and a woman choose. In the contemporary world, young adults may live together to deepen their relationships, as a trial period prior to a commitment to marriage, or as a temporary or a permanent alternative to marriage.

In order to maintain the sacredness of the martial relationship in the sacrament of Holy Matrimony, The Church has generally been opposed to the actions of couples choosing to live together without ecclesiastical or civil ceremony. Opposition has been and is expressed both in direct statement and by silent tolerance. The effect of the opposition has been to separate those couples from the ministry of the Church, to the detriment of the quality of their relationship, of the spiritual growth of the individuals, of their involvement in the mutual ministry of the Church, of their contribution to the building up of the Christian community. Current research documents that persons living under these circumstances are less likely to profess an affiliation with an established religion or to attend church. And yet these persons might well benefit from a church affiliation.

To minister to or engage in ministry with those who choose to live together without marriage does not denigrate the institution of marriage and life-long commitments. Rather it is an effort to recognize and support those who choose, by virtue of the circumstances of their lives, not to marry but to live in alternative relationships enabling growth and love.

In a community in search, all benefit from mutual support and concern. Although living among persons of differing lifestyles can be threatening, it can provide those who have committed themselves to a lifelong relationship in marriage the opportunity to renew, to reform, to recreate their loyalties and vows in an atmosphere of alternative possibilities.

We emphasize that the Church's focus should be on persons as they seek to understand and order their lives and relationships. All relationships are to be assessed in terms of their capacity to manifest marks of the Realm of God: healing, reconciliation, compassion, mutuality, concern for others both within and beyond one's immediate circle of intimacy. Extending the image of the Church as a community of persons in search raises pastoral implications. A community in search seeks wisdom, understanding and truth in the experience and hopes of each of its members and from those (too often ignored) who choose not to participate in that community.

Both at the diocesan and congregational levels, the Church can actively engage in education and discussion on all issues of sexuality. Members of the congregation, persons from specific disciplines in the secular world, and persons who have in their own lives wrestled with pertinent issues can all be asked to participate in such efforts. Congregations should encourage open, caring conversation, leading to trust and mutual, supportive acceptance. This makes more credible the Church's claim to faithfulness to the Realm of God.

Persons who have been ignored or rejected by the Church's ministry, or who have assumed such rejection, can only be reached and loved by a community that witnesses in deed to its faith that God calls all people to new hopes, to new possibilities, by a community that knows it does not have all the answers and in which each member contributes to its growth and future wholeness in the Realm of God.

B. "Post-Married" Adults

Some mature persons, by life-long choice or because of divorce or the death of a spouse find themselves unmarried but desiring an intimate relationship. We affirm that there can be life-enhancing meaning and value for some adult single persons in sexual relationships other than marriage. Economic realities may militate against traditional marriage arrangements. For example Social Security payments are reduced for two individuals who marry; channeling inheritances for children can become legally expensive and complicated where re-marriage occurs; maintaining a one-person household is for many persons prohibitively costly.

The choice of celibacy or estrangement from the Church for such persons who choose not to marry is not consonant with the Church's hope of wholeness for all persons in the Realm of God. Our understanding of the Church is one of inclusiveness. As we struggle to understand what the Church is called to in our time, one of our goals is inclusion in the Christian body of persons who have thoughtfully chosen lifestyles different from that of the mainstream.

Because we are whole human beings, and not, in the last analysis, separate compartments of body and soul, therefore the spiritual, mental, emotional, physical and sexual aspects of our personalities are all to be nurtured and expressed in responsible ways if we are to continue to grow towards wholeness in our mature years. We are created sexual beings, and our spiritual health, no less than any other aspect of health, is therefore linked to sexuality. When therefore, mature single adults choose to celebrate their love and live their lives together outside of marriage, provided that they have considered and responded sensitively to the public and personal issues involved, we believe that their decision will indeed be blessed by God and can be affirmed as morally acceptable and responsible by the Church.

C. Homosexual Couples

Changing patterns of sexuality and family life confront pastors and congregations with new challenges and opportunities for understanding and for ministry. Rather than arguing about these issues we need first to listen to the experience of those who are most directly involved. Where homosexuality is concerned, fear, rejection, and avoidance by the heterosexual community is common and entrenched; we believe that pastors and congregations must meet members of the homosexual community person to person. The first step toward understanding and ministry is listening.

We need as much as is possible to bracket our judgments and listen to persons as they are. The Church needs to acknowledge that its historic tendency to view homosexual persons as homosexual rather than as persons has intensified the suffering of this 5%-10% of our population. A congregation's willingness to listen is a first step toward redeeming our homophobic past.

Listening is also a first step toward acknowledging that our own understanding needs ministry. Those of us fearful and angry regarding homosexuality need liberation, and this can only come through person to person communication. So the Church's response includes permitting itself to be ministered to by the homosexual community.

This process will help the Church recognize that whatever our historical experience, we encounter each other as we are with all our many limitations and potentialities. What we may become is a function of our open meeting of each other and of the reconciling, empowering spirit of God active in such open meeting.

Such person to person meeting, by means of open forums, small group discussions, and one to one conversations needs to be accompanied by the study of Biblical, historical, theological, and social scientific perspectives. Accurate information and informed opinion are important counterbalances to the fear and distortion which have so often inhibited the Church's ability to respond appropriately.

Listening opens the door of hospitality, which has so long been firmly shut. Such words as ministry and hospitality, however, still suggest a relationship of inequality, we and they. As such they perpetuate the image of the Church as separate from the homosexual community. In fact, however, we believe that the Church should be as inclusive of homosexual persons as it is of heterosexual persons. In this light, all the normal avenues of inclusion should be available to homosexual persons.

Criteria for membership, for participation in church committees, choirs, education, vestries, etc. and for ordination should be no different for any given group. Some persons express fear that including homosexual persons in the full round of church life will influence others—especially children—to become homosexual. In fact, we know of no evidence or experience to confirm that such association can bring about a homosexual orientation.

Ideally, homosexual couples would find within the community of the congregation the same recognition and affirmation which nurtures and sustains heterosexual couples in their relationship, including, where appropriate, liturgies which recognize and bless such relationships.

VI. Recommendations

Sexuality is an integral part of our God-given humanity. The Church must devote more attention to sexuality in its child, adolescent, and adult educational programming. As we understand more about the nature and meaning of our sexuality we will learn how to respond more appropriately to persons of many different circumstances.

Change in the Church's life is an ongoing process. We therefore urge education and discussion at all levels of diocesan life.

Specifically we recommend the following:

1. That all collegial groups such as the Commission on Ministry, the Newark Clergy Association, and all other regular commissions and committees of the diocese address these issues as they impact their areas of responsibility and concern.
2. That the March/April Clergy day, 1987, and the June, 1987 Religious Education Conference include sexuality among the issues to be considered.
3. That Congregations develop programs appropriate to their setting and circumstances which enable education and discussion regarding issues of sexuality and the Church's response to changing patterns of sexuality and family life. In addition to providing structured educational programs, the Church should be a community where persons can discuss their experience and clarify their self-understanding relationships and courses of action. We would urge congregations to provide space and time, for example, for parent groups whose children are gay or lesbian and who want to discuss the implication of this for their own lives. Likewise, gay and lesbian couples may want to meet with each other or non-gays for support and friendship.
4. That Convocations support and perhaps sponsor such programs as suggested above.
5. That a group similar to this Task Force be established to facilitate discussion at the congregational level, to monitor the process, and to report to the Diocesan Convention of 1988, perhaps with recommendations or resolutions.

Notes: *Few documents on the current debates concerning sexuality in general and homosexuality in particular stirred as much controversy as this report prepared by the Diocese of Newark (New Jersey) of the Episcopal Church. In January 1985, the diocesan convention mandated a task force to prepare a study of nontraditional patterns of sexual behavior and organization of family units; homosexuals were one group targeted for* *consideration. During its two years of work, the task force involved a number of the diocese's congregations in a process of study and discussion of the issues.*

The report has its base in historical and cultural studies and supports a general approach of cultural relativism. Families have followed a variety of patterns. The report also approaches the Bible as a set of documents at the fountainhead of Christian tradition rather than a book of moral rules to be slavishly followed. It calls for the establishment to make a contemporary, creative, and appropriate response to homosexual couples, and calls for the church to accept and affirm such relationships.

This report stands on the extreme liberal wing of Protestantism. Its specific recommendations have found some support among Episcopalians, but have not won approval from the Episcopal church as a whole.

EPISCOPAL CHURCH

RESOLUTION ON THE REPORT OF THE TASK FORCE ON CHANGING PATTERNS OF SEXUALITY AND FAMILY LIFE (1987)

BE IT RESOLVED:

That the 113th Convention of the Diocese of Newark receives with great appreciation the report of the Task Force on Changing Patterns of Sexuality and Family Life, prepared at the request of the 111th Convention.

BE IT FURTHER RESOLVED:

That the Task Force enable an educational process for congregations, convocations, and the Diocese as a whole, utilizing resource persons and a study guide to be prepared that fairly represents the theological diversity among the people of God within this diocese.

AND BE IT FURTHER RESOLVED:

That the Task Force collect and monitor the responses to this diocesan-wide process and present specific recommendations and resolutions to the Diocesan Convention of 1988.

Notes: *The 1987 convention of the Episcopal Church's Diocese of Newark received one of the most controversial reports on human sexuality to appear during the decade. It recognized the existence of practicing homosexuals and called for their inclusion in the life of the church, especially homosexual couples. This document, which was designed to implement the findings of the report, calls for the inclusion of practicing homosexuals in the church's congregational life. It was passed by a substantial majority of both clergy and lay delegates. While much more open to homosexuals than the Episcopal Church nationally, the position of the diocese has been allowed to stand without punitive action by the national church.*

EPISCOPAL CHURCH

STATEMENT ON HOMOSEXUALITY (1988)

We, the undersigned, Bishops in the Church of God, wish to endorse and affirm the November 1987 resolution of the General Synod of the Church of England on the subject of human sexuality which stated that:

This Synod affirms that the biblical and traditional teaching on chastity and fidelity in personal relationships is a response to an expression of God's love for each of us, and in particular affirms:

1. that sexual intercourse is an act of total commitment which belongs properly within a permanent marriage relationship;

2. that fornication and adultery are sins against this idea, and are to be met by a call to repentance and the exercise of compassion;

3. that homosexual acts also fall short of this idea, and are likewise to be met by a call to repentance and the exercise of compassion;

4. that all Christians are called to be exemplary in all spheres of morality, including sexual morality, and that holiness of life is particularly required for Christian leaders.

Alex D. Dickson
Gordon T. Charlton
Harry W. Shipps
Maurice M. Benitez
C. Fitzsimons Allison
John H. MacNaughton
C. Brinkley Morton
James B. Brown
Clarence C. Pope, Jr.
Alden Hathaway
Charles F. Duvall
Gerald N. McAllister
B. Merino, Colombia
William C. Wantland
Donald M. Hulstrand
David B. Reed
Bob G. Jones
John Joseph Meakin Harte
John L. Thompson
Francis C. Gray
Robert O. Miller
Edward H. MacBurney
Earl N. McArthur
Donis D. Patterson, Dallas
Donald J. Parsons
Robert M. Moody
Edward Haynsworth
David S. Ball
A. Carral
John F. Ashby
William G. R. Sheridan
Don A. Wimberly
Howard S. Meeks
Alexander D. Stewart
A. Donald Davies
Robert H. Cochrane
William L. Stevens
Victor M. Rivera
Scott Field Bailey
Charles I. Jones
Robert M. Wolterstorff
David S. Rose
Jose Saucedo
Herbert D. Edmondson
Roger J. White
Joseph T. Heistand
William C. Frey
L. Garnier
Stanley Atkins
Robert L. Ladehoff
Duncan M. Gray, Jr.
Robert C. Witcher

Notes: *In 1988, a number of bishops in the Episcopal Church reacted to their colleagues signing a statement which essentially approved the ordination of homosexuals. Instead of approving that statement, the bishops affirmed a 1987 resolution of the General Synod of the Church of England which limited sexual activity to marriage. While this statement against homosexual relations is the majority opinion at present, the minority opinion has strong support.*

EPISCOPAL CHURCH

RESOLUTION ON VIOLENCE AGAINST HOMOSEXUALS (1988)

Resolved, the House of Deputies concurring, that this 69th General Convention decries the increase of violence against homosexual persons and calls upon law enforcement officials across the land to be sensitive to this peril and to prosecute the perpetrators of these acts to the fullest extent of the law; and be it further

Resolved, That the Executive Council be directed to communicate with the Attorney General of the United States, and the Attorney Generals of the several states the expressed wishes of the General Convention that such violence be decreased markedly; and be it further

Resolved, That all Bishops, and especially the Presiding Bishop, be encouraged to speak openly and publicly to repudiate the misconception that the Church encourages such violence, and to counter the public declarations of those who claim that AIDS is the punishment of God upon homosexual persons; and be it further

Resolved, That the actions of the 65th General Convention, which declared that ''. . . homosexual persons are children of God who have a full and equal claim with all others upon the love, acceptance, and pastoral concern and care of the Church'' be re-emphasised to all members of this Church.

Notes: *At its 1988 general convention, the Episcopal Church passed a number of resolutions supporting the homosexual community. This resolution opposes acts of violence against homosexuals, particularly acts committed because of the perceived connection between homosexuality and AIDS.*

EPISCOPAL CHURCH

RESOLUTION COMMENDING STUDY OF HUMAN SEXUALITY (1988)

Resolved, the House of Deputies concurring, that this 69th General Convention thank the Standing Commission on Human Affairs and Health for their work in the areas of human sexuality, and especially homosexuality, during the past triennium; and be it further

Resolved, That the Standing Commission on Human Affairs and Health be asked to continue their work; and be it further

Resolved, That on every question, the Commission consult with and/or coopt persons who have a special interest and/or expertise in the question under discussion.

Notes: *This resolution, one of several passed at the church's 1988 general convention, states the church's support of a study completed by its Standing Commission on Human Affairs and Health, which has responsibility for issues of human sexuality.*

EPISCOPAL CHURCH

RESOLUTION ON DIALOGUE ON HUMAN SEXUALITY (1988)

Resolved, the House of Deputies concurring, that this 69th General Convention affirm that the Biblical and traditional teaching on chastity and fidelity in personal relationships is a response to, and an expression of, God's love for each one of us; and that all Christians are called to be exemplary in all spheres of morality, including sexual morality; and that holiness in life is particularly required of Christian leaders. In this context, be it further

Resolved, That this Convention, responsive to the call of the Standing Commission on Human Affairs and Health ''to find a non-judgemental occasion to listen and talk,'' and in the spirit of the Presiding Bishop's statement that ''there will be no outcasts in this Church,'' strongly urge each diocese and congregation to provide opportunities for open dialogue on human sexuality, in which we, as members of this Church, both heterosexual and homosexual, may study, pray, listen to and share our convictions and concerns, our search for stable, loving and committed relationships, and our journey toward wholeness and holiness, and be it further

Resolved, That the accepted sources of authority for Christians, namely Scripture, tradition, reason and experience, supplemented by the 1976, 1979, 1982 and 1985 statements from the General Convention on human sexuality, the resolution adopted by the General Synod of the Church of England in November, 1987, and the 1988 report of the Standing Commission on Human Affairs and Health, and ongoing scientific research be commended for use in this dialogue; and be it further

Resolved, that each diocese report its findings and experiences to the Standing Commission on Human Affairs and Health no later than December 1990 and that the Standing Commission evaluate the reports and produce a composite report for presentation to the 70th General Convention.

Notes: *Among those who hope for change in traditional attitudes concerning homosexuality, providing the context in which new information and perspectives can be shared and discussed is of vital importance. Such discussions have traditionally led to a liberalizing of the views of those who participate. With no mention of any prior agenda concerning homosexuality, the Episcopal Church used this statement to call for a broad discussion of homosexual issues.*

EPISCOPAL CHURCH

RESOLUTION ON SUICIDE AMONG GAY AND LESBIAN YOUTH (1988)

Resolved, the House of Deputies concurring, That this 69th General Convention of the Episcopal Church recognize with love and compassion the tragic suffering of gay and lesbian youth and the loss of life of these children and others who felt compelled to end their lives; and be it further

Resolved, That this Episcopal Church pledge pastoral support of troubled youth, including exploration of the root causes of why many gay and lesbian children are driven to suicide; and be it further

Resolved, That the Youth Ministries Office of the Education for Mission and Ministry Unit be requested to include in their present resources information on the diverse dimensions of suicide, including gay and lesbian, for distribution to dioceses and congregations throughout the Church.

Notes: *This resolution, one of several passed at the 1988 general convention of the Episcopal Church, raised the issue of suicide among homosexual youth due to their alienation from society and a resulting sense of hopelessness.*

EVANGELICAL CONGREGATIONAL CHURCH

STATEMENT ON HOMOSEXUALITY (1983)

Homosexuality was the sin of Sodom for which that city was destroyed (Genesis 19), and is uniformly seen as a perversion of sex in the New Testament (Romans 1:26-27; Colossians 3:5). Therefore a homosexual relationship is not acceptable as an alternative life-style, and any homosexual act, even between consenting adults is a violation of the Biblical ethic.

Notes: *This brief statement from the 1983 edition of* The Creed, Ritual and Discipline of the

Evangelical Congregational Church *is a concise restatement of the conservative Protestant position.*

EVANGELICAL FREE CHURCH OF AMERICA

HOMOSEXUALITY, A CHRISTIAN EVALUATION AND RESPONSE (1978)

Introduction

The phenomenon of homosexual behavior has increased so drastically in visibility during the last decade that it now confronts every institution of society, religious and secular, with new and substantial problems. It would seem that a certain amount of homosexual behavior has always existed among human beings. Because of the fact that statistical evaluations of such behavior have been developed only in recent decades, and because, until recently, the accuracy of such statistics has been open to doubt, it is extremely difficult to demonstrate that there has been a marked increase in homosexual behavior in our day. There can be no doubt, however, that homosexuality is much more publicly displayed in our day than at any time since pagan antiquity. It seems reasonable to assume that the tremendous increase in public visibility reflects something more than greater openness, namely a corresponding increase in the practice.

For Christians concerned with a theology of history, i.e. with discerning the hand of God in history, it is important to know, not merely that homosexual conduct has been noted since the days of Lot (Genesis 19), but that at certain times it has proliferated (cf. Romans 1:24-27). If it is indeed proliferating in our own day, and in our own society, it may well be under precisely the same circumstances and for the same reasons as those described by Paul in Romans 1: widespread public and private refusal to acknowledge God and to be thankful to Him. If this is the case, then the proliferation of homosexuality represents not an "alternate life style," nor even merely the symptom of a psychological disorder, but the result of spiritual and moral confusion visited upon society by God as part of His judgment for society's ingratitude and lack of reverence towards Him.

For this reason it is necessary to note that our pastoral concern for homosexual persons and our attempt to minister to them the word of reconciliation, while essential, may not blind us to the fact that homosexual practice is not merely offensive to God as all sin is, but specifically cries out to Him for judgment upon society (Genesis 18:20). Hence our concern for the individual homosexual in his predicament must be paralleled by a concern for the future of society as it may develop under his influence. From a Christian perspective, homosexuality cannot be called a "victimless crime." First of all, of course, the practitioners themselves are its victims, in that they thereby incur guilt in the sight of God; in addition, society as a whole suffers great consequences when this "private" practice becomes widespread and even public.

Although homosexual practice has been documented since antiquity, no society has ever treated it as equally acceptable with heterosexuality.[1] Historically, almost all social and educational material from every society has been opposed to homosexuality and has exalted heterosexuality, especially in the context of marriage and the family. If society today begins to treat homosexuality as an acceptable "alternate life style," it may contribute greatly to the increase of a practice that is odious in God's sight and harmful to society. It would be misguided and wrong for the church to contribute to such a fearful development. If this seems severe and condemnatory, we must consider the fact that it does reflect the intense seriousness of the Bible's condemnation of the practice. While it should be our endeavor as Christians to speak the truth in love to sinners, indeed to all men, it would be untruthful to gloss over the intensity of the reproach brought by the Scripture to homosexual conduct.

Hence it must be the concern of congregations, ministers of the Word of God, and individual Christians to avoid promoting or appearing to condone the spread of homosexuality, even while endeavoring to show the greatest compassion and most effective witness to the homosexual.

Even Plato, although a citizen of a society in which homosexuality appears to have been tolerated or even esteemed, warns of the need to "take precautions against the unnatural loves of either sex, from which innumerable evils have come upon individuals and cities."[2]

It certainly behooves Christians of our day to be at least as circumspect as that ancient philosopher. For this reason we should beware of attempting to create a total separation between the moral-theological issue, as it relates to personal standards of behavior, qualifications for church membership, and suitability for various occupations including the ministry, and the social-political issue, as it relates to laws and public policies. The two, as Plato indicates, are and will remain interwoven.

The Scriptural Attitude Towards Homosexuality

In view of the fact that God ordained sexual reproduction prior to the fall of man (Genesis 1:28), we have no difficulty in acknowledging human sexuality as a good gift of God. At the same time, we recognize that it is a gift to be used and enjoyed within the framework of God's plan, within a life-long relationship between married people (cf. e.g. Ecclesiastes 9:9). While married love is exalted and even described in suggestive poetic imagery in the Song of Solomon, extramarital sexual relations are universally condemned in the Scriptures. Adultery ranks close to murder in the Bible as an affront to our covenant God and is frequently used as a metaphor for idolatry.

In this context, recognize that while heterosexual relations are good within marriage and condemned outside it, there is no similar gradation with respect to homosexual practices. On every occasion when they are mentioned in Scripture, whether as the sign of the social degeneracy of a particular town (Genesis 19), as connected with pagan cult worship (e.g. I Kings 14:24), or as part of what we might call in modern parlance a "swinging life-style" (Romans 1:24-28), homosexual acts are unequivocally condemned. It was then and is now symbolic of low moral state. It is true, and should be stressed, that those who have sinned through homosexuality can, like other sinners, be "washed, sanctified, and justified" and become part of the congregation of God's people (I Corinthians 6:11). There is nevertheless no possible way on scriptural grounds to approve or condone the practice.[3]

In view of the loathing with which many heterosexuals look upon homosexual acts and individuals, it is important to place the scriptural condemnation of homosexuality in the Bible's own perspective, which we see in I Corinthians 6:9-11. There it is placed in context with fornication, effeminacy, robbery, covetousness, drunkenness, contemptuousness, and extortion as a practice that bars its devotees from the kingdom of God, but—and this is crucial to communicate—does not bar a penitent from cleansing, sanctification, and justification. Christians should certainly try to avoid the attitude coming to be called "homophobia" (literally, fear of the same, but now used to mean hatred of homosexuals). On the other hand, it is hardly correct to say, as some misguided Christians have done, that homophobia rather than homosexuality is the great moral failing.

Homosexual Conduct and Homosexual Orientation

In recent times, some Christian leaders have argued for the acceptance of certain homosexual behavior on the grounds that it is "natural" for those who have a basic homosexual orientation. This argument derives from Paul's use of the term "unnatural" in his discussion of homosexual behavior in Romans 1:26-27, which, in this view, is to be understood as promiscuous homosexuality, i.e. homosexual behavior outside the context of loving and committed relationships. Advocates of this position argue that the Bible really does not discuss homosexual orientation, an understanding of which would alter our interpretation of homosexuality. Following this line of thought, when an individual whose sexual orientation is homosexual, engages in homosexual behavior in the context of a loving, committed relationship, it is ''natural'' and calls for our Christian approval.

It is true that the Bible does not distinguish between homosexual orientation and homosexual behavior, a distinction which is helpful to clarify. First, it is important to understand the idea of sexual *orientation*. This has to do with one's basis sexual identity, whether heterosexual *or* homosexual. The fact is that some individuals have an orientation toward members of their own sex which is as powerful for them as orientation toward members of the opposite sex is for others. At the present, explanations of how this orientation is caused are indeterminate; they range from the idea that sexual orientation is ''constitutional,'' i.e. genetic, to the idea that it is learned in the very subtle psycho-sexual development of the first few years of life. Most recent explanations lean toward the latter view, but in any case the reality and dynamics of a basic sexual orientation is widely acknowledged.

How does this affect the Biblical view? It must be remembered that the Bible condemns immoral sexual acts, not sexual orientation. It categorically prohibits all homosexual activity under any circumstances, and all heterosexual activity outside the bonds of marriage. What is at issue is not orientation since as is obviously evident in heterosexuality, the basic orientation does not fall under the censure of Scripture, but only immoral heterosexual acts.

This, of course, does not eliminate the Biblical distinction between sexual ''lust'' and sexual deed, or between motives and actions. Lust, which is to be distinguished from sexual orientation, involves an act of the mind which *entertains* immoral desire. Sexual orientation, on the other hand, involves basic sexual preference, i.e. whether one is homosexually or heterosexually inclined.

Since most people are heterosexually oriented, the scriptural condemnation of homosexual acts appears to be just even for those who claim no particular commitment to Biblical perspectives. But when the idea of a basic homosexual orientation is introduced into the discussion, the scriptural condemnation of homosexual behavior seems for man, even some Christians, to be unjustly harsh. It should be remembered, however, that the Bible is not insensitive to the tragic complexities of sin; it recognizes the impact of sin in its corporate and generational dimensions: ''The sins of the fathers are visited upon the children to the third and fourth generation. . . .'' (Exodus 20:5). Sin, as a root cause, works powerfully and subtly in human experience, and its influence touches every person. We are all subject to a variety of powerful orientations which have the potential for bringing forth sin. For each of us, including the homosexual person, the only hope is the marvelous grace of God.

Further, it is important to clarify that, while Scripture condemns homosexual behavior, it speaks with approval of deep affection between members of the same sex, even using the term ''love'' to describe such relationships (e.g. I Samuel 18:1-3). It is not the presence of such affection which is sinful, but its distortion into biblically prohibited conduct. Care must be taken not to give the impression that friendship between persons of the same sex should be avoided, or that such friendship implies either homosexual orientation or conduct.

And while Scripture does treat homosexuality in severe terms, it is nevertheless wrong to suggest that it is the ''unpardonable'' sin. Such an implication could easily result from the desire to avoid an attitude of indifference in light of the growing acceptance of homosexuality in society. Individual Christians and congregations must first of all be careful to represent the grace of God as the answer for this sin ''. . . for such were some of you'' (I Cor. 6:9-11), while at the same time examining their words and acts to avoid communicating any misconceptions about this important issue.

Homosexuality is a Legal Problem

Some Christians have argued that it is necessary to make a categorical distinction between biblical teachings as the standard for each Christian's life and as guidelines for society. In this light, they have argued that, while Christians should themselves shun the practice of homosexuality and bar practicing homosexuals from church office and even from communicant membership in their churches, they should permit or even urge the enactment of laws favorable to homosexual acts and persons. There seem to be two basic reasons behind such a view: (1) the contention that biblical values have no place in American law; (2) the contention that we as Christians enjoy the protection of our civil rights because minorities are protected under American law, and that we therefore ought to support the establishment of minority rights for all minorities, lest we imperil our own.

If it is a person's conduct that makes him a member of a "minority" the important factor is to consider his conduct, not his minority status.

Biblical values and American law. In the United States, thanks in no small measure to the influence of Oliver Wendell Holmes, law had tended more and more to reflect the momentary will of those with the power to make laws rather than any eternal principle. This corresponds to the cynical attitude of Thomas Hobbes in the seventeenth century: *Non veritas sed auctoritas facit legum* ("Authority, not truth, makes law").[4] According to the noted British legal scholar, Sir Norman Anderson, British and American law has tended to be "positive law," representing only the sovereign will (of ruler or people), not the law of God or natural law. But, he points out, "When a despotic government proceeds to enact and enforce laws which are both cruel and oppressive, men's minds instinctively turn to law of eternal validity by reference to which all positive law may be evaluated and judged."[5]

Prior to World War II, German legal scholars tended to stress positive law, free from any tutelage to religious or moral values. Since that time, however, German legal theory has returned in a large measure to the concept of natural law, and even divinely-sanctioned, God-given law.[6] If American laws are simply to reflect the will of the sovereign, in other words, the will of whoever is in power, then Christians have just as much right to make their will into law as anyone else. If, on the other hand, as Sir Norman Anderson indicates, men's minds instinctively seek "a law of eternal validity," then we as Christians should not hesitate to place that true law, the Law of God, in the marketplace of ideas and in the forum of public discussion.

Christians do not have the power, under our Constitution, to *impose* biblical values on the nation as a whole. Nevertheless, they do have the right to attempt to persuade others of the desirability of adopting such values. As Christians we clearly have this right, and the Scripture appears to make it a duty: "Knowing therefore the terror of the Lord, we persuade men" (II Corinthians 5:11). Paul is writing, in the context, of Christians as ambassadors, it is the duty of an ambassador to make known to others, not only his Sovereign's *offers,* but also his *wishes* and *requirements.*

As Christians, we should be careful not to accept the insinuation that if we so much as speak of our biblical values, we impose them on others. In a representative democracy such as ours, no values will be imposed unless the majority are persuaded that they are good. There is no reason for us to refrain from communicating our biblical values with our fellow-Americans—many of whom, as the Scripture teaches, are more or less clearly aware of them in their hearts before we enunciate them (cf. Romans 1:32, "knowing the judgment of God . . ."). If people will not heed us, that is their responsibility, but if we fail to share biblical values with them because of the misguided impression that we have no civil right to do so, that is our responsibility.

Minority rights and Christian rights. Before approaching the question of homosexual rights, it is necessary to make an important distinction, one unfortunately often overlooked, between "freedom rights" and "entitlement rights."[7] In some cases, homosexuals are demanding entitlement rights—the claim to jobs, housing, and the like—where the law does not accord them freedom rights, i.e. the right to engage in homosexual acts as they see fit. It would be very strange indeed to grant entitlement rights to groups of citizens engaged in conduct that violates existing laws, yet this is precisely what the homosexual community sought for, and obtained from, the Dade County, Florida, County Commission, until it was overruled by a popular referendum. Certainly entitlement rights cannot logically be granted unless and until freedom rights have been established. The usual argument for homosexual rights is based on the classification of homosexuals as a minority and runs something like this:

Major Premise: Society should protect the rights of minorities,

Minor Premise: Homosexuals are a minority,

Conclusion: Therefore society should protect the rights of homosexuals.

To the extent that Christians believe that they are entitled to rights only because they fit the category of "minority," some Christians feel that it is in their interest to defend all minority rights, even those of socially destructive groups such as homosexuals. To this contention we must respond with the observation that the syllogism itself is invalid because one of its terms is far too vague: minority. Society cannot be governed by the principle of "protecting minorities" unless it has a fairly clear idea what it means by "minority." Traditionally the term has applied to racial and religious minorities. But to apply it to any defined group that constitutes less than a majority of the population is clearly to broaden it to the point of making it unworkable. Homosexuals are a minority, but so are murderers, tax-collectors, rabbis, and opera stars. To the extent that one is a member of a minority by nature or even by religious persuasion (as in ethnic or religious minorities) it is reasonable to offer legal protection to him. To the extent that it is one's *conduct* that places him in a "minority" group, it will first be necessary to see whether the conduct is socially desirable or permissible before determining whether he should be entitled to protection. If American society ever reaches the point where the law is incapable of making a meaningful distinction between Christians and homosexuals as candidates for civil rights protection, then it will already have reached such a point of irrationality that no amount of constitutional protection for minorities will suffice to protect Christians from society's abuse.

Under these circumstances, the important thing for Christians to do as members of a free society is to help society identify and follow those eternal principles that should be reflected in human law. Christians should be a source of values clarification in American society, in this way functioning as biblical salt, and certainly not a source of values confusion.

While acknowledging that homosexual conduct is a sin, some Christians argue that in our secular society it should not be illegal, much as blasphemy is generally not illegal but comes under freedom of speech. Advocates of explicit protection for homosexuals that goes beyond existing general civil rights legislation are advocating special privilege for offenders against biblical standards, rather as though freedom of speech guarantees were explicitly expanded to protect the blasphemous, not merely from legal penalties, but from the effects in housing and employment that might result from popular disapproval of their conduct.

Many believe that in the area of homosexual rights, more concessions have already been made than are desirable. Homosexuals need not the misguided protection of society, but God's message of sin and forgiveness. To the extent that homosexual rights legislation might encourage the practice of homosexuality or give greater tranquility to the conscience of those engaged in it, Christians should be very cautious about endorsing it. Certainly we should not succumb to the mistaken notion that the rights of Christians in American society depends upon those of homosexuals or of any other arithmetical minority.[8] It is important for Christians, including ministers of the Word and individual Christian citizens to understand this issue clearly, particularly in view of the fact that, in terms of political logic, it is relatively straightforward. If we fail to see clearly here, other issues will press upon us even more difficult to resolve.

Christians should uphold both the specific provisions as well as the general principles of biblical morality. The laws of God are more righteous than any others (Deut. 4:8). If many or more non-Christian members of society choose to "decriminalize," i.e. make legal, or even to protect, conduct that the Bible condemns, Christians, finding themselves in the minority, may be obliged to submit and to accept the majority's decision, provided it does not oblige them to transgress or forbid them to obey God. It is not our Christian duty to demand legal enforcement of every biblical principle. However, Christians should always bear witness against evil conduct. We should be careful not even to appear to condone in others, because they are non-Christians, conduct which the Bible condemns. Christians should oppose legal and social harrassment and mistreatment of sinners—as indeed one would oppose mistreatment of those accused of crimes. But we should never willingly acquiesce in the enactment of laws that appear to create social approval and legal protection for homosexuality, but ought rather to oppose. Advocacy of homosexual conduct, like blasphemy and anti-religious propaganda, is already protected by laws regarding free speech. For the church or Christians to support or even remain neutral towards special, explicit protection for such advocacy, explicitly to insulate it from the ordinary social condemnation that follows such advocacy, is inappropriate. Our own civil right to preach the Gospel does not depend on a generalized, absolute right to freedom of speech, but on the explicit constitutional guarantees of free exercise of religion.

The Church's Ministry

The church must be very sensitive and sensible in its approach to the homosexual situation as it continues to become more prominent and open in our society, particularly through the media coverage in addition to speaking out in the public form. There are several things the church can do in ministry to homosexual persons:

1. First of all, while we endeavor to be sensitive and compassionate to the individuals concerned, we must recognize that scripture deals with homosexuality as a sin, at the same time we must be careful not to treat it as an unpardonable sin.
2. We must acknowledge that we are all sinners, just as are homosexuals, recognizing that Scripture says, "for such were some of you" (I Cor. 6:9).
3. We need to declare that God in His grace is able to deal with this sin in the life of the individual and to bring cleansing and forgiveness.
4. A spirit of love and compassion toward the individual caught in this web must be shown by the proclamation of the truth that God is able and willing to cleanse and forgive (I John 2:2).
5. The local church must endeavor to develop within itself people of compassion who will dedicate themselves to helping, in a non-condemnatory way, those individuals caught in this sin to gain victory over sin in their lives. Such people must be carefully chosen for spiritual maturity, a good self understanding, and a wholesome outlook of life.
6. We must endeavor to integrate these cleansed and forgiven individuals into full fellowship of the church.

If we are able to accomplish these things in a gracious and loving way, we may find many sinners turning to the church, recognizing that it is truly a caring and loving community.

Footnotes

1. Cameron Paul, "A Case Against Homosexuality," *Human Life Review,* Vol. IV., No. 3 (Summer, 1978), pp. 31-35.
2. Plato, *The Laws,* VIII, 836. Although Plato is reputed to have engaged in homosexuality himself, in his writings he consistently argues against it; love and esteem between members of the same sex was exalted as long as it did not result in overt homosexual behavior; this is "platonic" love.
3. See Clarence Williams Landis's excellent article, "Homosexuality from a Biblical Perspective," in *Trinity Journal,* Vol. VI, No. 1 (Spring, 1977).

4. Hobbes, Thomas, *Leviathan* (Latin ed., Longon, 1670), Pt. III, c. 26.
5. Anderson, Sir Norman, *Morality, Law and Grace,* Inter-Varsity Press, Downers Grove, 1973, p. 65.
6. See the discussion by Edgar Bodenheimer, "Significant Developments in German Legal Philosophy since 1945," in *American Journal of Comparative Law,* Vol. III, No. 3 (July, 1954), pp. 379-396.
7. Bahnsen, Greg L., *Homosexuality, A Biblical View,* Baker, Grand Rapids, 1978, offers a very helpful analysis of this question, pp. 99-105.
8. Of course, if we are speaking of a genuine ethnic or religious minority, the situation is different. When the rights of Jews, or blacks, or Jehovah's Witnesses, are threatened, then the rights of Christians are also imperiled. But the same is not true of every numerical minority.

Notes: *In one of the strongest statements against the practice of homosexuality, the Evangelical Free Church of America admonishes all ministers and members into active opposition to homosexuality. It specifically directs members to avoid any activity that might legitimize homosexual behavior.*

EVANGELICAL LUTHERAN CHURCH IN AMERICA

SEX, MARRIAGE, AND FAMILY (1970)

Sex, marriage, and family are gifts of God in which to rejoice. Their essential goodness cannot be obscured by any crisis of our time.

As traditional moral codes are being challenged, there is a profound struggle to formulate bases of ethical judgment which have meaning for contemporary men and women. Powerful forces of social change, joined with discoveries in the medical and life sciences, influence all aspects of human existence. The church is concerned not only with specific issues and controversies, but with the basic Christian understanding of human sexuality.

Human Sexuality

Who are we? We are responsible persons made in the image of God. God created male and female, making sexual interdependence serve the divine intention for life-in-community. Scripture portrays us as relational beings whose true humanity is realized in faith and love with God and neighbor.

True humanity is violated by sin, which is our broken relationship with God and each other. This alienation expresses itself in all facets of life, including sex, marriage, and family. At the same time God works in these broken relationships, healing and freeing the forgiven to devote their efforts to the well-being of others.

Human sexuality is a gift of God for the expression of love and the generation of life. As with every good gift, it is subject to abuses which cause suffering and debasement. In the expression of human sexuality, it is the integrity of our relationships which determines the meaning of our actions. We do not merely have sexual relations; we demonstrate our true humanity in personal relationships, the most intimate of which are sexual.

Some Current Issues

The following statements are not to be thought of as categorical laws or "Christian" solutions to the problems involved. Nor are they intended to furnish easy answers to hard questions. They are offered as guidance to pastors and laity in their ethical decision-making.

1. Some Issues Related to Sexual Expression

Within the realm of human sexuality, intercourse is a joyful means of giving oneself in the mutual expression of love. It is within the permanent covenant of marital fidelity that the full potential of coitus to foster genuine intimacy, personal growth, and the responsible conception of children is realized.

Because the Lutheran Church in America holds that sexual intercourse outside the context of the marriage union is morally wrong, nothing in this statement on "Sex, Marriage, and Family" is to be interpreted as meaning that this church either condones or approves premarital or extra-marital sexual intercourse.

Scientific research has not been able to provide conclusive evidence regarding the causes of homosexuality. Nevertheless, homosexuality is viewed biblically as a departure from the heterosexual structure of God's creation. Persons who engage in homosexual behavior are sinners only as are all other persons—alienated from God and neighbor. However, they are often the special and undeserving victims of prejudice and discrimination in law, law enforcement, cultural mores, and congregational life. In relation to this area of concern, the sexual behavior of freely consenting adults in private is not an appropriate subject for legislation or police action. It is essential to see such persons as entitled to understanding and justice in church and community.

Sexual exploitation in any situation, either personally or commercially, inside or outside legally contracted marriage, is sinful because it is destructive of God's good gift and human integrity.

The church recognizes the effects of social environment and cultural traditions on human behavior. It seeks, therefore, to respond understandingly to persons who enter into relationships which do not demonstrate a covenant of fidelity.

Notes: *The Evangelical Lutheran Church in America was created by a merger on January 1, 1988, of the American Lutheran Church, the Lutheran Church in America, and the Association of Evangelical Lutheran Churches. Until the new church is able to reconsider its position on particular social issues, it has republished and circulated statements previously issued by its constituent bodies. In 1970, the Lutheran Church in America issued this relatively mild statement. It noted that homosexual practice was a departure from the heterosexual norm, but did not single it out as especially sinful. It also called for an end to homophobia and demanded justice for homosexuals in the civil realm.*

The statement initiated denomination-wide discussion of the issue.

EVANGELICAL LUTHERAN CHURCH IN AMERICA

STATEMENT ON HOMOSEXUALITY (1977)

1. Advocates for public acceptance of homosexual behavior currently gain wide coverage on television, radio, the printed page, the stage, and motion pictures. These advocates appeal to the American traditions of tolerance and fair play. They build on the foundations of public acceptance for such movements as human rights, racial equality, women's liberation, and sexual freedom.

2. The homosexual community presses for an end to barriers and discrimination in education, employment, housing, and civil liberties. It wants repeal of laws limiting the private behavior of consenting adults. It wants recognition and acceptance of its values as co-equal with those of the dominant heterosexual world. Some of its members want the right to marry, receiving joint income tax benefits, property ownership and transfer rights, the right to adopt children, and other protections equal to those given the usual man/woman marriage.

3. This pressure forces review of prevailing attitudes and actions toward practicing homosexuals and toward homosexuality in general. Society as a whole is challenged to rethink its laws and their enforcement, its customs and traditions, and its myths and stereotypes about men and women who seek love and companionship primarily from persons of their own sex. The American Lutheran Church, too, is called upon to re-examine its own teachings and practices, doing so in the light of its understanding of the whole of the Scriptures.

4. The church need not be caught up in the conflicting theories as to how widespread homosexuality is, the factors which cause or foster homosexuality, and whether it is an illness, an arrested stage of sexual development, a form of deviant behavior, or a sexual expression of human nature. These are matters for the various scientific disciplines to debate and resolve. The church, however, is concerned that some human beings created in God's image are involved in homosexual behavior, that many people are hurting because of their own homosexuality or that of a loved one, and that the Scriptures speak to the entire issue.

5. Among major passages of Scripture relevant to the issue of homosexuality are: Genesis 1:27; Genesis 2:18-24; Genesis 18:16-19:29; Leviticus 18:22 and 20:13; Judges 19:1-30; Matthew 19:4-6; Romans 1:24-32; Romans 3:21-26; Romans 6:1-11; I Corinthians 6:9-10; and I Timothy 1:10. We recognize that persons of differing theological traditions interpret differently the meaning and intent of any or all of these passages. Nevertheless, we believe that taken as a whole the message of Scripture clearly is that:

   a. Homosexual behavior is sin, a form of idolatry, a breaking of the natural order that unites members of the human community;

   b. Homosexual behavior is contrary to the new life in Christ, a denial of the responsible freedom and service into which we are called through baptism;

   c. God offers the homosexual person, as every other person, a vision of the wholeness He intends, the assurance of His grace, and His healing and restoration for the hurting and broken.

6. We realize that this is a restatement of the traditional Christian position. For this we make no apology. We believe it unwise to reject our heritage of teaching and practice unless compelling reasons so direct. We find none such. We choose not to yield to the spirit of the times.

7. Nevertheless, we recognize the cries of our homosexual brothers and sisters for justice in the arena of civil affairs. We cannot endorse their call for legalizing homosexual marriage. Nor can we endorse their conviction that homosexual behavior is simply another form of acceptable expression of natural erotic or libidinous drives. We can, however, endorse their position that their sexual orientation in and of itself should not be a cause for denying them their civil liberties. They as well as we uphold standards of public decency, protection of the young, the weak, and the dependent, and efforts to end entrapment, exploitation, and oppression. They, too, need recognition and acceptance of themselves as human beings, participating and contributing members of the community.

8. It is in our congregations that our homosexual brothers and sisters—and their loved ones—best should find this spirit of care, concern, and community. Their sexual orientation should not deprive them of their opportunities to hear the Word, to receive evangelical pastoral care and the renewing power of forgiveness, and to experience the understanding and the compassionate ministry of other members of the Body of Christ. Such care, concern, and community do not give sanction to homosexual behavior. They offer the love of God, the comfort and challenge of the Gospel, and the power of the Holy Spirit for ethical living sensitive to the person's own situation.

9. Members of our congregations may need to change their attitudes and actions toward the homosexual person. They may need to open channels of honest, two-way, communication. They may find that they are guilty of words and deeds that harden the homosexual community against the heterosexual world and against the compassionate Christ. Members of our congregations may need to be more understanding of and more sensitive to life as experienced by the homosexual person. They may need to take leadership roles in changing civil laws and practices that deny justice to and exploit homosexually involved persons. Their Christian commitment to truth, justice, and love prompts the whole of their responsive and responsible ministry to the brother or sister who may be homosexual as well as to every other sinner in the congregation.

Notes: *In 1977, the Office of Research and Analysis of the American Lutheran Church (a constituent part of the Evangelical Lutheran Church in America since 1988) issued a draft document on homosexuality. The document suggests that many of the issues of the public debate on homosexuality are irrelevant and that the church's primary concern is with homosexual behavior. The paper's position is traditional and conservative—homosexuality is a sin and is contrary to the Christian life, but God can heal the homosexual and make him/her whole.*

The document does address the issue of civil rights in a positive fashion, but denies the call to legitimize homosexual marriages. It offers full participation as members in the church, but does not discuss the possibility of ordination.

EVANGELICAL LUTHERAN CHURCH IN AMERICA

A PASTORAL LETTER: THE CHURCH AND THE HOMOSEXUAL PERSON (1978)

During the past several months much attention has been focused on the issue of civil rights and homosexuality. According to reports in the press, we will continue to hear much about it in the ensuing months.

It may be that here in Minnesota enough of the emotional overtones have subsided by now so that we can take a more measured and careful look at the issue. Because I have taken what some consider to be a controversial position on this question, you deserve to know the background out of which I came to certain conclusions.

Let me begin with several preliminary observations:

1. I do not pose as an expert on this subject. So much has been said and written about homosexuality in the past 3-5 years that one would have to devote a massive amount of time to achieve a comprehensive view. I share this pastoral letter in the hope that it will, first, stimulate you to study more extensively on your own and, second, that it will make you more sensitive to the need for understanding and pastoral care for those who struggle with their personal understanding of sexuality.
2. Those who cannot think of a homosexual person in any terms other than "pervert", "freak" and "sinner" will not find these pages helpful since what I have to say is aimed precisely at one of the most prejudicial attitudes to be found in our church and society today.
3. Contrariwise, those who look for complete acceptance of all forms of homosexual behavior will be equally disappointed. They will find this pastoral letter quite inconclusive. I simply am not ready to give final answers to questions as complex as those surrounding this issue.
4. The section of the paper devoted to biblical references to homosexuality will probably cause much discomfort for those who interpret these passages literally or who believe

that every scripture must bear equal weight in making applications to our contemporary world.

5. Because this is not intended to be a scholarly paper, I will not include footnotes to resources. Specific bibliographic references are available on request.

In what follows I will address myself to six areas that relate to homosexuality: history, biblical references, nature, the church, ordination and civil rights.

I. History

Historically, homosexuality has only recently come into the open as a subject for discussion and examination. Much has been written about the nature of homosexuality, but little has been written about its history. Those who have investigated the question historically are widely divided in their views. Let me cite just two authors who come out a opposite extremes.

Ruth Tiffany Barnhouse, a clinical assistant in psychiatry at Harvard Medical School and fellow of the American Psychiatric Association, argues that no stable culture has ever held homosexuality as an ideal. She insists that the homosexual apologists of the Greek Classical period actually rewrote the old lore, attributing homosexuality to the ancient gods and heroes. This was done only to justify their own behavior, says Barnhouse. In point of fact, homosexual behavior was never considered legal anywhere except in the city of Elis. Furthermore, the flourishing of homosexuality in ancient Greece came at a time when the position of women had deteriorated badly. Even Plato, often quoted in support of homosexual behavior, condemned it later in life as unnatural and degrading, writes Barnhouse.

Barnhouse traces this same pattern through Western cultures and concludes that the incidence of homosexuality has probably been rather constant at three to five percent of the male population. Citing Karlen, she maintains that the only time a society tolerates homosexual behavior is when there are special circumstances, such as war or imprisonment, which make heterosexual relationships difficult. If current attempts to declare homosexuality a normal alternate life style succeed, says Barnhouse, we will be the first human civilization to do so.

Dr. John Boswell comes with credentials as impressive as those of Barnhouse. A professor of history at Yale University, he has specialized in the study of minorities, including Blacks, females and Jews. In a forthcoming book he will argue, contrary to Barnhouse, that homosexual behavior was accepted as quite normal in many cultures in history. The Athenians, for example, assumed that the best soldiers and wisest rulers were homosexuals. Plato, says Boswell, took for granted that there are as many homosexuals as heterosexuals in his country.

Furthermore, says Boswell, the Greeks believed that if you loved someone of the opposite sex, you were in danger of becoming like them. Thus, for a male to become passionately in love with a female might make him effeminate and vice versa. To have a wife and produce children was a duty, but not necessarily an act of love.

Boswell traces this same pattern to the Romans where marriage to someone of the same gender was quite common. Fidelity to one's lover was expected, but the lover might be of the same sex. Highly developed mores were common, but they did not run along heterosexual/homosexual lines. In fact, says Boswell, homosexuality was so accepted that it is difficult to find clear terms to distinguish it from heterosexuality. A relationship of affection, love and commitment was paramount, regardless of the gender of one's partner.

Boswell's study includes Western cultures that came under the influence of Christianity. He claims that the general attitude of the church was not hostile until about the 13th century. Boswell says that homosexual behavior fell into disfavor during a time comparable to the McCarthy era in the United States. Jews, Turks and homosexual persons became the scapegoats for the ills of society. Because Jews and Turks could not hide their identity, they continued to be the objects of scorn in succeeding centuries. Homosexual persons, however, went underground and retreated into anonymity.

It was not until the last decade, says Boswell, that they have begun to emerge again. A specific incident initiated the change. At a gay bar in Greenwich Village in 1968 a group of homosexual persons decided they had had enough. Tired of being harrassed by police and hauled into court, they resisted arrest. Their action had a ripple effect in clandestine gay communities across the nation. There has been a decided turnabout in the willingness of homosexual persons to identify themselves. The result is that for the first time in many centuries we are having to deal with homosexual persons who have few problems uncommon to others, who do not necessarily end up on the psychiatrist's couch and who ask to be treated as normal, law-abiding, contributing members of society. This is not to say that homosexual persons do not have problems related to their sexuality. The fact that they are a minority in a society which does not understand their peculiar needs means that they face the difficulties of any unaccepted minority.

The evidence that we are unprepared to deal with out-of-the-closet homosexual persons is documented by the events in Dade County, St. Paul, Wichita and other places. All of this leads Boswell to conclude that contemporary Western culture is probably the most anti-homosexual—or "homophobic"—the world has seen to date.

Each of us would do well to try to acquaint ourselves with the history of the treatment of homosexual persons in order to better understand our own attitudes and prejudices.

II. Biblical References

What follows is a very preliminary and sketchy attempt to suggest ways of looking at some of the more common references.

Genesis 1 and 2 are a good place to begin. There are some ethicists who use these chapters to insist that the unitive and procreative elements must always be considered in a sexual relationship. That is to say, one cannot separate sex as re-creation and sex as procreation. The procreative purpose may rarely and possibly never be the first purpose of the sexual relationship, but it is always a part of the relationship even if only symbolically, says this school of thought.

As most of you know, the ALC Office of Research and Analysis issued a brief statement on "Homosexuality" some months ago which asserted, among other things, that Scripture treats homosexual behavior as "sin, a form of idolatry and a breaking of the natural order that unites members of the human community." The statement does not deal extensively with any specific passages. Nevertheless, Genesis 1 and 2 are implicit as background references, particularly with regard to the "natural order" allusion.

The Community of Christ, an ALC congregation in Washington, D.C., has developed a document of its own in which it questions the assumptions of the ALC paper based on Genesis 1 and 2. Do these chapters prove that God had in mind that heterosexuality should be normative for all human sexual relationships? Is being heterosexual what is meant by "the image of God?" Is it not true that the Genesis accounts are more concerned with telling the story of creation from the peculiar point of view of the early Israelites rather than setting standards for human sexuality? Set in a world where a plethora of gods and goddesses were all defined through sexual identities and where sexual acts were sacralized, the accent for the Israelites is first and foremost on the mutuality of sex, reads the statement from the Community of Christ.

It is difficult for me to conceive of the Genesis account, in and of itself, as being supportive of anything other than a heterosexual pattern for sexual relationships. It may be asserted that it does not exclude other relationships, but it seems to be stretching a point to say that it argues from silence. In other words, I do not see the Genesis texts as being germane to our current debate. We simply have to say that the text describes a male/female relationship in which both procreation and re-creation are essential to the development of the human family. We do not know whether the writers did or did not approve of homosexual relationships.

Genesis 1 and 2 raise other interesting questions. In the Roman Catholic tradition, how can celibacy be accorded the status of "gift"? It could be argued that celibacy defeats the "natural order" of Genesis 1 and 2, especially if it is deliberately chosen. In the Protestant tradition, we have affirmed the decision of a married couple to forego parenthood in order to serve in a setting where it would be difficult to raise a family.

Genesis 19, the Sodom account, often comes to mind because it is set before us in the form of a story. The people of this inhospitable city demand they be given Lot's guests, seemingly for sexual purposes. Lot, in order to defend his guests, offers his daughters—an interesting moral question in and of itself! At the urging of his guests, Lot and his family escape the cities before fire and brimstone consume them.

If we ask, "What was the sin of Sodom and Gomorrah?," it is common to hear a single answer: "Homosexual perversion." Biblical scholars are asking us to take a second look. For example, if we consider Sodom from the standpoint of subsequent references, we find no suggestion that homosexual acts were the essence of their sin. Instead, it is clear that lack of hospitality is seen as the basic issue. Neither Ezekiel nor Jesus (Ezekiel 16:48-50; Matthew 10:14-15; Luke 10:10-12) mention homosexuality in referring to Sodom and Gomorrah. Both cite inhospitality—a cardinal sin in that culture—as the primary allegation. If Jesus wanted to condemn homosexual acts, he did not choose to do so on this occasion.

Does it follow then that sexual perversion was not a part of Sodom's sin? Of course not. However, it is important to see that both heterosexual and homosexual perversion are involved and, further, that one cannot take either form of sexual behavior at Sodom and project it as a broadside against all subsequent sexual behavior. To put it more succinctly, Genesis 19 is not intended to be understood on the narrow grounds of sexuality.

Leviticus 18:22 and 20:13 need not occupy our attention to any large extent since they are part of the Levitical code designed specifically for Israel in its infancy. Attempts at ferreting out part of the code for contemporary application while ignoring other parts as archaic only confuse the matter. If one is to use a part of the Levitical code, one must begin by establishing principles of selection. Most such attempts will founder on the grounds of inconsistency. Furthermore, we who champion evangelicalism in its historic sense will hardly want to retreat to the Levitical code for our understanding of the Gospel.

In the Gospels there are no clear references to homosexuality. If Jesus had an opinion on the subject, he either did not express it or else the Gospel writers did not consider it of enough importance to preserve it for us.

To argue from this that Jesus approved homosexual behavior is, of course, ridiculous. We must simply agree that we do not know the mind of Christ on this matter. If we were to argue that Jesus did not wish to destroy "one jot or tittle" of the law, thus affirming the Levitical code, we would soon find ourselves embroiled once more in the question of which part of the Levitical code he upheld and which he did not. We have no choice but to let it rest.

Romans 1:26-27 condemns women and men who "exchange natural relations for unnatural" and who are "consumed with passion for one another. . . ." Some scholars remind us again to look at the context before we jump to conclusions about the text. The broader issue in Romans 1 is idolatry. Our primary relationship is to God. Even nature witnesses to the existence of God, argues Paul. When there is disorder in that vertical dimension, the horizontal dimension soon falls into chaos and we find ourselves in disharmony with others. That disharmony shows itself in perverted expressions of evil including "dishonorable passions . . . unnatural relations . . . wickedness, evil, coveteousness, malice . . . envy, murder, strife, deceit, malignity, etc." It can be seen that both here and again in I Corinthians 6, sexual perversion is grouped with a number of social sins.

How shall we understand Paul in these citations? McNeill, the Roman Catholic priest whose book caused much controversy in his church, cites one possibility. He suggests that the sexual sins Paul has in mind are those of a person who goes beyond his or her own sexual appetites—one's "natural inclination"—to indulgence in any and every form of sexual activity imaginable. It becomes a very deliberate choice of a behavior contrary to one's normal inclination as, for example, homosexual activity by one who is "normally" heterosexual.

To be quite candid, I find myself unable to accept this understanding of Paul's mind on this question. A few scholars are even trying to convince us that the translation is false, that the Greek, if understood more precisely, does not refer to homosexual behavior at all. But until there is more evidence to the contrary from a larger body of responsible exegetes, I will continue to understand Paul to mean that homosexual acts, along with numerous other social sins, are contrary to God's intended order for believers and unbelievers alike.

This then settles the issue, does it not? If one believes that Paul includes homosexual behavior in a catalogue of sins, it is also safe for us to condemn it. Right? Wrong! Or at least we must say, "Not necessarily."

Even a strict fundamentalist—though he or she may not admit it—does not take the Bible literally. In spite of the New Testament position on divorce, for example, we have come to understand that an evangelical interpretation of the Gospel, coupled with an appreciation for a society far more complex than that of first century Palestine, may allow for exceptions. While we still take the vows seriously and invite a man and woman to pledge fidelity "till death do us part," we nevertheless acknowledge that it is sometimes in the best interests of all concerned if there is a separation and a severing of the bond.

The same can be said for the role of women. Again, even fundamentalists look past Paul's insistence that no woman teach or have authority over men. For example, they invite Anita Bryant, a woman without formal biblical training, to speak freely on a question that has deep biblical and religious roots! For us, the role of women should pose no great problem because we recognize, first, that Paul had a higher ideal—"there is neither male nor female"—and, further, that opportunities for education afforded women today make them as effective as men for teaching and other ministries.

What is the point of these two illustrations? It is simply to open your mind to the possibility that homosexuality may also need a new look in view of what we are learning about its nature. We may all reject the form of homosexual behavior condemned by Paul in Romans and I Corinthians. We may join him in declaring that all forms of selfish, irresponsible and hedonistic sexual behavior by a heterosexual or a homosexual person are alien to God's intended purpose for sex.

But this does not deliver us from the need to look at homosexuality from a more comprehensive vantage point. Just as we acknowledge that added knowledge and a changed social order have altered our view of divorce and the role of women, so we may have to take a new look at homosexuality. In order to do so, we will have to call upon the deeper currents of the gospel as well as our evangelical tradition.

There may be some who cannot accept the possibility of a reconsideration of homosexuality. For them, it may be well to recall that the ethical prescriptions of the New Testament are drawn from a wide variety of sources, including the Old Testament, the teachings of Jesus, first century Judaism, Hellenistic moral codes, and the experience of the early church. Unlike the Pharisees, Christians do not (or should not) compile a list of New Testament commandments comparable to the 613 rules of the Torah, all held to be forever binding. The New Testament foundation for ethics is agape. We live with a freedom which allows us to reexamine a particular issue with the possibility that the Spirit of God may lead us to a new or different understanding of that issue.

As I forewarned you in the introduction, those who tend to biblical literalism will of necessity have to part company at this juncture. If every passage of Scripture is thought to have equal application for Christian ethics, there is no room for further discussion. But for those who accept the fact that all of life stands under both judgment and grace and that the Spirit continues to work in the Church to help us understand the mind of Christ, there is room for exploration and new insight.

With that in mind, we can proceed to a discussion of the nature of homosexuality.

III. The Nature of Homosexuality

More than twenty years ago Alfred Kinsey shocked us with his reports about sexual behavior. His research suggested that 50% of males and 60% of females are exclusively heterosexual. The balance of his subjects ranged on a scale from primarily heterosexual to exclusively homosexual. He found that more than half of all males had some kind of homosexual experience during childhood and youth.

Though they have been doubted and, at times, ridiculed, the findings of Kinsey have been surprisingly durable. Current estimates are that 7-10% of the population is primarily or exclusively homosexual in orientation, with some researchers insisting on lower or higher figures. Quibbling over percentages, of course, is beside the point. The fact is that some persons, made in the image of God and with no conscious intention on their part, are drawn primarily to the same sex rather than to the opposite sex.

Until recently it was assumed that the cause for this sexual orientation was entirely environmental. The dominant mother/weak father configuration was thought to be consequential in the case of male homosexual persons. Others believed that an encounter with a homosexual adult predisposed a normally heterosexual child to homosexuality.

These and other myths have been increasingly questioned in the past few years. More definitive research, coupled with the emergence from the closet of healthy and well-adjusted homosexual persons, has resulted in a new look at all aspects of sexuality. This is not to say that we now have answers that once eluded us. In fact, suggestions range all the way from one study which points to fetal chemical conditions to the insistence that every person approaching adulthood can make a conscious decision regarding his or her sexual orientation. One can find few researchers who take either of these extreme positions. Most are content to say that the cause remains an enigma, but that one's sexual die is cast by two or three years of age.

Until recently it was difficult for most of us to accept the idea that one could be both homosexual and well-adjusted, to say nothing about being homosexual and Christian. In order to be a well-adjusted Christian, it was assumed that a homosexual person had to change his or her sexual orientation either through conversion or extensive psychological and/or psychiatric counseling.

It isn't surprising that we should have thought along these lines. The only homosexuals who dared cross the threshold of most pastors' studies were those who had such intense problems that they quite literally "fell out of the closet." Because they brought with them a combination of intense personal problems and a homosexual orientation, we assumed that the two were always related. It never occurred to us that we gave heterosexual persons the benefit of the doubt when they came with the same personal problems. That is to say, we did not assume that personal problems were directly related to a heterosexual orientation.

The same can be said about physical characteristics. The masculine woman or feminine man stereotype does not hold. The weak wrist and high pitched voice may serve as a vehicle for sick humor, but it says nothing whatsoever about the typical homosexual. I once had the opportunity to visit in a setting where there were more than fifty male homosexuals. If I were to judge by physical appearance alone, I would say that the trim, physically fit men I saw in that group were far more masculine than some of the flabby, pot-bellied macho males I have seen in other settings. Physical appearance is not a measure of one's sexuality.

The conversion myth has also gone by the boards. "If these people would just get right with God, they would have a normal sexual orientation," is typical of statements sent to me during the St. Paul controversy. The assumption is that if one is "born again" the result will be a heterosexual orientation. Dr. Anthony Campolo, a conservative Baptist who is professor of sociology at the University of Pennsylvania, believed this until one of his colleagues suggested that there was no clinical evidence that persons with an exclusive homosexual orientation could change their sexual preference. Not willing to accept this at face value, Campolo made his own investigation. To his surprise he found that, with one dubious exception, converted homosexual persons became Christian homosexual persons.

The child molester myth has also been demolished. Just as some perverted heterosexual men have molested younger girls, so some perverted homosexual men have molested younger boys. We need strong legislation to protect us from both. But we have no more right to project the immorality of a few homosexual persons on all homosexual persons than to project the immorality of a few heterosexual persons on all heterosexual persons. In fact, one study suggests that while 7-10% of the adult population are homosexual in orientation, only 3% of child molestations are committed by homosexual persons. If we want to protect our children from sexual molestations, it may be that we should work most intensively with heterosexual persons!

A very recent and comprehensive study by Bell and Weinberg *(Homosexualities: A Study of Human Diversity)* concludes that homosexual males do not indulge in sexual violence as often as heterosexual males, they are not as likely to make objectionable sexual advances as are heterosexual males, and homosexual teachers are not as apt to make sexual overtures to their students as are heterosexual teachers.

Pittinger's comment is to the point:

> "Of course there are entirely promiscuous types, especially among men. Of course some homosexuals are unpleasant people. Of course there are those who resort again and again to the employment of prostitutes. These are by no means typical homosexuals. . . . The 'run of the mill' homosexual male as well as the ordinary homosexual woman is a very different sort of person than that stereotype. Most of those I have come to know are entirely decent people, coming from all classes of society working in all sorts of trades and professions, not at all obvious or blatant. Indeed it is almost impossible to identify who is and who is not a homosexual simply by looking at him or her."

Because of the stereotypes, the homophobic cast of our culture, and our general misunderstanding of sexuality, it is little wonder that someone with a homosexual orientation may encounter emotional difficulties. A young boy or girl may begin to discover at age 12 or 13 that there is little or no strong attraction to persons of the opposite sex. Everything in their world tells them they ought to be other than what they are. In their peer group they start picking up impressions about "fems", "faggots", "freaks", "fairies", etc. They hear jokes about homosexual persons and often repeat them in the hope they can cover their own identity. In church they may hear allusions to "perverts" and "sinners." Before long they develop an intense self-hatred. They may hear themselves pleading with God, "I can't help it; please change me." Meanwhile, the depression grows deeper. For some, it ends with suicide.

It is a fairly well-known fact that the American Psychiatric Association in 1973 changed its description of homosexuality from "sexual deviation" to "sexual orientation disturbance." It applied the latter, however, only to those who were disturbed by their orientation and wanted to change. Homosexuality itself was categorized simply as one form of sexual behavior.

Barnhouse claims that the decision of the APA was not without political overtones. She also points out that many psychiatrists who have studied homosexuality very intensively continue to raise a vigorous protest against the decision of their colleagues. (For what may be a helpful new look at the nature of homosexuality as related to environmental factors, you will want to look for a soon-to-be-published book by Bell and Weinberg.)

In the April, 1978 issue of *Currents in Theology and Mission,* Harold I. Haas summarizes the question of the nature of homosexuality in what I would judge to be an exceptionally insightful comment. It is probably the best that can be said at this juncture:

> "The cause of homosexuality is a puzzling problem at best. The fact that homosexuality is found in diverse cultures with a large array of attitudes toward sexuality and child rearing customs may indicate that there is some biological substrate to homosexuality. But the fact that homosexual behavior itself takes such varied forms (as does also heterosexual behavior) argues that socio-psychological factors influence the form it will take. This implies that homosexual orientation is essentially an acquired characteristic. If so, the acquisition is slow, subtle, extends over several years and is not a matter of deliberate choice."

Where does all of this leave us? I believe it leaves one with a great sense of caution. The evidence is simply too conflicting for anyone to make conclusive judgments. The Bible-expounding demagogue who summarily declares homosexual orientation a perversion frightens me. And so does the statistic-citing researcher who declares that we must accept all homosexual behavior as normative.

IV. The Church and the Homosexual Person

This brings us to the point where I may offend some readers. I will argue on the basis of a premise that may seem inconsistent and, in the minds of some, unfair. I'm sorry for this, but I do not judge this line of thought to be necessarily inconsistent and, further, cannot be honest with myself unless I take this approach.

What I propose is that at this point in time in the debate over homosexuality we may have little choice in the church except to say that we accept the person, but question the behavior. Note that I avoid using the terms "sinner" and "sin". The LCA statement on "Sex, Marriage and Family" states that "persons who engage in homosexual behavior are sinners only as are all other persons . . . alienated from God and neighbor."

I am completely at ease with our LCA position. When we say, "All have sinned and fallen short of the glory of God" (Romans 3), we mean exactly that. There is no distinction based on one's nature, and surely not on one's sexual orientation.

We do, however, make judgments on the basis of one's behavior. The LCA statement says that "Homosexuality is viewed biblically as a departure from the heterosexual structure of God's creation." As I understand this, we are saying precisely what I suggested above, namely, that we accept the person but question the behavior.

We recognize, of course, that such an attitude will be small comfort to a homosexual person who desires to live out his or her sexual inclinations and who longs for open acceptance in the church. To such a brother or sister in Christ we can only plead for patience as we promise to get on with a deeper study of this difficult issue. We are looking at a mountain. Mountains are not moved in a day, especially when we do not know which parts and how much of the mountain should be moved.

In the meantime, we are faced with the question of how to relate to homosexual persons in our congregations. Here in the Minnesota Synod I doubt we have more than one or two congregations where a person living in an open homosexual relationship would find acceptance. There are some other places in our country, however, where this hurdle has already been passed. Known homosexuals are active members of some congregations. Once the initial curiosity subsided, these persons were accepted as any other member. They are as little likely to be singled out for special attention—positive or negative—as any other member of the congregation.

What would I do if I were the pastor of a local congregation and a homosexual person identified himself or herself as such and asked to become a member? Based on my present understanding of homosexuality, I would probably begin by trying to ascertain what kind of person I was dealing with. If I am speaking to one who has accepted himself or herself as a homosexual person (often after strenuous but unsuccessful attempts to change that orientation), but who has chosen to remain celebate, I would not hesitate for a moment to accept him or her and recommend membership.

But what about the person who has chosen to maintain a sexual relationship with someone of the same gender? Here I would make another distinction. In my dealings with these homosexual persons I have found that they, like heterosexual persons, are of two kinds. There are those who are promiscuous, immoral and without any sense whatever of devotion to and commitment to another person. Their milieu is the public restroom and the gay bar. Their goal is to arrange for a one night stand with any available partner. Some of these may have a preference for younger boys, in the case of males, and may have no qualms about perverting an adolescent.

My approach to such a person would be one of pastoral concern, but without the slightest encouragement of his or her lifestyle. I would make it clear that the church can under no circumstance approve of his or her behavior and that I could not recommend membership. I would assure such persons of my continuing availability to them and would try to relate them to counseling resources such as Lutheran Social Service.

There is, however, another kind of homosexual person who poses a far different and far more difficult situation for us. I have in mind the individual who has a profound sense of devotion to a single person of the same gender. This person would no more think of being unfaithful or promiscuous than would a heterosexual person with a sense of devotion to his wife or her husband. Furthermore, in the case of a male, the thought of perverting a young boy is absolutely out of the question.

Contrary to popular notion, there are such people. Not long ago I met a man who lived with his first partner for eight years until his friend died of leukemia. His grief for his friend and partner was genuine. Since then he has lived with another partner with whom he will soon celebrate the 25th anniversary of their relationship. He is actively involved in the affairs of his church and community, currently serving as director of an important social ministry program for a major metropolitan area.

How should we deal with homosexual persons of this kind? My inclination would be to treat these persons quite differently from promiscuous homosexual persons. I would inform them of the position of the LCA. I would point out the basically non-judgmental nature of our stance. I would also forewarn them of the resistance they are likely to face in the church if they intend to speak openly about their sexuality and try to ascertain if they are prepared to deal with it constructively. I would urge them not to make their sexual preference an issue in the life of the congregation other than in settings where the total question of sexuality is being considered.

Through all of this I am making an assumption that surely should not be taken for granted. That assumption is that with these persons, as with all new members, we seek to ascertain their personal relationship with Christ. For those without church background, this will be accomplished through instruction classes. For others, at the very least, there will be some form of orientation. And for all, there will be personal contact through counseling and/or home visitation. For those who have a personal relationship with Christ and who feel free in conscience to practice their homosexuality in a setting of devotion to a single person I would say, "Our church regards your sexual practice as a departure from the heterosexual pattern of creation. But we want you to be assured that all of us in this church are sinners under judgment who are saved by grace. Because you confess personal faith in Christ, we welcome you."

In his report to the 1978 convention of the LCA, President Robert Marshall addresses this issue. Beginning with the LCA statement that those who engage in homosexual behavior are sinners only as are other persons, he maintains that the consequences of this position

> "should lead congregations to receive homosexuals into the Christian fellowship without any qualifications. The (LCA) statement calls for the right and privacy and equal opportunity for homosexuals. While some associate homosexuality with the exploitation and abuse of others, it must be remembered that the accusation would apply to only some homosexuals and that some heterosexuals are equally guilty of the exploitation of others."

Let me summarize to this point: In my judgment, the sexual orientation of a homosexual person should be as incidental for his or her membership as that of a heterosexual person. As we would exclude from membership the immoral heterosexual person, so we should exclude the immoral homosexual person—but neither without the offer of pastoral care. As we would accept the Christ-confessing and moral heterosexual person, so we should accept the Christ-confessing and moral homosexual person.

I realize that some pastors cannot now—and probably never will—accept the idea that one can be Christ-confessing and a practicing homosexual person at the same time. I don't ask that you change your view. I only ask that you be patient, considerate and understanding when other pastors choose to be more open on this matter.

After our Synod convention one delegate is reported to have said, "I just wish those homosexual persons would stay in the closet and leave us alone." That might be the wish of many. But it is unrealistic. All the referendums in the world will not make the issue go away. Nor will the church escape the question. Some pastors and churches will turn away all homosexual persons, including the celibate. Others will accept only the celibate. Some may accept practicing homosexual persons under certain conditions.

My prayer is that during these next years all of us will exercise the utmost restraint in making judgments. The church has weathered many storms through the years and it will come through this one as well. Not without some bumps and bruises, but the better for having struggled with the question. I have a great and fundamental confidence in the Holy Spirit, the Creator and Sustainer of the church. God's grace is as powerful in the church today as ever. As we pray for the guidance of the Spirit, he will give us wisdom and help.

V. The Ordination of Homosexual Persons

Most of you have read the accounts in the media about the debate among the Presbyterians regarding the ordination of homosexual persons. If I have understood their position, I believe I am in complete accord with them. That is to say, I believe that a celibate homosexual person who meets all other requirements should be allowed ordination. I believe that an avowed, practicing homosexual person, regardless of all other qualifications and considerations, should not be allowed ordination.

Again, some may judge this to be an inconsistent and unfair stance. But let me explain what I believe is a viable position. To do so, we must go back to the basics. In the church all are sinners, all are under judgment, all are saved by grace through faith. It is by grace and through faith that we become members of the household of God where all are called to priesthood and servanthood. All are one in Christ. There is neither slave nor free, male or female. Neither is there a distinction to be made on the basis of sexual orientation.

Does this mean that ordination should be the option of any and all? By no means. The church has every right—indeed, an obligation—to set standards for acceptance into and continuation in ordained ministry. Our view is that ordained ministry is an office into which one is called. The call has two sources—from God and from God's people in the church.

Unless the call from God is confirmed by a call from the church, there can be no ordination. And if in the judgment of the church one who is ordained no longer qualifies for that office, ordination can be withdrawn by the church.

So far as our LCA is concerned, the authority to ordain has been vested with the various synods. While standards and guidelines are adopted by the national church, they are interpreted and implemented by the synods.

At the present time the LCA "Guidelines for Problem Situations" states only that "homosexuality disqualifies one for the ordained ministry of the Lutheran Church in America." It is clear that this leaves the door open for interpretation by each synod. Some read the Guideline to mean that no homosexual person should be granted ordination—neither the practicing nor the non-practicing homosexual person. Other synods read the Guideline to refer only to practicing homosexual persons and have been open to the possibility of ordaining an avowed *non-practicing* homosexual person. I know of no synod that has ordained a practicing homosexual person.

Citing again his report to the 1978 convention of the LCA, we find that President Marshall is quite content with this flexibility of interpretation among synods. "I believe the LCA has the ideal practice," writes Marshall. "The matter is dealt with in personal counseling by the assigned synodical authorities and judged according to each individual situation."

While I affirm the need for individual consideration, I believe the time has come when the national church should adopt a statement that is less ambiguous and open to interpretation by individual synods. The "assigned synodical authorities", while no doubt envisioning professional preparation committees and examining committees, are in fact none other than the synod presidents. If a synod president is open to the ordination of homosexual candidates, it will happen. If he is opposed to all such ordinations, it will not happen. I believe a more consistent churchwide policy is needed.

I have sometimes used the analogy of priesthood in the Roman Catholic Church to explain our current position. At this point in time the Roman Church forbids the ordination of a married priest. A man may have a strong heterosexual desire to be married. He may even have in mind the exact person he wishes to marry. But the Church says to him, "If your call to be a priest is your highest call, then you must forego your call to marriage."

Our Lutheran Church in America says the same to a homosexual candidate. We make no judgment regarding the person's sexuality. But we do make judgments regarding the standards for ordained ministry. At this point in time we say to the homosexual person, "If you call to be an ordained minister is your highest call, then you must forego the practice of your homosexuality." The same would hold true for a celibate homosexual pastor who decides that he or she wishes to form a sexual relationship with another person. Our policy precludes such a relationship and would call for resignation from the ministry or disciplinary action.

I recognize, of course, that the phrase, "practice your homosexuality," is open to misunderstanding. In its broadest context, sexuality refers to a wide variety of activities and associations, including many that have no direct association with physical contact. In this context, I am referring to it in its narrowest sense, that is, genital sexual behavior.

VI. Civil Rights

In many respects the civil rights aspect of this issue appears to be the most complex of all. Once more, however, I find it helpful to remember that one's sexual orientation *per se* is not what determines the quality of one's character. As we underscored earlier, one cannot judge all persons with a homosexual orientation by a single standard any more than we can do so in the case of all persons with a heterosexual orientation.

One purpose of law and order is to protect us from the unlawful and immoral behavior of those who flaunt law and morality, regardless of sexual orientation. Contrariwise, the purpose of civil rights legislation is to guarantee equal protection of the law, regardless of sexual orientation. Those who break laws and disregard morality cannot expect society to stand by and permit such behavior to go unchecked.

In the area of sexuality, this means that we can expect and should encourage *prosecution* of those who use others for the purpose of exploitation. At the same time, we can expect and should encourage the *protection* of those who respect our laws and work for equality and justice in society. It is out of concern for the latter that the LCA Statement on Sex, Marriage and Family suggests that the behavior of consenting adults in private "is not an appropriate subject for legislation or police action."

If we insist on civil rights for persons regardless of sexual orientation, does this mean that the church must open the doors for employment of homosexual persons at all levels? We discussed the ordained clergy earlier. But what about deaconesses, college presidents, staff and faculty, social service agency personnel, professional lay workers in the church? Does a civil right in all cases imply that one's sexual behavior cannot be taken into consideration when making employment decisions? I would argue for the right of the church to consider this as one factor among others. We must reserve the right to refuse employment or appointment for a variety of reasons, as is the case now. In some areas of employment we may insist that it would be inappropriate for a practicing homosexual person to hold a given position.

Does the state allow for such latitude? I believe it does. When one of our colleges, for example, looks for a president, we openly announce that he or she must be a Lutheran. The state respects our traditions and allows for this. It is not seen as unlawful. Likewise, the church may take a stance on homosexuality which, while pastoral and sensitive, suggests that persons who are practicing homosexual persons may not be best suited for certain positions.

Again, I know there are whose who shudder at possible consequences if the state should press the issue. Institutions and agencies which receive sizeable government grants would be particularly vulnerable. I have no easy answers.

I can only raise the counter question: Shall we absolutely close the door to every person with a homosexual orientation, no matter what position of employment is under consideration? Based on the principle of separation of church and state, I believe we should insist on the right to make judgments in this matter.

VII. Conclusion

I hesitate to use the term "conclusion" since I have no intention of concluding this letter in the usual manner. By now it is clear to you that I have few "conclusions" as such. I have only attempted to open your minds to the possibility of a further and deeper look at homosexuality. And that can only happen when we look even more broadly at sexuality. In spite of all of the efforts at sex education in this country in the last twenty-five years, it is evident that the church has failed in its task and that we must dig in for a long and intensive study of this issue. Out of it will come a better understanding of homosexuality and we will all be the better for it.

In the meantime, it may be well for every pastor to consider the suggestion that comes out of Washington's Community of Christ congregation:

> "The congregation's pastoral ministry to homosexual persons should be discussed and defined in the context of a discussion of its pastoral ministry to heterosexuals. Whatever is said of the one should apply to the other. All persons should be helped to establish and maintain wholesome, responsible, loving relationships with themselves, their families, and other persons."

—Herbert W. Chilstrom

Notes: *Since its formation in 1988, the Evangelical Lutheran Church in America has been led by Herbert W. Chilstrom, formerly bishop of the Minnesota Synod of the Lutheran Church in America. This statement from Chilstrom is not an official church statement, but because of his position in the church, it has been widely circulated during this period as the* *new church struggles with ongoing contemporary issues, especially the ordination of homosexuals. Chilstrom offers a conciliatory approach which carefully explains each position taken under the assumption that he is advocating a more liberal stance than that of the members in his synod. His most controversial positions concern the acceptance of homosexuals who live either celibate lives or in a committed relationship to one partner.*

Immediately after the formation of the Evangelical Lutheran Church in America, two congregations attempted to force the issue of accepting homosexual ministers by ordaining two homosexuals without church approval. After a period of consideration, the church expelled both congregations for their precipitous actions.

EVANGELICAL LUTHERAN CHURCH IN AMERICA

HUMAN SEXUALITY AND SEXUAL BEHAVIOR (1980)

G. Considering Homosexuality

1. We note the current consensus in the scientific community that one's preferred sexual behavior exists on a continuum from exclusively heterosexual to exclusively homosexual and that homosexual behavior takes a variety of forms. We believe it appropriate to distinguish between homosexual orientation and homosexual behavior. Persons who do not practice their homosexual erotic preference do not violate our understanding of Christian sexual behavior.
2. This church regards the practice of homosexual erotic behavior as contrary to God's intent for his children. It rejects the contention that homosexual behavior is simply another form of sexual behavior equally valid with the dominant male/female pattern.
3. We have reviewed the challenges to the traditional interpretations of those scripture passages that appear to proscribe homosexual behavior. We are not convinced by the evidence presented. Among passages cited as requiring interpretations different from the traditional interpretation are Genesis 18:16-19:29; Leviticus 18:22 and 20:13; Romans 1:24-32; I Corinthians 6:9-10; I Timothy 1:10. While we see no scriptural rationale for revising the church's traditional teaching that homosexual erotic behavior violates God's intent, we nonetheless remain open to the possibility of new biblical and theological insights.
4. We agree that homosexually-behaving persons need God's grace as does every human being. We all need the care and concern of the congregation. We all need opportunity to hear the Word, to receive the sacraments, to accept the forgiveness God offers, to experience the understanding and the fellowship of the community of Christ. We all need the power of the Holy Spirit for ethical living sensitive to our own individual situations. So saying we nevertheless do not condone homosexual erotic behavior. Nor do we condone idolatry, pride, disrespect for parents, murder, adultery, theft, libel, gossip, or the other sins known in our circles. The sacrifice God finds acceptable from each of us is "a broken spirit, a broken and contrite heart." Then he can answer our prayer for a "clean heart . . . a new and right spirit within me." (See Psalm 51.)
5. Truth, mercy, and justice should impel members of congregations of The American Lutheran Church to review their attitudes, words, and actions regarding homosexuality. Christians need to be more understanding and more sensitive to life as experienced by those who are homosexual. They need to take leadership roles in changing public opinion, civil laws, and prevailing practices that deny justice and opportunity to any persons, homosexual or heterosexual. We all need recognition and acceptance as human beings known to and loved by God.

Notes: *This statement was issued by the American Lutheran Church, now a constituent part* *of the Evangelical Lutheran Church in America. During the 1970s, arguments circulated in the church calling for a liberalizing of the church's traditional position. Partially in response to those arguments, as well as the general public debate on the subject, the church's Office of Research and Analysis issued this preliminary statement, which was finally approved by the church's general convention. It was not as conservative as the earlier draft document, but more traditional than that of the Lutheran Church in America.*

Homosexual behavior is rejected as another sexual pattern and such behavior violates God's intent for humans. Homosexual behavior is compared to murder, adultery, and theft. Nevertheless, the statement leaves room for further discussion and calls for a compassionate relationship with homosexually oriented people.

EVANGELICAL PRESBYTERIAN CHURCH

POSITION PAPER ON HOMOSEXUALITY (1986)

In our society today, there are many issues which concern the people of God. One such issue is the rise in acceptance of and openness toward homosexual activity. We of the Evangelical Presbyterian Church believe there is a need to state clearly our understanding of the Biblical teaching about homosexual activity. It is also our desire to set forth our position regarding the appropriate response of Christians and the Church to this critical issue especially in light of the trend in some Christian bodies toward the ordination of practicing homosexuals. Let us first consider the Biblical teachings on this subject.

Biblical Teachings

We believe the Scriptures of the Old and New Testaments to be the infallible Word of God, the final authority in all issues of life. Therefore, contemporary sexual attitudes and behavior are to be judged in the light of the Bible, rather than the Bible being reinterpreted, modified, or overturned by current cultural trends in thought and behavior.

We find our first problem with homosexuality in the first two chapters in the Bible. No reference to homosexuality is found here, but we do find, in the prototype family, Adam and Eve, God's perfect design for marriage and sexual expression. How beautifully simple and yet profoundly revealing is Adam's own description of Eve when God brought her into Adam's presence: "This is now bone of my bones, and flesh of my flesh, she shall be called woman, because she was taken out of a man." (Gen. 2:23)

God's commentary, spelling out the sanctity and intimacy of marriage, the bonding of male and female in physical oneness follows: "For this cause a man shall leave his father and his mother and shall cleave to his wife; and they shall become one flesh" (Gen. 2:24). This statement is reaffirmed by Jesus (Mt. 19:5) and by Paul (Eph. 5:31), expanding the succinct utterance of Genesis 1:27: "So God created man in His own image, in the image of God He created Him; male and female He created them."

Here we find the very foundation of human sexuality and discover the distinctives that give man and woman their God-ordained sexual identities. In the benediction that follows, we see not only God's provision for male and female completeness, but also His plan for the propagation of the human race: "And God blessed them; and God said to them, 'Be fruitful and multiply, and fill the earth and subdue it. . ."

When God saw that Adam was not complete alone, but needed something beyond all the wonders of the beautiful animal creation, He observed, "It is not good for the man to be alone; I will make him a helper suitable for him" (Gen. 2:18). The result was woman, not another male companion. A woman with her likeness to man, but with all her beautiful distinctiveness.

Today, we see the folly of modern man attempting to deal with human sexuality without knowing who he is. The result is often a confused and fragmented view of the nature of man and woman. G.C. Berkouwer reminds us that a man's nature is not self-enclosed, but must be understood in terms of its relationship to God. This understanding is found at the very beginning of the human race as described to us in the opening chapters of the Bible. Berkouwer states, "Here we see in Genesis 1 and 2 man and woman as the crowning jewel of God's creation, His image and likeness."

Homosexuality is a gross distortion of the "imago Dei" as still reflected in fallen man, and a mocking perversion and ignominious caricature of the sexual relationship as God intends it to be. Helmut Thielicke puts it more vividly: "He who no longer knows what man is, also cannot know what it is on which his peculiarity as a sexual being is based. He who disregards this anthropological motif of sexuality degrades it to a mere biological question."

God's judgment on this perversion of human sexuality emerges in the Law, i.e., Leviticus 20:13—"When a man is with a male as with a woman, both have committed something perverse; they will certainly be put to death; their blood guilt rests on them." Significantly, adultery and incest draw the same penalty.

Genesis 19:4-18 tells the story of the destruction of Sodom and Gomorrah, two cities given over to homosexual lust and murderous hostility. In recent years an attempt has been made to minimize the charges of homosexuality as relating to God's judgment on those cities. Writers such as J. McNeil, S.J., contend that the word "yadah" rendered "know" in Genesis 19:5 and 8, more frequently is used to mean "to be aware of." McNeil states that here we have a group of citizens who in a brash manner tried to "get acquainted with" Lot's guests.

Such an interpretation is absurd in the face of Lot's pleas to the mob, begging them, ". . . do not act wickedly . . ." and his effort to protect his angelic guests by offering instead his virgin daughters, "who have not had relations with man . . ." to do with as they pleased. Moreover, when the mob was smitten with blindness by the angels, they spent the rest of the night milling around Lot's house in flaming lust to gratify their homosexual desires. To confuse such activity with a desire to be "hospitable" is inexcusable nonsense for any serious commentator to indulge.

Letha Scanzoni's "explanation" that what Lot was seeking to avoid here was "gang rape" instead of private homosexual activity between two consenting adults (which she seems to accept as legitimate) is unworthy of refutation.

What must be acknowledged is that homosexuality is classified in the Levitical Law, or "Holiness Code," with other behavior such as incest, adultery, obeisance to Molech, bestiality, all of which are condemned.

Moving to the New Testament, we find no record in the Gospels of Jesus referring directly to homosexuality. However, our Lord made clear that He came not to destroy the law but to fulfill it. He not only fulfilled it, He strengthened it. For example, it was not enough to refrain from the act of adultery. He declared that everyone who looks at a woman lustfully has already committed adultery with her in his heart (Mt. 5:27, 28). He thus clarified the Mosaic Law, rather than dismissing it, as some exegetes contend.

Turning to the Pauline epistles, we find specific statements which speak directly to the issue: Romans 1:26ff, I Cor. 6:9, and I Tim. 1:10. The Romans passage is the most detailed and the most devastating! Here Paul begins his attack with the phrase, "For this reason . . . , " which refers back to the previous verses 24 and 25. These verses trace immorality and self destructive behavior which they describe to having exchanged God's truth for falsehood (shades of Satan in the Garden) and having turned to idolatry, which is the worshipping and serving of the creature rather than the Creator, Who is blessed forever. Amen.

Because of this, "God gave them over to their degrading passions. . . ." Women perverted natural relations into unnatural (lesbianism), and men forsook their natural relationships with women and burned in their lust for one another (homosexuality), committing shameless acts with men. They acquired in their persons the penalty that was coming to them because of their wrong behavior. (Rom 1:26, 27)

There are various ways by which professing Christians in the homosexual community have sought to bypass the clear meaning of Paul's words. For example, some people contend that for them the natural way can be homosexuality, and that God is pleased with this. With the same rationale, many heterosexual persons with strong sex drives could say, "It's natural for me to be promiscuous; therefore, I feel that in God's eyes promiscuity is approved for me." God will not accept this kind of causistry. Romans 1:26 points back to the natural way God established at the dawn of human history.

In I Corinthians 6:9, Paul uses two different Greek words to refer to homosexuals: *"malakoi"* probably refers to the passive in homosexual liaison, while *"arsenokoitai"* appears to designate the active partner. Only the most irresponsible sophistry can avoid the conclusion that Paul knew exactly what he wanted to say when he warned; ". . . Do not be deceived; neither fornicators, nor idolators, nor adulterers, nor effeminate, nor homosexuals, nor thieves, nor the covetous, nor drunkards, nor revilers, nor swindlers, shall inherit the kingdom of God. And such were some of you; but you were washed, but you were sanctified, but you were justified in the name of the Lord Jesus Christ and in the Spirit of our God." (I Cor. 6:9-11)

Paul reiterates in I Timothy 1:9, 10 the warning he has given in the previous passages. Here again he uses the term *"arsenokoitai"* with reference to the active homosexual partner. Significantly, he included them with the lawless, rebellious, ungodly, the unholy and profane, those guilty of fratricide and other kinds of murder, kidnappers, liars, and perjurers. For these, Paul says, the law was made with its consequent penalties to law breakers (I Tim. 1:9).

Christian Response

The position regarding homosexuality taken by the Evangelical Presbyterian Church goes beyond a written statement. We recognize Christ's loving gift of Himself on the cross as an act of God in human history excluding no one from the offer of its benefits. We believe that:

> "The Worship of God has, as its natural consequences, the response of commitment and service to Him. This finds expression as God's people gather to worship, then scatter into the world to serve Him. Such service includes witnessing to all peoples the marvelous deeds of Him who calls us out of darkness into His wonderful light. It includes, as a first duty, the proclamation of a grace that reaches out to forgive, to redeem, and to give new spiritual power to live for Him, through Jesus Christ, and the infilling of the Holy Spirit. . . It includes a witness to God's love and compassion . . . *(Book of Worship, Section 1-3)*

How can this witness to forgiveness, redemption, and new spiritual power to live for God be expressed towards those in the homosexual community and those in the church who struggle with their sexual identity?

A. EDUCATION

Through sermons, classes and study groups, the understanding of human sexuality as part of God's image in us from a Biblical perspective helps to lay the groundwork of understanding for all. Those experiencing homophobia, or a fear of homosexuality, can be freed from this fear through understanding; those seeking answers to their sexual confusion can likewise begin the journey towards wholeness through reading, teaching and discussion.

B. THE FRIENDSHIP FACTOR

The incarnation of God in Christ is our constant reminder of the absolute necessity of a genuine identification with those we try to reach. Homosexuals need to know an acceptance of their person beyond the sexual concerns they bring with them, and that the church views their sexuality as only a part of their total being. The basis for friendship must be recognition of our common need of the grace of God.

C. THERAPEUTIC RESOURCES

"Therapy" comes from a Greek New Testament word, *"therapeuo"* meaning "to heal." Healing in the area of sexual identity and behavior comes through a number of channels which individual Christians and local churches can offer. These include worship, small group and one-on-one covenant relationship, pastoral counseling, prayer, and the services of committed Christian psychologists. Local church programs can draw on the resources of such groups as Sexaholics Anonymous and Exodus International as they seek to establish ministries to homosexual persons. As individuals seek to move away from homosexuality in thought and act, they sometimes need the regular availability of caring and supportive Christians who can be trained by the local church for such a ministry.

D. INTERCESSION

The value and place of prayer cannot be overstated. Combined with education, friendship, and therapeutic resources, prayer says to all involved that the risen Lord has power to redirect individual lives and to heal personal images of sexual identity. Both prayer with individuals and private intercessory prayer for individuals function in the mystery of the working of God to free, redeem and heal.

Conclusion

While we acknowledge the reality of this problem, and do not take lightly the grip of homosexuality upon countless persons in our society, both within and without the church, we reach the following conclusions:

1. Biblical teaching makes it clear that the practice of homosexuality is a sin. We affirm that while God hates the sin, He loves the sinner.

2. Since the practice of homosexuality is incompatible with a Christian life-style, and since officers of the church must be "examples to the flock" we cannot condone the ordination of practicing homosexuals as Deacons, Ruling Elders, or Teaching Elders.

3. As Christians, who are ourselves sinners redeemed by the grace of God, we must reach out to those persons who are struggling with homosexuality, offering them education, friendship, therapy, and intercession, to the end that they may experience true wholeness through the freeing, renewing grace of God in Jesus Christ. "If therefore the Son shall make you free, you shall be free indeed." (John 8:36)

Notes: *The 1986 general assembly of the Evangelical Presbyterian Church adopted this thoughtful, traditional statement of the Christian position against homosexuality. It condemns the practice of homosexuality, denies ordination to homosexuals, and offers the church's ministry to homosexuals. The church also supports the work of several groups which attempt to convert homosexuals to evangelical Christianity while assisting in changing their sexual orientation.*

FREE METHODIST CHURCH

STATEMENT ON HOMOSEXUALITY (1985)

18. Homosexual Behavior

342. Homosexual behavior, as all sexual deviation, is a perversion of God's created order (Genesis 1-3). The sanctity of marriage and the family is to be preserved against all manner of immoral conduct (Exodus 22:16-17; Deuteronomy 22:23-28; Leviticus 20:10-16).

Homosexual behavior is contrary to the will of God as clearly stated in Scripture (Leviticus 18:22; 20:13; Romans 1:26-27; I Corinthians 6:9-10; I Timothy 1:8-10).

Persons with homosexual inclinations are accountable to God for their behavior (Romans 14:12).

The forgiving and delivering grace of God in Christ is all-sufficient for the homosexual (I John 1:9; Hebrews 7:25; Luke 4:18; I Corinthians 6:9-11).

The church has a personal and corporate responsibility to be God's instrument of healing, restoring love to the homosexual seeking recovery of Christian conduct and life-style (I Corinthians 2:7-8).

The church opposes legislation which makes homosexual conduct or life-style legitimate.

Notes: *In 1979, the Free Methodist Church made a definitive statement on homosexuality beyond its traditional assumption that sexual acts are limited to heterosexual monogamous marriage. The statement printed above, from the 1985* Discipline, *is substantially the same as that printed in 1979. It opposes homosexuality and any public accommodation of homosexual lifestyles.*

GENERAL BAPTIST CONFERENCE

STATEMENT ON HOMOSEXUALITY (1987)

Homosexuality (Adopted 1987)

Whereas the practice of homosexuality is soundly condemned as a sin in the Bible, and whereas homosexual behavior contributes to the spread of AIDS and other incurable diseases, therefore be it resolved that the delegates to the 1987 annual meeting of the Baptist General Conference hereby state our opposition to the practice and promotion of homosexual behavior, and to encourage the members of the Baptist General Conference to seek biblical means of ministering to the homosexual community.

Notes: *In 1987 this conservative Baptist group with Swedish roots passed a brief statement against homosexuality.*

GREEK ORTHODOX ARCHDIOCESE OF NORTH AND SOUTH AMERICA

HOMOSEXUALITY/HOMOSEXUALS (UNDATED)

A. Homosexuality

The Bible and Holy Tradition, the sources of the faith condemn homosexuality. It is, and shall remain for Orthodox Christians a grave sin, because:

1. Bible and tradition so reveal.
2. It is intrinsically promiscuous and breeds promiscuity.
3. It often preys upon the young and innocent, corrupting their morals with devastating effects upon their psychic structures.
4. It undermines the family unit as an institution of our society through the advocacy and promotion of legislation permitting, popularizing, and facilitating the existence and growth of a form of cohabitation which is a mocking parody of the family.
5. It frustrates the self evident purpose of sex within the order of creation, and as such is an abnormality. Orthodoxy distinguishes between the procreative purpose of human sexuality, and the feelings of desire which are attributed to the fallen nature of man, whereas the former is a property of the Primordeal nature of man and not the result of sin. Thus mutual fulfillment through the stilling of desire can not be looked upon as a purpose of sexuality and marriage nor can we divorce the potentiality of procreation from normal sexuality.

B. The Homosexual

The homosexual is viewed as a person with a sexual abnormality. As a person, he is entitled to basic human rights, and the protection of the law. The protection of his person as a citizen must not be extended to the protection of his abnormality, which would, in essence comprise a legal sanction of homosexuality.

Movements that seek to remedy the intrinsic guilt or self-consciousness of the homosexual, through the organization and formation of a subculture whose existence is predicated upon sexual misorientation; and the use of public funds to condition society to accept homosexuality as a socially and morally acceptable alternative life style, as remedial measures, beg the true issue of the causes of the plight of the homosexual by treating the symptom rather than the cause, and result in a disservice both to the homosexual and to society.

Thus the enactment of legislation which seeks to legislate immorality, serves only to perpetuate the problems and weaken society. In humanitarian consideration of homosexuals as fellow human beings we advocate the increased availability of counseling, psychiatric, and medical services to treat the cause wherever treatable, and legal social structuring necessary to discourage the growth of homosexuality as a sociological phenomenon.

Only by our unrelenting efforts to override the age-old temptations that beset the citizens of any society blessed with bounty and abundance will we subdue the plethora of problems that now besiege us, and of which abortion is only one.

It is our firm conviction that one day the laws of God and man will coincide, and toward the achievement of that divine day of destiny we pledge ourselves to the protection of human life, born and unborn, as a sacred trust of man's eternal covenant with God.

Notes: *The position of the Greek Orthodox Church is based on the church's understanding of the Bible and the Christian tradition. Its stance is somewhat distinctive, viewing homosexuality as an abnormality ultimately derived from the fallen nature of humanity. Ultimately everyone is susceptible and one of the dangers of homosexuals is their ability to* *corrupt the youth. For this reason, the church opposes any public or legal acceptance of homosexuality.*

The church has played an important role in keeping openly homosexual churches out of the National Council of Churches. Leaders see the Orthodox Church's participation in the council as dependent upon its exclusion of radical pro-homosexual groups, such as the Universal Fellowship of Metropolitan Community Churches.

HUNGARIAN REFORMED CHURCH IN AMERICA

HEIDELBERG CATECHISM (1563)

Q. 87. Can those who do not turn to God from their ungrateful, impenitent life be saved?

A. Certainly not! Scripture says, "Surely you know that the unjust will never come into possession of the kingdom of God. Make no mistake: no fornicator or idolater, none who are guilty either of adultery or of homosexual perversion, no thieves or grabbers or drunkards or slanderers or swindlers, will possess the kingdom of God."

Notes: *This brief statement is from the Heidelberg Catechism, one of the traditional Reformed doctrinal statements of the sixteenth century. The catechism has played an important role as the standard of the Reformed churches on the continent of Europe (as opposed to the English-speaking churches, which usually look to the Westminster Confession and Catechism). More recently the Heidelberg Catechism was included as one of several traditional doctrinal statements included in the* Book of Confessions *of the Presbyterian Church (U.S.A.).*

INDEPENDENT FUNDAMENTAL CHURCH OF AMERICA

RESOLUTION ON HOMOSEXUALITY (1977)

1977 - Winona Lake

WHEREAS, there is in our nation a growing movement of homosexuals which is demanding recognition and rights of respectability; and

WHEREAS, there are those in places of political and religious power who are willing to yield to these demands, both for social and economic benefits and for places of leadership and ordination in church circles; and

WHEREAS, the Bible is so very clear that homosexuality is a gross and grievous sin, in such passages as: Romans 1:26, 27, "For this cause God gave them up to vile affections: for even their women did change the natural use into that which is against nature; and likewise also the men, leaving the natural use of the woman, burned in their lust one toward another; men with men working that which is unseemly, and receiving in themselves that recompence of their error which was meet," and in such other passages as: I Corinthians 6:9, 10; II Peter 2:6, 7; and Jude 7, each of which refers to the sin of homosexuality; and

WHEREAS, God has declared His blessing on the nation that is righteous and His judgment on the nation that is evil; and

WHEREAS, nations have fallen before because of such sins as the cities of Sodom and Gomorrah fell;

BE IT THEREFORE RESOLVED, that the members and delegates of the Independent

Fundamental Churches of America meeting in annual convention June 25-July 2, 1977 at Winona Lake, Indiana, go on record as being opposed to any move that would recognize homosexuality as anything but gross sin which will bring the judgment of God as it has in the past; and

BE IT FURTHER RESOLVED, that while we view this as gross sin, we view those who are involved in homosexuality as objects of the grace of God to be reached and won from that and other sins to the Lord Jesus Christ, the great Saviour of sinners; and

BE IT FURTHER RESOLVED, that our churches be urged to pray for and reach by scriptural methods those caught by Satan in this sin, saving "with fear, pulling them out of the fire; hating even the garment spotted by the flesh," (Jude 23); and

BE IT FINALLY RESOLVED, that members of our movement see that copies of this resolution be sent to national, regional, and local leaders, and the media.

Notes: *One of the principle fundamentalist denominations in the United States, the Independent Fundamental Church of America, passed a resolution in 1977 that follows the traditional Christian teaching on homosexuality.*

INTERNATIONAL PENTECOSTAL CHURCH OF CHRIST

STATEMENT ON HOMOSEXUALITY (UNDATED)

BELIEVING that the Bible speaks out strongly in condemnation of sin and unrighteousness in all forms; and

BELIEVING that the Scriptures explicitly pronounce judgement on sexual deviance, namely, the book of Romans, chapter one, which refers to the guilt of mankind expressed in shameful worship, perverted passions and corrupted minds; and

BELIEVING that increased public tolerance of homosexuality can be attributed to various factors, including the acceptance of moral relativism and the contraceptive ethic which separates sex from any natural or necessary connection to procreation thus serving to promote the legitimization of homosexual activity; and

BELIEVING that whether the result of moral laxity, social acceptability or physiological change, the number of homosexuals seems to be increasing to the point that both men and women belong to this identity, now, according to published statistics in the literature, equal or exceed twenty percent (20%) of our total population; and

BELIEVING we must always be cognizant of the fact that all men regardless of their sins need God's redeeming love as expressed in Jesus Christ;

The INTERNATIONAL PENTECOSTAL CHURCH OF CHRIST issues this statement of its basic position addressing this subject, and

AFFIRMS that the infallible Word of God condemns homosexuality and believes this means of consensual activity between members of the same sex is not open for debate;

CONDEMNS the role and influence of the Feral Judiciary in the legitimization of homosexual conduct in the American society;

CALLS UPON professionals within our community for expanded research on the subject and urges our churches to extend the healing ministry to individuals who seek deliverance from this perversion and desire to feel the expression of God's love and grace as demonstrated by a caring body of believers.

Notes: *This strong statement against homosexuality and attempts to legitimize it, publicly, follows traditional Christian teachings on the subject.*

JEHOVAH'S WITNESSES

YOUR VIEW OF SEX—WHAT DIFFERENCE DOES IT MAKE? (UNDATED)

What of homosexuality? As we have seen, this practice is covered by the word *por-nei'a* ("fornication"), used by Jesus and his disciples. The disciple Jude used that word when referring to the unnatural sex acts of the men of Sodom and Gomorrah. (Jude 7) Homosexuality there caused degradation that produced a loud "cry of complaint" and led to God's destruction of those cities and their inhabitants. (Genesis 18:20; 19:23, 24) Has God's view changed since then? No. First Corinthians 6:9, 10, for example, lists "men who lie with men" among those who, if continuing such a practice, will not inherit God's kingdom. Also, describing the results to persons who 'dishonor their bodies in uncleanness,' going after "flesh for unnatural use," the apostle Paul writes that they "became violently inflamed in their lust toward one another, males with males, working what is obscene and receiving in themselves the full recompense, which was due for their error." (Romans 1:24, 27) Not only do such persons fall under God's condemnation. They also receive a "recompense" of mental and physical corruption. Today, for example, there is much syphilis among homosexuals. The high standard set out in God's Word, rather than depriving us of something good, protects us against such harm.

Notes: *In the matter of sexual ethics, the Jehovah's Witnesses are in complete agreement with the traditional Christian stance which limits sexual activity to marriage. Their 1979 booklet* True Peace and Security—from What Source? *contains a chapter in which their teachings on sexual behavior are laid out in systematic fashion. Homosexuality is denounced in the strongest terms as ungodly and unhealthy.*

LUTHERAN CHURCH-MISSOURI SYNOD

HUMAN SEXUALITY: A THEOLOGICAL PERSPECTIVE (1981)

I. Man as Male and Female

Robert Farrar Capon has written:

> Suppose I wrote a book called *The Sexual Life of a Nun.* You know what people would think. They would be curious—or shocked. They would expect to find it either a big joke or a compilation of a slightly prurient propaganda. How many would be able to see that, on the real meaning of the word *sexual,* it is a perfectly proper title? For a nun's life of course is utterly sexual. She thinks as a woman, prays as a woman, reacts as a woman and commits herself as a woman. No monk, no celibate, ever embraced his life for her kind of reasons. He couldn't if he wanted to. Of course she omits, as an offering to God, one particular expression of her sexuality; but it is only one out of a hundred. The sexual congress she does not attend is not life's most important meeting, all the marriage manuals to the contrary notwithstanding.[2]

Capon's point, made in fairly amusing fashion, is an important one. A study of human sexuality from the standpoint of Christian theology cannot begin with a discussion of marriage. Rather, it must begin with the creation of man as male and female, with what Karl Barth called "being-in-fellow-humanity."[3]

This is, after all, where the Scriptures begin. "So God created man in his own image, in the image of God he created *him;* male and female he created them" (Gen. 1:27; italics added). The suggestion here is that it is impossible to come to know the significance of our humanity without reference to the sexual differentiation between male and female. To be human simply *is* to exist in this male-female duality.[4] Consequently, it will be insufficient to say that God has created two kinds of human beings, male and female. Rather, we should say that God has created human beings for fellowship and that the male-female polarity is a basic form of this fellowship. To stress that human beings are created for community as male *and* female necessarily involves an equally firm insistence that they are male *or* female.[5] We are created not for life in isolation but for community, a community which binds those who are different. We are not simply "persons," however important that claim may on occasion be as a protest against inequities.

When the Scriptures deal with human beings as man and woman, created to realize not themselves but their fellowship as a harmonious union of those who are different, they view man and woman as *embodied* creatures. Men and women are not mere persons who meet in a purely spiritual union. On the contrary, the body has its own integrity. What we do in our bodies is done by *us;* there is no inner, purely spiritual self which remains untouched by our physical commitments (I Cor. 6:18). We are, quite simply, created as embodied creatures: as male and female. Thus we do not find in the other simply an image of ourselves, an alter ego; rather, the fellowship for which we are created is a fellowship of those who are different and who yet are joined in a personal community of love.

There is a further reason why we must begin not with marriage but with the creation of man as male and female. Not every human being need enter the order of marriage (I Cor. 7:1-7). Celibacy is also in accordance with the will of God. Despite the justifiable polemic of the Reformers against the view of medieval Christendom which institutionalized celibacy as a way of life more acceptable to God than the marital union of husband and wife, we cannot allow that polemic to determine everything we say about the fellowship of man and woman. The church today must certainly make clear to its people that marriage is ordained by God and sanctified by Him and that, indeed, the fellowship of man and woman is ordered toward the physical union which stands at its center and is the most intimate form of this fellowship. Nevertheless, the church must also assure those who do not enter the order of marriage that they also please God.

No human being can escape existing within, or in opposition to, the male-female distinction as the fundamental form of fellow-humanity. However, not every human being need marry.[6] We remain free to enter with God's blessing into the order of marriage and there to live out our obedience to Him. We are also free, however, while granting the inestimable importance of marriage as a sign and realization of our creation for fellow-humanity, to live out our commitment to our fellows in the unmarried state. We may expect that marriage will remain the norm, but we must make room for Jesus' own recognition that there may be some who "have made themselves eunuchs for the sake of the kingdom of heaven" (Matt. 19:12), that is, some who have chosen to forego marriage in order to live out their vocations in service to the Lord. And we recognize that some who do not choose the single state may, nevertheless, live such a life. They too exist within the duality of male and female. The too live as male and female.

> *The Christian community needs to be sensitive to the needs of all single persons in its midst, including those who for various reasons are unable to marry or who may have lost their spouse through death or divorce. Many unmarried persons bear the burden of loneliness and feel "left out" of the life and activities of their congregations and sometimes are given the impression, intentionally or unintentionally, that they have a less-privileged status. The Christian community must assure all those who are married that their situation is in no way inferior to the state of those who are married. Rather, they too, apart from the earthly institution of marriage, have been called to be members of God's family and to devote themselves to the work of Christian service (Eph. 4:12). To them may even belong opportunities for well doing which are not open to those who have the responsibilities of married life. In a spirit of mutual encouragement, married and unmarried alike must make it their aim to help each other secure their "undivided devotion to the Lord" (I Cor. 7:35).*

A further reason why marriage cannot be made a necessity lies in the fact that, despite its immeasurable importance for our lives, it remains an earthly order. This is made unmistakably clear not only by Jesus' words in Mark 12:25, where He says that in the resurrection there is no more marrying, but also by St. Paul's discussion in I Corinthians 7. In this chapter the apostle does not demonstrate a negative attitude toward sexuality as such, though this is often alleged.[7] His advice to the Corinthian Christians must be seen together with his statement in v. 31: "The form of this world is passing away." Because the end-time has entered our history in the person of Jesus Christ, no earthly reality such as marriage can be institutionalized as a necessary form of obedience to God; that is to say, marriage is not an institution which everyone must enter. Paul suggests that those who are unmarried may be better able to devote themselves to the work of the Lord, free of earthly cares and responsibilities which marriage brings. As Paul himself recognizes, however, this is true only of those to whom such a gift is given (v. 7). For others it might be true that only within marriage could they give themselves with a glad heart to the doing of God's will. While marriage is limited to earthly life, as a divine institution it can be pronounced good and entered with a good conscience (Gen. 2:24-25). . .

C. Homosexuality

Homosexuality comes under a categorical prohibition in the Old and New Testaments (Lev. 18:22, 24; 20:13; I Cor. 6:9-10; I Tim. 1:9-10). Paul writes in Romans 1 of the "dishonorable passions" to which God gives up those who worship the creature rather than the Creator and says: "Their women exchanged natural relations for unnatural, and the men likewise gave up natural relations with women and were consumed with passion for one another, men committing shameless acts with men . . ." (Rom. 1:26-27). In a discussion of homosexuality one might stop here with the fact of the condemnation uttered in such passages. If we consider homosexuality in the light of the total Biblical context regarding the purpose of marriage and the man-woman duality discussed above, however, we may come to a clearer understanding of why Christian thought has condemned and should continue to condemn homosexual lusts and acts.

The creation of human beings for covenant community finds its original expression in the fellowship of male and female. This fellowship, as we have stressed above, requires a commitment to the integrity of our sexual identity. The fellowship of male and female implies a recognition that we are male and female and that we should not strive to transcend that distinction. The ultimate fellowship for which God is preparing us, of which the man-woman polarity is an intimation, is not a merging of those who are alike into an undifferentiated oneness. It is a harmonious fellowship of those who, though different, are united in love. From this viewpoint we may say that the homosexual relationship approaches too closely the forbidden love of self and minimizes the distinction between lover and beloved. The male-female duality as the created pattern of human fellowship requires of us fidelity to our sexual identity, a willingness to be male *or* female.

Second, and very obviously, a homosexual relationship is nonprocreative, and it is so not merely by choice or accident but because the nature of the relationship itself could under no circumstances be procreative. Some, of course, may regard this as mere biological fact, irrelevant when the possibility of deep affection and love in a homosexual relation is considered. Nevertheless, the Scriptures do not place love in such "splendid isolation." "Mere" biology becomes very important when Christian teaching about human nature takes seriously the fact that we have no personhood except one that is incarnate. Furthermore, when we point to the fact that the homosexual relationship is nonprocreative, we do so against the background of the significance we found in suggesting that the one-flesh union of a man and woman is ordinarily expected to be fruitful.

Hence, we can say on Christian premises that mutual consent or even genuine affection is not enough to justify a homosexual relationship. The human being is, according to the Scriptures, more than mere freedom to define what he or she will be. There are acts or relationships to which we cannot consent without stepping beyond the limitations our

Creator has set for His creatures (Rom. 1:26 ff.). Sexuality provides an excellent example of this truth. Mutual consent alone between partners does not, on the Christian understanding, make heterosexual intercourse permissible. (See Section II above on marriage and its purposes.) Similarly, mutual consent alone, even when joined with affection, cannot justify a homosexual union. An unwillingness to make such affirmations is part of a "flight from creation" which besets the contemporary world and contemporary Christendom. It ought to be resisted in the name of the Redeemer who is also our Creator.

In discussing the sins which follow upon man's refusal to honor God as Creator of all things (Rom. 1:26-32), the apostle Paul singles out the sins of homosexual behavior for special comment. Such behavior comes under God's judgment not because it is any more heinous than the 21 vices listed in 1:29-31, but because it, too, illustrates man's rebellion against his Creator. Like these sins, homosexual behavior is illustrative of how rebellious man turns in upon himself and makes "an agony of the common life that should in God's intent have been a blessing to mankind."[36]

The apostle's condemnation, however, is not meant to deprive those guilty of these sins the help which God would extend to them. While not minimizing the threat of God's wrath against all forms of enslavement to sin, the church needs to recognize in its efforts to help the homosexual that all people are born in need of deliverance from the effects which sin has imposed on their lives. With this in mind it is important to realize that there are those persons who, apart from any deliberate choice on their part, have a predisposition toward homosexuality and have no desire to enter into a relationship with a person of the opposite sex.[37] In order to offer such persons the compassionate help they need, the church, having condemned all homosexual acts engaged in by such persons or by those of a heterosexual orientation, must stand ready to offer its assistance to those who seek to overcome the temptations which beset them and who desire to remain chaste before God despite their homosexual orientation.

> *It must be said that a predisposition toward homosexuality is the result of the disordering, corrupting effect of the fall into sin, just as also the predisposition toward any sin is symptomatic of original sin.*[38] *Furthermore, whatever the causes of such a condition may be—e.g., environmental or genetic—homosexual orientation is profoundly "unnatural" without implying that such a person's sexual orientation is a matter of conscious, deliberate choice. However, this fact cannot be used by the homosexual as an excuse to justify homosexual behavior. As a sinful human being the homosexual is held accountable to God for homosexual thoughts, words, and deeds. Such a person should be counseled to heed the church's call to repentance, trust in God's promise of deliverance (Ps. 50:15), and order his/her life in accord with the Creator's intent.*

We should stress that the judgment made here is moral and theological, not legal. The question whether homosexual acts between consenting adults should be legally prohibited is one about which Christian citizens may disagree. Not all matters of morality are fit subjects for legislation. Although law does play an educative role and must, therefore, shape moral convictions, questions of morality are especially fit subjects for legal codification when they impinge on the *common* good. Whether homosexual acts privately engaged in damage the common good in such a way that public concern and control are needed is difficult to judge. Even if one felt that such relationships were not a fit subject for legislation, however, the law would still have a legitimate interest in protecting children from homosexual influence in the years when their sexual identity is formed. At any rate, the judgment of informed Christians may well differ as to precisely where the legal lines ought more properly be drawn.

We cannot conclude without noting that the discussion above suggests that Christian counsel for the homosexual is that he seek to control his sexual orientation at least in the sense that he abstain from homosexual acts. We should not overlook the burden of loneliness which this places upon the homosexual. If the discerning eye of God created woman as the answer to man's loneliness, the homosexual who abstains from the sexual relationship to which he is inclined must feel that there is no "other" to answer to his loneliness. He must be helped to bear that burden, not merely exhorted to struggle nobly against his inclinations. It is right to remember, of course, that Christian counsel to heterosexuals will also often involve asking them to restrain their impulses and refrain from acts to which they are inclined. Finally, we should note again that, while marriage can be said to be the center of the male-female polarity, it is only a created reality. As we stressed above, marriage has limits, and entrance into a marital union is not a necessity. The person of homosexual orientation must be constantly made aware that fellowship in the church and a share in the hope of the heavenly kingdom is also offered to him/her through faith in Christ, whose death has atoned for all sins.

Endnotes

[2] Robert Farrar Capon, *Bed and Board: Plain Talk About Marriage* (New York: Simon and Schuster, 1965), p. 49.

[3] Karl Barth, *Church Dogmatics,* trans. A. T. Mackay *et al.* (Edinburgh: T. & T. Clark, 1961), vol. 3, part 4, pp. 116-240.

[4] This scriptural assertion implies that the subject of human sexuality includes much more than the male/female relationship in marriage. While it has been necessary to limit this study to a basic discussion of the male/female duality as it pertains to marriage and certain other problems, such as homosexuality, the Commission recognizes that more could and needs to be said about how our creation as sexual beings affects a whole variety of relationships such as between parents and children, friends of the same sex as well as friends of the opposite sex, male and female colleagues, employers and employees, and many other personal encounters between the sexes.

[5] In general cf. Barth, pp. 149-168.

[6] It is true that in the days of the Old Testament the unmarried state was regarded with disfavor. This was because of the Israelite stress on procreation as the continuation of the people, the seed of Abraham, from whom the Promised One was to come. We, however, who are of the new Israel and who confess that the Promised One has indeed come to His People, stand under no such necessity. (Our discussion here follows Barth, pp. 149-168.) The barren and the fruitful, the married and the unmarried are alike members of a new fellowship and family (Gal. 3:28).

[7] For a brief but helpful discussion of this chapter cf. Stephen Sapp, *Sexuality, the Bible, and Science* (Philadelphia: Fortress Press, 1977), pp. 68-73. . . .

[36] Martin H. Franzmann, *Romans* (St. Louis: Concordia Publishing House, 1968), p. 43.

[37] It is not uncommon today to distinguish between the pervert—for whom heterosexuality is natural but who nevertheless engages in homosexual acts—and the invert—who, as far as he knows, has never experienced heterosexual attraction and for whom a homosexual orientation seems perfectly natural.

[38] For a discussion of the distinction between "propensity" and "behavior" as these terms apply to the question of homosexuality the reader may wish to consult the Lutheran Church in Australia's 1975 "Statement on Homosexuality," pages 1-2. This report was distributed to the Synod by the CTCR in April 1975 as "a worthy contribution to the discussion" of this sensitive issue of human sexuality.

Notes: *In 1981, the Commission on Theology and Church Relations of the Lutheran Church-Missouri Synod issued a lengthy report on the nature of sexual life, in which homosexuality was treated as a special issue. This statement has been taken from that report.*

Homosexuality is treated as one question which emerges out of a discussion of sexuality and its purpose in creation. The creation of humans as sexual creatures, male and female, is part of the Creator's pattern. Given the purposes and the nature of creation, the prohibitions against sexuality in the Bible are understood. Homosexuality is to be condemned morally. The question of the criminalization of some or all homosexual activity is a matter about which Christians can and do disagree.

MUSIC SQUARE CHURCH

GUILT BY ASSOCIATION (UNDATED)

This unrestraining power in this bulldozing, bully, antichrist government regime says homosexuality is a third sexual preference, and that it should be taught in school. God says that homosexuality is a demon possession and one of the things that he despises most and that we must not associate ourselves with it or support it. I repeat, God says that it is a demon possession, not a third sexual preference. God hated those lewd, unrepentant, disgusting, vile creatures so much that he destroyed them in the city of Sodom. This satanic one-world government now has the audacity to say that we must allow our children to be taught by homosexuals (perverts, those whom God despises), and are saying it is now lawful to teach our children that homosexuality is a third sexual choice. They want to make homosexuals out of our children and gain more revolutionists that our children and us may be destroyed with them. Misery loves company. In Romans, the first chapter, and in other passages in God's word, God said that if we fellowship or take pleasure in, associate with, or support homosexuals, that we will be made to believe a lie, then in the end, be sent to the same hell that these unrepentant, unconcerned clamorous ones are going to. These in the time of Sodom as well as in the hour that we are now living in are driven by the relentless, unrestrained power of Satan himself. They actually attempted to force holy angels into compliance with their vile passions and lewdness, giving their city a name of infamy throughout all generations. Should we not agree with God and his angels and discriminate against such by paying heed to God's angels as just Lot did and flee and separate ourselves from this wickedness and not be left with the sinful multitude when the angels cried: ". . . Up, get you out of this place; for the Lord will destroy this city . . ." (Genesis 19:14). Then on the final day to them that did not flee and disassociate themselves, will stand before the Judgment Bar of God hearing the Father and His Son's words, ". . . Depart from me, ye cursed, into everlasting fire, prepared for the devil and his angels:" (Matthew 25:41).

God said all these things would happen in the last days. "Woe unto them that call evil good, and good evil; that put darkness for light, and light for darkness; that put bitter for sweet, and sweet for bitter!" (Isaiah 5:20).

Notes: *Music Square Church, also known as the Alamo Christian Church, is one of the Jesus People groups which emerged in the late 1960s. While occasionally branded as a cult, it follows a traditional Christian stance and Protestant values. It harshly denounces some things it sees as particularly important contemporary sins, among them abortion and homosexuality. This brief consideration, from one of the church's tracts, makes its opposition to homosexual activity quite clear.*

NATIONAL ASSOCIATION OF EVANGELICALS

STATEMENT ON HOMOSEXUALITY (1985)

The Scriptures declare that God created us male and female. Furthermore, the biblical record shows that sexual union was established exclusively within the context of a male-female relationship (Genesis 2:24), and formalized in the institution of marriage. The partner for man was woman. Together they were to be one flesh. In the New Testament, the oneness of male and female in marriage pictures the relationship between Christ and His church (Ephesians 5:22-33).

Everywhere in Scripture the sexual relationship between man and woman within the bonds of marriage is viewed as something natural and beautiful.

Homosexual activity, like adulterous relationships, is clearly condemned in the Scriptures. In Leviticus 18:22 God declares the practice of homosexuality an abomination in His sight. In Romans 1:26-27 the practice of homosexuality is described as a degrading and unnatural passion. I Corinthians 6:9-10 identifies the practice of homosexuality as a sin that, if persisted in, brings grave consequences in this life and excludes one from the Kingdom of God.

The Apostle Paul, strong in his condemnation of the practice of homosexuality, also testifies that those once engaged in homosexuality were among those who were forgiven and changed in the name of the Lord Jesus Christ (I Corinthians 6:11). This declaration offers hope both for forgiveness and for healing. Individual Christians, ministers, and congregations need to maintain the belief that all human beings have sinned, and that all Christians have received God's mercy while helpless, ungodly, and hostile to God. In the name of Christ we proclaim forgiveness, cleansing, restoration and power for godly living for all who repent and believe the gospel.

We believe that homosexuality is not an inherited condition in the same category as race, gender, or national origin, all of which are free from moral implication. We believe that homosexuality is a deviation from the Creator's plan for human sexuality. While homosexuals as individuals are entitled to civil rights, including equal protection of the law, the NAE opposes legislation which would extend special consideration to such individuals based upon their "sexual orientation." Such legislation inevitably is perceived as legitimatizing the practice of homosexuality and elevates that practice to the level of an accepted moral standard. While maintaining our opposition to proposed so-called "Gay Rights" legislation, where such legislation has been enacted into law, NAE strongly urges that churches and religious organizations be exempted from compliance by amendment to the law. The position and practice of such organizations regarding homosexuality are determined by their religious convictions. This we hold to be a grave matter of religious freedom.

Individual Christians, ministers, and congregations should compassionately proclaim the Good News of forgiveness and encourage those involved in homosexual practices to cease those practices, accept forgiveness, and pray for deliverance as nothing is impossible with God. Further, we should accept them into fellowship upon confession of faith and repentance, as we would any other forgiven sinner (I Corinthians 6:11).

We further call upon pastors and theologians, along with medical and sociological specialists within the Christian community to expand research on the factors which give rise to homosexuality and to develop therapy, pastoral care and congregational support leading to complete restoration.

Notes: *The National Association of Evangelicals consists of approximately 40 conservative evangelical Christian denominations. Its statement follows traditional Christian condemnation of homosexual behavior. The association accepts civil rights for homosexuals, but opposes attempts to grant special civil privileges. In addition, it is strongly opposed to forcing churches to adhere to any civil rights legislation that would grant job protection to homosexuals. Because most Churches oppose homosexuality for religious reasons, the association feels beingforced to employ homosexuals would infringe upon their rights.*

NATIONAL ASSOCIATION OF FREE WILL BAPTISTS

HOMOSEXUALITY AND ADULTERY (1976)

Whereas,

There is a widespread move by some modern advocates who want to consider Christian love as a basis for tolerating all kinds of sexual "freedom," and

Whereas,

These same persons advocate that homosexuality, adultery, and fornication are satisfactory ways of life even for Christians; and,

Whereas,

There is a growing sentiment and toleration among some church people toward homosexuality, adultery, and fornication; and

Whereas,

The Bible is replete with references (See note below.) exposing and condemning such actions on the part of any person, whether that person claims to be a believer or not; and,

Whereas,

Free Will Baptists believe the Bible is our rule and guide for faith and practice; therefore,

Be it resolved:

1. That the National Association of Free Will Baptists continue to denounce homosexuality and adultery as sinful, unChristian, and already condemned by God in His Word.
2. That the National Association of Free Will Baptists recommend that all pastors and church leaders continue to strongly denounce this unrighteous conduct and urge purity to prevail, ". . . for God has not called us unto uncleanness, but unto holiness" (I Thessalonians 4:3, 7).

Special Note: Bible references supporting the above resolution: Genesis 13:13; 19:5, 7; Levitucus 18:22; 20:13; Deuteronomy 23:17; Judges 19:22, 23; Romans 1:24-27; I Corinthians 6:9, 10; 7:2; Jude 7, 18, 19.

While many other references could be attached, there are more than adequate to support the above resolution.

Notes: *In 1976, the National Association of Free Will Baptists saw the need to go on record as opposed to the increase of sexual freedom, of which the growing toleration of homosexual activity is one symbol.*

NATIONAL ASSOCIATION OF FREE WILL BAPTISTS

STATEMENT ON HOMOSEXUALITY (1977)

Whereas,

The National Association of Free Will Baptists in its 1976 session passed a strong resolution against homosexuality and adultery; and

Whereas,

Homosexuality has come increasingly to the forefront gaining widespread acceptance even among many so-called Christians; therefore,

Be it resolved:

That we reaffirm our belief that according to the Bible homosexuality is sin; its participants are sinners; and the practice and the participant are condemned by God.

Notes: *This second resolution denouncing homosexuality came in reaction to Christian views which were perceived as supportive of homosexual behavior.*

NATIONAL ASSOCIATION OF FREE WILL BAPTISTS

RESOLUTION ON BIBLICAL VALUES (1984)

WHEREAS, the greatest needs of our nation are spiritual revival and return to God and Biblical values, and

WHEREAS, the current movements for rights of homosexuals, disregard for the sacredness of human life as created by God, such as abortion on demand and euthanasia, the equal rights amendment, pornography, secular humanism, and other such evils are in direct conflict with a return to God and spiritual renewal,

BE IT RESOLVED, that this body go on record as opposing the said evils, and

BE IT FURTHER RESOLVED, that our people be encouraged to work for the election of public officials, regardless of political party, who are supportive of Biblical values. *(Adopted as amended)*

Notes: *In 1984, the National Association of Free Will Baptists saw homosexuality as one of the many symptoms of the slide of society into evil and a major blockade to spiritual renewal.*

NORTH PACIFIC YEARLY MEETING OF THE SOCIETY OF FRIENDS

GAY AND LESBIAN FRIENDS (1986)

Since its beginning, North Pacific Yearly Meeting has been concerned with homosexuality. We had been clear that the civil rights of homosexual people should be protected. Beyond that, there was no unity and very little understanding of the subject.

During our 1982 annual session the host college where we met (and to which we planned to return in 1983) placed a number of behavioral restrictions upon us. The last one was that if gay and lesbian Friends were to identify themselves and meet together, they do so inconspicuously. A special meeting of Steering Committee was called to deal with the hurt and anger that this and the earlier restrictions generated. One Friend expressed dismay that we even felt a need to discuss the matter. If we had been told that black Friends, or our children could be included on campus only if they remained inconspicuous, we would know without question how to respond. A shock of realization of the truth to which this Friend pointed swept through the meeting.

Out of that experience the Steering Committee wholeheartedly affirmed that gay and lesbian Friends are an integral part of our Yearly Meeting family. Henceforth the Yearly Meeting would not participate in any situation that rejected or restricted them. This leap of insight was a turning point in the maturation of our Yearly Meeting. It opened the door to increasing our understanding of homosexuality and fully accepting the people whose lives are touched by it. Since then the gay and lesbian Friends of NPYM have begun to relax in the security of this acceptance, and in many caring ways have been sharing their experience with the rest of us. We hope that in time, with their help, we will all reach a clear understanding of this subject.

Notes: *The Society of Friends (Quakers) have been widely divided on the issues of sexuality, from those who represent a conservative holiness position to those who have been very accepting and supportive of homosexuals. Actions to restrict homosexual members of the North Pacific Yearly Meeting in the early 1980s led to a reconsideration of the meeting's stance and a complete reversal. The meeting now represents the most liberal wing of Quaker thinking.*

NORTH PACIFIC YEARLY MEETING OF THE SOCIETY OF FRIENDS

MARRIAGE (1986)

IN A MARRIAGE, a man and woman enter into a covenant with each other and with God. Early Friends perceived that no mortal being could join two others together in marriage; only they could marry each other through a public declaration of their commitment. In a Meeting for Worship specially called for that purpose, the couple publicly affirm and celebrate their commitment to each other. Before allowing the marriage, the Meeting, through a marriage committee, counsels with the couple, seeking to establish their clearness in what they are undertaking. If the committee so recommends, and the Meeting agrees, the marriage is taken under the care of the Meeting. This means that the couple is surrounded by a loving community which may take action as necessary to support the well being of the two individuals, of the relationship itself, and of any children who may result.

Traditionally, such public affirmation of commitment to one's partner in a Meeting for Worship has been limited to heterosexual couples. In recent times, committed homosexual couples have requested the opportunity to declare publicly their commitment to each other and to have their relationship taken under the care of the Meeting. Meetings may wish to honor such requests to take a homosexual committed relationship under their care by following the traditional clearness procedures and having a Meeting for Worship in which the couple publicly affirm and celebrate their commitment to each other.

Notes: *Following the emergence of a new perspective towards homosexuals and homosexuality, the North Pacific Yearly Meeting reexamined their understanding of marriage and came to an acceptance of "marriage" between committed homosexual couples. This new stance was embodied in the newest edition of their* Faith and Practice, *published in 1986.*

OPEN BIBLE STANDARD CHURCHES

STATEMENT ON HOMOSEXUALITY (1984)

Whereas one of the by-products of the increasing mood of permissiveness in our society is a growing awareness of a community not previously recognized, namely, the practicing homosexuals in our midst, and

Whether the result of moral looseness, social instability or physiological change, the number of homosexuals seems to be increasing.

The Bible speaks out strongly in condemnation of sin and unrighteousness in all forms. The Scriptures explicitly pronounce judgment on sexual deviance. The first chapter of Romans refers to the guilt of mankind expressed in shameful worship, perverted passions and corrupted minds.

Nevertheless, we must remember that all men regardless of their offenses need God's love as manifest in Jesus Christ. All too often we have both overtly and covertly rejected the person of the sexual deviant.

Therefore, we resolve as the Open Bible Standard Churches, Inc.

1. to stand firm in the belief that the Holy Scriptures condemn practicing homosexuality and give no basis for approving this as an acceptable lifestyle, and

2. to extend the healing ministry of the entire Christian community to individuals who seek forgiveness and deliverance from the sin of homosexuality.

Notes: *The Open Bible Standard Churches originally adopted this statement in 1980 and amended it to its present text in 1984. It follows the standard traditional Christian condemnation of homosexuality.*

PRESBYTERIAN CHURCH (U.S.A.)

WESTMINSTER CATECHISM (1647)

Q.139. What are the sins forbidden in the seventh commandment?

A. The sins forbidden in the seventh commandment, besides the neglect of the duties required, are, adultery, fornication, rape, incest, sodomy, and all unnatural lusts, all unclean imaginations, thoughts, purposes, and affections; all corrupt or filthy communication, or listening thereunto; wanton looks, impudent or light behavior, immodest apparel; prohibiting of lawful, and dispensing with unlawful marriages; allowing, tolerating, keeping of stews, and resorting to them; entangling vows of single life, undue delay of marriage; having more wives or husbands than one at the same time; unjust divorce, or desertion; idleness, gluttony, drunkenness, unchaste company; lascivious songs, books, pictures, dancings, stage plays; and all other provocations to, or acts of uncleanness, either in ourselves or others.

Notes: *The issue of homosexuality was not a primary concern of the Puritan (Presbyterian) leaders who authored the Westminster Catechism during their famous gathering in London. The Catechism and the associated Westminster Confession became the definitive doctrinal statements of English-speaking Presbyterianism. Though not a major issue, the subject of homosexuality was raised in the catechism in passing and as such set the tradition for most Presbyterian churches.*

In the 1960s, the United Presbyterian Church in the U.S.A. adopted a new Confession of Faith. Partially in reaction to those who suggested that the new confession meant a denial of the Westminster standards, the Church created a Book of Confessions, *which combined a number of doctrinal statements of the ancient church and the Reformed Church of the sixteenth and seventeenth century. A revised edition of the* Book of Confessions, *appeared in 1983, at the time of the merger which produced the Presbyterian Church (U.S.A.). (The Presbyterian Church (U.S.A.) was formed through the 1983 merger of the United Presbyterian Church in the U.S.A. (UPCUSA) and the Presbyterian Church in the U.S. (PCUS).)*

According to the Westminster Catechism, the seventh commandment forbids sodomy and all unnatural lusts (i.e., homosexuality). The more conservative Presbyterian denominations, such as the Orthodox Presbyterian Church, tend to accept this position literally, while the Presbyterian Church (U.S.A.) has moved to a different position in its more recent documents.

PRESBYTERIAN CHURCH (U.S.A.)

SEXUALITY AND THE HUMAN COMMUNITY (1970)

4. Male and Female Homosexuality

In the course of a normal pattern of growth, there are many factors which influence the shaping of one's sexual identity. God created us male and female, but the process of creation is not finished, either chemically or psychologically, at birth. There is a development process which continues through childhood and adolescence, the end of which is the establishment of a comfortable identity with one's given sexuality, including an acceptance of those features of the opposite sex which coexist with the given sexuality in all of us.

While it is not a universal phenomenon, the great majority of persons of both sexes encounter, at some point in this learning process, some form of homosexual feelings or experiences. That is, they experience some degree of sexual pleasure with and attraction toward a person of their own sex.

In some persons' development process, these homosexual feelings and experiences become fixed as the definition of their sexual identity, either wholly or in part. The roots of this condition may be in part chemical, in part psychological. In such persons, there may develop a need to find sexual relationship and gratification exclusively with another person of the same sex. Or such a person may develop occasional homosexual relationships which exist alongside an otherwise heterosexual behavior pattern.

So far in the history of our culture, both church and society have tended to deal with this pattern of sexual conduct almost exclusively by taboos, condemnatory attitudes, and repressive legislation. The essentially negative attitudes of church and society toward the phenomenon of homosexuality has often resulted in aggravated suffering and grievous injustice for homosexual persons. The taboos attached to the phenomenon have led society to treat homosexuals as criminals. Such responses have had the effect of inhibiting the possibility of change in homosexual persons who are unhappy with their state of affairs, but who hesitate to approach anyone for help because of the fear attached to any open acknowledgement of their circumstance.

The ethical reflections and personal attitudes of the Christian community should be such that homosexual persons will not be made to feel that their sexual preference is in irresolvable conflict with their membership in the Christian fellowship. Toward that end, the following ethical considerations might be kept in mind:

1. There is a difference between homosexuality as a condition of personal existence and homosexualism as explicit homosexual behavior.[7]
2. The condemnation of homosexualism found in St. Paul's writings[8] are given in the context of lists of antisocial and personally destructive forms of conduct which characterize "the unrighteous." It is not singled out as more heinous than other sins, but is discussed with other forms of behavior which betoken man's refusal to accept his creatureliness.[9]
3. The contexts in which Paul's condemnations appear suggest that he objected to the element of disregard for the neighbor more than he did to acts in themselves. Thus, prostitution does not call into question responsible heterosexuality. Perhaps pederasty, homosexual prostitution, and similar neighbor-disregarding forms of behavior ought not to overshadow our entire response to the human condition of homosexuality.[10]
4. St. Paul treats sexual sins as one set of symptoms of the universal experience of apostasy. No one is exempt from the experience of alienation from God, neither the homosexual nor the heterosexual person. Therefore, presumably both are eligible for the experience of reconciliation to which all men are invited in Christ.[11]

Since the state of knowledge about homosexuality is far from fully developed in our society, we urge the church to support further and more adequate research into this phase of human sexual behavior and to participate actively in the theological and ethical reflection on the matter which may be prompted by the new insights resulting from such research. We also urge that Christians in all those vocations which might include care for and counsel with homosexuals give attention in their initial or continuing professional training to the need for a fuller understanding of homosexuality and its processes, so that the desire for change can be more effectively elicited and encouraged.

If the function of sexual differentiation is best understood in terms of a covenant relationship which encourages both mutual personal fulfillment and the freedom to establish a family, then homosexual behavior is essentially incomplete in character. It is therefore important to guard against the development of fixed homosexual patterns during childhood and adolescence, by developing in children and young people an understanding of homosexuality, including their own feelings or experiences with it. One function of such an understanding is to spare young people from thinking they are destined to homosexuality because of some developmentally normal experience.

It should be a concern of the church to re-examine the various unisexual institutional structures of our society (schools, Penal Institutions, Military, etc.) to see where they may, knowingly or unwittingly, contribute to the formation or continuation of the very homosexual patterns we have for so long condemned. Separate men's and women's schools and colleges, for example, may create pressures of a homosexual sort by merely perpetuating their traditions of separate education. In the penal system, by contrast, heterosexual contact is often deliberately refused to a prisoner as part of his punishment. It is not unknown for homosexual assaults among prisoners to be encouraged as part of the punitive pattern.

Overcrowded conditions, underpaid and undertrained staff, and skeletal budgets for rehabilitation programs are common afflictions of the American penal system. Recent investigations of prison conditions in Arkansas[12] and Rikers Island, New York,[13] have included charges of sodomy. It is not surprising, but neither is it tolerable, that poor prison conditions and isolation from heterosexual contact would give rise to homosexual assaults.

The church has a more than passing obligation to look sharply at such institutional phenomena in our culture and to support, for example, in penal institutions, the development of such practices as conjugal visitation rights for prisoners, furlough in the community, family as well as vocational rehabilitation, etc.

Another concern of the church on this topic is that of developing an awareness among parents and young people of the possible psychological pain that can follow from being the object of homosexual advances by adult persons committed to this pattern.

To the latter end, some enlightened legal measures governing the overt and public behavior of homosexual persons can properly be supported by Christians. It is our opinion, however, that laws which make a felony of homosexual acts privately committed by consenting adults are morally unsupportable, contribute nothing to the public welfare, and inhibit rather than permit changes in behavior by homosexual persons. To overturn such laws would also eliminate the need for those surveillance practices which can become more odious than the so-called crime under scrutiny.

Endnotes

7 *Dictionary of Christian Ethics,* John MacQuarrie, Ed. Westminster Press, 1967, p. 152.

8 Notably Rom. 1:26 *et seq.* and I Cor. 6:9 *et seq.*

9 *The Ethics of Sex,* Helmut Thielicke, Harper & Row, 1964, p. 278 *et seq;* see also the exegesis of Rom. 1:18 by John Knox, *The Interpreters' Bible,* Vol. 9, p. 395.

10 *Sex and Love in the Bible,* William Graham Cole, Association Press, gives a sketch of the sexual attitudes and customs of the ancient world, to which St. Paul was responding in his writing. Cole's description makes clear that the early church was struggling against odds

to preserve a sensitivity to convenantal relationships between persons in a world which had commercialized every form of sexual liaison.

[11] *Theology of the New Testament,* R. Bultmann, Chas. Scribner's Sons, 1951. Vol. I, p. 250 *et passim.*

[12] *The New York Times,* July 12, 1969, p. 41.

[12] *The New York Times,* December 23, 1969, pp. 1 and 39.

Notes: *In 1970, the United Presbyterian Church in the U.S., which merged in 1983 with the Presbyterian Church in the U.S.A. to form the Presbyterian Church (U.S.A.), published a lengthy report on sexuality. Prepared as a congregational study document, it had narrowly been accepted by the General Assembly only after a lengthy and heated debate. Among the more controversial aspects of the report, the section on homosexuality suggested that in some cases homosexual relations might be accepted and that disapproval of unneighborly behavior associated with homosexuality (such as promiscuity) should not limit possible positive reactions to other behaviors. It also clearly supported the decriminalization of homosexual behavior between adults.*

PRESBYTERIAN CHURCH (U.S.A.)

STATEMENT ON THE ORDINATION OF HOMOSEXUALS: POLICY STATEMENT AND RECOMMENDATIONS (1978)

Policy Statement and Recommendations

Introduction

The General Assembly was asked by the Presbyteries of New York City and of the Palisades to give "definitive guidance" concerning the eligibility for ordination to the professional ministry of persons who openly acknowledge homosexual orientation and practice. One thing has become very clear in consideration of this request. The church must respond to this issue. Numbers of persons both within the church and outside it experience homosexuality, either as a transient part of their growth as persons or as a continuing force in their own lives or in the lives of family members and friends. New data in psychology and the social sciences have appeared that challenge the church's traditional posture on this matter. The time has come for the church to confront this issue, to reexamine and refresh its theological understanding of homosexuality in the light of God's revelation to us in Jesus Christ, and to renew its practical approach to mission and ministry among homosexual persons.

The issue submitted to this General Assembly is a call for guidance to individual Christian persons, congregations, and presbyteries concerning the status of self-affirming, practicing homosexual persons within the church. Specifically, the presbyteries seek guidance on the matter of ordination to the ministry of Word and Sacrament. Difficult questions are involved in this request. Should the General Assembly foster the creation of a new situation in the church, in which practicing homosexual persons would be free to affirm their lifestyle publicly and to obtain the church's blessing upon this through ordination? Or should the church reaffirm its historic opposition to homosexual behavior? These questions must be dealt with in the context of the whole life and mission of the church. To answer them, we must examine the nature of homosexuality according to current scientific understandings, interpreted within the context of our theological understandings of God's purpose for human life. To this purpose, in all its rich variety, the Scripture attests. Church membership, ordination, pluralism and unity in the church, and the Christian response in ministry and mission must then, in turn, be examined.

Homosexuality Within a Theological Context

New data and hypotheses in psychology, sociology, endocrinology, and the other secular disciplines cannot in themselves determine a shift in the church's posture on this issue. Very frequently these disciplines shed new light upon our understanding of homosexuality and how the church should respond to it. Frequently the results of scientific inquiry are tentative and inconclusive, neutral in their theological and ethical implications, or even weighted with unspoken values and assumptions that are misleading against the background of biblical faith. Therefore, we must address the task of theologically interpreting these extrabiblical data, while at the same time renewing our understanding of Scripture and tradition in the light of those data in the sciences.

Medical and psychological theories concerning homosexuality and its causes are complex and often contradictory. Among the multitude of hypotheses and conclusions currently being entertained, a small but significant body of facts emerges that enlarges our understanding of what homosexuality is and how we should respond to it. It seems clear that homosexuality is primarily a matter of affectional attraction that cannot be defined simply in terms of genital acts, although the homosexual orientation may be so expressed.

Most human beings experience occasional homosexual attraction, although not always consciously. It is reasonably certain that somewhere between 5 and 10 percent of the human population is exclusively or predominantly homosexual in orientation. Exclusively homosexual persons appear to be remarkably resistant to reorientation through most psychiatric methods. Most exclusively homosexual persons believe that their condition is irreversible. Some secular therapists working with those motivated to change report some success in reversal, and counselors employing both the resources of Christian faith and psychotherapeutic techniques report a higher rate of success. It appears that two critical variables are involved. First, do therapist and client believe that change is possible? Second, how convinced is the client that change is desirable?

The causes of homosexuality now appear to be remarkably numerous and diverse. There is no one explanation for homosexual affectional preference, and thus neither the persons involved nor their parents can be singled out as responsible for the homosexual orientation. Most authorities now assume that both heterosexuality and homosexuality result primarily from psychological and social factors affecting human beings during their growth toward maturity, with some possible influence from biological factors. Most homosexual persons do no consciously choose their affectional preference, although they do face the choice of whether to accept it or to seek change, and of whether to express it in genital acts or to remain celibate. However, although homosexual affectional preference is not always the result of conscious choice, it may be interpreted as part of the involuntary and often unconscious drive away from God's purposes that characterizes fallen human nature, falling short of God's intended patterns for human sexuality.

Human sexuality has a dynamic quality. Within the constraints of nature, nurture serves to transform both sexual identity and intersexual preference. Our sexuality is vulnerable to shaping influences from many directions.

As the embryo develops, the single root organism unfolds and differentiates, sometimes making a boy, sometimes a girl, sometimes a sexually ambiguous being. Following an initial gender assignment, we believe and nurture ourselves and one another into authentic or inauthentic sexual beings.

We find here a parallel to the Genesis account of the creation of humankind, which speaks of the precious and precarious balance of male and female life together that perpetually needs both our affirmation and God's upholding grace. Genesis offers polemic against deviations from the wise separation of humankind into man and woman. It is this separation that makes union possible. In creation, God separates woman from man so that they are constituted with yearning for each other. Becoming one flesh they portray the glory of his image in the earth.

To say that God created humankind male and female, called man and woman to join in partnership as one flesh, and commanded them to multiply (Genesis 1:27-28; 2:24) is to describe how God intended loving companionship between a man and a woman to be a fundamental pattern of human relationship and the appropriate context for male-female genital sexual expression. However, to say that God created humankind male and female, called man and woman to join in partnership as one flesh, and commanded them to multiply is not to state that God intended to limit the possibility for meaningful life to heterosexual marriage. Jesus' own celibate lifestyle and his commitment to his own ministry rather than to the biological family (Matthew 12:46-50; Mark 3:31-35; Luke 8:19-21) demonstrates the blessing of God upon life lived outside the covenant of marriage.

This biological and theological argument has implications for homosexuality. It appears that one explanation of the process in which persons develop homosexual preferences and behavior is that men and women fall away from their intended being because of distorted or insufficient belief in who they are. They are not adequately upheld in being male and female, in being heterosexual, by self-belief and the belief of a supporting community.

Therefore, it appears that what is really important is not what homosexuality is but what we believe about it. Our understanding of its nature and causes is inconclusive, medically and psychologically. Our beliefs about homosexuality thus become paramount in importance. Do we value it, disvalue it, or find it morally neutral? Do we shape an environment that encourages movement toward homosexuality or one that nurtures heterosexual becoming?

We conclude that homosexuality is not God's wish for humanity. This we affirm, despite the fact that some of its forms may be deeply rooted in an individual's personality structure. Some persons are exclusively homosexual in orientation. In many cases homosexuality is more a sign of the brokenness of God's world than of willful rebellion. In other cases homosexual behavior is freely chosen or learned in environments where normal development is thwarted. Even where the homosexual orientation has not been consciously sought or chosen, it is neither a gift from God nor a state nor a condition like race; it is a result of our living in a fallen world.

How are we to find the light and freedom promised to us by our Lord through the Holy Spirit in such a world? Where do we find norms for authentic life, which in truth transcend the conditioning of history and culture, and the power to live by them?

We dare begin no other place than with the living Word, Jesus Christ, who in risen power transcends time and space and the limitations of our values, norms, and assumptions to confront, judge, and redeem us. It is here that all theological confession and affirmation must begin—in the light of God as revealed to us in the incarnate and living Word, Jesus Christ. It is his exposure of our sin, his obedient sacrificial love, and his being raised in power to continue his activity of redemption of this world (I Cor. 15:20-28) that brings us new light. This same God in Jesus Christ comes to make us whole, to redeem creation, and to restore it to the goodness proclaimed at creation. Yet the prelude to this redemption is divine judgment.

To look at the Christ is to see at once the brokeness of the world in which we live and the brokenness of our own lives. This comes as the supreme crisis in our life.

Yet, in the moment of this crisis, the Spirit of God brings the confirmation of divine forgiveness, moves us to respond in faith, repentance, and obedience, and initiates the new life in Christ.

Jesus Christ calls us out of the alienation and isolation of our fallen state into the freedom of new life. This new life redeems us as sexual beings but is impossible without repentance. To claim that God's love for us removes divine judgment of us is to eliminate the essence of divine love and to exchange grace for romantic sentimentality. There is a necessary judgment in God's love—else it cannot redeem. It was this Christ who said to the woman in adultery, "Go and sin no more" (John 8:1-12), and to the rich young ruler: "One thing you still lack. Sell all that you have and distribute to the poor . . . and come, follow me." (Luke 18:22 and parallels.)

Jesus Christ calls us out of the alienation, brokenness, and isolation of our fallen state into the freedom of new life in Christ. We deny that this new life liberates us to license and affirm that it frees and empowers us for lives of obedience whereby all of life becomes subject to his Lordship.

Scripture and Homosexuality

We have already indicated that we must examine scientific data but must move beyond them in order to understand what our sexuality means and how it should be expressed. We anchor our understanding of homosexuality in the revelation in Scripture of God's intention for human sexuality.

In order to comprehend the biblical view of homosexuality, we cannot simply limit ourselves to those texts that directly address this issue. We must first understand something of what the Scriptures teach about human sexuality in general. As we examine the whole framework of teaching bearing upon our sexuality from Genesis onward, we find that homosexuality is a contradiction of God's wise and beautiful pattern for human sexual relationships revealed in Scripture and affirmed in God's ongoing will for our life in the Spirit of Christ. It is a confusion of sexual roles that mirrors the tragic inversion in which men and women worship the creature instead of the Creator. God created us male and female to display in clear diversity and balance the range of qualities in God's own nature. The opening chapters of Genesis show that sexual union as "one flesh" is established within the context of companionship and the formation of the family. Nature confirms revelation in the functional compatability of male and female genitalia and the natural process of procreation and family continuity.

Human sin has deeply affected the processes by which sexual orientation is formed, with the result that none of us, heterosexual or homosexual, fulfill perfectly God's plan for our sexuality. This makes it all the more imperative for revelation to make clear for us how our sexual relationships are to be conducted so as to please God and challenge us to seek God's will instead of following our own. Though none of us will ever achieve perfect fulfillment of God's will, all Christians are responsible to view their sins as God views them and to strive against them. To evade this responsibility is to permit the church to model for the world forms of sexual behavior that may seriously injure individuals, families, and the whole fabric of human society. Homosexual persons who will strive toward God's revealed will in this area of their lives, and make use of all the resources of grace, can receive God's power to transform their desires or arrest their active expression.

Within the context of general biblical teaching on human sexuality, a number of passages dealing specifically with homosexuality are significant for our response to this issue. These are, of course, complementary to the wider biblical themes of creation, fall, and redemption.

Three Scriptures specifically address the issue of homosexual behavior between consenting males: Leviticus 18:22, Leviticus 20:13, and Romans 1:26-27. Romans 1:26-27 also addresses the issue of homosexual behavior between consenting females. These three passages stand in an integral and complementary relationship. Leviticus 20:13 regards homosexual behavior as an "abomination."

In the Reformed tradition, the Leviticus passages are considered part of the moral law and thus are different in kind from Levitical proscriptions against certain foods, for instance, which belong to the ritual law. Jesus declared "all foods clean" (Mark 7:19)—one declaration among many that the ritual law of the Old Testament is transcended and fulfilled in him. Moral law in the New Testament is not the means of salvation, for that is Christ alone. Rather, obedience to the moral law is a fruit of grace and salvation.

Genesis 19:1-29 and Judges 19:16-26 show that homosexual rape is a violation of God's justice. II Peter 2:6-10 and Jude 7 suggest a wider context of homosexual practice in

Sodom, implying that such rape was but one expression of prior homosexual practice in the population.

Romans 1:26-27 speaks to the problem of homosexual passion, describing it as ''dishonorable,'' as well as to homosexual behavior, which is described as ''unnatural.'' By ''unnatural'' the Scripture does not mean contrary to custom, nor contrary to the preference of a particular person, but rather contrary to that order of universal human sexual nature that God intended in Genesis 1 and 2.

We emphasize that Paul here includes homosexual behavior in a larger catalog of sins, which includes pride, greed, jealousy, disobedience to parents, and deceit. Homosexual behavior is no greater a sin and no less a sin than these.

Two other texts, I Corinthians 6:9-10 and I Timothy 1:9-10, show further New Testament opposition to homosexual behavior. I Corinthians probably distinguishes between the more passive partners or catamites *(malakoi)* and the more active partners *(arsenokoitai)*. Homosexual relationships in the Hellenistic world were widespread. We may safely assume that some were characterized by tenderness, commitment, and altruism. Yet the New Testament declares that all homosexual practice is incompatible with Christian faith and life. No Scriptures speak of homosexuality as granted by God. No Scriptures permit or condone any of the forms of homosexuality. In Matthew 19:1-12, Jesus reaffirms God's intention for sexual intercourse, enduring marriage between husband and wife, and affirms godly celibacy for those not entering the marriage covenant.

The biblical revelation to Israel, reaffirmed in the teaching of Jesus and Paul, portrayed in the *theology and human creation,* specifically reflected in the ethical teaching in both the Old and New Testaments, and confirmed in nature, clearly indicates that genital sexual expression is meant to occur within the covenant of heterosexual marriage. Behavior that is pleasing to God cannot simply be defined as that which pleases others or expresses our own strong needs and identity; it must flow out of faithful and loving obedience to God. Sin cannot simply be defined as behavior that is selfish or lustful. Many unselfish deeds ignore God's expressed intentions for our lives. Homosexual Christians who fail to recognize God's revealed intent for sexual behavior and who move outside God's will in this area of their lives may show many gifts and graces. They may evidence more grace than heterosexual believers who so readily stand in judgment over them. This does not mean that God approves their behavior in the area in which they are failing to be obedient.

To conclude that the Spirit contradicts in our experience what the Spirit clearly said in Scripture is to set Spirit against Spirit and to cut ourselves loose from any objective test to confirm that we are following God and not the spirits in our culture or our own fallible reason. The church that destroys the balance between Word and Spirit, so carefully constructed by the Reformers to insure that we follow none other than Jesus Christ who is the Word, will soon lose its Christian substance and become indistinguishable from the world. We have been charged to seek ''new light from God's Word,'' not ''new light'' contrary to God's Word.

Church Membership

Persons who manifest homosexual behavior must be treated with the profound respect and pastoral tenderness due all people of God. There can be no place within the Christian faith for the response to homosexual persons of mingled contempt, hatred, and fear that is called homophobia.

Homosexual persons are encompassed by the searching love of Christ. The church must turn from its fear and hatred to move toward the homosexual community in love and to welcome homosexual inquirers to its congregations. It should free them to be candid about their identity and convictions, and it should also share honestly and humbly with them in seeking the vision of God's intention for the sexual dimensions of their lives.

As persons repent and believe, they become members of Christ's body. The church is not a citadel of the morally perfect; it is a hospital for sinners. It is the fellowship where contrite, needy people rest their hope for salvation on Christ and his righteousness. Here in community they seek and receive forgiveness and new life. The church must become the nurturing community so that all whose lives come short of the glory of God are converted, reoriented, and built up into Christian maturity. It may be only in the context of loving community, appreciation, pastoral care, forgiveness, and nurture that homosexual persons can come to a clear understanding of God's pattern for their sexual expression.

There is no room in the church for all who give honest affirmation to the vows required for membership in the church. Homosexual persons who sincerely affirm "Jesus Christ is my Lord and Savior" and "I intend to be his disciple, to obey his word, and to show his love" should not be excluded from membership.

Ordination

To be an ordained officer is to be a human instrument, touched by divine powers but still an earthen vessel. As portrayed in Scripture, the officers set before the church and community an example of piety, love, service, and moral integrity. Officers are not free from repeated expressions of sin. Neither are members and officers free to adopt a lifestyle of conscious, continuing, and unresisted sin in any area of their lives. For the church to ordain a self-affirming, practicing homosexual person to ministry would be to act in contradiction to its charter and calling in Scripture, setting in motion both within the church and society serious contradictions to the will of Christ.

The repentant homosexual person who finds the power of Christ redirecting his or her sexual desires toward a married heterosexual commitment, or finds God's power to control his or her desires and to adopt a celibate lifestyle, can certainly be ordained, all other qualifications being met. Indeed, such candidates must be welcomed and be free to share their full identity. Their experience of hatred and rejection may have given them a unique capacity for love and sensitivity as wounded healers among heterosexual Christians, and they may be incomparably equipped to extend the church's outreach to the homosexual community.

We believe that Jesus Christ intends the ordination of officers to be a sign of hope to the church and the world. Therefore our present understanding of God's will precludes the ordination of persons who do not repent of homosexual practice.

Pluralism and Unity in the Church

We of the 190th General Assembly (1978) realize that not all United Presbyterians can in conscience agree with our conclusions. Some are persuaded that there are forms of homosexual behavior that are not sinful and that persons who practice these forms can legitimately be ordained.

This is wholly in keeping with the diversity of theological viewpoint and the pluralism of opinion that characterize the United Presbyterian Church. We are concerned not to stifle these diverging opinions and to encourage those who hold them to remain within the church. As Paul clearly teaches in Eph. 4:1-16, as members of Christ's body we desperately need one another. None of us is perfect. No opinion or decision if irreformable. Nor do we mean to close further study of homosexuality among the presbyteries and congregations. Quite the contrary, the action we recommend to the judicatories includes a firm direction to study this matter further, so that fear and hatred of homosexual persons may be healed and mission and ministry to homosexual persons strengthened and increased. The pluralism that can bring paralyzing weakness to the church when groups pursue their vision in isolation from one another can bring health and vigor when they practice pluralism-in-dialogue.

We want this dialogue to continue. Nevertheless, we judge that it cannot effectively be pursued in the uncertainty and insecurity that would be generated by the Assembly's silence on this matter at this time. On the basis of our understanding that the practice of homosexuality is sin, we are concerned that homosexual believers and the observing world should not be left in doubt about the church's mind on this issue during any further period of study. Even some who see some forms of homosexual behavior as moral are concerned that persons inside and outside the church will stumble in their faith and understanding if this matter is unresolved.

Ministry and Mission

In ministry the church seeks to express and portray the grace and mercy of Christ in worship, nurture, evangelism, and service to those within the covenant community. In mission the church proclaims to all the good news of redemption and reconciliation, calls persons and nations to repentant faith in Christ, and promotes and demonstrates the advance of his rule in history through healing works of mercy and prophetic witness that aim at justice and liberation.

In its ministry and mission the church must offer both to homosexual persons and to those who fear and hate them God's gracious provision of redemption and forgiveness. It must call both to repentant faith in Christ, urging both toward loving obedience to God's will.

The church's grappling with the issue of homosexuality has already energized its membership in a remarkable awakening of prayer and theological study. Our study should continue with the aim of reaching harmony in our diverging positions on homosexuality and other crucial issues. Our prayer should now be concentrated upon this process of internal reconciliation and also upon the creation of ministry with homosexual persons. Great love and care must be exercised toward homosexual persons already within our church, both those who have affirmed their sexual identity and practice and those who have in conscience chosen not to do so. We urge candidates committees, ministerial relations committees, personnel committees, nominating committees, and judicatories to conduct their examination of candidates for ordained office with discretion and sensitivity, recognizing that it would be a hindrance to God's grace to make a specific inquiry into the sexual orientation or practice of candidates for ordained office or ordained officers where the person involved has not taken the initiative in declaring his or her sexual orientation.

The Christian community can neither condone nor participate in the widespread contempt for homosexual persons that prevails in our general culture. Indeed, beyond this, it must do everything in its power to prevent society from continuing to hate, harass, and oppress them. The failure of the church to demonstrate grace in its life has contributed to the forcing of homosexual persons into isolated communities. This failure has served to reinforce the homosexual way of life and to heighten alienation from both church and society. The church should be a spiritual and moral vanguard leading society in response to homosexual persons.

Through direct challenge and support the church should encourage the public media—television, film, the arts, and literature—to portray in a wholesome manner robust, fully human life expressing the finer qualities of the human spirit. It should call upon its members and agencies to work to eliminate prejudicial and stereotypical images of homosexual persons in the public media.

Decriminalization and Civil Rights

There is no legal, social, or moral justification for denying homosexual persons access to the basic requirements of human social existence. Society does have a legitimate role in regulating some sexual conduct, for criminal law properly functions to preserve public order and decency and to protect citizens from public offense, personal injury, and exploitation. Thus, criminal law properly prohibits homosexual and heterosexual acts that involve rape, coercion, corruption of minors, mercenary exploitation, or public display. However, homosexual and heterosexual acts in private between consenting adults involve none of these legitimate interests of society. Sexual conduct in private between consenting adults is a matter of private morality to be instructed by religious precept or ethical example and persuasion, rather than by legal coercion.

Vigilance must be exercised to oppose federal, state, and local legislation that discriminates against persons on the basis of sexual orientation and to initiate and support federal, state, or local legislation that prohibits discrimination against persons on the basis of sexual orientation in employment, housing, and public accommodations. This provision would not affect the church's employment policies.

Conclusions

I. Response to Overture 9 (1976)

The Presbytery of New York City and the Presbytery of the Palisades have asked the General Assembly to give "definitive guidance" in regard to the ordination of persons who may be otherwise well qualified but who affirm their own homosexual identity and practice.

The phrase "homosexual persons" does not occur in the Book of Order of the United Presbyterian Church. No phrase within the Book of Order explicitly prohibits the ordination of self-affirming, practicing homosexual persons to office within the church. However, no phrase within the Book of Order can be construed as an explicit mandate to disregard sexual practice when evaluating candidates for ordination. In short, the Book of Order does not give explicit direction to presbyteries, elders, and congregations as to whether or not self-affirming, practicing homosexual persons are eligible or ineligible for ordination to office.

Therefore, the 190th General Assembly (1978) of The United Presbyterian Church in the United States of America offers the presbyteries the following definitive guidance:

That unrepentant homosexual practice does not accord with the requirements for ordination set forth in Form of Government, Chapter VII, Section 3 (37.03): . . . "It is indispensable that, besides possessing the necessary gifts and abilities, natural and acquired, everyone undertaking a particular ministry should have a sense of inner persuasion, be sound in the faith, live according to godliness, have the approval of God's people and the concurring judgment of a lawful judicatory of the Church."

In relation to candidates for the ordained ministry, committees should be informed by the above guidance.

II. Recommendations

Consistent with this policy statement and conclusions, the 190th General Assembly (1978):

1. Adopts this policy statement and directs the Office of the General Assembly to send a copy of the policy statement to all congregations, presbyteries, and synods and to provide it for widespread distribution.
2. Receives the background paper of the Task Force to Study Homosexuality as a study document, and directs the Office of the General Assembly to provide copies to all congregations, presbyteries, and synods and to make such copies available to others upon request.
3. Urges judicatories, agencies, and local churches to undertake a variety of educational activities, using both formal and informal church structures and organizations.
   a. Since homosexuality is one issue that helps clarify our general responsibility to God in the world and focuses many dimensions of belief and action, such educational activities should probe such basic issues as (1) the strengthening of family life; (2) ministry to single persons and affirmation of their full participation in the Christian community; (3) nurturing lifestyles in our families, congregations, and communities that celebrate the values of friendship with peers of one's own sex and the opposite sex, committed choice of life-mates, joyous and loving fidelity within marriage, the establishment of homes where love and care can nurture strong children able to give loving service to others, and the fashioning of an atmosphere of justice, truth, and kindness that signals Christ's presence; (4) understanding how

to extend ministries of deep concern and challenge to those who through choice or circumstance are sexually active, homosexually or heterosexually, outside the covenant of marriage; (5) helping those whose ability to show loving concern is destroyed by homophobia—the irrational fear of and contempt for homosexual persons.

b. Workshops in synods and presbyteries should be conducted both to explore ways to help homosexual persons participate in the life of the church and to discover new ways of reaching out to homosexual persons outside the church.

c. Courses on sexuality should be initiated by seminaries, colleges, and churches to provide officers and members with a systematic understanding of the dynamics of human sexuality as understood within the context of Christian ethics.

d. Contact and dialogue should be encouraged among groups and persons of all persuasions on the issue of homosexuality.

4. Urges presbyteries and congregations to develop outreach programs to communities of homosexual persons beyond the church to allow higher levels of rapport to emerge.

5. Urges agencies of the General Assembly, as appropriate, to develop responses to the following needs:

   a. Support for outreach programs by presbyteries and congregations to homosexual persons beyond the church to allow higher levels of rapport to emerge.

   b. Encouragement of contact and dialogue among groups and persons who disagree on whether or not homosexuality is sinful per se and whether or not homosexual persons may be ordained as church officers.

   c. Development of structures to counsel and support homosexual persons concerned about their sexuality and their Christian faith.

   d. Development of pastoral counseling programs for those affected or offended by the decision of this General Assembly.

6. Urges candidates committees, personnel committees, nominating committees, and judicatories to conduct their examination of candidates for ordained office with discretion and sensitivity, recognizing that it would be a hindrance to God's grace to make a specific inquiry into the sexual orientation or practice of candidates for ordained office or ordained officers where the person involved has not taken the initiative in declaring his or her sexual orientation.

7. Calls upon the media to continue to work to end the use of harmful stereotypes of homosexual persons; and encourages agencies of the General Assembly, presbyteries, and congregations to develop strategies to insure the end of such abuse.

8. Calls on United Presbyterians to reject in their own lives, and challenge in others, the sin of homophobia, which drives homosexual persons away from Christ and his church.

9. Encourages persons working in the human sciences and therapies to pursue research that will seek to learn more about the nature and causes of homosexuality.

10. Encourages the development of support communities of homosexual Christians seeking sexual reorientation or meaningful, joyous, and productive celibate lifestyles and the dissemination throughout the church of information about such communities.

11. Encourages seminaries to apply the same standards for homosexual and heterosexual persons applying for admission.

12. Reaffirms the need, as expressed by the 182nd General Assembly (1970) for United Presbyterians to work for the decriminalization of private homosexual acts between

consenting adults, and calls for an end to the discriminatory enforcement of other criminal laws against homosexual persons.

13. Calls upon United Presbyterians to work for the passage of laws that prohibit discrimination in the areas of employment, housing, and public accommodations based on the sexual orientation of a person.

14. Declares that these actions shall not be used to affect negatively the ordination rights of any United Presbyterian deacon, elder, or minister who has been ordained prior to this date.

    Further the 190th General Assembly (1978) calls upon those who in conscience have difficulty accepting the decisions of this General Assembly bearing on homosexuality to express that conscience by continued dialogue within the church.

Notes: *Following the adoption of* Sexuality and the Human Community, *which represented the triumph of the most liberal wing of the United Presbyterian Church in the U.S.A., a more positive attitude toward homosexuals developed in many sections of the church. The new attitude and perceived support of homosexuals raised the possibility that open, practicing homosexuals could be ordained as Presbyterian ministers (teaching elders). As the debate spread through the church, presbyteries began to express their opinion on the issue and petition the general assembly to clarify its position. In response to several petitions, the Assembly appointed a task force which in 1978 presented a lengthy report.*

The report states that currently practicing homosexuals are not to be ordained, but that both homosexuals who are currently leading and intend in the future to lead a celibate life or former homosexuals who have left their homosexual life behind are fit candidates. This statement largely laid to rest the issue of homosexuality in the Presbyterian Church (U.S.A.).

In 1979, this document was also adopted by the Presbyterian Church in the U.S., which in 1983 merged with the United Presbyterian Church in the U.S.A. to form the Presbyterian Church (U.S.A.). The Presbyterian Church in the U.S. had recommended this document for use in its congregations in the years prior to the merger.

In 1986, the Presbyterian Church (U.S.A.) again recommended this document rather than writing a new position paper for the merged church.

PRESBYTERIAN CHURCH IN AMERICA

STATEMENT ON HOMOSEXUALITY (1977)

Overture No. 11. . . That the General Assembly encourage Christians to recognize their responsibility to petition the powers that be that such men and women who practice, approve, or condone any of these activities not be invested with the authority to teach in schools or be in a position where they can influence our nation, which professes ''In God we trust.''

8. . . . That the Fifth General Assembly of the Presbyterian Church in America affirm the Biblical position for our denomination which states that:

1. The act of homosexuality is a sin according to God's Word;
2. Churches should actively seek to lead the homosexual person to confession and repentance that he might find justification and sanctification in Jesus Christ, according to I Corinthians 6:11; and
3. In light of the Biblical view of its sinfulness, a practicing homosexual continuing in this sin would not be a fit candidate for ordination or membership in the Presbyterian Church in America.

Notes: *The Presbyterian Church in America, which represents the continuing conservative wing of the former Presbyterian Church in the U.S. (the Southern Presbyterian Church), has adopted a strong stance against homosexuality and succinctly stated its opposition to the practice.*

PRESBYTERIAN CHURCH IN CANADA

STATEMENT ON HOMOSEXUALITY (1969)

HOMOSEXUALITY

The Board of Evangelism and Social Action reported to the 95th General Assembly that it had sent the following communication to the Justice Committee of the House of Commons with regard to the proposed legislation, which was later passed to remove homosexual acts between consenting adults in private from the Criminal Code.

The Board of Evangelism and Social Action of the Presbyterian Church in Canada is comprised of ministers and lay people appointed by the General Assembly of the Presbyterian Church to consider issues of concern and make recommendation to the General Assembly. Since the General Assembly will not meet until June 1st and because of the present discussion on homosexuality in the House of Commons, the Board of Evangelism and Social Action speaks on its own behalf in the following statement:-

The Church and Homosexuality

With regard to the proposed amendment to the Criminal Code re Homosexuality, the Board of Evangelism and Social Action of The Presbyterian Church in Canada takes the following position:

1. There is wisdom in what is proposed for these reasons:-
    a. It is not practical to insist that civil law should coincide at every point with canon law or to contend that every sin ought to be the object to criminal prosecution.
    b. The effect of the proposed amendment is simply to recognize in law what is presently the case in fact, namely, that legal action is not now being taken against homosexual practices when committed in private between two consenting adults.
2. The Christian Church does not condone homosexuality, nor we believe, does society as a whole. Homosexuality is contrary to nature according to the word of God. It is important to understand that the proposed amendments do not in any sense oppose this view, but rather seek to protect minors from corruption and to prohibit public offenses.
3. Nevertheless, in a proper understanding of homosexuality, we must take into serious account the psychological factors that in many cases explain this form of aberration. This is not to deny that in other instances, homosexuality may be the result of wrong association and habit. In many people, there is some degree of ambivalence of sexuality; what happens in the life of an individual may depend on his own inner discipline and the degree to which he regards himself as subject to the authority of the Word of God. But no matter where the root causes of homosexuality may lie, the homosexual person ought always to be the object of deep compassion. The responsibility of the Church is to proclaim to the homosexual, equally as to all men, obedience to the law of God, and at the same time, the limitless possibility of forgiveness and renewal in Jesus Christ.

    With such observations, we would support the proposed amendment to the Criminal Code concerning homosexuality.

Notes: *In the late 1960s, Canada decriminalized homosexual behavior between consenting adults. Prior to that action, the Board of Evangelism and Social Action of the Presbyterian*

Church in Canada had supported the move to decriminalization. The law was passed before the 1969 meeting of the General Assembly, and at that time the church went on record as approving the action.

PRESBYTERIAN CHURCH IN CANADA

STATEMENT ON HOMOSEXUALITY (1985)

The task of preparing a draft response to Overture No. 14 of the Presbytery of Cape Breton was laid upon the Church Doctrine Committee by the 110th General Assembly. That overture asks the Assembly to "affirm to our people that the Presbyterian Church in Canada holds to the teaching of Holy Scriptures that homosexual practice is sinful."

It is to be noted that the prayer of the overture here refers not to homosexual orientation, but to "homosexual practices." We shall therefore, for the most part confine ourselves to a consideration of the rightness or wrongness of homosexual acts rather than the condition known as homosexuality. It seems reasonably clear, as we shall see, that this is also the focus of those Biblical texts that must be considered here.

The problem of the rightness or wrongness of homosexual practice involves to a degree unusual in ethical issues the testimony of psychiatrists and other scientists. It is clearly impossible to discuss the issues involved without considering their contributions. We cannot, however, abdicate to the psychiatrists our responsibility as a church to make our own ethical decisions. The question, after all, is not whether homosexual acts are insane but whether they are sinful. Psychiatrists are not necessarily competent to make that judgment. They are, for example, regularly called in to court to testify as to the sanity of people charged with criminal offenses; they are not asked to comment as to the rightness or wrongness of those acts. An act can be quite sane and yet sinful.

Moreover, we are not called upon as a church to determine the causes of homosexuality. (That would be clearly outside our competence.) Furthermore, psychiatrists and other scientists do not agree as to the cause of homosexual orientation. But the questions of the origin of orientation and the ethical estimation of homosexual acts are not the same. It may be true that the orientation arises either from genetic causes or from experiences so early in childhood that the person cannot be held responsible for that orientation. This is not exclusively true of homosexuality, however. The causes of violent behavior or of sexual orientations such as paedophilia may also be genetic or environmental yet the indulgence of those tendencies must clearly be considered sinful. In short, homosexual orientation may well not be culpable but the practice that can spring from that orientation may be so.

We must not adopt an obscurantist attitude with respect to the empirical sciences and the contributions they can make to ethical discussion. Nor ought we from any misplaced sense of inferiority grant them too much weight. There is no reason to abandon those resources with which the church has always approached ethical questions, the witness of Holy Scripture and the wisdom of our forebears in the faith, when we consider this difficult issue.

We are also dealing with currents in the social atmosphere in our day. These are not as easily analyzed as the writings of scientists or theologians and yet they are of immense importance. First, we must take note of the widespread existence of "homophobia," the irrational fear and loathing of homosexuals, in our society. Interviews with homosexuals show the real pain and discrimination this attitude causes. Certainly, we must oppose this form of hatred as vigorously as any other. On the other hand, we must beware of those who label as homophobic anyone who hesitates to accept homosexuality as an equally valid alternative lifestyle. The issue is too serious for name-calling, sloganeering, or labeling, by either side.

It also must be noted that our society is fundamentally antinomian. This is, of course, not confined to homosexual issues. Our society respects little in the way of restraint on heterosexual activity as well. Societies are always most prone to attack those sins into which they are least likely to fall. This being the case, there will be many warnings in our time from both society as a whole and the church embedded in it against "legalism." It must be remembered, however, that both legalism and antinomianism are equally heretical.

The Witness of Scripture

Overture No. 14 declares its adherence to the Bible as "the rule of faith and life". With this general statement we, of course, agree. We have recently declared as a church that the Bible is "the standard of all doctrine by which we must test any word that comes to us from church, world, or inner experience. We subject to its judgment all we believe and do". (*Living Faith* 5.1) For us, therefore, a consideration of the texts relating to homosexual practices is vital.

Respect for the authority of Scripture demands great care in the application of its various texts to our present life. We must be sure we thoroughly understand those texts both as to their meaning and their enduring significance. Neither simple-minded "proof-texting" nor evading the meaning of passages to serve a pre-determined theory can be acceptable. Both informed exegesis and thoughtful hermeneutics are necessary.

The overture refers us to four texts, Lev. 18:22; Rom. 1:26-27; I Cor. 6:9, 10 and Jude 7. Doubtless the Presbytery does not insist that we confine our attention to these passages. It should be noted that these texts are all "negative", that is they all speak against a form of sexuality. There are "positive" passages which must also be considered, passages which speak of God's positive will for our sexuality. Although we must consider those passages to which the Presbytery of Cape Breton calls our attention, it would be a grave error in any study of human sexuality to focus only on passages which speak negatively of certain aspects of human sexuality.

Lev. 18:22. This verse and the very similar Lev. 20:13 are quite clear as to their meaning. A translation such as "No man is to have sexual relations with another man" (TEV) is entirely accurate. The real problem here is, in fact, not exegetical but hermeneutical. To what degree are these passages authoritative for us?

It has often been noted that we do not obey a number of the regulations of the Holiness Code, the collection of laws in which our two commandments are embedded. We are "people of the New Covenant". We do, however, also maintain a number of the laws of Leviticus, most notably, perhaps, a certain injunction to love one's neighbor. Many of the regulations that deal with sexual matters, laws dealing with incest, bestiality and adultery, are also still widely accepted. Moreover, many are finding new value in the laws there which deal with the poor. In other words, we may neither automatically accept or reject as authoritative any particular commandment in Leviticus. We must always consider them in their wider canonical context. Does the law in question accord the key themes in the rest of Scripture? Is it contradicted or declared invalid at some other point in scripture? Does it accord with the work and witness of Jesus Christ?

The Old Testament does not merely or even mainly condemn sexuality. It has a consistent viewpoint with respect to human sexuality which may be summed up simply as, "Committed heterosexuality is a good and joyful gift of God." This basic insight is affirmed in the two creation accounts of Genesis 1 and 2, in the entire Song of Songs and underlies many accounts of male/female relationships throughout the length of the Old Testament. Heterosexuality is considered to be a basic and fundamental part of human nature as God created it. There is no point in the Old Testament at which it can be said that homosexual acts are viewed with any favor at all. The basic understanding of Genesis that humans are created to be heterosexual is accepted by the Jesus of the gospels, Mt. 19.3-12 Mk. 10.2-12. The regulations of Lev. 18 and 20 are fully in accord with this key Biblical line of understanding. They are part of a trajectory which simply cannot be justifiably removed from the Bible.

The New Testament texts mentioned in the overture confirm this basic understanding. Romans 1:26-27 presupposes the creation stories of Genesis. For Paul the "natural" is not merely what may be observed all around us; it is always rooted in the will of God disclosed in Scripture. The natural is not simply what is "there" but that which properly reflects the will of the creator. In this passage, therefore, Paul is not simply using a natural law argument; this passage is an extension of the trajectory we have already identified in the Old Testament. Homosexual relations are part of the general brokenness of a humanity infected by sin. This understanding is by no means laughable, nor has it been rendered untenable by modern psychiatry. It must be noted that those who engage in homosexual acts are not here separated from the rest of humanity; this passage is part of a section of the epistle which aims to show that "all have sinned and fallen short of the glory of God". Homosexuals and heterosexuals alike need the grace of God appropriated in faith. Those who engage in homosexual practices are no less and no more culpable than those who engage in heterosexual licentiousness, verses 24-25, or the sins of the mind and spirit listed in verses 29-31.

I Cor. 6.9-10. Here it is declared that "malakoi" (literally, the "soft") and "arsenokoitai", among others, will not inherit the Kingdom of God. The latter word also appears in a second sin list in I Tim. 8-10. It is a relatively rare word (the Pauline usage is its earliest appearance) and a valiant attempt has been made by various scholars to deny that it necessarily refers to homosexuals at all. While detailed arguments cannot be presented here, it must be noted that the unusual word is very probably a literal translation of the rabbinic term for male homosexual activity "mishkav zakur", or "lying with a male". The Greek word is a compound one, made of the words for "male" and"bed". The latter is used euphemistically in a way that should not be unfamiliar to us. The two words are found in the Septuagint version of the laws of Leviticus considered earlier.

It is sometimes argued that these two passages, inasmuch as they are sin-lists containing traditional material widely circulating in the early church, have no authority for us. The logic of this position is not immediately apparent. Why should material that was accepted by the whole church, including Paul, be less authoritative than material that stems from Paul alone?

Finally, the overture asks us to consider Jude 7 which speaks of the destruction of Sodom and Gomorrah. It appears that the sin of Sodom is here interpreted sexually, perhaps following the example of the intertestamental work Jubilees. Little more can be said about this enigmatic passage.

It cannot be said that the Bible very often speaks of homosexual practices but where it does, it speaks of them with disfavor. On the other hand, it frequently celebrates the joys of committed heterosexuality. Its voice with respect to homosexual practices is, therefore, quite clear and consistent, in fact, unusually so. We cannot find any hermeneutical principle which will allow us to ignore this clear word. Nor does any general theological approach to scripture which emphasizes love or liberation to the exclusion of the demand of holiness commend itself to our approval.

The New Testament does not record any words of Jesus regarding homosexual practices. In the gospels Jesus maintains the validity of the Law of the Old Covenant (Mt. 5.17-19,, Lk. 16.17) but retains an attitude both of freedom and authority with respect to it (Mt. 5.21-47). It must be said, however, that Jesus generally uses this freedom to extend the Law rather than to curtail or to deny it. "Unless your righteousness exceeds that of the Scribes and Pharisees, you will never enter the Kingdom of Heaven." Mt. 5.20. It would be invalid to suggest that his silence with respect to the Law's prescriptions against homosexual acts should be interpreted as rejection of those regulations.

Perhaps the attitude of Jesus can best be deduced from a consideration of the story of the woman taken in adultery (John 7.53-8.11) in most of our Bibles). This story was considered to be of such importance that it was preserved outside of the regular Gospel tradition. Here Jesus is presented with a woman caught in the very act of adultery, an activity also forbidden in the Law. Despite the penalty laid down in the Law and despite the false righteousness first claimed by her accusers, he offers to the woman both forgiveness and acceptance, "Nor do I condemn you." But he also accepts the Law's estimation of the sinfulness of her actions and lays upon her the stern command, "Go and sin no more".

Our society wishes to present us with two alternatives, either to share in the homophobic cruelty so widely practiced in our culture, or to accede to the antinomian ethical indifference which often passes for wisdom in our time, to condemn entirely or to condone. For us the task is to proclaim a middle way, to point sinners both heterosexual and homosexual to the grace and mercy of Jesus Christ and to declare before all his unconditional demand for holiness. Perhaps our word can be that of our master, "Neither do we condemn you; go, and sin no more".

Notes: *Though the Presbyterian Church in Canada had approved the decriminalization of homosexual activity in 1969, it had never spoken in one voice on the issue of homosexuality. It generally affirmed the older Presbyterian doctrinal statements (such as the Westminster Catechism) which denounced homosexuality and stood for the traditional Christian stance of limiting sexual acts to married couples. However, in 1985, the church was asked to address the issue and passed this resolution condemning homosexual acts.*

REFORMED CHURCH IN AMERICA

HOMOSEXUALITY: A BIBLICAL AND THEOLOGICAL APPRAISAL (1978)

INTRODUCTION

At the 1977 General Synod session a motion was made and supported that General Synod "go on record affirming the human and civil rights of homosexuals and lesbians." This motion was referred to the Theological Commission for study and recommendation (*MGS*, 1977, p. 204f.). In formulating its response the Commission deemed it necessary to broaden the scope of its inquiry. This study begins with a biblical and theological appraisal of homosexuality. This appraisal provides the essential foundation for the Commission's response to the referral concerning homosexual rights. The church's pastoral ministry to homosexual persons is the subject of an additional study being prepared for presentation to the General Synod in 1979.

Homosexuality has become a subject of major controversy in society and in the church. While homosexual practices have been recorded since the dawn of human history, they have also been proscribed in western civilization since the beginning of the Christian era. Efforts to legitimate the homosexual experience and accord full human rights to homosexual persons constitute a social movement of recent origin. This movement for homosexual liberation has received both impetus and opposition from members of the churches. The moral and legal status of homosexual persons and their place in church and society raise complex questions with deep personal, social and pastoral dimensions which must be addressed.

Any responsible inquiry concerning the biblical perspective on homosexuality requires careful consideration of a new, emerging theological context. Speaking from within this context are committed Christian persons, both homosexual and heterosexual, whose biblical exegesis and theological reflection leads them to the opinion that a homosexual relationship may express the divine will for human life. Heretofore, that possibility was not considered. Paul, Luther, Calvin, and more recently, Karl Barth assumed the sinfulness of homosexual activity without question. Given the issues raised in the homosexual context, this assumption must give way to a careful re-examination of the scriptural witness in this matter.

The contribution of the human sciences to our understanding of homosexuality is an invaluable aid to biblical and theological reflection. Truth, as Calvin averred, is "of God" wherever it is found. However, the human sciences may not be used to abrogate the biblical witness. We must seek to evaluate all human wisdom in light of the Scriptures so that our moral judgments and conduct may conform to the Word of God.

Our norm is Holy Scripture, not our prior assumptions about a biblical perspective on homosexuality. Doctrinaire opinions, pro or con, concerning homosexuality should not be the starting point of an inquiry or be projected onto the texts. When one presumes to know in advance what Scripture will say to him, he reduces it to a mere human possession and hears what he wishes to hear. Thus, Scripture ceases to be for him that quick, sharp and discerning word which is always intended to address and question its hearers (Heb. 4:12). With humility, and with compassion for persons who will be affected by our study, we propose a fresh look at the biblical material, careful exegesis, and interpretation that is both faithful to the historic Reformed witness and aware that always "God has yet more truth to break forth from His Holy Word."

Explicit Biblical References

It may be vexing to note that a major contemporary issue receives incidental attention in Scripture. Passages which make explicit reference to homosexuality are few in number, both in the Old and New Testaments. It should be acknowledged that neither the Old Testament prophets nor Jesus himself ever mentioned the subject. However, the texts which do refer to homosexual activity are unequivocal in their condemnation of the practice. It is not possible or necessary to offer detailed exposition of each of the explicit texts. To avoid repetition; key, representative passages will be considered. Brevity also prevents a detailed description of the various interpretations emerging from the homosexual context and in opposition to it. This spectrum of opinion is part of the research which informs this study and will be referred to at key points. This study is prescriptive rather than descriptive. It presents our conclusions drawn from the biblical material rather than enumerating the wide variety of current opinions.

Old Testament References

The following passages contain explicit reference to homosexual acts: Genesis 9:21-27; 19:4-11; Leviticus 18:22; 20:13; Deuteronomy 22:5; 23:17; Judges 19:16-26; I Kings 14:24; 15:12; 22:46.

The story concerning the men of Sodom (Gen. 19:4-11) merits consideration in some detail only because it has been a traditional *locus classicus* for homosexual condemnation, and it figures prominently in current biblical re-appraisal. The key sentence is found in verse 5: "Bring them out to us, that we may know them." The men of Sodom importune Lot to release his male guests to them. The verb "know" *(yadha)* in this context bears a sexual meaning, as it does elsewhere, e.g., Genesis 4:1. The intent is homosexual rape. Thus Lot's plea: ". . . do not act so wickedly" (v. 7).

It has been objected that this traditional interpretation rests on faulty exegesis. The sin involved is not homosexual aggression, but a breach of the sacred law of hospitality. *Yadha* bears a wide range of interpersonal meanings from making an acquaintance to sexual coitus. Apart from this passage, the verb has sexual meaning only in 10 of its 943 appearances in the Old Testament. In each of these 10 instances, the verb refers to heterosexual intercourse. The Hebrew term normally used in reference to both homosexual intercourse and bestiality is *shakhabh*. Thus critics of the traditional interpretation maintain that the focus of the text is on Sodom's sin of pride and inhospitality which provoked divine retribution, not on homosexuality.

Despite linguistic considerations, this demurrer is not convincing. To excise the sexual import of the text one must translate *yadha* in two completely different senses within the short span of four verses. Lot offers his virgin daughters "who have not known man" to the men of Sodom, urging "do to them as you please; only do nothing to these men . . ." (v. 8). Lot is obviously attempting to placate their homosexual lust with the offer of his daughters for sexual use. It is, of course, the sacred law of hospitality which motivates Lot to seek his guests' protection at such high cost. The men of Sodom do perpetrate a frightful violation of this law. However, the text stresses the reprehensible nature of the violation as strongly as the fact of the violation itself.

Granting the obvious sexual import of the passage, we must add that a responsible interpretation cannot justify the excessive homosexual condemnation and retribution which tradition has sought to deduce from it. Homosexual conduct is nowhere portrayed in Scripture as the only or chief sin which brought divine judgment upon the city. The heinous sins of Sodom are variously catalogued by the prophets Isaiah, Jeremiah and Ezekiel. Homosexuality is not mentioned as one of them. Beyond the passage under discussion, the sole canonical reference to homosexual acts as a sin of Sodom occurs in Jude which refers to the "unnatural lust" of the wicked twin cities (v. 7). Of primary interpretive importance is the tenor of mob violence, terror, aggression and assault which pervades the passage. The categorical difference between mob sexual assault and a consenting act between two persons need not be demonstrated. This text (and its obvious parallel in Judges 19) may be interpreted as a clear condemnation of persons who would force homosexual acts upon unwilling partners. The text by itself will not justify a blanket condemnation of homosexuality.

Leviticus 18:22 and 20:13 are found in that body of Hebrew cultic and ethical laws known as the Holiness Code (Lev. 17:1-26:46). The theological foundation of this legislation is the exhortation to Israel to be a holy people even as Yahweh their God is holy (20:26). As a separate people, bound in covenant to the Lord of history, Israel must exemplify his righteousness and shun the idolatrous practices of the "people of the land" who consort with pagan gods of nature and fertility. Among the many laws governing Israel's cultic and moral purity are two which refer to male homosexual acts.

It is clear that the law condemns such acts. The substitution of homosexual intercourse for heterosexual is one of the "abominations" punishable by death. The reasons for this proscription and its extreme punishment raise questions of interpretation. Numerous scholars have demonstrated that homosexual behavior in Israel could never be considered a neutral act because it figured so prominently in the fertility cults of Israel's Canaanite neighbors. In the Hebrew mind homosexuality was inextricably linked to the odious practice of sacred male prostitution, one of the on-going threats to the integrity of Israel's worship. This concern is seen vividly in the texts of Deuteronomy and I Kings noted above.

Examination of the Leviticus texts in their context indicates, however, that they cannot be dismissed solely as the expression of a cultic bias which no longer has relevance. The proscription of homosexual acts in Leviticus 18 is one in a series of laws governing the proper sexual relations which must obtain among a holy people. Here cultic bias is not prominent. Thus a case against homosexual behavior is clear-cut if Leviticus 18 can be accepted as a normative statement of divine will, as universally binding as the Ten Commandments. However, serious problems, biblical and theological, hinder such acceptance. While Leviticus 18 condemns adultery, incest, bestiality, and male homosexuality on moral grounds, the same passage accepts polygamy without question, forbids sexual intercourse with a menstruating woman, and says nothing at all about female homosexuality. Not without reason did Calvin refer to the "shadowy" character of Old Testament legislation (*Institutes*, II. vii. 16 and viii. 28, 29.)! Only by a casuistic picking and choosing can one find justification in the Old Testament laws for a condemnation of homosexual persons in our own time. How can one condemn a male homosexual according to the law without, at the same time, advocating his capital punishment, shunning women in menstruation, tolerating polygamy, and ignoring lesbianism? Such causistry, not unknown among the people of God, always involves the imposition some extra-biblical principle of interpretation upon the text. Further, it leaves the casuist foundering in a legalistic morass. It is precisely this dilemma to which the New Testament speaks, proclaiming the good news of Jesus Christ; "For Christ is the end of the law, that everyone who has faith may be justified" (Rom. 10:4); ". . . love is the fulfilling of the law" (Rom. 13:10). For a true reading of Scripture in this matter we must consider the explicit New Testament texts and, then, the sense of Scripture as a unified whole summed up in the person and work of Jesus Christ.

New Testament References

Explicit references to homosexuality in the New Testament are few. In addition to the Jude text cited above there are three, each penned by Paul: Romans 1:26f.; I Corinthians 6:9-10; I Timothy 1:9-10. While Paul's rejection of homosexual activity is beyond question, it should be noted that in none of the passages does Paul make it his theme or the object of an independent statement. Homosexuality is always mentioned as one among many manifestations of a deeper human problem. The Romans passage will be considered here because it is Paul's most familiar statement on the subject and his sharpest rejection of homosexual behavior. Also, by focusing on this text we may by-pass the complex exegetical debate as to whether the Greek *malakoi* and *arsenokoitai* in I Corinthians and I Timothy were ever intended to refer to homosexual behavior.

Paul's specific references to homosexuality in Romans 1 have as their context his general diagnosis of the human condition (1:18-3:20). All men stand condemned before God's righteousness, enslaved to sin, and incapable of saving themselves. Salvation is afforded, not on the basis of law, but through that righteousness which is appropriated only by faith (1:16-17). Apart from faith, man stands under "the wrath of God." To demonstrate his case, Paul begins with the moral failure of the Gentiles. The truth of God as creator and Lord is plainly visible in the created order. However, man does not honor the Creator or live in grateful obedience, i.e. faith. In self-willed rebellion he chooses to worship and glorify himself. Man's basic problem, then, is the sin of idolatry. He seeks to be his own god. Thus, a frightful "exchange" (v. 23) takes place in which the worship appropriate to the Creator is misdirected to the created order. Seeking a higher place than God ordained for him, man falls prostrate before the gods of his own making. Paul concludes his diagnosis with an observation characteristic of the biblical view of man. The disruption in the vertical, God-man relationship necessarily foments a disruption on the horizontal plane of human relationships. Idolatry leads to moral depravity not by chance but as the direct result of God's judgment in "giving man up" (v. 24) to the dishonorable consequences of his bad exchange.

Having diagnosed the human predicament, Paul goes on to offer his own illustrations. The evil results of idolatry are sensual vices (vv. 24-27) and anti-social vices (vv. 29-31). He cites lesbianism and homosexuality to illustrate sensual vice or "dishonorable passions." Paul is one with his Jewish forebearers in loathing homosexual conduct as the prime example of idolatrous perversion. Cultic homosexuality was common, not only in ancient Canaan, but also in Paul's Graeco-Roman environment. Significantly, the same verb which indicates the vertical exchange (v. 25) is repeated to describe this horizontal perversion: "Their women exchanged *(metellaxan)* natural relations" (v. 26) thereby acting "against nature" *(para phusin)*, and the men did "likewise" by "giving up" natural relations with women to vent their burning passions in shameless acts with men (v. 27).

Of passing interest is the fact that Paul, sometimes accused of slighting the role of women, here not only refers to lesbianism but gives it first mention! Far more important are the conclusions about homosexual behavior which are to be drawn from the text. First, we note that Paul is condemning a form of sexual activity that results from a conscious choice. He understands homosexuality to be the intentional perversion of one's natural, heterosexual orientation. Homosexual acts are a self-chosen sexual "exchange" for which a person is responsible and held accountable. The horizontal perversion is parallel to and occasioned by the vertical act of self-willed rebellion, the original idolatrous exchange. One who dishonors God will dishonor his own body as well.

Secondly, it is apparent that homosexual perversion is one among many consequences of man's sinful state. It is not singled out as an especially heinous form of depravity which merits a more stringent opprobrium. Paul goes on to censure with equal force covetousness, malice, envy, gossip, disobedience to parents, and other sins of the mind and heart. The pervert and the gossip, side by side, stand in need of redemption. Further, lest anyone take particular delight in Paul's condemnation of homosexuals, we must note that his indictment continues in Romans 2 and 3 to include a similar condemnation for any of God's people whose idolatry consists in the aspiration to be judge and lord over their fellow creatures.

Finally, we disagree with those within the "homosexual context" (see p. 1) who dismiss Paul's censure of homosexual acts as merely another instance of Jewish cultural bias. His conclusion rests on firmer ground—a carefully constructed theological foundation. This is apparent in his assertion that persons who exchange heterosexual relations for homosexual are acting "against nature" *(para phusin)*. Those who claim that Paul's use of *phusis* is ambiguous or an extraneous borrowing from Stoic thought fail to appreciate the extent to which Paul's use of Hellenistic terminology is colored by his profound understanding of salvation history drawn from the Old Testament and his personal encounter with Jesus Christ. Paul's perspective on homosexuality presumes a theology of creation, not simply an aversion to sex orgies in the name of divine worship. Thus we must move on from explicit references to consider the broader biblical themes that have bearing on the subject.

The Sense of Scripture

The Reformed tradition has never been content to make theological judgments based on isolated biblical texts. Rather, it seeks to determine God's will for human life in the light of Scripture as the unified witness to God's saving acts culminating in the person and work of Jesus Christ. Christian ethical reflection is informed by those key doctrines which present the "sense" of Scripture as a coherent whole. A biblical perspective on homosexuality involves the broader understanding of human sexuality as a vital component of the self. Full treatment of the broader subject is far beyond our scope. However, it can be said that the Scripture's repeated endorsement of heterosexuality as the Creator's express intent is far more significant for our understanding than the few negative pronouncements concerning homosexuality. Further, when God's will for *human* sexuality becomes the focus, we approach the subject in a way that implicates all of us.

When Paul rejects homosexual acts on the grounds that they are "against nature" he expresses and reaffirms the clear sense of Scripture: Human sexuality was created for heterosexual expression. This is not to say that human sexuality *must* result in physical acts. The New Testament legitimates sexual abstinence and affirms the celibate life as a gift of the Spirit given to some persons (I Cor. 7:1-7). The above conclusion only means that when human sexuality becomes functional, the nexus should be male-female. When the subject of homosexuality is raised, the majority of modern opinion is expressed with fear, loathing or recrimination, as is often the case, it must be pitied and resisted. When the same statement is made in humility and with compassion, it may be considered biblical:

> Have you not read that he who made them from the beginning made them male and female . . . and the two shall become one (Matt. 19:4-5)?

The differentiation of the sexes is an indelible mark of creation (Gen. 1:27; 2:18ff.), an enduring constant despite its distortions in the fall (Gen. 3:17), and one necessary focus of Christ's redemptive work.

In the second creation narrative (Gen. 2) the Lord God detects only one dissonant note in the creative harmony. "It is not good that man *(ish)* should be alone" (v. 18). Man's restless incompleteness remains until the Lord God acts to make the "fit helper" for him. Woman *(ishah)* is extracted from the man's very self, yet she is so enticingly different! The man's ecstatic song of joy (v. 23) celebrates both their oneness and their essential differentiation. Man and woman come to know themselves fully only in the presence of one another. They are driven to seek union and completeness in the physical act by which they again become "one flesh." The creation account in Genesis 1 is more terse but equally significant:

> So God created man in his own image, in the image of God he created him; male and female he created them (Gen. 1:27).

One humanity is created but again in definite sexual distinction. The plural "he created them" is an intentional contrast to the preceding "he created him." This juxtaposition rules out any notion of an originally androgynous being. Both male and female appear when mankind is created. Each is an equal bearer of the image of God. Each is created as "Thou" for the other. In their sexual separateness, each is complemented and completed only by the other.

The purpose of this essential sexual differentiation now becomes clear. "One flesh" implies much more than a physical union. The image of God as relatedness includes sexual oneness while extending far beyond it. Genesis 2 stresses sexuality as a bodily drive toward psychic fulfillment, interpersonal wholeness, the completion of the total self in a relationship of communion on all levels of being. Genesis 1 shares this emphasis while identifying the other *telos* of human sexuality. God instructs the male and female: "Be fruitful and multiply . . . (v. 28). This command may seem less urgent in an overpopulated world, but it has theological significance. The procreative purpose makes the Creator's heterosexual ordering of creation even more apparent. Roman Catholic thought has tended to accentuate the procreational purpose. Protestant tradition has cited the relational intent as sufficient reason to free sexual intercourse from procreational necessity. But neither have doubted that God's will is fully expressed only in the unity of the two. It is not convincing to argue, as some in the homosexual context do, that the divine relational purpose of sex can stand alone to justify any homosexual act done in love. Procreation need not result from every sexual act, but it testifies to the fact that within the sexual act is a divinely ordered potential which only man and woman can make actual.

The Bible makes no grudging or reluctant admission of human sexuality. Heterosexual love is celebrated! The original man greets his bride with ecstatic song (Gen. 2:23). Proverbs urges a husband to faithfully "rejoice with the wife of thy youth" (5:18). The Song of Solomon spares little detail in its rhapsody of sensual delight. The psalmists and prophets compare Yahweh's covenant with his people to a marriage bond. Paul urges mutual love and submission in marriage (I Cor. 7:4) and sees in the mysterious, mutual attraction of husband and wife a metaphorical expression for the love which binds Christ to his church (Eph. 5:32). Thus, the sense of Scripture expresses rejoicing that human beings are heterosexual by nature, that is, by God's creative intent. Man and woman together become sexually fulfilled only within a binding relationship of interdependence, fidelity and self-giving love.

We have now reached a conclusion which is both reassuring and fraught with danger. Heterosexuality is not only normal; it is normative. Homosexual acts are contrary to the will of God for human sexuality. These statements may be distressing to some homosexuals and a matter of indifference to others. They may bring a healthy reassurance to the Christian heterosexual seeking moral guidance in evaluating a complex contemporary issue. They may offer counsel to youth, parents, and others in an era of sexual confusion and exploitation. But our conclusion may also be a grave stumbling block to the church, an occasion for pride and hypocrisy. It is one matter to affirm that self-chosen homosexual acts are sinful. It is quite another to reject, defame and excoriate the humanity of the person who performs them. This distinction has often been missed. It is possible and necessary on biblical grounds to identify homosexuality as a departure from God's intent. However, as the creation story makes clear, *all* human sexuality suffered in the fall (Gen 3:16).

The conclusion to Paul's diagnosis of the human condition is most relevant:

> For there is no distinction; since all have sinned and fall short of the glory of God . . . (Rom. 3:22-23).

No man or woman may claim that their sexual life or any other aspect of their fallen humanity fulfills the Creator's original intent. Heterosexuality in itself is no "righteous work" which can justify a person before God. No sexual act is an expression of pure, self-giving love. No marriage achieves the complete, "I-Thou" communion which Scripture terms "one flesh". Selfishness, exploitation, promiscuous thoughts (Matt. 5:28) if not actions, and other evils taint every heterosexual in their sexuality. Persons who populate Reformed church pews should need no lecture on total depravity, only encouragement to apply this sense of Scripture to the subject at hand. Despite the compulsive fear and loathing which homosexuality arouses in our society, there are no theological grounds on which a homosexual may be singled out for a greater measure of judgment. All persons bear within them the marks of the fall.

The above statements do not imply a suspension of ethical judgment or a leveling of all moral conduct. They do mean that all persons, regardless of sexual orientation or conduct, stand in need of God's redeeming grace in Jesus Christ and the sanctifying power of the Holy Spirit. The righteousness which we do not possess and cannot establish by good works, sexual or otherwise, is given as a free gift of grace (Rom. 5:17). It is through faith and not moral rectitude that we are saved. To complete the gospel message, however, we must note carefully that Jesus preached repentance as the doorway to the kingdom, and Romans 6 follows quickly upon Romans 5:

> Are we to continue in sin that grace may abound? By no means! How can we who died to sin still live in it (Rom. 6:1-2)?

The love of God is not indiscriminate nor is his grace "cheap." Faith can never license a life-style of intentional sin. New life emerges only from the "death" of the old. Paul, and later Calvin, demonstrated the essential link between justification and sanctification. Man is accepted by God on the basis of Christ's perfect righteousness and then given power to begin acting according to that righteousness in his own life. Sin remains, but it has been dethroned (Rom. 6:14).

> For just as you once yielded your members to impurity and to greater and greater iniquity, so now yield your members to righteousness for sanctification (Rom. 6:19).

The Christian life necessarily entails a putting to death of sin and the progressive renewal of the self in every area of personality. The Holy Spirit is the dynamic force which empowers this transformation of life and leads to personal wholeness (Rom. 8:11; Gal. 5:16ff.).

The gospel is good news to all persons in their sexual brokenness. In an age when curative functions have been largely handed over to the physician and therapist, the church must not underestimate the decisive role which the Spirit can play in a person's quest for wholeness or fail to emphasize the healing potentialities inherent in the good news which Jesus proclaimed and demonstrated. To those who practice homosexual perversion (see crucial distinction between perversion and inversion, below.) the gospel offers not only a mandate to change, but also spiritual resources to draw upon in that struggle. To the church in its dealings with the homosexual, the gospel offers not only a mandate to Christian love, but also the spiritual resources needed to become a redemptive community.

Scripture affirms that it is within the body of believers and through the body that the Holy Spirit works to bring life and growth, strength and healing to its members and to those outside. The time is overdue for the homosexual to be accepted by the church as one who bears the image of God no less than others and whose need of God's saving grace is equally great. This does not mean that a homosexual's journey toward wholeness is not a steep, uphill climb. The path is often marked by profound inner conflicts, anxiety and loneliness. Preachments and platitudes will not help nor will a spirit of judgment. A caring, person-centered ministry is imperative. The homosexual must be affirmed as a person even while his/her acts of perversion cannot be. And this caring affirmation of the person must precede and extend beyond any rejection of the person's acts. In the church's pastoral ministry, ignorance must give way to knowledge of the complexities involved in the homosexual condition and the immense obstacles to its resolution. Finally, while calling the homosexual to repent of his/her perversion, the church must also repent of its revulsion and fear. The Holy Spirit does his work among those whose mutual dependence upon God's grace is acknowledged and shared. Only in that climate of grace are persons freed to face themselves honestly and to become open to the transforming love of Christ as it becomes embodied in the fellowship of believers.

The Human Sciences

Responsible biblical interpretation must take into account the relevant empirical evidence concerning its subject. While use of the term homosexual (or heterosexual) is necessary, it must be recognized as an abstraction. By referring to a segment of humanity on the basis of sexual behavior, one makes discourse about them possible, but at the cost of their individual personhood. Sexuality is but one dimension of the self emerging from and expressing each inimitable and complex individual gestalt. Beneath every individual act, sexual and otherwise, are the complex inner drives and motivations which give rise to it. Similar acts result from a diversity of motivations and these motivations, in turn, from a myriad of biological, psychic, and social sources.

Nowhere is this complexity more obvious than in the homosexual phenomenon and the plethora of scientific opinion as to its nature, cause and cure. Theories abound among therapists, physicians, sociologists and other experts, but a consensus is not within sight. Is homosexuality a disease? Four years ago the board of the American Psychiatric Association determined that it is not. A recent poll of 2500 member psychiatrists revealed that 69 percent disagree.[1] What causes homosexuality? Factors most frequently hypothesized include hormonal imbalance, genetic abnormality, distorted psychosexual development due to unhealthy parent-child relationships and external factors such as adolescent experimentation with conditioning effects and peer group pressure. Of these factors, the weight of scholarly opinion points to some form of distorted psychosexual development. Homosexuality has no identifiable common cause but results from a combination of one or more factors in varying degrees in different individuals.

This conclusion has significance for biblical interpretation and Christian ethical reflection. A considerable body of scientific research and opinion distinguishes between homosexual *perversion* and homosexual *inversion.* Kinsey's widely-quoted research revealed that 37 percent of the male population surveyed had at least some overt homosexual experience to the point of orgasm. Ten percent of white males were preponderantly homosexual for at least three years between the ages of 16 and 65, while four percent were and apparently remained "exclusively" homosexual after the onset of adolescence.[2] (Research among females or minority groups is less extensive or conclusive.) Shocking as Kinsey's statistics may be, they do support the distinction between pervert and invert, and give further indication of the complexity of the homosexual phenomenon. The term perversion is used to designate homosexual acts engaged in by persons whose basic sexual orientation remains heterosexual. Perverts choose to act contrary to their predominant orientation. Such perversion may include temporary adolescent experimentation, neurotic adult pleasure-seeking, or situational instances in which heterosexuals engage in homosexual acts while isolated from persons of the opposite sex, e.g., in prisons, the military, etc.[3] Kinsey's research suggests that the vast majority of homosexual acts (33 out of 37 percent) are instances of heterosexual perversion.

When we consider the remaining four percent, however, we are dealing with representatives of very different homosexual type. Homosexual inversion is a condition resulting not from conscious choice but from determinative factors over which the person has no control: genetic, hormonal, or psychosocial damage done in infancy and early childhood. Unlike the pervert, the invert does not *decide* to become a homosexual. Rather, his/her orientation comes as a painful discovery during some developmental stage, usually adolescence. The homosexual invert has no more choice in the matter of sexual attraction than does the "normal" heterosexual. It must be noted further, that homosexual inversion has not lent itself readily to medical or psychotherapeutic treatment. While statistics regarding invert reorientation are not promising, nonetheless, change cannot be ruled out and help should be sought.

The distinction between homosexual perversion and inversion is crucial to Christian ethical reflection. First, its recognition demonstrates a willingness to face the homosexual issue with some regard for its inherent complexity and with the awareness that simple answers are not always adequate to complex reality. Secondly, this distinction should serve to strengthen the church in its normative stance. When it is understood that most homosexual acts are performed by persons with some measure of heterosexual orientation, the urgency of the church's moral witness becomes obvious. Contrary to popular opinion, evidence suggests that most homosexuals do have some measure of choice. Thus, the church cannot abandon the adolescent struggling to achieve sexual identity, the ambivalent adult, or the neurotic gay bar "cruiser" to the painful vagaries of a promiscuous culture or the ethical relativism of our time. While avoiding simplistic and obnoxious social crusades, the church must affirm through its preaching and pastoral ministry that homosexuality is not an acceptable, alternative lifestyle. God's gracious intent for human sexual fulfillment is the permanent bond of heterosexual love. This redemptive word must be spoken, with sensitivity, caring and clarity to any person who would make a perverted sexual choice, and to society as a whole.

Finally, the distinction noted above means that the church must learn to deal differently with persons who are homosexual by constitution and not by choice. Although a minority, they are numbered in the millions. One has no reason to doubt that inverts are also numbered among laity and clergy of the Reformed Church in America. The inverts' presence, often clouded by fear of discovery, loneliness, and guilt, and the shape of the church's ministry toward them are the most challenging issues which emerge from a study of the biblical perspective on homosexuality. As demonstrated above, Paul's indictment and the sense of Scripture as a whole define homosexual behavior as a conscious act of horizontal rebellion, a willful perversion of one's basic heterosexual nature, a bad "exchange" made by choice. Scripture does not refer to the problem of homosexual acts which emerge in accord with one's conscious, sexual orientation and not against it. As Jesus remained silent on the entire subject, so the biblical writers did not address the human condition now known as homosexual inversion. It does not follow from this fact, however, that the heterosexual norm is less binding, as many in the homosexual context aver, or that any sexual act accords with God's will if it is performed in fidelity, trust and love. The norm expressed in creation and reaffirmed in Jesus' own teaching is not abrogated by the fact that some persons *cannot* conform to it, any more than it is set aside because some persons *will not* live by it.

We cannot fail to recognize, however, one basic axiom of ethical reflection and common sense; a person cannot be blamed for a situation over which he/she has neither control nor choice. There is firm biblical support and every humane reason to understand the invert's predicament as evidence of the problem of evil, rather than sin. As the Bible makes clear, the tragic effects of the fall were precipitated by a chosen act of rebellion, but they extended far beyond it. Sin's result is cosmic disorder on a grand scale in which the innocent suffer along with the guilty. Evil erupts in natural disasters, accidents and disease, while the whole creation "groans in travail" and longs for its redemption (Rom. 8:22f.). Stated simply, the homosexual invert is no more to be blamed for his/her condition than a retarded child. It follows, then, that the church's ministry to the invert may best begin with the attempt to lift a burden of guilt that need not be carried. Inverts may not idealize their orientation as a legitimate alternative, but neither should they blame themselves for their sexual orientation.[4]

The most vexing ethical question is posed by persons who maintain that although homosexual inversion is not a sin, the decision to act it out is. Here the church's tolerance of ambiguity will be tested by the need to offer hope as well as morality. Here, also, the intersection of Christian ethics and pastoral ministry is clearly focused. Ethical judgments weigh upon the lives of real people whose aspirations and needs are at once spiritual, psychological and physical. Judgments must be made, but not without regard to the amount of weight each individual is able to bear. The homosexual person's decision will not be made with the objectivity of the ethicist or the discrimination of deliberative, ecclesiastical body. If the church is involved at all in the personal decision, we may hope it will be through the ministry of a sensitive and skilled lay or clergy counsellor. Here the church's primary role must be pastoral. Informed by biblical interpretation and theological reflection, the church's ministry to homosexual persons should receive careful consideration. The scope of a pastoral ministry to homosexuals will be the subject of an additional study which the Theological Commission will submit to General Synod in 1979.

Homosexual Rights

Approval of the homosexual orientation or acts is not a prerequisite to firm support of basic civil rights for homosexual persons. Sexual conduct is primarily an ethical question and not the concern of criminal law, except when sexual acts are committed against minors or public decency or when they involve rape or prostitution. Criminal laws to deter such acts are in force and applicable to both heterosexual and homosexual persons. Statistical evidence denies any allegation that homosexual persons are more inclined to commit violent crimes than heterosexual persons. Further statistical comparisons indicate, for example, that a child is no more likely to be seduced by a homosexual teacher or youth worker than by a heterosexual in the same role. Therefore, legislation specifically directed toward homosexual persons is unnecessary and constitutes a prejudicial attempt to legislate private morality.

Sincere and legitimate concern is sometimes expressed by parents and other adults concerning the possible negative effects of homosexual role models on children and adolescents. While this concern is valid in instances where homosexuality is espoused or flaunted, parents should recognize that negative sexual role models abound in our permissive and promiscuous society. Human sexuality is debased and exploited in advertising, in the media and on the street in many unseemly ways. Inevitably, young people will observe some persons who act out their sexuality in an irresponsible manner. Although youth cannot be isolated from such influences, they do need guidance in discerning right from wrong and making moral judgments in sexual matters. Here the teaching ministry of the church as well as the healthy sexual modeling and nurturing role of parents in the Christian home are crucial to a child's maturing sexual awareness and identity. The church should also respond to the need for a constructive Christian social witness in matters of sexual values and conduct. Concern for youth is better expressed in these positive ways than through blanket, discriminatory sanctions against all persons of one sexual type.

While we cannot affirm homosexual behavior, at the same time we are convinced that the denial of human and civil rights to homosexuals is inconsistent with the biblical witness and Reformed theology.

Endnotes

[1] Reported in *Time Magazine,* February 20, 1978, p. 102.

[2] Alfred C. Kinsey *et al., Sexual Behavior in the Human Male* (W. B. Saunders Co., 1948), pp. 651ff. While the Kinsey reports are weak at certain points, they represent the most

exhaustive scientific studies available and must be relied upon until better research is forthcoming.

[3] H. Kimball Jones, *Toward a Christian Understanding of the Homosexual* (New York: Association Press, 1966), pp. 20ff.

[4] Lewis B. Smedes, *Sex for Christians* (Grand Rapids: Mi.: Wm. B. Eerdmans Publishing Co., 1976), p. 71f. Cf. Helmut Thielicke, *The Ethics of Sex* (New York: Harper and Row, 1964), p. 283f.

Notes: *In 1977, the General Synod of the Reformed Church in America asked its Theological Commission to offer an opinion concerning the issue of supporting civil rights for homosexuals. The issue was considered at two meetings in 1977 and 1978, and a decision was made to broaden the report into a general statement on homosexuality. In this endeavor, the commission was moving in concert with other groups which were also giving major consideration to the issue.*

The Commission concluded that heterosexuality was both normal and normative for humanity, but like all aspects of human life, suffered from the fall and is imperfect (less than what God intended). That leaves room for further discussion of the presence of homosexuality in human life. The Commission made a distinction between the person who engages in occasional homosexual actions and the person who seems to be constitutionally homosexual. The pastoral tone of the document does not hide the final conclusion, however: that homosexual behavior, whether by simple choice or in working out one's homosexual nature, is sin.

The Commission saw need for further reflection on the pastoral issues raised by exploring the issues of homosexuality. That would become the subject of another year's inquiry.

Although it opposed homosexuality, the commission saw no need to criminalize homosexual behavior.

REFORMED CHURCH IN AMERICA

CHRISTIAN PASTORAL CARE FOR THE HOMOSEXUAL (1979)

In its 1978 report to the General Synod of the Reformed Church in America, its Theological Commission presented a study document entitled "Homosexuality: A Biblical and Theological Appraisal." That document serves as the theological context for this paper. The commission sets forth in this study the responsibility of the church to the homosexual who turns to it for help.

The story of the church's dealings with the homosexual is mostly a story of ignorance, ineptitude, and ill will. For centuries, both church and society have used legal punishment and severe moral censure to control or eradicate homosexuality. The approach proved worse than useless, and in employing it the church denied its essential nature and failed the homosexual. Falling readily into the role of the elder brother (Luke 15:25-30), the church either drives homosexuals underground, or, if acknowledging them, at best extends conditional affection. At worst, the church excludes homosexuals leaving them the choice either of isolating themselves or joining the homosexual community. Through this paper the Theological Commission voices its conviction that when the church is true to her Lord's intention for her she will be God's instrument for extending refuge, new beginnings, and healing to all whom life has damaged or overwhelmed, excluding no one.

The Church's Pastoral Responsibility

During his final days on earth Jesus instructed his followers to cultivate mutual love and unity of spirit (John 17:20-23), to do works of mercy (Matt. 25:37-40), and to bear witness to God's good news in Christ. Jesus made no exceptions to these instructions. "Come to me, *all* you who are weary and burdened, and I will give you rest" (Matt. 11:28). He did not demand instant sanctification of those who responded nor did he impose on them severe sanctions for failure. "Take my yoke upon you and learn from me, for I am gentle and humble in heart, and you will find rest for your souls. For my yoke is easy and my burden is light" (Matt. 11:29-30). The Christian fellowship is instructed to extend Christ's invitation freely to all.

The climate of the Christian church is to be receptive, gentle, and humble. Christians are to think of themselves as a household, a grateful family of redeemed sinners and not as a club for the socially approved. In this fellowship there is time to learn what faith in Christ is to mean for one's character and pattern of life. The faithful are to understand that becoming mature in Christ is at best uneven and often painfully slow. The Good Shepherd entered the lives of those who needed him without condescension. He responded to people's needs with respect, concern, solace, healing, and challenge to new life. This spirit marks his church whenever it is faithful to her Lord. Jesus teaches us that what is basic and most important about a person is always larger and deeper than anything negative presently associated with him or her.

Toward the penitent, Jesus was unfailingly compassionate. The guilt-ridden and the despised found him an unfailing source of forgiveness, renewal and hope. As Christ's agents on earth, the church must be conscious of persons who understand the biblical teaching on forgiveness but who cannot appropriate God's forgiveness unless and until they experience the forgiveness of fellow Christians. When the Christian withholds his forgiveness from those whom God has freely forgiven, he presumes to sit in judgment on God as well as on the penitent. Maturing in Christ begins with confession of sin. Freedom to confess openly and fully requires a climate of love, trust, and forgiveness. John Calvin sums up the destructiveness of an unforgiving spirit with his comment that "without the hope of forgiveness, men are stupified in their sins."[1] The spirit of judgment silences the penitent. In his enforced silence he is desolate. In Dietrich Bonhoeffer's words, "He who is alone with his sin is utterly alone."[2] The church must come to the penitent and the guilt-ridden as the expression of Christ's forgiveness and hope and joy.

The Homosexual's Perspective: Reasonable Expectations of the Church

The ministry of reconciliation to the homosexual must not be left to the "gay" church. While a certain affinity grouping within the church seems unavoidable, given the world as it is, the body of Christ is fractured when groups are segregated or find it necessary to segregate themselves from much of the church in order to feel accepted and free to be open about their deep concerns. We believe, however, that people now turning to affinity groups should have an option. There should be a place for the homosexual in the Reformed Church in America as well. John McNeill points out what the homosexual, and all others, may rightfully expect from a Christian congregation:

> Homosexuals will never be able to master their sex drive in a positive way and integrate it successfully into their whole personality development until they are aware of themselves as persons of dignity and worth, worthy of their fellow human's respect and consideration. For that matter, neither will anyone else.[3]

If the church is serious about ministering to the homosexual, there are areas of congregational life with which it must come to terms.

Toward elimination of the double standard of morality applied to the homosexual. - The church seems arbitrarily to have placed certain sins, homosexuality conspicuously among them, beyond its own responsibility for ministry and, by implication, beyond the reach of God's grace. As is stated in the previous study, homosexuality is not a sin that is to be singled out for special condemnation. In the Scriptures it appears as one in a list of offenses (e.g. Ex. 18:7-23; 20:9-21; I Cor. 6:9-11). There is, after all, nothing in the Christian faith which guarantees exemption from marital problems, cancer, or broken legs. Christians struggle with all the temptations and difficulties of mankind, including a wide range of sexual problems. The Christian faith does, however, provide a helpful perspective on human problems and promises resources for dealing creatively with them. The church's mission to the homosexual is in most respects the same as it is to the heterosexual: to preach God's good news of grace and forgiveness through Christ, release to those in bondage and liberty to the oppressed (Luke 4:18).

The church should acknowledge its sins against the homosexual. - The church is obliged to reflect her Lord's openness to all persons. This includes such obligations as learning what people are really like. If an aggressive apology on behalf of homosexuality is to be deplored, so is homophobia, a compulsive, irrational fear and loathing of those suspected of homosexuality, rooted in ignorance and triggering expressions of rudeness and hatred. Homosexuality is neither to be celebrated nor persecuted. Homophobia must be replaced by a sense of common humanity, the desire to understand, and the determination to put away the sins commonly committed against the homosexual, which include:

1. Caricaturing or stereotyping fellow human beings by identifying all homosexuals with the blatant, flaunting "fairy" or female "butch."
2. Labeling: reducing a person to some aspect of his behavior, i.e., identifying a person's sexual orientation with the totality of his being.
3. Enjoying disparaging humor at the homosexual's expense. Most church members would probably not go out of their way to do a homosexual person a bad turn. They are not so much hostile as unconcerned, disinterested in the homosexual's difficulties, and quite willing to join in derogatory "humor" at his expense or similar expressions of contempt.

The church should make a genuine effort to understand homosexuality. - As explicated in the prior paper *(Homosexuality: A Biblical and Theological Appraisal)*, homosexuals frequently have been subdivided into "inverts," who are regarded as exclusively homosexual, and "perverts," who have capacity for heterosexual response but who for a variety of reasons practice homosexuality. The church must be willing to understand and deal with the concrete life situation in which the sexual invert finds himself. It is most unlikely that any invert ever faced himself in the mirror and said to himself, "I'm going to be homosexual." Malcolm Boyd probably speaks for all inverts when he says,

> I don't understand why I'm involved (in homosexuality) and I might just as soon not be because who wants any more problems. But I didn't dig it up . . . this is something that has intruded itself directly into my life. . . .[4]

The sexual invert finds himself trapped in a sexuality he did not deliberately choose yet is expected to contain, a sexuality which is looked upon by society as something not only wrong but revoltingly unclean. He hears people like himself referred to as "queers" and "perverts." How, then, is a decent, sensitive person to cope with the feeling of being unclean and false? Guilt, self-loathing and a fear of close relations readily becomes a prominent part of his life. The resulting loneliness makes him vulnerably prone to expect too much too soon from others, e.g., instant, unqualified approval. Such a response is altogether unlikely, leading to disillusionment and despair. Moreover, to be preoccupied with one's homosexuality, something difficult to avoid, encourages a person to minimize his abilities and qualities of character and to neglect cultivating them. A pervasive sense of futility paralyzes the will and prevents constructive decisions.

There is much we do not know about homosexuality, but we do know that it is a complex phenomenon. The word embraces a wide spectrum of behavior and psychological experiences. Homosexuality is found at all socio-economic levels, in all ethnic groups, in urban areas and in rural areas. Some homosexuals function well in everyday life, while others are maladjusted in varying degree, some to the point of severe disturbance. Some have learned to make their homosexuality a relatively incidental part of their lives while others are dominated by it, sometimes to the point of obsession. Also, there is a wide divergence in sexual responsibility. Homosexuals who become sexually involved only with another consenting adult in the context of a long-term, affectionate relationship must be viewed differently from those promiscuously given to "one night stands." There is, then, as wide a personality variation among homosexuals as among heterosexuals.

The church should know that the pivotal issues in researching homosexuality are by no means definitively resolved. Evelyn Hooker delineated four unresolved major issues.[5]

1. Is the human being psychosexually neutral at birth, so that learning fully determines homosexual object choice, or are there inherent sexual dispositions which influence selectively one's learning?
2. What is the nature and content of the learning processes by which a homosexual object choice develops? Is it a matter of a deviant developmental role model for the child? A model whose personality, motives and gender indentifications are incompatible with adult relations with the opposite sex?
3. What are the critical periods in the developmental process for homosexual object choice? Early childhood? Adolescence?
4. Are parent-child relations in the nuclear family crucial in determining whether a person becomes homosexual? Or are peer relations in childhood and adolescence and/or deviant subcultures in adolescence or early adulthood of equal or even greater importance?[5]

A fifth issue was delineated by Dr. Henry W. Riecken in a letter to the Director of the National Institute of Mental Health.[6]

5. The persistence or plasticity of homosexual phenomena. Are they enduring and unchangeable, as some therapeutic efforts would suggest? Or are they highly transient and temporary, as some anecdotal reports about . . . exclusively male societies would suggest.

These unresolved issues underscore the fact that in considering homosexuality we are indeed dealing with a complex, imperfectly understood phenomenon about which facile pronouncements are inappropriate. Consensus of scholarship points to multiple causation of the disorder and agrees that it is at best a persistent state which is not easily modified.

The homosexual should reasonably expect personal acceptance and an understanding of the process of sanctification. - Healing and growth toward Christian maturity begins with an experience of grace. The church, as a healing fellowship, is to be the earthly expression of God's gracious acceptance of the penitent. Within this fellowship of love the homosexual must be accepted in his homosexuality. If this is not the case he is left with the choice of leaving the fellowship, wearing the mask of heterosexuality, or being contemptuously condemned. Most choose the mask. The effect is to leave the homosexual feeling hypocritical, unwanted, and unknown. He lives in fear of exposure because this spells rejection. Christian congregations seem more concerned with "instant righteousness" or the appearance of righteousness than with the patient, often painful process of growth in godliness.

Sanctification begins with genuine, responsible, self-confrontation before God: "If we confess our sin, he is faithful and just to forgive . . . and to cleanse . . ." (I John 1:9). That is to say, if we are to "become mature, attaining to the whole measure of the fullness of Christ" (Eph. 4:13b), we must begin by removing our masks of propriety and spiritual attainment and joining our fellow Christians in the task of growing together in godliness.

If honesty and responsibility are the preconditions God has laid down for personal healing and growth to take place, it follows that self-justification, self-deception, or self-concealment prevent healing and growth. Whenever a person feels bound to hide important aspects of himself, personal relations, however cordial, remain shallow. Trust is tenuous.

One fears putting much stress on a relationship lest it be destroyed. But the homosexual has found the sanctions of society so severe that honesty has seemed a bad bargain. To acknowledge his homosexuality is to invite loss of job, social ostracism, and even physical cruelty.

The difficulty Christian congregations face in any effort to deal openly with homosexuality or any other troublesome problem is that they rarely deal openly with one another about their sins and spiritual struggles. The homosexual in his closet is, then, by no means the only member of the congregation living a double life. Snared in the American obligation to be a success, people feel free to share only their victories. In a context such as this, the idea of anyone's emerging from his closet, whatever his temptation and sin, poses a severe threat. This is the dilemma as the church tries to be the healing fellowship it is intended to be.

Is there a way out of the dilemma? Not if the church persists in looking for easy victories. The way out will require humility, a teachable spirit, prayer, faith, and courage. The church must learn once more that healing and growth in the personal realm is not a case of ever upward and onward. Progress is uneven. Lapses are universal. Christians should be warned against demanding a smooth, effortless, error-free movement toward maturity. Nor should they expect to be able to do it alone, but as members together of Christ's body (Rom. 12:4, 5). In a context such as this idolaters, the covetous, the homosexual, slanderers, the sexually immoral, those who oppress and exploit people, and sinners of all stripes can find the hope and the help they need to become more fully the person God knows and intends them to be.

The Church's Perspective: Reasonable Expectations of the Homosexual

Just as the homosexual who turns to the church for help brings with him certain reasonable expectations of the church, so the church has reasonable expectations of the homosexuals who seek its help.

Little can be done to help anyone who does not commit himself actively and unreservedly to a life of discipleship. The church may reasonably expect that the homosexual and all others who seek her help will participate regularly in the worship and submit themselves to the authority of the Word of God. As the sinner receives God's gracious acceptance through Jesus Christ, he is freed to respond to "the upward call of God in Christ Jesus" (Phil. 3:4) and be transformed by the "renewal of [one's] mind" (Rom. 12:2). The homosexual ought not react helplessly to his homosexuality, but seek instead through maturing in Christ as far as possible to modify or eradicate its negative effect on his life.

As one who has been redeemed, the homosexual is given a new way to think of himself. "For you did not receive a spirit that makes you a slave again to fear, but you received the Spirit of sonship. . . . The Spirit himself testifies with our spirit that we are God's children. Now if we are children, then we are heirs, heirs of God and co-heirs with Christ . . ." (Rom. 8:15-17). He ought not, then, identify himself primarily with his homosexuality. It is not the most important thing about him. A person's standing before God as one redeemed and cleansed through Christ is what is most important. The redeemed are to think of themselves as necessary and contributing members of Christ's body who are being transformed by the power of God so as to "become mature, attaining to the whole measure of the fullness of Christ" (Eph. 4:13).

The church can also reasonably expect that the homosexual will not regard only that love to be genuine which affirms his homosexual behavior.

> Nothing can be more cruel than the tenderness that consigns another to his sin. . . . It is a ministry of mercy, an ultimate offer of genuine fellowship, when we allow nothing but God's word to stand between us, judging and succoring.[7]

One can love a person without approving those things in him which retard his fullest development.

The homosexual does well not to preoccupy himself with blaming others, though they may have contributed to his discomfort and unhappiness. Nor should he nurse a sense of injustice. We should in no way want to minimize the difficulties of homosexuality. Nursing a sense of injustice, however, furthers nothing constructive. The homosexual must learn to see his fellow Christians as unfinished products who are in many stages of maturity. He must learn to bear with those who cannot yet respond to him with love and encouragement and not let their distance or unkindness overweigh the efforts of those who can and do reach out to him. People need time to overcome negative conditioning. Giving people time to get acquainted often markedly changes attitudes. It is much easier to be hostile toward an abstract category than toward a fellow member of the congregation who sings in the choir and who is making efforts to grow as a Christian.

The church expects its people to be open to new possibilities. The homosexual must not place a ceiling on his capacity for growth. It is important that a person submit his whole self to Christ without excepting his homosexuality. This means letting go of the myth of incurability. A facile, overly optimistic view toward change and healing is unwise, but fatalism is even more so. With a teachable spirit, the desire and determination to find something better, a sense of the presence of Christ, who wills healing and growth, and support of the Christian fellowship much valuable growth can take place. Crucial to the process is the recognition of one's inability to deal with the problem alone, and the willingness to trust himself fully and openly to someone skilled and understanding.

The Contribution of the Pastor

If the pastor is to be of help to homosexuals, then he must be sensitive to the hopeless frame of mind in which they so often seek out the church. The homosexual needs to experience being known, understood, and loved unconditionally as a person. While the pastor has confidence in the healing power of Christ, this ought not lead him to expect or to suggest the possibility of quick, easy solutions. Premature reassurance fails to enter into the seriousness of the homosexual's situation. The homosexual should be expected to shoulder all appropriate responsibility but should be assured that he is not alone in his struggle.

Among the most important of the pastor's contributions is infusing an appropriate emotional climate by word and example. By steady emphasis upon the biblical teachings dealing with grace, forgiveness, reconciliation, and fellowship, he helps create a climate of mutual burden-bearing and an expectation of transformation.

The pastor serves as mentor for spiritual development. He is a key figure in sustaining the homosexual on his pilgrimage. The pastor will most likely be involved in any decision the homosexual makes concerning therapy. Pastors ought not be surprised nor dismayed when setbacks occur, but should be prepared to help the person deal with the paralyzing disappointment that can follow from a lapse.

In the final analysis responsibility for a life of discipleship rests with the homosexual himself. The pastor can help both homosexual and Christian community to see that this problem is not unique, but is of the same order as other problems with a strong compulsive element.

Endnotes

[1] John Calvin. *Commentary on the Psalms*. Vol. 5, p. 132 (Psalm 130:4)

[2] Dietrich Bonhoeffer, *Life Together,* New York, Harpers, 1954, p. 10

[3] John Mc Neill, *The Church and the Homosexual*. Kansas City, Sheed, Andrews and Mc Meel, Inc., 1976, p. 155

[4] Malcolm Boyd, ''Interview,'' *The Wittenburg Door*. Oct.-Nov., 1977, p. 33

[5] Evelyn Hooker, ''Homosexuality,'' in J. M. Livingood (ed.), *National Institute of Mental Health Task Force on Homosexuality: Final Report and Background Papers,* p. 12

[6] *Ibid.* p. 1

[7] Bonhoeffer, *op. cit.*, p. 107

Notes: *Following its development of a theological statement on homosexuality, the Theological Commission of the Reformed Church in America turned its attention to the pastoral questions raised by the initial inquiry. This second study begins with the observation that previous efforts to get rid of homosexuality by various forms of governmental and ecclesiastical suppression had failed.*

The thrust of the document is to emphasize compassion and acceptance of each person within the church and not isolate homosexuality as a particularly serious sin. All people have serious problems with sin and they must struggle with various forms of sin their entire life. The church must also see that one condition for the growth of the individual, including the homosexual, is the development of a sense of self worth. The church should provide individuals, including the homosexual, a safe place to openly struggle with their life condition and spiritual state.

The statement views all Christians as continually growing. The homosexual should be at least open to the possibility of growing beyond his condition.

Stopping far short of approving homosexuality, and attempting to honor the biblical record and Christian tradition, this statement is one of the most positive in establishing a view in which the homosexual can exist openly within the Christian community.

SALVATION ARMY

THE SALVATION ARMY'S POSITION ON HOMOSEXUALITY (1980)

The Salvation Army is vitally concerned with strengthening family life. Salvationists are disturbed by any behavior which is destructive to this basic unit of our society. The Scriptures affirm that healthy relationships between husband and wife and parents and children are necessary to satisfactory family life. Homosexual behavior, both male and female, promoted and accepted as an alternative life-style, is contrary to the teachings of the Bible and presents a serious threat to the integrity, quality and solidarity of society as a whole.

We believe, however, that we should seek, in the spirit of Jesus Christ, to understand and help the homosexual, differentiating between homosexual acts and the innate tendency which may or may not lead to that activity.

1. Homosexual behavior, like any deviant behavior, is capable of control. Not all homosexuals are incapable of normal heterosexual relationships. Some homosexuals achieve a happy heterosexual marriage.
2. Homosexuality, so long as it does not express itself in overt acts, is not blameworthy and should not be allowed to create guilt.
3. Homosexual practices unrenounced render a person unacceptable as a Salvation Army soldier, just as acts of immorality between heterosexual persons do. (From *Chosen to be a Soldier—Orders and Regulations for Soldiers of The Salvation Army,* page 48)
4. Homosexuals who are unable to develop mature heterosexual relationships can be helped by medical advice and/or psychiatric treatment, pastoral counselling, and pre-eminently by submission to the Lordship of Jesus Christ, liberating the whole person for a new quality of life.

Salvationists seek to alleviate the loneliness and alienation often felt by homosexuals by offering Christian love within Salvation Army fellowship and worship, which is open to all.

Notes: *The Salvation Army follows a traditional Christian approach to homosexuality. Seen as destructive to family values, it is strongly discouraged. Practicing homosexuals cannot be members of the Army, though they are welcomed to worship and fellowship at Army activities.*

SEVENTH-DAY ADVENTIST CHURCH

SOCIAL RELATIONSHIPS (1986)

The social instinct is given us of God, for our pleasure and benefit. ''By mutual contact minds receive polish and refinement; by social intercourse, acquaintances are formed and friendships contracted which result in a unity of heart and an atmosphere of love which is pleasing in the sight of heaven.''—*Testimonies,* vol. 6, p. 172. Proper association of the sexes is beneficial to both. Such associations should be conducted upon a high plane and with due regard to the conventions and restrictions which, for the protection of society and the individual, have been prescribed. It is the purpose of Satan, of course, to pervert every good thing; and the perversion of the best often leads to that which is worst. So it is highly important that Christians should adhere to very definite standards of social life.

Today the ideals that make these social relationships safe and happy are breaking down to an alarming degree. Under the influence of passion unrestrained by moral and religious principle, the association of the sexes has to an alarming extent degenerated into freedom and license. Sexual perversions, incest, and sexual abuse of children prevail to an alarming degree. Millions have abandoned Christian standards of conduct and are bartering the sweet and sacred experiences of marriage and parenthood for the bitter, remorseful fruits of lust. Not only are these evils damaging the familial structure of society, but the breakdown of the family in turn fosters and breeds these and other evils. The results in distorted lives of children and youth are distressing and evoke our pity, while the effects on society are not only disastrous but cumulative.

These evils have become more open and threatening to the ideals and purposes of the Christian home. Adultery, sexual abuse of spouses, incest, sexual abuse of children, homosexual practices, and lesbian practices are among the obvious perversions of God's original plan. As the intent of clear passages of Scripture (see Ex. 20:14; Lev. 18:22, 29 and 20:13; I Cor. 6:9; I Tim. 1:10; Rom. 1:20-32) is denied and as their warnings are rejected in exchange for human opinions, much uncertainty and confusion prevail. This is what Satan desires. It has always been his plan to cause people to forget that God is their Creator and that when He ''created man in His own image'' He created them ''male and female'' (Gen. 1:27). The world is witnessing today a resurgence of the perversions of ancient civilizations.

The degrading results of the world's obsession with sex and the love and pursuit of sensual pleasure are clearly delineated in the Word of God. But Christ came to destroy the works of the devil and reestablish the relationship of human beings with their Creator. Thus, though fallen in Adam and captive to sin, those who are in Christ receive full pardon and the right to choose anew the better way, the way to complete renewal. By means of the cross and the power of the Holy Spirit, all may be freed from the grip of sinful practices as they are restored to the image of their Creator.

It is incumbent upon the parents and the spiritual guides of the youth to face with no false modesty the facts of social conditions, to gain more fully a sympathetic understanding of the problems of this generation of young people, to seek most earnestly to provide for them the best environment, and to draw so near to them in spirit as to be able to impart the ideals of life and the inspiration and power of Christian religion, that they may be saved from the evil that is in the world through lust.

But to our young men and young women we say, The responsibility is yours. Whatever may be the mistakes of parents, it is your privilege to know and to hold the highest ideals of Christian manhood and womanhood. Reverent Bible study, a deep acquaintance with the works of nature, stern guarding of the sacred powers of the body, earnest purpose, constancy in prayer, and sincere, unselfish ministry to others' needs will build a character that is proof against evil and that will make you an uplifting influence in society.

Social gatherings for old and young should be made occasions, not for light and trifling amusement, but for happy fellowship and improvement of the powers of mind and soul. Good music, elevating conversation, good recitations, suitable still or motion pictures, games carefully selected for their educational value, and, above all, the making and using of plans for missionary effort can provide programs for social gatherings that will bless and strengthen the lives of all. The Youth Department of the General Conference has published helpful information and practical suggestions for the conduct of social gatherings and for guidance in other social relations.

The homes of the church are by far the best places for social gatherings. In large centers where it is impossible to hold them there, and where there is no social center of our own, a proper place free from influences destructive to Christian standards should be secured rather than a place that is ordinarily used for commercial amusements and sports, such as social halls and skating rinks, which suggest an atmosphere contrary to Christian standards.

Notes: *The Seventh-day Adventists have included a brief but clear reference to homosexual relationships in their more comprehensive statement on ''Social Relations,'' found in their* Church Manual. *Both male homosexual and lesbian relationships are denounced as perversions that threaten the Christian home. The church is called upon to make special efforts to educate young people in traditional Christian sexual mores including no sex outside of monogamous heterosexual marriage.*

SOCIETY OF FRIENDS

TOWARD A QUAKER VIEW OF SEX (1963)

III. Homosexuality

The task of taking a fresh look at homosexuality is not one which is undertaken with alacrity. That is because homosexuality conjures up more passion and prejudice than possibly any other subject except that of colour. The two attitudes have much in common; it is the fear and ignorance behind them that give them their venom.

The word ''homosexuality'' does not denote a course of conduct, but a state of affairs, the state of loving one's own, not the opposite, sex; it is a state of affairs in nature. One should no more deplore ''homosexuality'' than left-handedness. One can condemn or prohibit *acts* of course; that is another matter. But one cannot condemn or prohibit homosexuality, as such.

Secondly, the label of ''homosexuality'' is misleading. People are not either homosexual or heterosexual. Most people are *predominantly* one or the other; most in fact are predominantly heterosexual; many are predominantly homosexual; many are attracted to both sexes fairly equally and may be pushed one way or the other by circumstances, convenience, and social pressure. Before we assume that homosexuality is bad and heterosexuality is good, we should recognize that homosexuals are no more necessarily promiscuous than heterosexuals are necessarily chaste. They may be similar people (or even, it will be realized, *the same person*) and have similar moral values. But of course, where a heterosexual finds blessing in marriage, a homosexual cannot; and many of the pressures designed to hold lovers of the opposite sex together have the effect of tearing lovers of the same sex apart; it is hardly surprising then that most homosexual affairs (at least amongst men) are less durable than most heterosexual affairs.

Male Homosexuality

A homosexual orientation, as has been said previously, is usual among boys in the 11-17 year-old group, and may frequently find physical expression in such acts as mutual masturbation, more especially in all-male institutions. Many boys have countless rather casual contacts. At the same time, in dealing with adolescents, one should remember that their involvements, whether they have physical expression or not, can be far from casual: "A boy's first love is a love apart, and never again may he hope to recapture the glory and the anguish of it. It is heavy with portent and fearful with beauty, terrible as an army with banners; yet withal so tender and selfless a thing as to touch the very hem of the garment of God. Only once in a life comes such loving as this . . ." (Radcliffe Hall, 1957, p. 134). That first love will often be for another boy. The shock and bitterness of a boy who is denounced for having such feelings may well make it harder for him to reach a satisfactory sexual adjustment later. And the denunciation will not remove the feelings.

A factor in this adolescent homosexuality is that it may be and commonly is extremely promiscuous, even in the most respectable boarding schools. These very physical "affairs" usually seem to leave little behind them; often a mere sharing of physical experience, they may have little connection with any real homosexuality. It is not uncommon to observe that a boy who has been the terror of the Lower Fourth becomes a respectable married man with a large family; whereas a class-mate who may have lived chastely, horrified by so-called indecent activities, and conscious of not even the faintest interest in joining them, later turns out to be the seemingly permanent homosexual. "The lack of psychological contact with woman-kind may well be a more important contributing factor than the experience of sexual play in dormitories." (West, 1960, p. 127.) While we may say that in general the adolescent phase of homosexuality is usual and does no harm, we must not forget that it may be associated with activities causing acute suffering to sensitive boys. Mutual masturbation can become a gang activity at puberty, or even before, with severe cruelty shown on occasions towards the reluctant boy who through fear or distaste tries to stand out. Something like initiation rites may be established—again a source of terror to a sensitive boy. We cannot say that practices of this kind do no harm, however harmless the homosexuality itself may be; and it is clear that a continuing responsibility rests upon parents and teachers to be on the alert for all forms of bullying.

Seduction is probably a small or insignificant factor in forming homosexual inclination, and early promiscuity (especially with a much older person, which is what shocks society most) probably affects the boy concerned less than experiences at say 20 or 30, let alone 60. A man of 60 does not commonly have a new sexual relationship without a considerable involvement and crisis. A boy of 13 may hardly even remember it, especially if there was no emotional involvement. Society has inverted the significance of these matters: worse, the discovery by a parent of homosexual behaviour in a son is still often attended by a major uproar in the home and even attempts, involving a great deal of publicity, to prosecute the partner. What would have been forgotten then becomes a vivid experience. Since in relation to homosexuality people tend either to know everything or to know nothing (and it must be assumed that many readers of this chapter fall in the latter category) it is necessary to stress how *common* homosexual experiences are in the young. Kinsey thought that about a third of all males have some homosexual experience at some point. This may well be an underestimate. What one can say definitely is that (on the physical side) a great many boys at school are involved at some time in sexual play with others; sometimes frequently, sometimes not; sometimes with only one boy, sometimes with many—or even with several at one time. Males are very phallus-centred and particularly in early adolescence the experiment and relief offered by homosexual interchanges are pursued, usually, without harm or emotional upset.

These affairs will most often be with boys of the same age, and mainly physical. Less often but still commonly there may be an age gap of a few years, as between a 17 year-old and a 14 year-old boy. In the second case, these relationships may be far more emotionally charged, and physical satisfaction less routine, *but,* because in general more tense and deeper, they are more lasting. A genuine protectiveness and caring may be felt by the older boy, a real admiration by the younger; these emotions are not readily damped-down or forgotten. The romantic homosexual school literature—even the occasional poems which seek entry in the columns of the school magazine—relates to this latter type of affair.

But both these sorts of homosexuality, that which is mainly physical and shared with contemporaries, and that (marked by passion more than lust) linking those of different ages, flow naturally into heterosexuality and even marriage. The process may not be rapid: there are many affairs among young men of university age, and a really intense homosexual involvement may not occur until the early twenties; but all this may still be and often is but a natural precursor to the heterosexual life that is to come. One reader of *The Spectator* wrote to say that at school he had written sonnets to a younger boy; later he wrote them to his girl friend; the former was good practice for the latter. Even the mainly physical affairs explore, for the boys involved, their personalities and power, and make them sexually unafraid of later, heterosexual experience.

The Early Twenties

Passing on now to the early twenties, we may find that a tenth to a twentieth of the young men of our acquaintance are still mainly homosexual in outlook. Some may still be working out the entanglements of adolescence: their path through earlier sexual experience was perhaps not smooth or uninterrupted. They will have affairs with other young men, usually not boys, though there may well be an age difference. These affairs may still be very promiscuous—"one night stands"—or mainly emotional. But they are becoming more self-conscious: in the society of today those involved may be thinking of themselves as "homosexual"; and it is this age which knows real despair and may assume nothing else is ever to come. This is wrong; there is in society a small "hard core", but this is by no means necessarily the same group that had homosexual experiences at school or later. Many or most of the youths still predominantly homosexual in the twenties become normally heterosexual. Of those now becoming permanent homosexuals, many would not do so did not the pressures of law and of public opinion drive them into the only society where they can find acceptance, sympathy and apparent security.

On the other hand, many men come to discover strong homosexual feelings only late in life. But whatever the situation—and this, again, must be stressed—there are very large numbers of happily married men who could still regard themselves as "homosexual" and very many more who have occasional homosexual impulses and feelings. In neither situation is the marriage likely to be much prejudiced unless there has been a failure of complete candour between husband and wife; on this as on so many other subjects, a failure of mutual understanding may lead to disaster. A wife who knows that her husband has homosexual tendencies knows where she is; and it is quite remarkable how a problem of this kind can be carried. A wife who is ignorant is helpless to cope; she is likely to become suspicious and fearful, and disaster is always just round the corner. A husband in such a marriage is an easy prey to blackmailers; and when disaster comes it is not easily dealt with, since all involved assume the damage irreparable. The wife feels deceived and humiliated; the husband, that the only thing left is to abandon attempts at heterosexual interest, and if necessary wife and family as well. Many girls know nothing about homosexuality at the time of marriage; and for these it may be difficult to make useful and necessary explanations.

Later Years

In later years the picture becomes more set as people become (on the whole) more set in their habits. Most males with some degree of homosexual inclination have nevertheless achieved a successful marriage, but a substantial minority now think of themselves as definitely homosexual. These attempt long-term homosexual "marriages", some with success; they settle down, for years or for ever, with some compatible spirit, and given the right qualities of temperament and character achieve a viable relationship.

But then of course there are the others: those men for whom a happy sexual relationship with a woman is not possible. To these, homosexuality is natural; persecution will make them inhibited, mad, or suicidal, but it will not make heterosexuality any more natural for them, or increase the attractiveness of those who try to force them into it.

Those men are chiefly thought of by the public as "homosexuals", who are likely to attract public and police attention. For a number of reasons, not excluding natural promiscuity, they do not settle down with one another, but endure a lifetime of fragmented relationships and are always on the search for a partner. They may form the "queer" society; they will frequent "gay" bars, street corners, beaches and public lavatories. They tend to have an especially strong sense of persecution and, with it, they avoid being too responsible. By and large, they are not happy; although some, by demanding little of the emotions, are not dissatisfied.

This last group may include the men who are effeminate; but it cannot be too strongly urged that not all effeminate men are homosexual, and few homosexual men can really be described as effeminate. But there are some who quite obviously can; and they come particularly to the notice of the public when they are in this last promiscuous category. That is why the conventional image of the homosexual is that of an effeminate, promiscuous man, especially likely to be interested in boys. Men of this kind are likely, one day, to get publicity; the rest are unnoticed and pass—to acquaintances, friends and even relations—as heterosexual. Small wonder that most people are surprised at the extent of homosexuality; they do not know which of the people known to them are homosexual.

This necessarily dispassionate account may still fail to convey any particular problem. The reader is told that this happens and that happens; there seems nothing for him to *do* about it. But no account of homosexuality would be complete without reminding the normal reader that his own sexual emotion is welcomed by society, is encouraged by commerce, and features in films. What would it be like if every time he fell in love with a girl, he found he could not share or announce his love, and that if his affection were detected he would probably be written off as depraved by his fellows and expelled, if still at school? The homosexual learns guilt, secrecy and shame, which may follow him all the days of his life. The odd thing is that the greater his love, the greater the fear and shame. A boy may masturbate while at school with other boys for whom he feels nothing; his similarly uninhibited and perhaps contemporaneous heterosexual career will however distract attention from this; it will be said with truth, "Oh, that didn't mean anything to him", and an inglorious, unfeeling career of conventional seductions will attract nothing but mild admiration. But another will fall passionately in love, and stay in love for years, with another boy; his lack of girl friends will be noticed, and his affection deplored or, more likely, disbelieved. If and when his interest is noticed, he will probably find that many of his comrades credit him with nothing but a desire to commit sodomy. This may not even have entered his mind and his mortification and disgust may know no bounds.

Later in life it may be much the same; the promiscuous but discreet cannot expect acceptance, but if skilful they may avoid persecution. The chaste lover can expect no gratitude from society, which will only suppose, since he is chaste, that he is not homosexual. And, of course, two lovers, if both are male, can hardly expect to be urged together by the welcome pressure from society that a heterosexual engagement attracts. If they manage to set up house and stay together, they will not be favoured by praise in the local press on the silver anniversary of their union. This will seem absurd to most: but it is surprising how much the unrelenting hatred of society may eat into the soul; and man is a social animal.

Male Homosexuality in Britain

What is the present position concerning male homosexuality in Britain? Is it for example on the increase?

> It is widely believed that the prevalence of homosexuality in this country has greatly increased during the past fifty years and that homosexual behaviour is much more frequent than used to be the case. It is certainly true that the whole subject of homosexuality is much more freely discussed today than it was formerly; but this is not in itself evidence that homosexuality is today more prevalent, or homosexual behaviour more widespread, than it was when mention of it was less common. (*Wolfenden Report*, 1957, p. 19).

Yet, although homosexuality is discussed more freely, it is seldom that a public figure feels he can afford to disclose that he is in fact homosexually inclined. Consequently people do not realize that they know intimately men who are predominantly homosexual, and who go to some trouble to conceal it.

> "Oh, a deal of pains he's taken and a pretty price he's paid
> To hide his poll or dye it of a mentionable shade;
> But they've pulled the beggar's hat off for the world to see and stare.
> And they're taking him to justice for the colour of his hair."
>
> (Housman, 1962).

It is commonly thought that homosexuals are found only, or mostly, in certain occupations. They in fact exist in every rank and activity of society. Homosexuals are by no means unknown even in those places where, above all, society makes efforts to keep its figures impeccable and personally unassailable. "It would never do for the British public to hear the 'Weather Report' from the lips of a co-respondent." (Herbert, 1949.) Similarly, it is thought even less tolerable that nations should be administered by those, however able, who love their own sex; a series of broken marriages is considered preferable by the arbiters of public morals.

Because of all this, homosexuals are at a loss to know how to meet each other; and consequently pubs and bars, even street corners or particular beaches, become homosexual meeting places until the police decide to have a purge. When people hear that a particular lavatory is a meeting place for homosexuals, they shudder, and wonder at the lack of taste. But who has driven them there? If homosexuals could meet more openly and with less persecution, they would no doubt choose more aesthetic surroundings. One of the ironies of the last Wolfenden debate in the House of Commons, 29th June 1960, was Mr. Shepherd (M.P. for Cheadle) deploring homosexual contacts in public conveniences,[1] while Mr. Gardner (M.P. for Billericay) asked whether we were to be confronted with the spectacle of two males living together as lovers.[2] But surely from the point of view of public decency, the latter arrangement is preferable, and is indeed the alternative that those who urge reform of the law would candidly prefer to see.

Many people fear that a more permissive attitude to homosexuality would "open the floodgates" and result in unbridled licence. "It is true that a change of this sort would amount to a limited degree of such toleration, but we do not share the fears of our witnesses that the change would have the effect they expect. This expectation seems to us to exaggerate the effect of the law on human behaviour . . ." (*Wolfenden Report,* 1957, p. 23).

The Wolfenden Committee also rejected another common belief. Some people, they find, hold that "conduct of this kind is a cause of the demoralisation and decay of civilisations, and that therefore, unless we wish to see our nation degenerate and decay, such conduct must be stopped, by every possible means. We have no evidence to support this view, and we cannot feel it right to frame the laws which should govern this country in the present age by reference to hypothetical explanations of the history of other peoples in ages distant in time and different in circumstances from our own. In so far as the basis of this argument can be precisely formulated, it is often no more than the expression of revulsion against what is regarded as unnatural, sinful or disgusting. Many people feel this revulsion, for one or more of these reasons. But moral conviction or instinctive feeling, however strong, is not a valid basis for overriding the individual's privacy and for bringing within the ambit of the criminal law private sexual behaviour of this kind . . ." (*ibid.*, p. 22). We should go further, and question whether a feeling of revulsion, however strongly felt, is an adequate ground for moral censure. The situation is well painted by A. E. Housman in the poem for which we have quoted already:

"Tis a shame to human nature, such a head of hair as his;
In the good old time 'twas hanging for the colour that it is;
Though hanging isn't bad enough and flaying would be fair
For the nameless and abominable colour of his hair."

It has been left to professional writers to reveal as much as they dare in literature. Among the best fictional accounts of these matters are *The Heart in Exile* by Rodney Garland, which does a Baedeker's tour of homosexual society, *The City and the Pillar* by Gore Vidal, *Finistère* by Fritz Peters, and *The Charioteer* by Mary Renault.

In non-fiction, Donald West's *Homosexuality* must be one of the best and most thorough books on this topic ever written; others are Gordon Westwood's *Society and the Homosexual*, Peter Wildeblood's *Against the Law*, Anomaly's *The Invert* (an impressive 1929 Catholic viewpoint), and *Homosexuality and the Western Christian Tradition* by D. Sherwin Bailey.

Male Homosexuality and the Law

There has never been, anywhere, so far as is known, a law against homosexuality as such in any secular legal code. A man's feelings, emotions or orientations have never been the subject of this kind of attack. It is only with what he *does* that the law is concerned. Hence it is misleading to say "homosexuality is illegal". It is not, and one might say it cannot be. It has been said, "One cannot try the mind of man, for the devil himself knoweth not the mind of man."

Canon and Ecclesiastical Law. The Church has always frowned on homosexual practices. The ancient Jews distrusted them—apparently because they cannot lead to the procreation of children. The Mosaic law, embodied in the Old Testament and inherited by the Christian Church, was clear (*Leviticus* 18, v. 22; and 20, v. 13). St. Paul seems to have regarded homosexual behaviour itself with abhorrence, apparently because he was afraid women would be sexually neglected; and because such acts were "unnatural" (see Appendix A). "And likewise also the men, leaving the natural use of the woman, burned in their lust one toward another" (*Romans* 1, v. 27), suggests that St. Paul shared what has been called "the prairie fire" view of homosexual conduct—that it is naturally more attractive than heterosexual satisfaction, and if it were allowed legally and morally everyone would turn to it. This is plainly contrary to experience, although there may have been some historical reasons for this fear in St. Paul's day. It is to him, principally, that those wishing to attack homosexuals turn, for there can be no doubt as to his recorded views (I *Cor.* 6, v. 9). His opinions may have been personal ones, however, or part of the accepted Jewish thought of his day. Equally strong prohibitions, for example, that women should not pray with their hats off (I *Cor.* 11, v. 5), nor speak in church (I *Cor.* 14, v. 34), tend to be disregarded by most modern Christians, so that St. Paul's views are not, in themselves, final.

Gibbon, in his *Decline and Fall*, gives some account of these matters: "I touch with reluctance, and despatch with impatience, a more odious vice, of which modesty rejects the name and nature abominates the idea"; after discussing the laxities which abounded before Constantine, he goes on: "A new spirit of legislation, respectable even in its error, arose in the Empire with the religion of Constantine. The laws of Moses were revered as the divine original of justice. . . The lovers of their own sex were pursued by general and pious indignation." Justinian, after relaxing legislation concerning heterosexual matters, "declared himself the implacable enemy of unmanly lust, and the cruelty of his persecutions can scarcely be excused by the purity of his motives."

Justinian viewed homosexuality with abhorrence, believing that homosexual practices caused the earthquakes which were especially troublesome in his reign. Painful death, preceded by mutilation and castration, was the punishment for homosexual intercourse and two bishops, among many others, suffered this fate, and their dying bodies were dragged through the streets. "Perhaps these prelates were innocent," Gibbon adds dispassionately.

The Christian Church later also incorporated the ancient Jewish sex codes into Roman and Canon Law which formed the basis of the domestic law of medieval Europe. In medieval times, when clerical preoccupation with the sins of the flesh was at its height, and sexual pleasure was almost damnable in the strict meaning of that word, many men and also a few women were sent to their deaths for homosexual offences. The Church in general still regards homosexual practices as unnatural and gravely sinful, e.g. "Let it be understood that homosexual indulgence is a shameful vice and a grievous sin from which deliverance is to be sought by every means." (Archbishop of Canterbury, *Diocesan Notes*, November 1953).

Sodomy. Sodomy in England signifies sexual intercourse between two individuals involving penetration *per anum* by the penis. Nothing short of that is sodomy. (American State Legislatures sometimes give the word a wider meaning). The two individuals concerned need not both be male although obviously one must be. Sodomy is punishable under the statutes concerning *buggery*: buggery denotes both sodomy and anal intercourse between an individual and an animal, commonly called bestiality. We are here concerned only with sodomy.

Sodomy has been punishable since a statute of Henry VIII passed in 1533 (25 Henry VIII c. 6) by which it was punishable by death. It remained so punishable until Peel's reforms. The Offences against the Person Act 1861 provided, by Section 61: "Sodomy and Bestiality. Whosoever shall be convicted of the abominable crime of buggery, committed either with mankind or with an animal, shall be liable to be kept in penal servitude for life . . ." and Section 62 punished attempt, or assault with intent to commit buggery, with ten years imprisonment. These clauses were repealed by the Sexual Offences Act 1956 (Section 51, 4th Schedule) and replaced by Section 12 of that Act. "Buggery . . . (1) It is a felony for a person to commit buggery with another person or with an animal." The Second Schedule repeats the punishments of life imprisonment for the offence, and of ten years imprisonment for the attempt. It should be emphasized that no matter what the age of the parties, consent is no defence. Also that a boy under 14 cannot be charged with sodomy, and a passive adult partner might under this provision be imprisoned for life for an offence suggested by the boy.

It is not widely understood, even among some lawyers, that sodomy, although widely thought not only to be a homosexual, but *the only* homosexual act, may be either heterosexual or homosexual; that is, it may be committed between persons of opposite sexes. It may well be in fact more common among married people than between homosexual partners; and there is no evidence that homosexuals are drawn to sodomy more than others. Needless to say there are very few prosecutions against married couples for so undetectable an offence, which usually only comes to light in divorce proceedings, but they do occur. (Kinsey, Pomeroy and Martin, 1953, p. 370).

Homosexuals as such, therefore, are little more concerned with reform (which may well be needed) of the sodomy laws than others are; the chief legislation which affects them is that against "gross indecency between male persons". Ignorance about the nature and effect of this latter legislation is so widespread that, for instance, in the House of Commons debate on 29th June, 1960, the Conservative Member for Cheadle, in attacking the changes in the law proposed by the Wolfenden Committee, said in passing that he would be happy to see the total repeal of the "Gross Indecency" section—which meant going further than was suggested by the Wolfenden Committee.

Gross Indecency. Gross Indecency means, in this part of English Law, any sexual acts between male persons (including between boys) other than sodomy. Any sexual conduct involving the genitals is consequently prohibited, and consent is no defence. The law against "gross indecency" is relatively new, and arose in an unusual way in 1885 when Parliament appears to have created an entirely new offence unwittingly. It is thought desirable to give some account of the process of enactment as recorded in *Hansard*, to demonstrate this.

On 6th August 1885, the Criminal Law Amendment Bill was going through the Commons on its third reading, when Mr. Labouchère rose to move a fresh clause of which he had given notice on the Order Paper. Before he could say anything Mr. Walton rose on a point of order. He asked whether the clause about to be moved, which dealt with a class of offence totally different from that against which the bill was directed (protection of women and girls, and suppression of brothels) was within the scope of the bill. The Speaker ruled that anything could be introduced at this stage by leave of the House. Mr. Labouchère then proposed his clause:

"Any male person who, in public or private, commits or is a party to the commission of, or procures or attempts to procure the commission by any male person of any act of gross indecency with another male person shall be guilty of a misdemeanour, and being convicted thereof, shall be liable at the discretion of the Court to be imprisoned for any term not exceeding one year, with or without hard labour." *Hansard* continues, "That was his Amendment, and the meaning of it was that at present any person *on whom an assault* of this kind here dealt with *was committed* must be under the age of 13, and the object with which he had brought forward this clause was to make the law applicable to any person, whether under the age of 13 or over that age. He did not think it necessary to discuss the proposal at any length, as he understood Her Majesty's Government were willing to accept it. He therefore left it for the House and the Government to deal with as might be thought best." (Italics not in *Hansard*). Mr. Hopwood pointed out that under the existing law "the kind of offence indicated could not be an offence in the case of any person above the age of 13", but "he did not wish to say anything against the clause." Sir Henry James suggested two instead of one year's imprisonment. Mr. Labouchère had no objection. "Clause, as amended, agreed to." This clause was repealed and reenacted in Clause 13 of the Sexual Offences Act 1956 which provides as follows: Clause 13: "Indecency between men—It is an offence for a man to commit an act of gross indecency with another man, whether in public or private, or to be a party to the commission by a man of an act of gross indecency with another man, or to procure the commission by a man of an act of gross indecency with another man."

Firstly, it should be observed that consent and privacy are immaterial. Secondly, the Victorian legislature was so sure that *indecency meant sexual behaviour* that it was induced to prohibit gross indecency as such, without troubling to define it. So reluctant also have lawyers been to disturb this attitude that there is no recorded case of a defendant admitting acts as charged but denying their indecency. (It is hoped that it will not be thought frivolous if it is observed that Lord Curzon thought eating soup before lunch grossly indecent; it would have startled him if two men doing it together violated this Act). It is not the least remarkable factor of this legislation that it is supremely vague. This has led to difficulties in its application: actual contact between the parties involved, for example, has been held unnecessary. And although the originators of this legislation must have had something analagous in mind to sexual intercourse, a mutual love-making in some form, the interpretation by the courts is still getting wider and vaguer. Indeed in 1963 (R. *v*. Hall, Cr. App. R 253), it was held that the offence may be committed "with" another man without the consent of that other man, or his being a party to it.

Accordingly, under the law as it now stands, gross indecency may be used to signify any sexual behaviour involving the presence of two males, more usually such acts as mutual masturbation, but mutual, or even presumably unilateral, exposure of the genitals will suffice if the circumstances are those of sexual excitement.

It was under the 1885 clause we have been discussing that Oscar Wilde was tried in 1894, and under which most of the celebrated homosexual convictions in the early 1950s were obtained. It will be noticed that when Mr. Labouchère explained his clause, he seemed to be thinking in terms of *assaults*. The Rt. Hon. Sir Travers Humphreys, P.C., said in his preface to *The Trials of Oscar Wilde* edited by H. Montgomery Hyde: "It is doubtful whether the House fully appreciated that the words 'in public or private' in the new clause had completely altered the law. . . The reluctance of juries to convict in such cases is notorious, while no-one having experience in such matters would deny that the words 'in private' have naturally assisted the blackmailer in his loathsome trade."

Most men prosecuted under this clause are convicted on their own confession, or that of an accomplice turning Queen's evidence, and it has been suggested that no less than 90 per cent of cases of successful blackmail involve a threat to disclose such an offence.[3] There are even cases where a man has come forward to disclose blackmail by criminals, yet prosecution has followed against him for gross indecency. Thus a man has not been able to expose a blackmailer without the possibility of incurring prosecution, perhaps for an entirely private act with the blackmailer himself.

Recent Developments. In the House of Commons of 24th October 1963, Mr. Shepherd (M.P. for Cheadle) asked the Secretary of State for the Home Department what steps he was taking to ensure that persons complaining to the police about alleged blackmail in respect of homosexual practices receive adequate protection against prosecution in respect of those practices. Mr. Brooke, replying for the Government, said "This is a matter for the discretion of the chief officers of police; but my information is that it has for some time now been the usual practice that the Director of Public Prosecutions is first consulted, and that proceedings are taken only in grave or exceptional circumstances or where the complaint is not made *bona fide*". Persons who are blackmailed in respect of homosexual practices can therefore report the blackmail to the police without fear generally that they will themselves be prosecuted.[4]

The Government has so far declined to introduce legislation to bring the law on homosexual conduct into line with that on heterosexual conduct, preferring to await a clear gathering of public opinion in favour of this move. The reasons given in one debate (1960) for resisting legislation were:

1. (as was the case) the majority of M.P.s were not in favour of early legislation, and
2. the present Act is on the statute book (even if it would not now be passed in its present form) and to remove it might seem to give moral approval to the acts prohibited.

A private Member's bill to reform the law was introduced in March 1962 by Mr. Leo Abse, M.P. for Pontypool. It was talked out, but public comment was far more sympathetic than that which followed the 1960 debate. This favourable trend continues.

Most English-speaking countries have followed England in having legislation similar to this "gross indecency" section. Continental and other countries, except West Germany, have never had similar legislation. Austria has recently provided by statute for an age of consent of 18 years. The Wolfenden Committee, appointed by the Home Secretary, reported in 1957 as its principal recommendation on homosexuality that acts between consenting adults in private should no longer be a criminal offence. It also recommended *inter alia* that questions relating to "consent" and "in private" be decided by the same criteria as apply in the case of heterosexual acts between adults; that except for some grave reason proceedings be not instituted in respect of homosexual offences incidentally revealed in the course of investigating allegations of blackmail; that the age of "adulthood" for the purposes of the proposed change be 21; and, finally, that "research be instituted into the aetiology of homosexuality and the effects of various forms of treatment". (*Wolfenden Report*, 1957, Para. 355).

On 15th July 1964 it was announced that the new Director of Public Prosecutions had circularized Chief Constables suggesting that his consent should be obtained for all prosecutions of consenting males in future. This might well achieve uniformity of prosecution, but it appears doubtful whether it will see the end of this kind of prosecution altogether in the light of the statement of the Attorney General in the House of Commons on 28th July 1964 that no change in the enforcement of the law was intended. We hope that it will, nevertheless, result.

The offence of gross indecency finds no place in the common classification of crimes in text books, namely (1) offences against the State, (2) offences against property, and (3) offences against persons. It is perhaps the office of a logical system of criminal jurisprudence to exclude it, and leave private conduct to private morals and to pastoral and medical advice. All these are hindered by the present law, which also embarrasses frank consideration of moral standards, the examination of public welfare and much-needed research. Masturbation is not a crime, nor, in England, are fornication, adultery or sexual acts between women. Gross indecency with children of either sex under the age of 14 is prohibited by the Indecency with Children Act, 1960. Were the adult 'gross indecency' legislation to be repealed, it would still remain an offence indecently to assault a male person, with a minimum age of consent of 16. (Sexual Offences Act, 1956, S. 15.) This would deal satisfactorily with the difficulties raised by the present law.

Female Homosexuality

Homosexuality is probably as common in women as it is in men. Although with girls today heterosexual social relationships start early, the early adolescent phase may still be a time of passionate friendships and of an adoration of an older girl or woman. Close physical contact is common: girls will dance together, share a bed, or walk arm in arm, often without any strong emotional feeling. Many women continue to attach themselves to others of their own sex beyond the phase of adolescence, but owing to their nature and to society's different attitude, homosexuality in women takes forms differing from those in men. Female homosexuality is free from the legal, and to a large extent from the social, sanctions which are so important in the problems of male homosexuals. Analysis of the two forms, their differences and similarities, may therefore suggest what might happen if these sanctions were to be modified for men.

Any personal relationship between two people carries a sexual element, the nature of which will depend upon the balance of the male and female in each of the two personalities. A friendship between two individuals, one predominantly male and the other predominantly female, as with the normal man and woman, is different from one between two men in whom maleness predominates or between two women in whom femaleness predominates. In the first case the relationship is enriched by the stimulus of two very different mental patterns, in the second and third the richness lies in the freedom of a common background of thought process. A man, however, will sometimes enjoy in a woman a vigour of mind which he regards as masculine and the woman will equally welcome in a man an intuitive sympathy and tenderness which she regards as feminine. Similarly, at moments in a friendship between men, one may show "feminine" tenderness and care for the other and between women one may show "masculine dominance". (The latter is not always easily distinguishable from maternal dominance). These simple facts, though rarely formulated, are widely accepted and none would criticize a marriage, or a friendship between two persons of the same sex, in which they appear.

Society's criticism begins when the female element in a man or the male element in a woman is permanently and overtly dominant, a criticism which is almost as much directed against a married couple where the woman "wears the trousers", as in a relationship between two members of the same sex which has a homosexual element. Social structure has a further influence on this type of situation, however, since there is a strong feeling of condemnation of two persons of the same sex so linked that neither is likely to marry, a condemnation based on a conviction, which is probably socially valuable, that marriage and the procreation of children is a major responsibility of members of society.

Such criticism is far less violent against homosexual relations between women than those between men, and the reasons for this tolerance merit examination:

1. Maternal tenderness in a woman, expressing itself in kisses and embraces, is socially acceptable and it is probably for this reason that society is neither offended nor disturbed by seeing two women of any age or of very different ages kissing and embracing in public, nor by seeing two little girls or young women going about hand in hand, arm in arm, or with their arms around each others' waists.
2. The giving of maternal tenderness is so profound a need in a woman that much of the satisfaction from caresses between women will be of this kind. Society values this need in a woman and calls upon it freely, and there is considerable tolerance of its expression.
3. A very large number of women involved in homosexual relationships would frankly admit that they would prefer or are looking forward to a heterosexual one. The adolescent girl whether adoring an older woman or more closely involved with a contemporary would usually reject indignantly the idea that this precludes or replaces the male lover or husband and family to which she looks forward. The pair of middle-aged women, which society on the whole views with such tolerance, often have heterosexual experiences behind them or have been deprived of marriage, as by death or by an unhappy love affair, and thankfully find comfort, consolation and happiness in each other without in any way minimizing the value of the experiences they have had or missed. Even pairs of younger women of marriageable age—the types of female homosexuality on which society looks more askance—are often at least apparently seeking male society with a view to finding husbands. This acceptance of heterosexuality as good and desirable makes for tolerance of female homosexual pairs by society.
4. Tolerance of the pair of older women, in this country at least, probably developed when it was socially unacceptable for a single woman to live alone and it was therefore taken for granted that two single women should set up house together. This tolerance was probably reinforced in this century by the long period following World War I when there was a large surplus of women.
5. It should be emphasized that two women have often lived together in a companionship which replaces many aspects of the companionship of married life and yet in which few if any caresses are exchanged—probably true of some male partnerships as well. It is recognized that such partnerships between older women, with or without physical expression, can form a useful unit in society, each partner pursuing her avocations the better for the strength of the companionship and tenderness she finds at home, and the pair together able to offer a generous and welcome hospitality.

This is the positive side. Before considering the effect which a comparably more tolerant attitude in society would have on male homosexual relationships, it is necessary to examine the negative, and to see whether what is harmful and regrettable in female homosexuality has the same form or is similar in origin to what is harmful in homosexuality among men.

The first and most conspicuous feature is that female homosexuality is often associated with deep unhappiness. In the young girl unhappiness is probably at the minimum when the object of adoration is remote, but may even then become deeply disturbing if the emotion is so dominant that it throws life entirely out of proportion. An adolescent girl is probably more likely to be subject to this kind of disturbance than is a boy, since her emotions have often developed faster than her intellect, and she has no other dominant interest to distract her such as sport, engine-spotting or the constant care of a bicycle.

When in early life the relationship is more intimate, many of the features already noted as harmfully characteristic of male homosexuals may again be present: we find again the restless jealousy, possessiveness, and the torments of changing partnerships. These are often associated with an overt or unacknowledged sense of guilt or of resentment at being involved in what is not giving full satisfaction. This fact is probably far more important than would ever be acknowledged by the partners and, while some homosexuals are accurate when they say they do not want heterosexual relationships, many more, in their determined proclamations of this, are in fact doing violence to fuller impulses, which they are unable to perceive. The sense of guilt may at times be stronger in a young girl than in a man because she cannot, if she is at all feminine, escape the feeling of frustration at thus avoiding motherhood.

The same tensions and frustrations occur in unhappy partnerships of later life. The emotional strains, the deep bitterness arising from a continued search to find in another woman the satisfaction that only a man could give, produce the twisted embittered woman, only too familiar to psychiatrists. She may become cut off from society by her own self-absorption, for in such a situation self-absorption is dominant. She is a menace to her friends and colleagues and spreads unhappiness wherever she goes. Society is rightly critical and wrongly unsympathetic—yet sympathy is hard to give, for it is demanded on false grounds and when offered is often fiercely rejected.

This is the picture, then, of the positive and negative in female homosexuality. What can be deduced from it as to the possible course of male homosexuality if legal restrictions were removed and moral ostracism diminished? The most conspicuous feature that appears to be missing altogether from female homosexuality, even with the freedom which society allows it, is the brief contact of a purely or almost purely physical nature which is so characteristic of a certain section of male homosexual society. This is probably inherent in the different nature of the physical sexual responses of a man and a woman. It seems easier for most men than for most women to have physical relations without emotional involvement with the partner. The experience is thus phallus-centred and produces excitement without deep commitment. In heterosexual life a man may have fleeting affairs with other women without of necessity betraying his emotional fidelity towards his wife; in homosexual relationships he may be forever changing the partner. Women, on the other hand, are more often committed with the whole of their being; they are less likely to be genital-centred in their physical experience, but can achieve sexual satisfaction from various parts of the body. They are more personally involved, and more dependent on the partnership apart from physical contact. Women, therefore, will often try to work towards a lasting partnership, whether in marriage, in extra-marital love or in homosexual friendship.

It is important for society to recognize that young men need tenderness and affection just as much as do young girls and that an expression of these is no more to be wondered at or deplored in the one than in the other. Were this recognized, above all by the young men themselves, then many could pass through a homosexual phase of affection without a sense of guilt, and without believing that their need for this affection was evidence that they could not have normal heterosexual relationships. An easier attitude towards relationships of affection between young men, however expressed, far from spreading permanent homosexuality, would help to make it more transient.

Unless the balance in numbers between the sexes becomes seriously upset, giving a preponderance of males, it is unlikely that paris of older men will ever be as familiar a sight in society as pairs of older women will continue to be for several decades; but is there any reason to doubt that a permanent and loyal companionship, with the strength and security of mutual trust and affection, could be as tolerable and even valuable to society as the corresponding partnership between two women?

A Christian Attitude

There now comes the difficult matter of a Christian attitude to homosexual problems. On

16th September 1962, in his sermon in Canterbury Cathedral, the Bishop of Woolwich appealed for reform of "our utterly mediaeval treatment of homosexuals" and went on to say "as with capital punishment, one more determined push will see reform of something that is a peculiarly odious piece of English hypocrisy."

It will be clear from all that has gone before that we do not regard the standards of judgment relevant here as being different from those that apply to other sexual problems. Surely it is the nature and quality of a relationship that matters: one must not judge it by its outward appearance but by its inner worth. Homosexual affection can be as selfless as heterosexual affection, and therefore we cannot see that it is some way morally worse.

Homosexual affection may of course be an emotion which some find aesthetically disgusting, but one cannot base Christian morality on a capacity for disgust. Neither are we happy with the thought that all homosexual behaviour is sinful: motive and circumstances degrade or ennoble any act, and we feel that to list sexual acts as sins is to follow the letter rather than the spirit, to kill rather than to give life.

Further we see no reason why the physical nature of a sexual act should be the criterion by which the question whether or not it is moral should be decided. An act which expresses true affection between two individuals and gives pleasure to them both, does not seem to us to be sinful by reason *alone* of the fact that it is homosexual. The same criteria seem to us to apply whether a relationship is heterosexual or homosexual.

> "I seek only to apply to my own life the rules which govern the lives of all good men: freedom to choose a partner and, when that partner is found, to live with him discreetly and faithfully." (Wildeblood, 1957, p. 175.)

Is the homosexual to have that freedom, or must he, in Housman's words, "curse the God that made him for the colour of his hair"?

It is now necessary to emphasize that we are not saying that all homosexual acts or relationships are to be encouraged. It is difficult shortly to suggest circumstances which may give them a quality of sin. But first of all any element of force or coercion, or abuse of some superior position, must obviously put an act beyond the pale and leave it to be condemned. The authors of this essay have been depressed quite as much by the utter abandon of many homosexuals, especially those who live in homosexual circles as such, as by the absurdity of the condemnation rained down upon the well-behaved. One must disapprove of the promiscuity and selfishness, the lack of any real affection, which is the stamp of so many adult relationships, heterosexual as well as homosexual. We see nothing in them often but thinly disguised lust, unredeemed by that real concern which has always been the essential Christian requirement in a human relationship.

But it is also obvious that the really promiscuous and degraded homosexual has not been helped by the total rejection he has had to face. Society has not said "if you do that, that is all right, but as to the other, we cannot approve of that". It has said "whatever you do must be wrong: indeed you *are* wrong".

Only if Society is prepared to revise this judgment and to accept even degraded homosexuals as human beings, can they be helped to face the moral implications of their selfish relationships. . . .

V. Conclusion

What we have put forward already, and what appears in the appendices, give some idea of the great range of problems which may be brought by troubled people to those whom they trust and respect. Helping to alleviate disorders of the sort we have described is profoundly difficult, let no one doubt that: other problems such as poverty or physical ill-health are nothing compared with the more deeply ingrained sexual disorders which root themselves within the personality and seemingly defy the best attempts at relief. Individual counsellors may feel uncertain and unprepared, and it is to them that this section is directed. An understanding humility is no bad equipment. Such understanding of these disorders as we are able to share in these pages is directed towards a single aim, to give help.

Experience from discussions in our own group, the help we have had over the past five years from those within and without the Society of Friends, and the correspondence in *The Friend* and elsewhere, convince us that the desire to understand, to think deeply and to help, is widespread both amongst Friends and in other churches, but mere personal concern is not enough in a counselling situation. The over-confident or clumsy "do-gooder" can do much damage by treading with heavy feet among the tender problems of those in trouble. It is, however, also true that it is unnecessary for all enquirers to be sent automatically to the nearest marriage guidance bureau or psychiatric clinic. Such facilities already have more work than they can cope with in handling the more serious disorders, and such a step may magnify a problem that could be dealt with through ordinary understanding friendliness.

Men and women in sexual trouble usually feel that they are alone, cast out and rejected. Sympathetic friends may be of inestimable help, and indeed with many passing problems a listening ear and the reassurance which that can give are often all that is required. Most of those, for example, who are anxious about masturbation do not need psychiatric treatment but they may need help in overcoming a dominating habit. In only a few will this anxiety be a symptom of deeper disturbance. Sexual worries are often short-lived. They may be stirred up by life's passing crises (overwork, an examination, courtship, the death of a relative) and soon pass into oblivion.

Counselling at any level makes certain demands: first and foremost that of accessibility. It is hard to discuss one's sexual difficulties with others and it can be assumed that anyone wishing to do so is in some desperation, only coming after much heart-searching and plucking up of courage. Tuesday week, or even tomorrow evening, may be too late: the magic moment passes, courage may fail, a temporary but ultimately unsatisfactory solution may offer itself or, as in a few known cases, actual suicide may occur. Accessibility is thus both crucial and a dual problem: the "right" person must also somehow be readily reached.

Next is the need to listen with compassion but without judgment. Sexually troubled people are often overloaded with guilt about their condition: automatic censure is nothing new to them and serves only to increase their distress and isolation. Emotional reactions from the counsellor, arising mostly from origins of which he or she is not aware, are unhelpful. The realities of sexual conduct are far more complex than many yet realize, as we have tried to show; the counsellor must therefore be interested but unshockable, neither gleefully inquisitive nor blatantly horrified. The interest shown by some counsellors has a vicariously erotic flavour, and this can help neither party. Finally there is the need for absolute discretion, a secrecy equal to that of the confessional. Intimate details must only be given away with the person's consent, and in effect this means only to those who may be called on to help more expertly in treatment. With homosexual disorders in particular, the illegal nature of certain types of conduct may place some counsellors in a difficult position, but their duty is as clear as it is to the priest.

Because of the complexity of many of the matters herein discussed, we believe it right that for Christians, especially in larger congregations, one or two experienced counsellors should be known to be available, but we recognize that in sparsely populated rural areas this may not be possible.

Those who are called upon to give intimate and personal counsel will soon be aware of changing attitudes to morality among their fellow-members and they may feel it necessary to initiate group discussion on sexual matters. There is a danger that any compassionate view that is published—like this present essay—may be misread. A reader here and there may accept *some* of our ideas, and then proceed to put his interpretation of them into action—imposing on his victims the consequences of a permissiveness that we appear to support. It must therefore be said that at no point does our approach approve of mere permissiveness. To the question "May we do what we like?" we do *not* answer "Yes, you may''. We have been led to ask what may be the actual and ultimate result in the persons concerned of love affairs involving coitus, and have implied that the result is not necessarily or invariably destructive. We do not, however, encourage anyone to think that it would be ''perfectly all right'' to make love with a casual friend who equally desires the experience.

The true answer to our open question might prove to be as critical of ''free love'' as of mere obedience to an external morality. Sexual actions can never be primitively ''innocent''. We are not in the Garden of Eden. We are a complex race of people with the imprint of a long history on our spirits. Sexual actions stir us far below the level of consciousness, and may do more than we know to shape our future. There is an almost overwhelming urge throughout society towards the trivializing of sexual actions and the separating of them from the rest of life. A young man, whose whole working life is given to preparation for a responsible career, may nevertheless think it all right to propose ''going to bed'' to a girl he has only just met and whose surname is unknown to him. We think it probable that to use one's capacity for love-making in so tenuous a relationship is to reduce ultimately one's capacity for any depth of feeling or commitment. For in many such liaisons there is a deliberate intention to steer clear of being involved, to have fun without commitment.

In trying to work out the implications of the high standard of responsibility demanded in this essay, we have been unable to avoid the continual challenge of the questions—*when is it right to have sexual intercourse?* and, *is it ever right outside marriage?* The problem of sexual behaviour outside marriage is everywhere under discussion at the present time, and the needs of many who want guidance are not met by the simple statement that chastity is right and un-chastity wrong. Such a statement leaves many untouched and some desperate.

We condemn exploitation in any form. Exploitation is using the partner to satisfy a physical or an emotional need without considering the other as a person. There are many forms of exploitation from the extreme of prostitution for material gain to exploitation in marriage. It is exploitation if the insecure boy enhances his sense of masculine adulthood by sexual adventures, without considering the girl's feelings. It is equally exploitation if the girl leads the young man into marriage by using her attraction as a bait without thinking about his welfare. Exploitation can also happen in non-sexual relationships when the stronger character accepts adoration from the weaker and the less mature, or when one person uses the other to enrich his or her status or self-confidence. This can occur not only between unequal, but also between equal partners. In marriage it is also exploitation if the man uses the woman to show his masculine prowess or the woman uses the man to establish her social status as a married woman, or as one who is attractive and valued. Neither partner has stopped to consider the other's value.

In seeking to find a truly Christian judgment of this problem, we have again and again been brought to the quality of human relationships as the only final criterion. To base our judgment on whether or not the sex-act has taken place is often to falsify that judgment fantastically. Is the girl who remains chaste, but leaves would-be lovers stimulated to the point where desire would almost certainly seek relief elsewhere, more or less blameworthy than the girl who surrenders, whether in mistaken generosity or in the pathetic desire to ''keep her boy''? *The Christian standard of chastity should not be measured by a physical act, but should be a standard of human relationship, applicable within marriage as well as outside it* (see p. 56).

Moreover, the problem of what to say to the early developing, over-stimulated youth of the present time is not the same as the problem of what to say to the responsible young men and women equipped by experience and education to analyse and evaluate a situation in which they find themselves. A simple ''thou shalt not'' meets the needs of neither.

When human relationships are judged by this criterion, it is found to result in an assessment of behaviour not very different from that of conventional Christian morality, but it brings us to a new realization of the true nature of chastity. True chastity is a quality of the spirit: it entails the deepest respect and a profound value for human relationships. It involves the most generous giving, which may mean the restraint of withholding, but it is not solely measured in physical terms. Further, there are lives which are being lived unconventionally with more true chastity than some lived in obedience to conventional codes.

If chastity means respect for oneself and others, then promiscuity is the final denial of it. It denies the importance of personality, and those who seek relief in this way of life imprison their true selves—they are sexual deviants damaging both themselves and their transitory partner by divorcing the physical from the spiritual and keeping impersonal what should involve the whole personality. Yet wherever the most transient relationship has, as it may have, an element of true tenderness and mutual giving and receiving, it has in it something of good.

Promiscuity cannot be countered by the mere statement that it is sinful: its causes need to be sought and understood. It is often the expression of loneliness and insecurity, born of a lack of experience of real relationships with others. Promiscuity is exploitation—one-sided or mutual—but the wrongfulness of exploitation cannot be realized unless the significance of personality is perceived, until it is recognized, as Von Hgel put it, that "caring is the greatest thing, caring matters most."

Easier to judge with compassion, but in some ways more difficult to contend with, are the boy and girl relationships where both believe themselves totally committed and so have intercourse together. Today the dangers of pregnancy must and should be clearly set forth, and the wrongfulness of irresponsibly creating a life is something which boy and girl should know before they are deeply involved. Even were society's attitude to the child born out of wedlock to become more charitable, still the fatherless child is deprived of the family background that is its natural, right environment.

We must be prepared, however, to look ahead to the time when contraception is completely reliable and pregnancy is not a danger, and consider what sanctions and what motives can then be put forward. It is right and proper that many boys and girls and young men and women should fall in and out of love a number of times before they marry—and this process will involve emotional heights and depths. If these experiences are to be educative, they must involve all the personality, but such a series of experiences will be, generally, less disruptive if the final sexual commitment is avoided. Society can and should offer educational relationships by giving opportunities for the young to do things together. While they have no resources but to sit entwined in the cinema, watching huge photographs of impassioned love scenes, they will learn no outlet for their feelings for each other save those of passionate love-making. But an activity shared with other couples may help a pair to look outward at life together rather than inward at each other, and so save them from being deeply committed physically before they are otherwise ready.

Impersonal exploitation, the dangers of pregnancy, the disruptive effect of a series of love affairs involving intercourse—these are heavy arguments in favour of continence in the young unmarried. Should we go further and say unequivocally that it is utterly wrong to have intercourse outside marriage, and if so on what grounds? Only those who remain virgin until marriage can tell the value of this in their married lives, and the number of couples who express their joy at having done this, constitutes an impressive argument to offer to the young unmarried. As one couple has said, "the trouble is that until you are married, you don't realize why it is so important not to beforehand". We feel, however, constrained to say, what we believe to be true, that many deeply rich and happy marriages exist when one or both partners has had previous sexual experience, and that it would be both cruel and untrue to suggest otherwise. This same truth is borne out in the experience of the many happy second marriages which abound. It is, of course, easy to say that the individual who has moved carelessly from one liasion to another is unlikely to be successful or faithful in marriage. Even this does not necessarily follow if the transitory affairs were the expression of an insecurity or immaturity which genuine love later enables him to supersede. Moreover, it must be recognized that there are those who before marriage allow themselves a sexual freedom which they would indignantly repudiate as permissible within the marriage bond.

It has indeed been claimed that marriages are more successful where there has been previous sexual experience. This claim can be neither proved nor disproved. Those who are happily married may attribute their happiness to whatever previous experiences they have had. Those who believe in sexual freedom before marriage may claim that their marriages are happy rather than admit the possibility that they were wrong; the same may be true of those who came virgin to marriage, and would be unwilling to acknowledge, or might even be unaware of, a lack of adjustment due to their inexperience. Where an experience previous to marriage has been one of depth and integrity, where the individual has learnt from it, even if the lesson were one of suffering, then the resulting growth of personality could be a strength and not a weakness in the marriage.

We have so far considered only pre-marital relationships with others than the future wife or husband. For a couple to have intercourse before marriage merely to see whether they really want to marry, is likely to be a disastrously misleading experiment. For some, harmony experienced before marriage disappears once they are committed in marriage; others may mistake for failure what is, in fact, a lack of mutual adjustment which experience could overcome. More important than either, perhaps, the atmosphere of tentativeness prevents the mutual abandonment essential to happy adjustment.

We have felt that a distinction should be drawn between this situation and that of the couple, who, with their wedding day fixed and imminent, deliberately anticipate it, in order that the moment when they take each other as man and wife shall be completely private to themselves alone. For them, their marriage begins then and there. Censure seems in such a case, impertinent; yet it must also be said that for others their great joy is to wait until they have gladly and publicly exchanged their promises. It should be stressed that, where either partner feels doubt or guilt, it would be dangerous for them to anticipate their wedding night.

Finally, something must be said of those who are adult and unmarried and find themselves deeply in love, in a situation where marriage is impossible. When two people are deeply committed to each other, but for some reason unable to marry, then the level of judgment is a totally different one. They may, in fact, live as husband and wife and their union may, in its inherent quality, be indistinguishable from that of a legally married couple. There are faithful, permanent and rich partnerships of this sort that deserve our deepest sympathy and often our respect. Yet such a relationship can affect others beside the couple concerned and the full cost of this has to be counted.

What then is chastity? It is the antithesis of what was recently described to one of us as "the hire purchase attitude of this age"—the attitude that implies: "I want it *now* and I must have it. I will pay later—perhaps—if I can". It is not rigid restraint nor refusal to be involved; it is not arid self-discipline nor living according to a moral pattern. It is a wholeness of personality, courtesy and charity, sincerity and purity of heart. It is not necessarily measured in physical terms; it is a total absence of exploitation; it is as necessary a part of marriage as of a single life.

There are no clear-cut answers to the questions we have posed, and this nearly every counsellor will be forced to admit if he seeks to understand fully a particular situation. This is precisely because we are dealing with human relationships at their deepest, the point where rules are irrelevant. But the point where rules cease to apply is also the point at which our first and greatest need is to seek the will of God. This at least we can say to our fellow members of the Society of Friends: that if the traditional code seems now to be of little value, either in restraining us or in pointing out the way to generous living, then more than ever we need the presence of God in our judgments and decisions. And Christianity, precisely because it is concerned with the quality of human relationships, is more relevant to the unforeseen and the intensely difficult than it is to the neatly patterned way of life.

What now can we say to those who do not accept God in their lives and may indeed reject any religious influence?—to the numerous boys and girls who tumble into sexual intimacy when they are little more than children, who are confused by what it does to them and escape from confusion into toughness; to the young adults whose bottle parties are followed by indiscriminate sexual indulgence; to those whose marriages are unsatisfying and who seek distraction elsewhere; to the homosexuals living in a hell in which they are torn between a genuine impulse to tenderness and an overwhelming sense of lust? For those who are already involved we can do little, except in so far as we meet particular cases; and then our approach has to be through compassion—the reverse of moral judgment. Through this we may be admitted to their lives and their problems, and our questions may become worthy of their consideration; it is by helping them in their self-questioning rather than by giving judgment that truth can be brought to light.

The response of Friends and counsellors generally to the problem as a whole must obviously be through a clearer concept of the purpose of education and of life in community. The fulfilment of our nature as distinctively human beings is through relationships that are *personal,* through the kind of friendship that is its own justification. To some this must seem so obvious as to make them forget that to an enormous extent the structure of society and the incentives it offers constitute a flat denial of this view. Almost the whole of the time spent in educational training is directed towards the study of groups and not of individuals; that is, towards a functional relationship, not a personal one, and significance is thought of as social significance, in terms of power and prestige. The recognition of personal relationship and the understanding of its nature are left to chance. This subject has been fully discussed by Rhymes (1964, pp. 53-56).

Some schools now admit counsellors trained by the Marriage Guidance Council to talk to their pupils about problems of sexual conduct and marriage, and a very important part of their work has proved to be a discussion of the nature of personal relationships, showing how young people can grow to maturity through them. It is clear that this is not self-evident to young people; the recognition of what is personal is not provided by instinct or common sense and it is confused by the meretricious attractions and influences of our urban and affluent society. A personal relationship is a loving relationship in its most meaningful sense—the sense implied by *"Thou shalt love the Lord thy God . . . and thy neighbour as thyself".* This is a love that has no ulterior purpose. It contains its own fulfilment in itself. Much has yet to be done to understand and clarify the nature of love. Too much attention has been given to love as an ideal, good or bad, noble or sentimental; too little to it as a form of action, a continuing and developing experience. Most novels are devoted to the analysis of the breakdown of love, the working out of its painful or tragic aspect in stock situations; few describe its fulfilment through the difficulties and crises of ordinary life. Everyone knows the passion, the excitement, the adoration that are the content of sexual experience in the first stage; but the nature of love as an established relationship is less easy to demonstrate in a convincing way to those who are caught in these first obsessions. This demonstration is an urgent necessity, for much more needs to be known as to what gives love stability and endurance and, conversely, what may leave it open to destruction.

The philosophic and religious approach to the nature of personal relationship has been explored by two outstanding thinkers in our time: Martin Buber and John Macmurray. It is to the latter that we owe the clearest exposition in English. His *Reason and Emotion,* first published in 1935, threw a new and startling light on sexual and general morality at a time when, because of the collapse of Western economy, many people were thinking furiously, and constructively, about the purpose of life and society. This book is equally relevant to our problems today. Those who wish to share our search for a new and effective morality will benefit from reading it, and, if obtainable, its predecessor *Freedom in the Modern World.*

Macmurray puts forward a new definition of chastity as "emotional sincerity", linking it with the sense in which a work of art can be said to be chaste and with the meaning of the words of Jesus, "Blessed are the pure in heart". Chastity, he says, is "sincerity in the expression of what we feel; and it is the fundamental virtue, from one point of view, of a Christian morality. . . . It is the condition of personal integrity." The awareness with which our group has done its work may well be put in these lines from *Reason and Emotion:*

> Though Europe has developed itself intellectually with a steady growth upwards, has progressed in its grasp of principle, in scholarship and understanding, in the organisation and control of life and the world, it has remained all but completely barbarous on the emotional side. Our civilization, for all its scientific and administrative capacity, has remained emotionally vulgar and primitive, unchaste in the extreme. We do not recognize this, of course, because it is simply the reflection of our own inner insensibility. That insensibility is the inevitable result of a morality based upon will and reason, imposing itself upon the emotions and so destroying their integrity. Until we insist upon emotional sincerity, until we cease playing ducks and drakes with our feelings in the mistaken desire to dragoon them into conformity with what we conceive to be our 'duties', until we begin to trust our emotional life, this state of affairs will necessarily go on. Our sex-morality, in particular, will remain blind, barbarous and unreal, a vulgarity and a scandal (p. 132).

It might be added that our sex-morality, because it has not met the needs of people as persons, has been unable to prevent, and may indeed have caused a great measure of personal tragedy between men and women and in the lives of their children.

Often it is the very idealism of a religious group that prevents its members from understanding the actions and needs of people. Idealism can be a sign of spontaneous and selfless devotion in an integrated personality. But too often it is the attachment of emotion to a pattern of ideas or morals, and this kind of idealism can be an escape from having to face the darker levels of our own nature. In this shadowed region of the personality, all that we consciously repudiate lives on, for the time being so overlaid by fine sentiments that we are unaware of its existence. It is in a crisis, when controls give way, that this shadow-life tends to become active and ravaged feelings make communication impossible just when it is most needed. A deeper morality must be concerned with the whole nature of man, not merely with his conscious intentions and sentiments.

In view of this, those who genuinely wish to give help to others in sexual confusion and distress will—if they really understand what their task is—be compelled to consider every aspect of family life and especially the relationships through which young people grow up. They must always reflect on the experiences that will decide whether their impulses and feelings remain confused and destructive under the surface of apparently good behaviour, or whether they will come to know themselves and discover the discipline through which their feelings and impulses can work towards a creative end.

Endnotes

[1] *Hansard,* Volume 625, Column 1484.

[2] *Hansard,* Volume 625, Column 1504.

[3] Rt. Hon. The Lord Jowitt. Medicine and the Law: *Journal of Mental Science,* 100, 35: 1954.

[4] *Hansard,* 24th October, 1963, Column 242.

Notes: *Printed above are two chapters from the book,* Towards a Quaker View of Sex. *Next to the Wolfenden Report, few religious statements on homosexuality had more of an effect on raising the issue in the Christian community (while suggesting that there was more to be said than a simple traditional condemnation of homosexuality) than this one. Though not an official document of any body, the study was prepared by a group of prominent British Quakers and published by the Friends Home Service Committee at Friends House in London. Thus it carried some official sanction. It originally appeared in 1963, and a* *revised edition (from which these selections are taken) appeared in 1964. The work grew out of pastoral concerns and the need of guidance for homosexual Quakers.*

The importance of Toward a Quaker View of Sex *was its adoption of what later became the position of those within the larger Christian community who found homosexuality an acceptable way of orienting the sexual aspect of one's life. The report stated, "The Christian standard of chastity should not be measured by a physical act, but should be a standard of human relationship, applicable within marriage as well as outside of it." The report condemned exploitation and promiscuity, but found a variety of situations in which sex outside of marriage could be considered acceptable behavior. Homosexuality, apart from exploitation and, promiscuity (a dominant pattern of behavior in the homosexual community), was possible.*

SOUTHERN BAPTIST CONVENTION

ON HOMOSEXUALITY (1976)

WHEREAS, Homosexuality has become an open life-style for increasing numbers of persons, and

WHEREAS, Attention has been focused on the religious and moral dimension of homosexuality, and

WHEREAS, It is the task of the Christian community to bring all moral questions and issues into the light of biblical truth.

Now therefore, be it *Resolved,* that the messengers to the Southern Baptist Convention meeting in Norfolk, Virginia, affirm our commitment to the biblical truth regarding the practice of homosexuality and sin.

Be it further *Resolved,* that this Convention, while acknowledging the autonomy of the local church to ordain ministers, urge churches and agencies not to afford the practice of homosexuality any degree of approval through ordination, employment, or other designations of normal life-style,

Be it further *Resolved,* that we reaffirm our Christian concern that all persons be saved from the penalty and power of sin through our Lord Jesus Christ, what ever their present individual life-style.

Notes: *The Southern Baptist Convention chose to speak on four occasions concerning homosexuality. In this first statement, it moved to counter the possibility that a local church might ordain a homosexual as a Baptist minister.*

SOUTHERN BAPTIST CONVENTION

ON HOMOSEXUALITY (1977)

WHEREAS, The precipitous decline of moral integrity in American society continues at an alarming pace, and

WHEREAS, A campaign is being waged to secure legal, social, and religious acceptance for homosexuality and deviant moral behavior at the expense of personal dignity, and

WHEREAS, The success of those advocating such deviant moral behavior would necessarily have devastating consequences for family life in general and our children in particular, and

WHEREAS, The radical scheme to subvert the sacred pattern of marriage in America has gained formidable momentum by portraying homosexuality as normal behavior.

Now therefore be it *Resolved,* that the Southern Baptist Convention meeting in Kansas City, Missouri, June 14-16, 1977, reaffirm the firm biblical resolution on homosexuality passed in Norfolk, Virginia in 1976 and commend Anita Bryant and other Christians during the recent referendum in Miami, Florida for their courageous stand against the evils inherent in homosexuality.

Be it further *Resolved,* that we show compassion for every person in our society regardless of lifestyle, and earnestly pray for the redemption of all persons.

Notes: *A second statement on homosexuality by the southern Baptist Convention was occasioned by the fight over passage of anti-homosexual legislation in Florida. It represents a first attempt to enter the public sphere on the issue.*

SOUTHERN BAPTIST CONVENTION

ON HOMOSEXUALITY (1980)

WHEREAS, All across our nation there is a concerted effort by ''Gay Activists'' and liberal humanistic politicians to pass ordinances which, under the deceptive guise of human rights, have the effect of giving public approval to the homosexual lifestyle, making it equally acceptable to the biblical heterosexual family lifestyle, and

WHEREAS, Southern Baptists have the opportunity to become involved in their own communities in this struggle.

Be it *Resolved,* That our Convention deplore the proliferation of all homosexual practices, unnatural relations of any character, and sexual perversion whenever found in our society and reaffirm the traditional position of Southern Baptists that all such practices are sin and are condemned by the Word of God.

Be it further *Resolved,* That while the word of God condemns such practices, relations, and perversion, our Convention affirms that the Bible also offers forgiveness for those who will seek and receive it.

Notes: *The Southern Baptist Convention tries to stay out of political issues and does not legislate for the local church. However, in its concern for the homosexual issue, it urges church members to become involved in fighting against special civil rights laws to protect homosexuals.*

SOUTHERN BAPTIST CONVENTION

ON HOMOSEXUALITY (1985)

WHEREAS, There is a concerted effort by some to pass public ordinances which, under the deceptive guise of human rights, has the effect of giving public approval to the homosexual lifestyle; and

WHEREAS, There is an effort to have homosexuals identified as a minority, thereby attempting to gain affirmative action protection and preference for hiring.

Be it therefore *Resolved,* That we, the messengers of the Southern Baptist Convention meeting in Dallas, June 11-13, 1985, deplore the proliferation of all homosexual practices, and reaffirm the biblical position of Southern Baptists that all such practices are sin and are condemned by the Bible; and

Be it further *Resolved,* That we oppose the identification of homosexuality as a minority with attendant benefits or advantages; and

Be it finally *Resolved,* That we affirm that while the Bible condemns such practice as sin, it also teaches forgiveness and transformation, upon repentance, through Jesus Christ our Lord.

Notes: *In its most recent statement concerning homosexuality, the Southern Baptist Convention reasserted its earlier opposition to attempts to in any way legitimize homosexuality or homosexual behavior.*

UNITED CHURCH OF CANADA

SEXUAL ORIENTATION (1984)

Acknowledgments and Affirmations

a. We affirm our acceptance of all human beings as persons made in the image of God, regardless of their sexual orientation.

   Accumulated social science research and the articulated experience of the vast majority of both heterosexual and homosexual men and women affirm that sexual orientation is not so much a matter of choice, as a ''given'' aspect of one's identity, resulting probably from a complex interaction of genetic and environmental factors.

b. We affirm salvation for all people is by grace through faith and that all believers in Christ are accepted as full members of the Christian church, regardless of their sexual orientation.

   We acknowledge that the church has encouraged, condoned and tolerated the rejection and persecution of homosexual persons in society and in the church, and call it to repent.

c. We affirm that the church is called to initiate and encourage communication and discussion with homosexual believers about sexuality in order that fellowship may be increased and misunderstanding, fears and hostilities lessened.

   In learning more about sexual orientation the church can benefit from the input of the homosexual community which is working to articulate its own history, understanding of sexuality and its relationship to the broader church and society.

d. We affirm that members of the church, individually and corporately, are responsible for becoming more aware of discrimination against homosexual persons, taking action to ensure that they enjoy their full civil and human rights in society, working to end all forms of discrimination against them, and for personally supporting the victims of such discrimination.

   In March 1977, the Department of Church in Society of the Division of Mission in Canada, passed the following resolution:

   ''. . . We affirm the right of persons regardless of their sexual orientation to employment, accommodation and access to the services and facilities that they need and desire.

   Recommendation: That in all areas covered by The Canadian Human Rights Act, provision should be made for prohibiting discrimination on the basis or 'sexual orientation'.''

e. We affirm the need, as the church engages its heterosexual and homosexual members in dialogue, to recognize the personal and professional risks to which homosexual persons open themselves as they respond to this invitation.

f. We affirm the need for all church members, both heterosexual and homosexual, to study and understand sexuality and lifestyles in the light of the gospel.

Notes: *As early as 1977 the United Church of Canada had passed a resolution calling for the protection of the civil rights of homosexuals. The church added to the resolution in 1984 with a broader statement on sexual orientation. It accepted homosexuals as church members and called for dialogue on important issues related to homosexuality and the life of homosexual people in the church. However, it did not invite homosexuals into the ordained ministry. In 1988, a church resolution was passed that accepted homosexuals into the ministry, an action that has led the church into an intense controversy that may lead to a schism.*

UNITED CHURCH OF CHRIST

RESOLUTION ON HOMOSEXUALS AND THE LAW (1969)

Preface

Christian love for God and our neighbor in God impels us to cherish the life and liberty of all men. Even while we proclaim a unity under God which transcends our division, and while we find in Christ our measure for being human, we still honor variations among men in their political loyalties, lifestyles, and sexual preferences. Love is meaningless which does not cherish in others the freedom to be different from ourselves. Faith in the sovereign God is likewise betrayed when it does not accord to Him rather than ourselves the ultimate judgment of the moral limits of human variation. This is our Christian warrant for championing the fullest civil as well as religious liberties.

In no other dimension of life is such liberality more difficult or more important than in attitudes towards sex. The weight of Christian tradition, while commending chastity as a vocation, has clearly stressed faithfully monogamous, heterosexual marriage as the normal context for personal growth, sexual fulfillment, procreation, and the rearing of children. Sexual intimacy in any other context still tends to be viewed by the church as a substitute for marriage or a lapse from it, but as reprehensible in any case.

Such a Christian ideal, worthy as it is, should not blind us to variations and limitations which may preclude that ideal for many. Nor should it lead Christians to a rigid and graceless moralism which proscribes and persecutes those unable by constitution or circumstance to fulfill their Christian hope. We believe that the Church, which has long honored both chastity and marriage as vocations, must also learn to cherish, and not merely to condemn, those whose sexual need and loneliness may prove importunate—though unmarried, unmarriageable, widowed, or homosexual.

Among these conditions, homosexuality has proved by far the most difficult for most of us to accept and to accord respect and freedom either in the church or in public life. Fortunately, new insight is available. For example, modern Bible scholarship suggests that, while homosexuality is condemned in the Old and New Testaments, its seriousness has been exaggerated by wrenching scriptural verses out of context. As elsewhere, e.g., Ephesians 6:5, "Slaves be obedient to those who are your earthly masters," censorious and self-righteous selection and use of Scripture has further obscured the truth as well as betraying canons of Christian charity.

Again, while even medical specialists are divided on the nature and the irreversibility of homosexuality, its causes are now better understood, its extent more accurately assessed, and cruel cultural myths alleging danger to society from homosexual persons have been dispelled. We also now understand that sexual differences in personality and preference constitute a continuum of variation rather than an absolute polarity.

According to the most conservative estimates, at least one out of every twenty men and women are predominately homosexual in orientation. The United States, Germany and Austria remain the only countries in the Western world still proscribing homosexual practices as a criminal violation. In our nation known homosexuals are excluded from civil as well as military service, widely denied jobs and residence, and socially ostracized. Those not known are forced into a clandestine double life of dishonesty and subterfuge, with constant risk of blackmail, unemployment, and criminal prosecution as well in all states except Illinois.

The Council for Christian Social Action believes that the time is long overdue for our churches to be enlisted in the cause of justice and compassion for homosexual persons as well as for other socially rejected minorities. Clearly there are profound pastoral responsibilities unmet by most churches for homosexual persons in their own midst. Yet our particular concern as a Council is for the legal establishment of civil liberties—for whose denial we in the churches bear substantial blame.

The members of our Council commend traditional Christian ideals of sex, marriage, and family life. Yet we believe that legal prohibition of sexual behavior should be limited to protecting men and women from sexual coercion, children from sexual exploitation, and society from offensive public display of sexual behavior.

In light of these considerations, we have adopted the following resolution:

Resolution

WHEREAS homosexual practices between consenting adults in private endanger none of the properly protective functions of civil law; and

WHEREAS laws against consentual homosexual practices between adults in private violate the right of privacy and are virtually unenforceable, except through the abhorrent practices of police entrapment and enticement; and

WHEREAS such laws have no effect on the degree of homosexuality (as indicated by various studies abroad showing that homosexuality exists to no greater extent in countries without such laws than in the United States); and

WHEREAS present laws and government practices regarding employment and military service of homosexuals are based on false assumptions about the nature of homosexuality in general and the danger of homosexuals to society in particular;

THEREFORE, the Council for Christian Social Action (CCSA) hereby declares its opposition to all laws which make private homosexual relations between consenting adults a crime and thus urges their repeal.

FURTHER, the CCSA expresses its opposition to the total exclusion of homosexuals from public employment and from enlistment and induction into the armed forces, especially the dismissal of less than honorable discharges from the armed forces for homosexual practices with consenting adults in private. The CCSA supports dismissal of homosexuals from public employment and from the armed forces and their prosecution under the law when they have been found guilty of homosexual practices in public, against children or minors, or where force is used.

FURTHER, the CCSA opposes, where they exist, police practices of entrapment and enticement in their attempts to enforce laws against homosexual practices and solicitation.

FURTHER, the CCSA encourages the United Church of Christ Conferences, Associations, and local churches to hold seminars, consultations, conferences, etc. for honest and open discussion of the nature of homosexuality in our society.

Notes: *The United Church of Christ has emerged as one of the most open Protestant Christian denominations regarding homosexuality. It was one of the first to deal with the issue, even before the famous Christopher Street riots in New York City in the summer of 1969. In the spring of 1969, the Council for Christian Social Action of the United Church of*

Christ passed a strong resolution calling for the decriminalization of homosexual acts between consenting adults. Included in the resolution were references to government service and the military, both still areas in which homosexuality is an important issue. No action on this resolution was taken by the general synod of the church.

UNITED CHURCH OF CHRIST

STATEMENT ON HUMAN SEXUALITY AND ORDINATION (1973)

The Executive Council, recognizing that Associations have final responsibility for ordination and standing and acknowledging that such responsibility must be exercised within the context of a clear understanding of the theology of ordination,

A. Recommends that congregations, Associations and Conferences initiate programs of study and dialogue with regard to the implications (meanings) of human sexuality, in all its mystery, at its broadest and deepest levels in the theological context.

B. Directs the Council for Church and Ministry and its successor body to continue its study of the relationship between ordination and human sexuality in consultation with congregations, Associations and Conferences for the purpose of developing resources for the study of human sexuality and developing a process for decision making that may be utilized by Associations in the matter of ordaining affirmed homosexuals.

C. Recommends to Associations that as they continue to clarify their understanding of the theology of ordination they give serious consideration to the position of the Council for Church and Ministry in the matter of human sexuality: "In the instance of considering a stated homosexual's candidacy for ordination, the issue should not be his/her homosexuality as such, but rather, the candidate's total view of human sexuality and his/her understanding of the morality of its (expression)."

D. Directs the Council for Church and Ministry and its successor body to make progress reports and possible recommendations to the Executive Council during the present biennium.

Notes: *In 1973 the executive council of the United Church of Christ raised the issue of ordination of practicing homosexuals. While making no specific recommendation to approve ordination of qualified homosexuals, the raising of the issue was perceived as a step toward endorsement.*

UNITED CHURCH OF CHRIST

PRONOUNCEMENT ON CIVIL LIBERTIES WITHOUT DISCRIMINATION RELATED TO AFFECTIONAL OR SEXUAL PREFERENCES (1975)

The purpose of this Pronouncement is to make a statement on civil liberties. It is not within the province of this Pronouncement to make an ethical judgment about same-gender relationships. However, this Pronouncement may well serve to further dialogue that will clarify the ethical issues involved in human sexuality.

There is, in the United States, a significant minority of persons whose civil liberties, and whose right to equal protection under the law, are systematically and routinely violated. Discrimination related to affectional or sexual preference in employment, housing, public accommodations, and other civil liberties, has inflicted an incalculable burden of fear into the lives of persons in society and in the church whose affectional or sexual preference is toward persons of the same gender.

Most directly affected are the 10% of the population whose affectional or sexual preference, according to the research of Alfred Kinsey, is predominately toward persons of the same gender. Also affected is the one-third of the American population which Kinsey found to have had at one time or another an adult same-gender sexual experience. Public revelation of even a single experience often results in the presumption that a person is same-gender oriented and thus subject to social sanctions including violations of her or his civil liberties. Even the civil liberties of persons whose affectional or sexual preference is a well-guarded secret are vulnerable. Inquiry by private investigatory agencies into the personal life of the individual is often a pre-requisite for employment. Draft records, insurance investigations, arrest records (even when charges have been dismissed or the defendant acquitted), and investigations instigated on the basis of anonymous accusation or rumor, all provide an employer, landlord, and other persons information used justify discrimination.

Discrimination Causes Suffering

A constant fear of losing one's job and home, and the economic and social consequences of such a loss, creates suffering in human life. Living as presumed heterosexuals, same-gender oriented women and men are intimidated into silence, forced into lives of duplicity and deception, by the hostility of the majority society. Such duplicity and deception, and their concurrent alienation, sometimes evolving into isolation and depression and culminating in suicide, are necessarily detrimental to the growth of the individual and to the growth of interpersonal relationships. Today, same-gender oriented persons, our sisters brothers in human community and in Christian community, are struggling to free themselves from the fear which the reality of discrimination, particularly in employment and in housing, has inflicted upon them. Such persons are taking a moral stance against discrimination and the violence that it does to human dignity. They seek to secure protection for their full civil liberties and equal protection under the law. The church must bear a measure of responsibility for the suffering visited upon same-gender oriented persons since often the traditional Judeo-Christian attitude toward same-gender relationship has been used as a primary justification for denial and violation of civil liberties and the perpetuation of discrimination against such persons.

The Religious Perspective

Christian love for God and our neighbor in God impels us to cherish the life and liberty of all women and men. We proclaim a unity under God which transcends our division, and find in Christ our measure for being human.

As Christians, we seek to personify the liberating Gospel of Jesus the Christ and to follow his example in our relationships with others. This means that we try to have love and respect for each other—for individual well-being, quality of life, personality, dignity, and self-actualization.

The Christian churches have a long tradition of concern for human justice and civil liberties. From the days of the Hebrew prophets, we have been charged to pursue justice for all who are oppressed. In its most faithful moments the church has been recalled to the words of Amos: "I hate, I despise your feasts, and I take no delight in your solemn assemblies. . . . But let justice roll down like the waters, and righteousness like a might stream." (Amos 5:21,24) Insofar as the church has been concerned for social justice, it also necessarily has been concerned for civil liberties. Historically, branches of the Protestant churches have been the most significant single influence in the rise of concern for basic civil rights in the Western world. The tradition of the United Church of Christ is a particularly rich heritage of such concern. First suffering the denial of liberty at the hands of both civil and ecclesiastical authorities in the Old World, our ancestors claimed these rights for themselves in the New World. Realizing that the rights of none were secure until the rights of all were secure, our ancestors-in-faith gradually extended their civil liberty concern to the whole of society.

In faithfulness to that biblical and historic mandate, we hold that, as a child of God, every person is endowed with worth and dignity that human judgment cannot set aside. Denial and violation of the civil liberties of the individual and her or his right to equal protection under the law defames that worth and dignity and is, therefore, morally wrong. Our Christian faith requires that we respond to the injustice in our society manifested in the denial and violation of the civil liberties of persons whose affectional or sexual preference is toward persons of the same gender.

Affirmation of Civil Liberties

THEREFORE, without considering in this document the rightness or wrongness of same-gender relationships, but recognizing that a person's affectional or sexual preference is not legitimate grounds on which to deny her or his civil liberties, the Tenth General Synod of the United Church of Christ proclaims the Christian conviction that all persons are entitled to full civil liberties and equal protection under the law.

Further, the Tenth General Synod declares its support for the enactment of legislation at the federal, state and local levels of government that would guarantee the liberties of all persons without discrimination related to affectional or sexual preference.

Further, the Tenth General Synod calls upon the congregations, Associations, Conferences, and Instrumentalities of the United Church of Christ to work for the enactment of such legislation at the federal, state, and local levels of government, and authorizes the Secretary of the United Church of Christ to commend this Pronouncement to the Conferences for distribution by them to their respective state legislators and representatives in the Congress of the United States.L

Notes: *In 1975, the general synod of the United Church of Christ addressed the issue of civil rights for homosexuals. Following the 1969 resolution by the Council for Christian Social Action, the church called for nondiscrimination against people because of their sexual preferences.*

UNITED CHURCH OF CHRIST

RESOLUTION ON HUMAN SEXUALITY AND THE NEEDS OF GAY AND BISEXUAL PERSONS (1975)

The General Synod adopts the statement on a Response to the Overture of the California, Northern Conference Concerning the Special Needs of Gay and Bisexual Persons in the Professional Leadership of the Church:

A. The United Church of Christ has a priority commitment to strengthen the local church. Wherever personal suffering must be silently endured without benefit of pastoral care or empathetic support, especially when the suffering occurs in the lives of the professional leadership of the church, the local church, and the church at every level, is weakened.

   Insofar as social, legal and religious condemnation of homosexuality has inflicted immeasurable emotional, psychological and, at times, physical suffering upon the lives of homosexual and bisexual persons and their families, the church has a responsibility to respond to the special needs of such persons. Of immediate concern are the needs of homosexual and bisexual ministers, directors of religious education, and others in the professional leadership of the United Church of Christ.

   Therefore, the Tenth General Synod responds to the special needs of homosexual and bisexual ministers, directors of religious education and others in the professional leadership of the United Church of Christ by directing the Office for Church Life and Leadership to:

   1. Compile and distribute a nation-wide listing of both church and non-church related

counseling resources that offer non-judgmental counseling for homosexual and bisexual persons and their families.

2. Compile and distribute an annually updated listing of vocational guidance and counseling agencies with experience in counseling homosexual and bisexual professionals.

3. Distribute a comprehensive bibliography of books, articles and audio-visual aids concerning human sexuality.

B. The United Church of Christ has not faced in depth the issue of human sexuality. Changing morality and ethics within American society present both problems and challenges to the church.

Therefore, the Tenth General Synod requests the Executive Council to commission a study concerning the dynamics of human sexuality and the theological basis for a Christian ethic concerning human sexuality, and to recommend postures for the church, to be presented to the Eleventh General Synod.

Notes: *The Tenth General Synod of the United Church of Christ dealt with the issue of civil rights for homosexual people. It also dealt with the fact that a number of people then in leadership positions in the church had become identified as homosexual, primarily because they had so identified themselves in the years since they had been ordained and/or hired. This situation, catching the synod somewhat unprepared, led to the initiation of a study of human sexuality, similar to the efforts being pursued or about to begin in sister denominations.*

UNITED CHURCH OF CHRIST

RESOLUTION DEPLORING THE VIOLATION OF CIVIL RIGHTS OF GAY AND BISEXUAL PERSONS (1977)

WHEREAS the Tenth General Synod declared by an overwhelming majority its commitment to an end to discrimination relating to sexual or affectional preference; and

WHEREAS in recent months we have witnessed the widespread violation of the civil rights of gay and bisexual persons in the name of Christianity; and

WHEREAS gay and bisexual persons have become victims of violence, including murder, allegedly as a result of fanatical prejudice kindled recently by those who publicly espouse and exploit irrational fear; and

WHEREAS the recent referendum in Dade County, Florida represents a new reactionary movement which may eventually erode the civil liberties of all; and

WHEREAS the United Church of Christ in its heritage and in this theology has a commitment to compassion for, and liberation of, oppressed minorities;

THEREFORE, BE IT RESOLVED that this Eleventh General Synod:

1. Reaffirms the action of the Tenth General Synod in its Pronouncement on Civil Liberties Without Discrimination Related to Affectional or Sexual Preference;

2. Deplores the use of scripture to generate hatred, and the violation of civil rights of gay and bisexual persons; and

3. Calls upon individual members, local churches, Associations, Conferences, and Instrumentalities to continue to work for the enactment of civil rights legislation at the federal, state and local levels of government.

Notes: *This resolution deals with the movement to pass anti-homosexual laws in Florida, a* *movement led by singer Anita Bryant and the conservative Christian community. The Church's solution is in the spirit of its previous pronouncements.*

UNITED CHURCH OF CHRIST

EQUAL EMPLOYMENT OPPORTUNITY POLICY (1980)

The Executive Council of the United Church of Christ affirms its moral and legal commitment to support and implement a program of Equal Employment Opportunity. It further calls upon the national agencies, Conferences, Associations, local churches, and church-related institutions of the United Church of Christ to adopt and implement a Program of Equal Employment Opportunity which does not discriminate against any employee or applicant because of race, color, national origin, sex, age, sexual preference, or disabilities.

Notes: *This resolution deals with homosexual church employees faced with discrimination from church leaders who are theologically or ethically opposed to homosexuality. A revised text was passed 1981.*

UNITED CHURCH OF CHRIST

EQUAL EMPLOYMENT OPPORTUNITY POLICY (REVISED) (1981)

The Executive Council receives the open letter from the United Church People for Biblical Witness;

The Executive Council revises Vote 80 4 EC 20 by changing the term ''sexual preference'': to ''sexual orientation'' and reaffirms its action to include the term;

The Executive Council reaffirms the October, 1973, statement (73 10 EC 34) on considering a stated homosexual's candidacy for ordination;

The Executive Council requests the Chairperson of the Council to write a letter to the United Church People for Biblical Witness interpreting to them the Executive Council's action.

Notes: *In reaction to pressure from the United Church People for Biblical Witness, an evangelical Christian caucus within the United Church of Christ, the church's executive committee altered its policy on employment of homosexuals within the church. Their action rejected the stance of the caucus, though a minor change was made in the original document.*

UNITED CHURCH OF CHRIST

RESOLUTION ON INSTITUTIONALIZED HOMOPHOBIA WITHIN THE UNITED CHURCH OF CHRIST (1983)

WHEREAS, social institutions have historically embodied the prevailing prejudices and mores of their age; and

WHEREAS, the United Church of Christ has been called on in the past to assess the extent to which its structures and instrumentalities reflect the prevailing values (e.g., racism and sexism); and

WHEREAS, homophobia (defined as the irrational fear of same-gender feelings, identification, and/or social-sexual expression which can be either conscious or subconscious) prevails in our culture and society; and

WHEREAS, lesbians, gay men, and bisexual persons suffer from institutionalized homophobia through isolation, devaluation, and discrimination to such an extent that they lead lives that are either hidden or ridiculed within the institutional church; and

WHEREAS, such treatment fosters emotional strain, alienation, a lack of self-worth, and in some cases a life where suicide appears to be the only option; and

WHEREAS, these same persons have gifts of ministry and faith to offer the United Church of Christ; and

WHEREAS, some Conferences, local churches, Associations, and national Instrumentalities have take steps in addressing institutionalized homophobia; and

WHEREAS, the United Church of Christ has at times demonstrated to lesbians, gay men, bisexual persons, lay and clergy, that they are not persons of equal worth in the life of the church by turning these persons away from access to jobs, decision-making processes, and other aspects of institutional life which are available with little constraint to those who are heterosexual;

THEREFORE, BE IT RESOLVED that the Fourteenth General Synod denounces institutionalized expressions of homophobia in all its forms, and calls upon all levels of the United Church of Christ to expose, to address, and in the light of the Gospel, to transform institutionalized homophobia eliminating its effects within the church.

Notes: *While most churches, even those which oppose homosexuality on biblical and theological grounds, oppose homophobia, it remains a common reaction of people in Western culture. Applying some of the same reasoning developed in the fight against racism, the United Church of Christ identified and denounced various forms of homophobia.*

UNITED CHURCH OF CHRIST

RESOLUTION IN RESPONSE TO THE CONCERNS OF SAME-GENDER ORIENTED PERSONS AND THEIR FAMILIES WITHIN THE UNITED CHURCH OF CHRIST (1983)

WHEREAS, God calls us into the family of faith to share our joys and our sorrows, to serve God by serving our neighbor, to proclaim justice and to do justice, to personify the liberating Gospel of Christ, and to celebrate our Oneness as the people of God; and

WHEREAS, same-gender oriented persons baptized and nurtured in the Christian faith in United Church of Christ congregations, and their families, are, no less than other United Church of Christ members, concerned about the welfare of the family; and

WHEREAS, serious pastoral concerns exist with regard to the oppressive attitudes which same-gender oriented persons and their families encounter in the church and in the society as a whole; and

WHEREAS, such attitudes often cause same-gender oriented youth and adults, spouses and children of same-gender oriented persons, parents of same-gender oriented persons, and other family members to experience alienation and isolation within the community of faith; and

WHEREAS, the Thirteenth General Synod of the United Church of Christ adopted Family Life as Priority of the United Church of Christ calling for "all families to be ministered to creatively and for all persons, regardless of their family patterns, to be affirmed and supported in the life of the church, manifesting our unity as a family in Christ", and

WHEREAS, the Family Life Priority Working Group has been commissioned with the responsibility to faithfully implement the Family Life Priority; and

WHEREAS, the concerns of same-gender oriented persons and their families are related to painful realities which merit serious consideration and action by the Family Life Priority Working Group, including, but not limited to, concern for recognition of the faithful familial relationships of same-gender oriented persons; affirmation for same-gender oriented youth and adults; reconciliation within families seeking to cope with the knowledge that their families include one or more same-gender oriented children, spouse, parent or relative; sensitivity to the discrimination faced by same-gender oriented persons who are hospitalized and are denied the comforting presence of their beloved; advocacy for same-gender oriented persons seeking custody of their children; and response to the isolation which many same-gender oriented elderly persons experience, many of whom look to the church to be a supportive community in the often difficult final years of life; and

WHEREAS, the entire church, and especially congregational life, will be enriched through deepened awareness of the constellation of family life which exists within every United Church of Christ congregation; and

WHEREAS, United Church of Christ pastors are in need of resources and educational opportunities to enable them to better serve the same-gender oriented persons within their congregations and communities, and their families;

THEREFORE, BE IT RESOLVED that the Fourteenth General Synod of the United Church of Christ reaffirms the Family Life Priority commitment that "all families be ministered to creatively and that all persons regardless of their family patterns, be affirmed and supported in the life of the church, manifesting our unity as a family in Christ:" and

FURTHER that the United Church Board for Homeland Ministries be requested to invite the United Church Coalition for Lesbian/Gay Concerns to participate as consultants to the Family Life Priority Working Group to articulate the concerns of same-gender oriented United Church members and their families.

Notes: *Through the 1980s, as the issue of homosexuality continued to cause concern and differences of opinion within the United Church of Christ, it was brought to the floor of the general synod in its many facets. One of the issues rarely considered in the discussion was that of the effects upon the homosexual's family due to the social condemnation of homosexuality. The church was called upon to react in pastoral and appropriate ways to the suffering encountered in these families.*

UNITED CHURCH OF CHRIST

RESOLUTION RECOMMENDING INCLUSIVENESS ON ASSOCIATION CHURCH AND MINISTRY COMMITTEES WITHIN THE UNITED CHURCH OF CHRIST (1983)

WHEREAS, St. Paul admonished the church in Rome to cease condemnation with these words:

> "Who will be the accuser of God's chosen ones? It is God who pronounces acquittal; then who can condemn? It is Christ—Christ who died, and, more than that, was raised from the dead—who is at God's right hand, and indeed pleads our cause." [Romans 8: 31-34]; and

WHEREAS, St. Paul affirmed the inclusive nature of God's grace and love with these words:

> "Then what can separate us from the love of Christ? Can affliction or hardship? Can

persecution, hunger, nakedness, peril, or the sword? 'We are being done to death for thy sake all the day long,' as Scripture says; 'we have been treated like sheep for slaughter'—and yet, in spite of all, overwhelming victory is ours through him who loved us. For I am convinced that there is nothing in death or life, in the realm of spirits or superhuman powers, in the world as it is or the world as it shall be, in the forces of the universe, in heights or depths—nothing in all creation that can separate us from the love of God in Christ Jesus our Lord.'' [Romans 8: 35-39]; and

WHEREAS, throughout the history of the Christian Church, God has called persons of every sexual orientation to the Christian ministry and such persons have brought to the ministry commitment to the Gospel of Christ, selfless dedication in the service of humanity, and the clarity and strength of their personal faith in Christ and the all-sufficient truth of God's abiding love and grace irrespective of their individual sexual orientation; and

WHEREAS, there is growing awareness within the United Church of Christ that same-gender oriented persons called by God to ministry have faithfully proclaimed the Gospel and served the church with honor and dedication while enduring immeasurable suffering because the church has been unwilling to affirm their full personhood, inclusive of their same-gender orientation, and has perpetuated discriminatory practices causing such ministers to fear the loss of employment and the violation of Christian vocation as ordained ministers; and

WHEREAS, lesbian and gay United Church of Christ seminarians, many of whom have been baptized and nurtured in the Christian faith in UCC congregations, have responded to God's call to ministry and are preparing themselves for Christian vocations, including the ordained ministry; and

WHEREAS, many such seminarians have already affirmed their lesbian and gay identities, have a comprehensive knowledge of their personal sexual orientation, live responsible and socially conscious lifestyles, and understand the dynamics of homophobic oppression in their own lives, in the church, and in the society as a whole; and

WHEREAS, United Church of Christ Associations which have elected lesbian and gay laypersons and clergy to Church and Ministry committees have found their contributions to the work of those committees to be invaluable in bringing understanding and sensitivity to the inclusive nature of God's love and God's liberating activity in calling same-gender oriented persons to the Christian ministry; and

WHEREAS, the church has a responsibility to affirm the inclusive nature of God's love for all persons and to cease its discriminatory practices towards persons seeking to serve God and humanity through Christian vocation; and

WHEREAS, lesbian and gay clergy within the United Church of Christ have been called to specific ministries, including parish ministry, and have and are demonstrating that irrational fears about their ability to exercise their ministries responsibly are unfounded;

THEREFORE, BE IT RESOLVED that the Fourteenth General Synod calls upon congregations, Associations, and Conferences of the United Church of Christ to be faithful in continuing educational efforts designed to increase understanding of same-gender oriented persons and their commitment to the Christian faith and to the church; and

FURTHER, the Fourteenth General Synod of the United Church of Christ recommends that Associations throughout the UCC be open to consideration of the nomination and election of avowed lesbian and gay laypersons and clergy to their Church and Ministry committees.

Notes: *One of four resolutions passed in 1983 by the Fourteenth General Synod of the United Church of Christ, this statement calls for inclusion of homosexuals, both gay males and lesbians, on the important committees which approve ministerial candidates for ordination. In the United Church, ordination is largely an affair of associations (the first level of church organization above the congregational level), and inclusion of gays on the ordination committees would make them more open to approving a gay candidate.*

This resolution more than any other comes the closest to stating approval of homosexual relationships and behavior.

UNITED CHURCH OF CHRIST

REPORT OF THE TASK FORCE FOR THE STUDY OF HUMAN SEXUALITY (1983)

Introduction

The Twelfth General Synod in June of 1979 voted to continue the study of human sexuality and to create a Task Force to facilitate that study. (See Appendix, page 30, for the full text of that vote: 79-GS-40.) At its meeting that fall, the Executive Council elected ten persons to serve on the Task Force. Subsequently, the United Church People for Biblical Witness voiced concern that the Task Force was not sufficiently inclusive; and the Executive Council authorized, and the President appointed, an eleventh member.

During these four years, health and other commitments have affected our membership. Rev. Lee Lawhead of Doylestown, Pennsylvania resigned, and a replacement was named by the President. Another member, Rev. Peggy Way of Nashville, Tennessee was unable to attend many meetings to the point where in her words, ''Although I affirm this report, it would be inappropriate for me to sign it since it is really the work of the other members.'' This, as we make this final report to the Fourteenth General Synod, the Task Force consists of the following members:

Kenneth Taylor, Chair
William Eichhorn
Yoshio Fukuyama
Jan Griesinger
William Irwin
David Kimberly
Frances Nye
Mary Terada
James Walker
Karen Werme

We met seven times in the course of our work. Many of us attended theThirteenth General Synod where we held an open hearing and met with Conference delegations. We are grateful to many people and groups throughout the Church who have contributed materials, information, and assistance: executives and staff members of instrumentalities and other national bodies; Conference Ministers, Conference staff and Association officers; the United Church Coalition for Lesbian/Gay Concerns and the United Church People for Biblical Witness; persons in local churches who have written to us both in response to our inquiries and at their own initiative; seminary faculty; pastors; and representatives of various church-related groups. Throughout our work, we have received excellent staff support from the President's office and Robert Noble, Assistant to the President.

Our experience has been challenging and difficult, and part of the challenge arises out of our diversity. Half of us are lay persons, half are ordained. We are Black, Asian, and Caucasian. We are members of churches in cities, rural towns, and suburbs from New England and the West Coast, and five states in between. Our occupations vary from probation officer to pastor, industrial chemist to law student, college chaplain to elementary public school teacher, homemaker to psychiatrist. We are married, single, divorced, parents and non-parents, gay and straight. Some of us grew up in other denominations. Our heritage includes Reformed, Congregational, Evangelical, and Christian. Our experience on this Task Force has confirmed for us ''the cost and joy of discipleship.''

We have encountered in one another the diversity of which we often speak in the United Church of Christ. It is real. It is an opportunity. But it is difficult. Our differences startled us. They angered, confused, and at times nearly overwhelmed us. We laughed at them, worked at them, and came to respect them.

Our convictions have not changed. If anything, we are more diverse than when we began, for our differences are more clearly defined. We come from the east and from the west, from the north and from the south, . . . and all the other places from which people come when considering human sexuality. But we have gathered together about a table, and experienced a mystery to which we cannot give words, only witness. We came to know and to trust that for each of us Christ truly sits at the head of the table. With us he has been broken; for us he has poured himself out; and over us his prayer remains: "that they may all be one." To the Holy Spirit who has enabled us to partake of that mystery, we are thankful.

This report contains three sections. Each corresponds to a portion of the task outlined in the vote of the Twelfth General Synod.

Section I describes our work in response to Paragraph C. of that vote which directed the Task Force to "encourage and facilitate the continuing study of human sexuality." Included in *Section I* is a description of a report which we sent to conferences indicating the kinds of materials and programs being used by churches, associations, and conferences as part of the continuing study of human sexuality within the UCC.

Section II of this report deals with the study which the Task Force made of the various materials referred to it by the Twelfth General Synod. Points of clarification which we have found to be important are included as well as observations about the process by which some of those materials came before the General Synod and the church.

Section III responds to Paragraph F of the General Synod vote which "Directs the task force to present a framework of Biblical and theological understanding, reflecting the diversity within the United Church of Christ and seeking comments from United Church of Christ theologians." The framework in its initial draft has been sent to 25 professors in the areas of Biblical studies, theology, and ethics on the faculty of seminaries related to the UCC and to 7 UCC members on other seminary faculties. Pastors are theologians, and we sought comments from 17 pastors suggested by Conference ministers. Ten Conference and national executives, and representatives of 10 UCC-related groups, were also included in our testing of this framework. However, this framework is ultimately a statement of and by this Task Force. In the UCC the task of Biblical and theological reflection belongs to all. Thus we present this framework, not for adoption by General Synod, but for sharing and learning within the church.

The action of the Twelfth General Synod which established this Task Force indicates that it has the authority to "present recommendations to the Fourteenth General Synod." To facilitate the work of General Synod, we have chosen to present our recommendations separately and to distinguish them from this report by placing them in another section which is attached at the end. We do this to maintain as clearly as possible the distinction between a report and a recommendation regarding policy or program. It is our hope that this arrangement will assist the General Synod first to receive the report requested, and then subsequently to deal with our own or any other recommendations regarding human sexuality as may be presented to it.

Section I

Encouraging the Continuing Study of Human Sexuality

Paragraph C of the vote of the Twelfth General Synod mandated the Task Force to:

1. "Encourage and facilitate the continuing study of human sexuality by all congregations, associations, conferences, and other groups within the church."
2. "Identify, test, and publicize various models of study" undertaken by those parts of the church.

3. "Observe, evaluate and monitor processes which continue the study" of human sexuality both within the UCC and in other denominations.
4. Seek reports and circulate information to the conferences.

Early in 1980 the Task Force sent through the conferences an open letter to members of the UCC, requesting information about how churches, associations, conferences, and other groups had been dealing with issues of human sexuality. The request was also reported in *Keeping You Posted* and *A.D. Magazine*. A follow-up letter to conference staff and association officers was sent in the fall of that year. Over 100 persons responded, either individually or on behalf of various groups who worked on sexuality issues within the church. They forwarded outlines of many different programs, lists of the materials used, samples of bibliographies developed, and observations about the kinds of events or study formats which they had tried and found helpful.

The Task Force reviewed all the materials received. We also studied work being done in other denominations such as the United Church of Canada, the Church of the Brethren, and the United Presbyterian Church (USA).

The Task Force prepared a four-part report which we sent to the Conferences during 1982:

Part I: The Special Bibliography

Given our limited budget, we could not ourselves test, or observe and evaluate, the hundreds of books, audio-visuals, and curricula recommended to us. But we were able to secure the help of the members of the UCC who had used them. Thus, we compiled a "Special Bibliography" of the materials commended to us, and listed beside each item the name and address of person(s) who are ready to share with others their experience and evaluation of that item.

Part II: Educational Models

From the many study outlines and program suggestions sent to us from across the church, we selected twelve to illustrate the kind of programming being done by various parts of the church. The following is an outline of the materials included:

1. *Why is Sexuality My Christian Concern*

   A sermon which introduces a local church adult education program, an outline of which is also included.

2. *A Christian Understanding of Human Sexuality*

   An outline of a 16 week course using both *Human Sexuality: A Preliminary Report* and *Issues in Sexual Ethics.*

3. *The Bible is Our Authority*

   Ten basic understandings used in study/discussion groups at a conference annual meeting.

4. *Sexuality and Confirmation*

   A description of a portion of a confirmation program.

5. *A Human Sexuality Course for 8th and 9th Graders*

   A letter of introduction to parents and outline of the curriculum.

6. *Homosexuality Information Day*

   A schedule and design.

7. *A Church and Ministry Committee's Study & Discussion Day on the Ordination of a Homosexual*

   A schedule of resources.

8-9. *Young Adult Weekend Retreats*

Excerpts from fliers from two such retreats.

10-12.*Areas for Continuing Work in a Church or Conference*

10. *"Some things a Local Church Might Do"*—An outline by a member of a local church given during a study group.

11. *"Observations by a Pastor"*—A description by a new pastor of what she sees happening.

12. *Areas for Further Study Listed by a Conference Task Force*

Part III: Other Bibliographies.

One was produced by a local church; another was developed by a seminary professor and students as part of a course on human sexuality; and a third was developed by the Office for Church Life and Leadership. These three included descriptions of most of the items listed. In addition, two short bibliographies prepared by the United Church People for Biblical Witness and the United Church Coalition for Lesbian/Gay Concerns were included to supplement the others.

Part IV: Synopsis of Statements by Protestant Denominations.

The synopsis from the National Council of Churches on many different topics in the area of human sexuality included portions of study materials prepared by various denominations.

By preparing and distributing these materials to the conferences, we hope that the Task Force has encouraged and facilitated the continuing study of human sexuality within the UCC through:

—identifying and publicizing some of the materials and types of study which have been undertaken and tested by various parts of the UCC.

—encouraging and facilitating the sharing of observations and evaluations about those materials and processes.

—adding to the information available about resources for dealing with the subject of human sexuality, including information about studies undertaken by other denominations.

Section II

Items Referred to the Task Force

Paragraph D of the vote of the Twelfth General Synod "refers to the Task Force for continuing study, clarification, and possible recommendations for policy development" a number of related items. They are:

—Recommendations 2-18 of the "Recommendations in Regard to Human Sexuality," adopted by the Eleventh General Synod 1977;

—A Minority Resolution on "Recommendations in Regard to Human Sexuality," presented to the Eleventh General Synod;

—Twelve overtures and resolutions submitted to the Twelfth General Synod in 1979 dealing with the area of human sexuality, many of which relate to Recommendations 2-18 voted by the Eleventh General Synod;

—*Human Sexuality: A Preliminary Study,* a report which the Tenth General Synod in 1975 requested the Executive Council to commission, and which the Eleventh General Synod in 1977 voted to receive and to commend to the churches for study and response (Recommendation 1 of the 18 "Recommendations in Regard to Human Sexuality");

—*Issues in Sexual Ethics,* a book published by the United Church People for Biblical Witness, which the Eleventh General Synod encouraged that the Task Force study.

The Task Force spent many hours considering these and other materials. We studied *Human Sexuality: A Preliminary Study* and *Issues in Sexual Ethics,* and would concur with the actions of the Eleventh and Twelfth General Synods which have encouraged the study of both books.

The adoption of the "Recommendations in Regard to Human Sexuality" by the Eleventh General Synod prompted the presentation of the Minority Report at that same Synod in 1977, and many of the resolutions and overtures to the Twelfth General Synod. Because these subsequent materials focused on Recommendations 2-18, we gave particular attention to these recommendations, and sought to understand the concerns they raised. To this end we also reviewed correspondence received by both the United Church People for Biblical Witness and the President's office of the UCC.

From our study it is clear to us that a variety of elements contributed to the concerns which were expressed. Obviously different people experienced and weighed each of them differently. As a group, we ourselves contain many of those differences. But through our work together we have come to appreciate the following as factors which can carry considerable significance:

A. The Time Element

In 1975, the Tenth Synod requested the Executive Council "to commission a study concerning the dynamics of human sexuality and the theological basis for a Christian ethic concerning human sexuality, and to recommend postures for the church, to be presented to the Eleventh General Synod" in 1977.

Although this action appeared to allow two years for the work requested, the actual work-period between Synods is less than eighteen months. Time is needed at the beginning to organize; and work must be completed months before Synod so that any materials or reports can be printed and mailed to delegates in the spring.

In the course of the work done on human sexuality between the Tenth and Eleventh General Synods, this time limit affected the process at both the beginning and the end. When the Executive Council authorized funds for the study to the Board for Homeland Ministries, the Board presented a prospectus in which it indicated that the study would have to be preliminary in nature because of the limited time available. The eventual title, *Human Sexuality: A Preliminary Study,* thus reflects the time limitation. Similarly, time was a factor in the months just before Synod. At its meeting in March of 1977, when it received the study, the Executive Council requested that it be sent to delegates as a separate section of the advance materials. But even so, some delegates did not receive a copy until shortly before the Synod convened.

Such difficulties have taught lessons which have since been put into practice. One role of the Executive Council is to monitor the implementation of General Synod actions. Where adjustments such as in the timeframe are required, it can act as General Synod *ad interim* to enable the action to be implemented more effectively. Both the Council and the General Synod have acknowledged the importance and appropriateness of this role. For example, the Twelfth General Synod in 1979 directed that the Executive Council "continue its monitoring of the implementation of General Synod Eleven sexuality actions."

It has long been a requirement that proposed pronouncements be sent to delegates and churches three months before General Synod. That practice and awareness has been extended. The reports of this Task Force, for example, are required to be mailed three months before Synod.

There is a difference of opinion on the Task Force whether the Tenth General Synod was realistic in its expectation that two years was sufficient time for the work which it was requesting, particularly given its own observation that the UCC had yet to face a subject which presented "both problems and challenges to the church." We are agreed, however, that study of human sexuality and the theological basis for a Christian ethic concerning human sexuality'' is a task for the whole church, year after year, and not just for one biennium.

B. Disagreement about the Relationship between the Recommendations 2-18 and Human Sexuality: A Preliminary Study

The Tenth General Synod in 1977 did not specify the relationship between the study to be commissioned and the postures to be recommended. That initial lack of clarity remained unresolved and is reflected subsequently in the ''Recommendations in Regard to Human Sexuality'' adopted by the Eleventh General Synod in 1979. The first recommendation ''receives the report, 'Human Sexuality: A Preliminary Study' with appreciation and commends it to the congregations, conferences, associations, and instrumentalities of the UCC for study and response.'' The remaining seventeen recommendations, numbered 2-18, deal with policies and programs which address issues of human sexuality in both the church and society. But there is no indication in the action of what the relationship is between the first and the following seventeen recommendations.

The phrase ''A Preliminary Study'' in the title of the report also contributed to some people's confusion because it implies a next step. Similarly the fact that the study was being forwarded throughout the church ''for study and response'' added for some to an impression that the study was preliminary to some subsequent development.

The action of the Tenth General Synod did not specify that there was to be a relationship between the study and the postures to be recommended. Neither did it indicate that there need not be. The Eleventh General Synod did not clarify that ambiguity. Subsequent references to Recommendations 2-18 in parts of the church nationally as well as locally indicate that the assumption continues to be made that they were based on the study. However, no such relationship is actually specified in the actions of either Synod.

This lack of specifity was a major factor contributing to what became for some a subsequent disagreement. It appeared to some to be inconsistent, and a violation of process, to forward a preliminary study to the church for its study and response while at the same time proceeding to establish policy and programs in the very subject to be studied. For others, however, it was entirely appropriate to reaffirm and establish policies and programs in an area where study was simultaneously being encouraged and where a resource for such study was being distributed.

From our work, it is also clear that for still others the situation was understood in terms of one General Synod having to find a way to deal expeditiously with a number of matters on the same subject, which were being presented for action at the request of the previous General Synod.

Similarly, some understood that the team of consultants who worked with development of the study were not involved with the development of the recommendations. Others did not. For still others, such questions about the preparation and process through which these materials had come to Synod were overshadowed by the fact that they were on the agenda and Synod had to have some way to vote on them.

Our study indicates that, in retrospect, most would agree that the process was complicated by the ambiguous relationship between the study and the recommendations. The lack of clarity, which existed from the beginning with the vote of the Tenth General Synod, contributed to the perception of some that the adoption of Recommendations 2-18 was inappropriate.

C. The Meaning and Implications of Recommendations 2-18

In our study we sought to identify the particular issues which caused concern to some people. With nine of the recommendations the Task Force found no such issues. We also did an analysis of correspondence and resolutions concerning Recommendations 2-18 which indicated that these particular recommendations were not a focus of concern. These nine recommendations, as voted by the Eleventh General Synod are:

3. Calls upon the United Church Board for Homeland Ministries to continue to provide leadership in developing resources concerning human sexuality for appropriate use by various age groups in local churches and to provide consultative services and training for conferences, associations and congregations who wish to sponsor programs concerned with human sexuality and family life.

4. Requests the UCC-related seminaries, conferences, and instrumentalities to continue developing courses and resources through which clergy, seminary students, and laity may be prepared to minister in the area of human sexuality and to address related policy issues.

5. Urges pastors, members, congregations, conferences and instrumentalities to support programs in which information about human sexuality can be made available through such major American institutions as elementary and secondary education, adult education, social welfare agencies, medical services, and the communication media.

8. Calls upon pastors, congregations, conferences, and instrumentalities to address, in their own programs and in those of public and private agencies, the concerns for sexuality and lifestyle of persons who have physical or emotional handicaps, or who are retarded, elderly, or terminally ill. Because of its faithful ministry through care of the young, handicapped, retarded, and aged, we urge the Council for Health and Welfare Services to encourage administrators and staff of member institutions to respect the needs for intimacy of adult persons served, and protect the right of sexual expression as important to self-worth, affirmation of life, and avoidance of isolation.

9. Urges the Board for Homeland Ministries, the Commission for Racial Justice, and the Office for Church in Society to work for the protection of persons threatened by coercive use of sterilization, medical treatment, experimental research, or the withholding of medical information, and to fully inform these persons of their rights under the law.

12. Calls upon instrumentalities to address the economic structures which victimize women (and men) and explore such strategies as compensation for housework and child care, Social Security for homemakers, programs for displaced homemakers, insurance benefits for pregnancies, and quality day care.

13. Affirms the wide public attention being given to issues related to sexuality and sex roles, particularly as they affect women, but expresses concern regarding the need to explore such issues as they affect men. The 11th General Synod urges the Board for Homeland Ministries, the Office for Church Life and Leadership, conferences, associations, and congregations to develop programs which take into account the needs, experiences and viewpoints of both males and females, and which encourage further understanding of sexual identity; the effects of sex role stereotyping and present economic, legal, political, and other societal conditions based upon gender.

With the remaining recommendations we identified particular issues and concerns. For example, Recommendation 11 deals with abortion and freedom of choice. It reads:

11. Affirms the right of women to freedom of choice with regard to pregnancy expressed by the Eighth General Synod and interpreted as a constitutional right in the January 22, 1973 decisions of the Supreme Court which remove the legal restrictions on medical termination of pregnancy through the second trimester. Pastors, members, congregations, conferences, instrumentalities and agencies are urged to resist in local communities or in legislative halls attempts to erode or negate the 1973 decisions of the court and to respect and protect the First Amendment rights to differences of opinion and freedom from intimidation concerning the issue of abortion.

    Deplores the June 20, 1977 decision of the U.S. Supreme Court and recent actions of the U.S. Congress that effectually deprive the poor of their Constitutional rights of choice to end or complete a pregnancy, while leaving the well-to-do in the full enjoyment of such rights.

Calls upon UCC members, congregations, associations, conferences and instrumentalities to assure that publicly supported hospitals provide medical service to women within their usual service area to exercise their Constitutional right to end or complete pregnancies; and to petition their State legislatures and the U.S. Congress to assure that the poor will be provided with medical services to exercise their Constitutional rights to end or complete pregnancies.

Within the UCC there are obviously persons who do not agree with the freedom of choice position which the above recommendation represents. The members of this Task Force do not all agree with that position. However, that position has been reaffirmed by both the Twelfth and Thirteenth General Synods and there is, in our judgement, no question as to the intent or meaning of Recommendation 11. Thus we found no particular difficulty with this recommendation other than the fact that some members of the UCC may not agree with it.

With some of the recommendations, we found that the way in which the statement itself was worded raised concern. With Recommendation 7, it was simply a matter of unclear wording. With others there was concern for something left unsaid. Thus, we agreed that Recommendation 10 could appropriately have included mention of the church's teaching of sexual ethics as part of the prevention of unwanted pregnancies. With Recommendation 14, we concurred that there is a need to affirm the integrity of Biblical translation and to make clear the distinction between translation and paraphrase. In Recommendation 18, we agreed that the statement seemed to minimize a concern for the exploitation of sex in the media by overemphasizing the rights of adults to sexually explicit materials and the need for First Amendment guarantees.

Part of the work of the Task Force involves clarification. Thus we developed the following rewordings of Recommendations 7, 10, 14, and 18, as we sought to clarify them in our own minds in regard to the concerns just noted. The original recommendation voted by the Eleventh General Synod is listed on the left, our own clarification on the right:

7. Calls upon the Board for Homeland Ministries, the Commission for Racial Justice, the Office of Communication, and the conferences to develop and share model programs that can help local churches minister to and educate their communities about the components of sexual violence, including rape, marital violence, child abuse, abusive medical practices, and domination and submission images in the media of relationships between women and men portrayed as exclusive expressions of human interaction.

7. Calls upon the Board for Homeland Ministries, the Commission for Racial Justice, the Office of Communication, and the conferences to develop and share model programs that can help local churches minister to and educate their communities about sexual violence. This should include rape, marital violence, child abuse, incest, unethical medical practices, and patterns of male domination/female submission.

10. Calls upon pastor, members, congregations, conferences and instrumentalities to encourage the extension of contraceptive information and services by both public and private agencies for all youth and adults as instrumental to

10. Calls upon pastors, members, congregations, associations, conferences, and instrumentalities to teach Christian sexual ethics, to foster responsible use of birth control; to foster responsible family planning; and to encourage availability

preventing undesirable pregnancies and fostering responsible family planning.

of contraceptive information and services in both public and private sectors.

14. Recommends to all instrumentalities, agencies, conferences, associations, and congregations that language they use reflect both feminine and masculine metaphor about God, and draw upon the diverse metaphor of God represented in the Bible, in the Christian tradition and in contemporary experience.

14. Recommends to all instrumentalities, and other national bodies, conferences, associations, and congregations that language used reflect both feminine and masculine metaphors for God, drawing upon the diverse metaphors for God represented in the Bible, in the Christian tradition and in contemporary experiences, maintaining a clear distinction between translation and paraphrase.

18. Deplores and condemns the dehumanizing portrayals of women and men, the abuse of children, and the exploitation of sex in printed and electronic media of communication, recognizes the rights of adults to access to sexually explicit materials, and affirms that efforts toward change must recognize First Amendment principles.

18. Deplores and condemns the dehumanizing portrayals of women and men, the abuse of children, and the exploitation of sex in printed and electronic media while recognizing the rights of adults under existing constitutional protections.

In recommendations, #2, 15, 16, and 17, we noted ambiguous wording which obscured meaning and allowed for various interpretations. For example, in #2, it is not clear whether "full participation" included ordination, and whether "other lifestyles" included gay and lesbian. In #15, the issue identified is whether the recognition "that diversity exists" indicated approval of such diversity, particularly in the "relevance of marital status, affectional or sexual preference or lifestyle to ordination." In #16, the issue identified was whether "to work for decriminalization" might indicate approval of all "sexual acts between consenting adults." In Recommendation 17, the issue noted is whether the recognition of "other stable living units" in addition to "traditional marriage" implies an acceptance of homosexual couples and/or persons of opposite sex living together in a sexual relationship outside marriage.

The substantive concern regarding all four of the above is whether these recommendations indicate that homosexuality and other sexual relationships outside of marriage were being approved by the affirmative vote of General Synod Eleven in adopting them. In our estimation it is impossible to determine what the delegates at that Synod thought these recommendations meant or what they meant by adopting them. The Task Force agreed that it would have been preferable to have the intent clearly stated. Ambiguous wording may have provided openness and flexibility which for some is a positive value. But the same ambiguity about meaning and intent has been a factor in the concern which these recommendations have caused for others.

Although we can not clarify the intent of General Synod Eleven, the Task Force members struggled at length to find the following rewordings which we all could support. The wording as voted by the Eleventh General Synod appears at left, our rewording on the right:

2. Reaffirms the present important ministries throughout the United Church of Christ and recommends the development of new liturgies, theology, and counselling services which enable the full participation and sharing of gifts of all persons: children, youth, older persons,

2. Recognizing that exclusion of persons on the basis of sex, marital status, sexual orientation, and family pattern occurs in the life of the church, encourages the UCC to continue its traditional ministries and develop new ministries with all individuals.

nuclear families, those who live alone, or choose other lifestyles.

15. Recognizes that diversity exists within the UCC about the meaning of ordination, the criteria for effective ministry, and the relevance of marital status, affectional or sexual preference or lifestyle to ordination and performance of ministry. It requests the congregations, associations, and conferences to address these issues seeking more full and common understanding of their implications. It requests the Office for Church Life and Leadership to develop resources to facilitate such understanding.

15. Recognizing that the responsibility and authority for ordination in the UCC rests in the associations, requests congregations, associations, and conferences to seek a more full and common understanding of the criteria of effective ministry, and the relevance of marital status, sexual orientation and sexual behavior to ordination and performance of ministry. It requests the Office for Church Life and Leadership to continue to develop resources to facilitate such understanding.

16. Urges congregations, associations, conferences and instrumentalities to work for the decriminalization of private sexual acts between consenting adults.

16. Urges congregations, associations, conferences and instrumentalities to work for the decriminalization of private sexual acts between consenting adults, recognizing that adults may voluntarily engage in private sexual acts which may or may not be what God intends for human beings

17. Urges that States legislatively recognize that traditional marriage is not the only stable living unit which is entitled to legal protection in regards to socio-economic rights and responsibilities.

17. Urges that congregations, associations, and conferences work with state legislators to achieve equal protection of socio-economic rights and opportunities for all family units comparable to those enjoyed by heterosexual married family households.

In #6, the issues identified are whether "rites to celebrate" included marriage, and whether "relationships of commitment" included homosexual relationships and heterosexual relationships outside marriage. Below is the text of the recommendation as voted by General Synod Eleven. On the right is a rewording which we developed out of our discussions.

6. Encourages the congregations of the United Church of Christ, assisted by conferences and instrumentalities, to study and experiment with liturgical rites to celebrate important events and passages in human experience (transitions, anniversaries, separations, and reunions) and relationships of commitment between persons. The Office for Church Life and Leadership and the Board for Homeland Ministries are asked to facilitate the sharing of such liturgical experience.

6. Encourages the congregations of the United Church of Christ, assisted by conferences and instrumentalities, to study and experiment with ceremonies to observe the religious significance of important events and passages in human experience, and requests the Office for Church Life and Leadership and the Board for Homeland Ministries to make examples of such ceremonies available.

The Task Force is aware that some people may wonder whether under our rewording homosexual relationships of commitment and heterosexual relationships outside of marriage could be included in such events. For those churches and individuals who choose to observe them, that would be possible, although some members of the Task Force would oppose such a practice.

We understood the rewording of the above recommendations as a way of clarifying and working with the concerns and issues which they raised for some in the church. We discovered that for each of them we could arrive at a comparable statement with which we could all agree, except for #6 as noted above. We have considered at length the possibility of presenting them to General Synod Fourteen as recommendation for it to consider and act upon. However, we have decided unanimously to include these rewordings here as part of our report, to be received by General Synod. These rewordings evolved over many months of focused discussion among ten people. We are not convinced of the feasibility or need to redo what is now a past action of a previous General Synod.

D. Understandings of General Synod

Another factor influencing the response to the adoption of 2-18 is the different perceptions of General Synod and actions which it takes. These are sometimes related to the various traditions which we brought together in the UCC. But other elements are involved as well.

There are those who view votes of the Synod as though they expressed a statement of, or set policy for, the entire UCC. Those of us whose heritage is the Evangelical and Reformed Church sometimes tend to view them this way remembering that actions of the Synod in that church carried that kind of authority. The same tendency occurs at times among those of us who joined the UCC from other denominations which have a more hierarchical pattern of organization and decision-making. Or sometimes we just assume that our church functions like more centralized, secular organizations. In addition, there is a natural tendency for those of us who agree with an action of General Synod to refer to it in our enthusiasm as some kind of precedent or standard which reflects what the entire church in all its parts does, or should, believe or want to do.

On the other hand, there are those of us who tend to view the votes of Synod as indicating little more than what a group of people at a particular meeting happened to think or do. Those of us who come from Congregational Christian traditions sometimes see Synod actions in this perspective. Also, those of us who once thought of Synod actions as authoritative for the entire church, and who have since been informed that they are not quite, sometimes view them in this light. In addition, for those of us who may disagree with a vote of the Synod, there is the natural tendency to isolate its relevance or to minimize its significance by viewing it as something voted by a particular group of individuals at some distant event which has only some vague relationship to us.

Each of the above perspectives is, to a degree, a caricature. But each is indicative of real perceptions which we have encountered in our work.

An understanding of the policy of the United Church of Christ and the role of General Synod is thus important. They are particularly relevant in or experience when issues of human sexuality are being discussed in the context of ordination and ministerial standing.

The Constitution and Bylaws of the United Church of Christ assigns responsibility for ordination and ministerial standing to the Associations of our Church. Therefore, General Synod by its own action can not set standards or establish criteria in those areas for the whole denomination. It may express itself in the form of recommendations to the Associations. But it must recognize, as we all must, that each Association has the authority and responsibility to determine whom it will ordain and to whom it will grant standing as a minister in the UCC.

One of the issues raised by the Overtures and Resolutions presented to the Twelfth General Synod is the ordination of lesbian and gay persons. However, given the particular way in which our Church is organized, that issue must be decided by each Association. To request General Synod to establish a church-wide policy in this area is to ask it to exceed its own powers and authority.

In considering ordination we would suggest that sexual orientation in and of itself not be a criteria for determining a candidate's qualification, although an Association might establish standards of behavior which apply to all candidates. Some of us on the Task Force make a distinction between sexual orientation and sexual behavior. Those members believe that sexual orientation, which refers to orientation of a person's feelings toward the same sex, the opposite sex, or both, is not a moral issue. However, they believe that sexual behavior does have moral significance. Others of us on the Task Force do not make this distinction between orientation and behavior. Those members find the crucial questions to be those of what constitutes responsible and irresponsible sexual expression, regardless of sexual orientation.

E. The Broad Scope of Recommendations 2-18

Recommendations 2-18 cover large general areas of the church's ministry as they relate to issues of human sexuality. For some people, that very scope became a complicating factor in subsequent decisions and proposed actions concerning them.

The recommendation include some areas where work in the denomination has been going on for many years. "Developing resources concerning human sexuality for appropriate use by various age groups in local churches" (#3) is one example. The development of "programs which take into account the needs, experiences, and viewpoints of both males and females" (#13) is another, as is the call in #12 "to address the economic structures which victimize women (and men)."

After the recommendations were adopted by the Eleventh General Synod, a number of resolutions and overtures were submitted to the next General Synod which called for the implementation of Recommendations 2-18 to cease. But to have done that would have meant that many long-standing programs and ministries of the church might have had to stop.

The recommendations also cover areas which have been the subject of other actions taken by the General Synod, at the same, Eleventh General Synod and at previous Synods. To suspend Recommendations 2-18 would raise questions about the status of numerous other actions of the General Synod and the appropriateness of various parts of the church to proceed or to continue on the basis of those actions.

Thus the very general and inclusive character of the recommendations has complicated discussions and considerations of them. That difficulty has been a source of frustration for some who wished to deal with specific implications of these broad recommendations.

F. Implementation

As mentioned above, implementation was also a concern for some in regard to Recommendations 2-18. The action of the Twelfth General Synod which established this Task Force assigned the actual monitoring of that implementation to the Executive council. However, we have received copies of the reports submitted by instrumentalities to the Council and discussed programs generally with representatives of the various instrumentalities. In studying the kinds of concerns raised and reviewing such implementation, we on the Task Force found it useful to remember the following:

Each of our instrumentalities and other national bodies has a directorate or board which is responsible for the programs and policies which it pursues. Thus, the work of these bodies is shaped and guided not only by the actions of the General Synod, but also by the action of boards of directors who are elected to serve on behalf of the whole church.

The UCC has two kinds of instrumentalities: Recognized Instrumentalities, which are existing agencies recognized by the General Synod to serve as an instrumentality of the UCC; and Established Instrumentalities, which have been created by the General Synod and which perform all their acts in accordance with the UCC Constitution and Bylaws and instructions given them by the General Synod. (Articles 47 and 48, UCC Constitution.)

The programs of instrumentalities are informed by requests and communication from all parts of the church. Their work is a result of actions taken by conferences, associations, local churches, and other UCC-related groups besides the General Synod. For example, the Office for Church Life and Leadership developed the "Study Guide on Ordination and Homosexuality" in response to a specific request from the West Central Regional Council for Mission Priorities to the Executive Council. Decriminalization of sexual acts between consenting adults generally requires changes in State laws. Therefore, it is more appropriate for action to be initiated in the Conferences than on a national level. Since the Office for Church in Society has not had requests from Conferences to address issues of decriminalization, it has not proceeded to implement Recommendation 16.

Thus, programs being implemented by an instrumentality may have been prompted by several General Synod actions taken over a period of time. Implementation may be based on more than one action or request initiated by one or many parts of the church. In our work as this Task Force, we found no indication that implementation in the area of human sexuality has been undertaken by instrumentalities and other national bodies solely on the basis of Recommendation 2-18.

Section III

A Framework of Biblical and Theological Understanding

A. Background

The vote of the Twelfth General Synod which outlined the work of the Task Force includes the following paragraph:

> "Directs the task force to present a framework of Biblical and theological understanding, reflecting the diversity within the United Church of Christ and seeking ccomments from United Church of Christ theologians." (Appendix).

Our life together in the United Church of Christ is based on a covenant of mutual care and trust in relation to God and to each other. It is the basis of our accountability to God and our responsibility for each other. We covenant together because of our human need to be related to each other, in spite of our differences, enabling us to sustain our relationships and to fulfill God's intention for us in our lives.

In formulating this framework of Biblical and theological understanding, members of the Task force quickly recognized the diversity of understanding that exists not only among members of the Task Force, but also among the many resolutions, overtures, letter and reports submitted during the past four years from throughout the United Church of Christ. Some of these differences we identified as "uncollapsible." There were some in the Task Force who would have liked to present a Biblical and theological framework that was clear and precise in its Biblical and theological affirmations; for others the diversity of historical and theological traditions out of which we come makes such a goal impossible to achieve.

We approached our task both deductively, reflecting on the traditional teachings of the churches, and inductively, listening to and reflecting on the questions and issues being raised throughout the United Church of Christ concerning human sexuality.

B. Questions

The questions being asked by members of our churches include:

—What is wrong or right about abortion? unwedded parenthood? sexual relations outside marriage? pre-marital, extra-marital sexual relations? living together in a sexual relationship without marriage?

—Should a woman have a right to choose an abortion?

—Can I continue to be a part of a church which is so oppressive to people of color, women, gays.

—Is homosexuality a sin or illness? Can homosexuality be "cured"? What is homosexuality? What is homophobia?

—How can the church help its members to overcome homophobia?

—Can we really accept a woman minister? a gay or lesbian minister?

—What is God doing to liberate those who are sexually oppressed?

—Is God masculine? Is women's liberation anti-family? Is gay liberation anti-family?

—Are marriage and celibacy the only options available for the Christian as a sexual being?

—What is our responsibility for sex education in the house, school and church?

—What are the economic and political forces which shape the moral choices of individuals and institutions?

—Are heterosexuality and sexual relations in marriage the only forms of sexuality which are part of the natural order?

—How should the Church respond to the increasing number of unmarried persons who are sexually active, including the rising number of teenage pregnancies?

—How can we stop violence against women, children and gays—rape, incest, battering, pornography?

—How do I decide whether a particular form of sexual behavior is responsible Christian action or not?

—What kinds of institutions nurture and sustain healthy sexuality?

C. Diversity of Theological Perspectives

In the Spring of 1982, we sent copies of a preliminary draft of our Biblical and theological framework to a select group of theologians, Biblical scholars and leaders in the United Church of Christ for their comments and suggestions. We include a sampling of their responses, underlining further the diversity of perspectives and concerns present in the United Church of Christ

There are those, for example, who emphasized the authority of Scripture and tradition, as being primary for our task:

> . . . *In the Reformed tradition we have always affirmed that the infallible criterion for faith is the written Word of God illuminated by the Spirit to the community of faith. . . . I would like a statement affirming that Scripture by the power of the Spirit is self-authenticating or self-validating. It does not need to be brought into harmony with the secular wisdom of any age; on the contrary, it always calls into question such wisdom.*
>
> . . . Either *you acknowledge the authority of Scripture and basic Christian tradition, and judge all actions and statements today in the light of them,* or *you accept all positions, which claim to be Christian, as valid. . . . The authority of the Scriptures has been lost in the UCC; its Reformed heritage is a thing of the past. . . .*
>
> . . . *There is a danger in trying to make inclusivity the ultimate goal. We can become so theologically inclusive that we end up having no theology at all; we end up standing for everything and yet standing for nothing. . . . With the multiplicity of views, approaches and opinions within our denomination, it will be very difficult if your task is to satisfy everyone. Our Lord wasn't able to do that while he was among us. . . .*
>
> . . . *I would hope that something could be said . . . about the shared history of*

understanding of human sexuality that we have with other protestant traditions, with Roman Catholics, and with Jews. . . .

. . . I do not presume to suggest that this biblical/theological affirmation document should try to discuss the whole of all human sexuality questions, but give some sign or symbol of the way that theological position does have specific leads, handles, or directions for issues—to help persons know how it is used in terms of getting at those substantive questions.

There were others who suggested a more inductive approach to formulating a Biblical and theological framework on human sexuality:

. . . We cannot continue to couch all our theological statements in traditional forms. We need to begin from where we actually are in our Church, apply social and political as well as theological analyses in order to grasp the essentials *of* who we already are. *We* are *a church which makes it a practice to affirm the full personhood of women and gay men and lesbians and this is a strength. We have accepted and have supported changing family mores; we are one of the few denominations which does so explicitly.*

. . . The vast preponderance of Christian writing on the subject (of sexual theology) has assumed largely a one-directional movement. Hence, the question has been "what do the scriptures and tradition and contemporary theology say about our human sexuality. . . ." Also important is "the other direction"—what does our experience as human sexual beings have to say to the ways in which we interpret the scriptures and tradition, and attempt to live out the meanings of the Gospel in our lives? Attending to this second question not only alerts us to fresh perceptions of God's activity and self-disclosure in the present, it also alerts us to ways in which the tradition needs reformation at significant points.

Still others were more prescriptive in their suggestions to the Task Force:

. . . It is our position that two modes of sexual expression are open to the believer and given as gifts of God: heterosexual monogamous marriage and celibacy . . . that biblical passages such as Leviticus 18:22 and 20:13, Romans 1:26, 27, and I Corinthians 6:9,10 speak plainly and authoritively to this issue. They clearly condemn homosexuality as sin, and as such not to be endorsed or encouraged, but rather avoided. Until such time as the UCC is ready to pronounce those passages (and similar ones throughout the Bible) null and void, it cannot with integrity affirm homosexual practice. . . .

. . . No sexual activity, when motivated by love, is ever wicked or sinful—all sexual love, *whether in or out of marriage, with or without a partner, or with a partner of the same sex, is intrinsically good—Anyone in whom eros acts in concert with agape lives morally, lives indeed in the spirit of Christ even if not strictly in accord with the moralisms of Christ's churches.*

The general sense of the Task Force, given the diversity of theological perspectives present in the United Church of Christ, can be illustrated by the following comments we received:

. . . Certainly here is no single method for interpreting the Bible which everyone holds. . . . I would think for example, that we might be able to say something like this: the United Church of Christ has generally employed the tools of modern biblical scholarship in interpreting the scriptures. I do not believe it is accurate to say that the United Church of Christ is predominantly allegorical, or literalistic, or legalistic in its interpretation of the scriptures.

. . . This diversity can be admitted . . . as a positive contribution the U.C.C. makes to the whole church—an experiment in such diversity under one denominational roof, acknowledging that others will draw boundaries of discipline and

perspective for the sake of having a more cohesive church that we have chosen not to draw. . . .

. . . . In our humanness the truth given to each is partial and being both partially truth and partially untruth—that witness is called to live in creative interrelationship with the truth and partialness of another witness. . . .

D. Our Understanding of the Church

We on the Task Force affirm the second article of the Preamble to the Constitution of the United Church of Christ. It expresses our understanding of the church:

> "The United Church of Christ acknowledges as its sole Head, Jesus Christ, Son of God and Saviour. It acknowledges as kindred in Christ all who share in this confession. It looks to the Word of God in the Scriptures, and to the presence and power of the Holy Spirit, to prosper its creative and redemptive work in the world. It claims as its own the faith of the historic Church expressed in the ancient creeds and reclaimed in the basic insights of the Protestant Reformers. It affirms the responsibility of the Church in each generation to make this faith its own in reality of worship, in honesty of thought and expression, and in purity of heart before God. . . ."

To acknowledge *"as its sole Head, Jesus Christ, Son of God and Saviour"* is to confess that we are bound together, responding to Jesus' call to discipleship and faith. We in the United Church of Christ may interpret that confession in different ways, using different metaphors and theological understandings, as well as the understandings gained from the natural and human sciences. Our individual and collective response to Jesus' call to discipleship is the central core of our identity as members of Christ's Church.

To *"acknowledge as kindred in Christ all who share in this confession"* affirms our vision of unity in Christ. Our confession of Christ challenges all that divides us in this world—differing theological and cultural traditions, our racial, ethnic and national backgrounds, differences in our marital, educational, and occupational statuses, our political, sexual, and family orientations—for in Christ we are one.

We *"look to the Word of God in the Scripture, and to the presence and power of the Holy Spirit, to prosper its creative and redemptive work in the world."* It is through the prompting power of the Holy Spirit that the authority and guidance of the Bible becomes manifest in our lives and in the world. Our unity is not based on a single method of interpreting the Bible or the Holy Spirit, but on an understanding which we share: that our faithfulness as Christians must continually be informed by our response to the Word as motivated by the Spirit. We believe John Robinson's famous words, "Remember that God has yet new truths to reveal from his Holy Word," are particularly relevant in a time of rapid social and technological change.

We claim as our own *"the faith of the historic Church expressed in the ancient creeds and reclaimed in the basic insights of the Protestant Reformers."* We affirm *"the responsibility of the Church in each generation to make this faith its own reality of worship, in honesty of thought and expression, and in purity of heart before God."* We value the richness and diversity of our immediate heritage—Congregational-Christian, Evangelical and Reformed—as well as the historic tradition of the Christian churches from its earliest beginnings. In inheriting and valuing this historic faith, we seek to interweave both what the tradition has to say about human experiences and what our experiences mean for the way in which we understand and attempt to live out that faith.

E. Affirmations about Sexuality

The following are theological and Biblical statements about human sexuality which we on the Task Force affirm and share with the church.

1. Our humanity is a creation of God and it is good. Our humanity includes our sexuality, a gift of God entrusted to us, which can be a source of joy and wholeness.
2. Human sexuality is an integral part of our humanity. As our humanity is prone to selfishness, our sexuality may be abused and misused. As we are created in God's image, our sexuality can be an expression of our faithfulness to God and neighbor.
3. Jesus Christ bears God's invitation to human wholeness and communion, for in God's redeeming love in Christ, our proneness to misuse and abuse our sexuality is overcome and our confession of sin heard and forgiven.
4. Human sexuality is profoundly personal. The physical expression of one's sexuality in relation to another ought to be based on loving commitment and accountability to God and one another.
5. Human sexuality is also social and can become a basis for injustice and oppression. Freedom from oppression is God's intention and activity, in order that we might be free to become fully God's people, living in just and caring relationships with one another.

F. Illustrations of Our Diversity

We share the affirmations about the church and about human sexuality described above. At the same time we experience real differences when we address particular issues. The following statements by two individual members of the Task Force illustrate some of those differences. The Section G which follows these two statements contains observations by the Task Force as a whole on the meaning of such differences.

Background and Implications for Two Concerns in Human Sexuality

The relationship between Scripture, Christian tradition, science, and experience provides the background for addressing two concerns: sexual oppression and sexual lifestyle.

Scripture: When we address ethical concerns, do we have a word from God beyond what we may already perceive in the created world and the human situation? The witness of the Church has been that the Old and New Testaments, the Scriptures, contain God's self-disclosure, revealing to humanity that which may not have been otherwise evident. The very existence of the Church itself derives from God's supreme act of self-disclosure in Jesus Christ. As affirmed by the Constitution of the United Church of Christ, it therefore behooves us to discern how the record of God's self-disclosure (i.e. the Scriptures) comments upon the concerns we have.

There are two issues, however, as we read the Scriptures. One is the question of interpretation, and the other is the question of authority.

As we interpret the Scriptures we must responsibly incorporate the full body of Biblical material pertaining to the subject. This guards us from isogesis, from reading into the Bible that which we have previously decided we want to come with. For example, during the 1800's Christians in England were working to abolish slavery at the same time that some Christians in America were fighting to preserve it. The difference was a comprehensive versus a selective reading of what the Bible says about humanity. The same is true when we bring our own questions to the Bible.

The other issue is that of authority. If the process of responsible interpretation has illuminated a Biblical principle, are we then willing to abide by it, even if we would have to change? If not, who or what has become our authority? In many areas we call society to change. What would it say about our commitment to Jesus Christ if we declined God's call when it was directed towards ourselves instead? We must follow.

Christian tradition: Christian tradition, while not equal to the authority of the Scriptures, does provide perspective. As we examine how the Church has understood the Scriptures in the past, we test our own perception of the Scriptures in the present. Scriptural warrant should be carefully and clearly described when substantial revision is advanced.

Science: Science imparts a different kind of knowledge than Scripture and Christian tradition. As Jesus identified in the Great Commandment, God's self-disclosure addresses humanity's problems in relation to God, to self, and to each other, and is often prescriptive. Scientific discovery observes, experiments, and derives date pertaining to the physical universe and therefore is descriptive.

At times science may provide discoveries and applications which affect human living, and which the Church must therefore address. The possibility of world-wide destruction through nuclear war, the coexistence of advanced agricultural knowledge with starvation, the ability to medically sustain life beyond what once was the case, all represent areas where the Church's ministry takes place in the context of scientific discovery.

Experience: Knowledge may be gained from the experience of others. The New Testament canon gradually emerged out of varied groupings of literature due to the self-authenticating quality of the canonical works in the experience of the early Church. The Biblical record as a whole may be described as depicting the experience of individuals and nations as they became the subject of God's self-disclosing activity. Listening to the experience of others may enlighten us to that which we had not been previously aware of, or even see themes in the Scriptures which our own experience may have prevented us from seeing. Conversely, human experience may be transformed as through the Scriptures we encounter the power of God.

When we survey the human condition, of course, we see a world which falls far short of God's intention. That is why as we listen to human experience we must also be conscious of the Scriptures. A fallen condition in human experience may govern our reading of the Scriptures rather than the reverse. For example, in medieval times the Church at one point debated whether or not women had souls. Church and society were dominated by men, and such discussion was entertained because the Church allowed the human situation to speak to the Scriptures rather than the reverse. Whenever the human condition is characterized by individual or institutional behavior which contradicts what may be manifest from God's self-disclosure, we must seek to faithfully live, teach and transform the world in accord with what God has said and done.

Two concerns. We see in the Genesis account that when God initially created the world God saw that it was good. Humanity was created in God's own image, male and female. Man and Woman were called into one-flesh union, and were also commissioned to be fruitful and multiply. These foundational truths have a number of implications for two concerns which the Task Force was conscious of: sexual oppression and sexual lifestyle.

Regarding sexual oppression: Because Man and Woman are both created in God's image, both are equal before God. Institutional, social, or personal actions which foster injustice or oppression fall short of God's intended design. A person's right to experience economic, vocational, and civil liberty is inalienably founded upon their creation in God's image. Where such liberty is supplanted by injustice or oppression because of sex or sexual orientation, God's intention for creation is violated.

Regarding sexual lifestyle: Because Man and Woman are both created in God's image, because God blessed the one-flesh union of Man and Woman, and because God commissioned Man and Woman to be fruitful and multiply, God's intention is that sexual union should be loving, honoring, uplifting, and take place in the context of a unique covenantal commitment (marriage) between a man and a woman. Where sexual union is unloving, dehumanizing, or exploiting, it falls short of God's intended design. Where sexual union takes place outside the context of the unique covenantal commitment between a man and a woman, it falls short of God's intended design. The Scriptures also affirm celibacy as the other meaningful and joyous lifestyle gift which God gives for human living.

In American society there has been an increasing acceptance of sexual activity outside the context of heterosexual marriage. Attitudes toward premarital, extra-marital, and homosexual relations are in a state of flux. For the Church it is important to note that whenever the Scriptures address heterosexual marriage, it is always uplifted and honored. No alternate contexts for sexual activity are ever affirmed. On the contrary, whenever alternate contexts are identified, they are described as fallen and/or prohibited. This unified voice throughout the Scriptures has been paralleled ecumenically as other denominations and churches have reexamined similar questions. Regarding the issue of homosexual behavior, at least eleven mainline Protestant denominations, as well as the Roman Catholic and Eastern Orthodox communions, have in the last decade reaffirmed that homosexual behavior departs from God's intention for sexual expression.

Some members of society have an inner sexual orientation primarily directed toward members of their own sex. Theologically, a primary erotic affinity for members of one's own sex may be understood to be one of the many distortions that the created world experiences as a result of the fall. However, homosexual persons have often been victims of irrational fear, prejudice, oppression, and violence at the hands of society, and sometimes of the Church also. Change in this regard is mandated by the Scriptures, and obviously overdue.

However, change is similarly being sought with reference to an understanding of homosexual behavior. Affirmation of homosexual behavior would contradict the theological and biological content and implications of Biblical teaching regarding sexuality. Such affirmation would therefore require either a substantial revision of the Scriptures, or a rejection of the authoritative role of the Scriptures in the life of the Church.

The developmental components of sexual orientation are still under investigation by the scientific community. The nature and components of reorientation are also under continuing study. When reorientation does occur two factors are present: 1) the belief that reorientation is possible, and 2) the belief that reorientation is desirable. Beyond the development of sexual orientation, over which we may have little conscious responsibility, it appears that our perceptions about our sexuality are also influential. Continued scientific research in these areas will hopefully inform the Church's understanding.

Some implications for the Church's ministry: On the basis of the preceding remarks, the following implications for the Church's life and ministry may be drawn.

Regarding sexual oppression: The Church should affirm and/or reaffirm:

1. *Legislative change that insures employment practices and opportunities.*
2. *Legislative change that guarantees equal compensation for equal work.*
3. *Legislative change that guarantees equal access to housing.*
4. *Legislative change that decriminalizes private sexual acts between consenting adults.*
5. *Legislative change that insures the elimination of violent acts perpetrated because of sex or sexual orientation.*
6. *Monitoring the media to eliminate harmful heterosexual and/or homosexual stereotyping.*

Regarding sexual lifestyle: The Church should also:

7. *Glorify God by uplifting heterosexual marriage and celibacy as God's intention and gift for human living.*
8. *Affirm that sexual orientation, in and of itself, should not be a relevant criterion in assessing qualifications for Christian service, but that conformity to the above understanding of sexual lifestyle is expected of all Christian people.*
9. *Extend a ministry of compassion, concern, and challenge to those who either through choice or through circumstance are sexually active outside the context of heterosexual marriage.*
10. *Provide support communities for homosexual persons concerned about their sexuality and the Christian faith. Such support communities would assist homosexual persons in*

developing a meaningful and fulfilling celibate lifestyle and/or reorientation for those who so desire.

11. Extend a ministry of compassion, concern, and challenge to those who are enchained by the irrational fear and oppression of homosexual persons.

These suggestions are not intended to be exhaustive. They represent only a beginning in seeking to address very real human concerns within our culture in the name and power of Jesus Christ.

The following second example illustrates a different theological method:

Living the Questions About Human Sexuality in a Biblical/Theological Perspective

Let us begin with the context—a variety of movements for social change which have surfaced over the last 15 years, in particular the women's and gay movements. They are the catalysts for renewed reflection on issues of human sexuality. These groups have testified within the UCC and elsewhere about the damage of oppression at the deepest emotional and spiritual levels and have called for a new language, new standard of behavior, and an end to discrimination. The questions they have raised have no clear answers in much of church tradition and Biblical interpretation. They are proceeding with an examination of institutionalized oppression, the systematic denial of their rights; they are enacting new modes of behavior and are seeking new ways of answering moral questions.

The questioning and acting in behalf of their own liberation reveals to thousands that God is active in this process of upheaval and is calling for renewal. It also becomes clear that methods of theological and Biblical interpretation have been used, not in the service of liberating the captives, but to preserve a particular way of understanding and wielding power in the world. How has this happened? Why? In whose interest? Does the Bible have anything to say about such mis-use of religion? How can the Christian tradition enlighten the current struggle for clearer answers?

This form of theologizing is happening everywhere—church school classes, adult Bible study groups, retreats, church women's conferences, youth gatherings, among groups of gay and lesbian Christians. Individuals also wrestle with decisions about their own behavior and often do not feel free to share even the questions with organized church groups (whether or not to have an abortion, for instance). People who seriously seek answers do not do so in a vacuum if they have any other alternatives. They talk to friends and family. They read books and magazines. They pray and meditate. They read the Bible and materials their churches provide. They go to support groups. They talk to people who have been through such decision making.

When people turn to the Bible in the midst of questions raised by these movements for social change, they discover a critical or liberating tradition in the Bible—the prophetic-messianic tradition. They find most of the Bible "is not written from the standpoint of world power but by those who take the side of the disadvantaged, the rural population against the landowners and urban rich, the small colonized nation against the mighty empires. . . . God judges those who 'grind the faces of the poor, the widow and orphan.' God 'puts the mighty down from their thrones and fills the poor with good things.' . . . the God-language of the Bible tends to be judgmental and destabilizing toward the existing social order and its hierarchies of power—religious, social and economic. . . . The primary vision of salvation in the Bible is that of an alternative future, a new society of peace and justice that will arise when the present systems of injustice have been overthrown. . . . Both testaments contain, as part of this prophetic perspective, a remorseless critique of religion. This attack is directed a degeneration of religion into cult and rote, especially the use of religion to justify those already in power and to ignore God's agenda of social justice. . . . The Synoptic Gospels are framed as a continual confrontation between the iconoclastic messianic prophet and the scribal and priestly leaders who 'tithe mint and cummin and neglect the weightier matters of the law: justice and mercy and faith. (Mt. 23:23).'' Rosemary Reuther, Christianity and Crisis, *11/10/79, pages 309-310.)*

The following themes are central:

1. *The Exodus, a historical redemptive event, the central event of Hebrew experience. God is experienced as breaking open the future. The slaves are liberated bodily. This is not just a spiritual liberation.*
2. *Jubilee, Leviticus 25—redistribution of land and possessions every 50 years, a commitment to material equality, a condemnation of those ''who add house to house and join field to field, until there is no more room.'' (Deut. 5:8).*
3. *Jesus' statement of his own mission—the setting at liberty of the captives (Luke 4:16-19). His way of being in the world among the outcast and despised, his refusal to get caught in the holier than thou games played by the Pharisees, his expectation that the kingdom of God was at hand and would make all things new. And his insistence that love of God and neighbor was the essence.*
4. *The separation of the sheep and goats (Mt. 25) where the only criteria is clothing the naked, feeding the hungry, welcoming strangers.*
5. *The common ownership of belongings among the early Christians (Acts 4:34) and distribution of goods to any who stood in need.*

These themes form a cannon within the cannon that can be used to judge other texts and motifs.

The task of Biblical interpretation was stated as follows by the Ohio Conference Theological Reflection Group:

1. *We believe that there is a distinction that needs to be drawn between the living ultimate Word of God and the pen and ink words of scripture.*
2. *We believe that the Word is never completely or fully understood.*
3. *We believe that both within the scriptures and together interaction with the reality of the Holy Spirit the Truth operates as a dynamic, living reality.*
4. *We believe that God reveals the Truth to those who remain open to it. This leads us to affirm that our historical context is different from those who penned the words of Scripture.*
5. *We affirm that because we are human beings with intellectual and emotional limitations all scriptural interpretation will be somewhat subjective. We must therefore rely upon the Grace of our God to be present in our lives and guide our study.''*

Thus the text is to be read in context, using the hard work of historians who try to understand the writer, the audience, and the situation at the same time Biblical material was written. We then reflect on the similarities and differences between our context and that of the Bible and look at how the text might be useful in answering the questions posed by our age. We must use imagination and the human freedom God gave us at creation.

This approach does not lead us to ask or expect the Bible to give a specific answer to individual moral questions like: ''Should I withdraw financial support from my daughter who lives with her boyfriend?'' ''Should I bring my gay partner to my parents' home for Christmas?'' ''Should I loan my sister the money for an abortion when I don't believe abortion is right?'' We must also resist the temptation to prescribe for another how they will decide.

We can be clear that many Biblical themes inform our decision making on specific issues:

—that loving commitment and mutual accountability are the key criteria in personal relationships;

—that exploitation of any kind and use of other persons for our own ends is immoral;

—*that systematic denial of human rights is contrary to God's will;*

—*that institutional policies which keep people poor and in fear for their livelihood are a distortion of the gospel.*

Our behavior and values are constantly re-evaluated in our contact with other Christians—in gay/lesbian support groups, church study groups, Christian education conferences. Serious Christians do not see this process of theologizing as "doing your own thing." Framing the questions, searching for answers, studying the tradition, acting for justice are collective and communal. Together we work at how faith points toward answers, relying on the grace of our God. By calling Scripture "the word of God" the church expresses confidence that in a faithful hearing of Scripture the will of God can, in fact, be encountered by human beings. When the Word of God becomes incarnate in people's actual struggle for justice and freedom, when it becomes flesh and blood in the offering of body and shedding of blood of those engaged in those struggles, then is our redemption at hand.

G. Regarding Our Differences

The Task Force was created to include many differing points of view. One level of those differences is the various positions which we hold on particular issues such as abortion. But beneath the level we have identified another which includes the following:

1. All of us see Scripture, the tradition of the Church, the findings of contemporary science, and our own experience as important elements in the decisions we make and the conclusions we reach as Christians. However, the weight which we may give to each of those elements varies. We also use them differently in varying combinations. Thus, there are basic differences in the ways by which we work toward our decisions and conclusions.

2. Some believe that it is important for the Church to be inclusive; it should support the religious quest of people wherever they may be on that pilgrimage. Others believe that the Church needs to be clear and definitive about its beliefs; it should provide explicit guidelines even though that may result in some people feeling that their own views have been excluded.

3. We have different understandings about how our sexual identity as males and females is established. To what degree is it biological, and therefore something which is essentially given or determined? To what degree is it something which develops as we grow, and is therefore culturally conditioned and changeable?

4. The same differences are reflected in different understandings of sexual orientation, sexual preference, and their relationships to behavior. Some see lesbian/gay orientation as a given, part of the natural order, intended by God, and therefore capable of being expressed in ways which are morally responsible Christian behavior. Others see same sex behavior as wrong; the preference for persons of the same sex as something which can be changed or adopted; and a same-sex orientation as something which is not natural and therefore not intended by God.

5. We also place different emphasis on the importance of sexual expression and the sexual discipline. For some sexual expression is a basic right. Sexuality is integral to our humanity, and its responsible expression is essential for human wholeness. For others, what is basic is the context in which it is appropriate to exercise that right. Self-discipline is seen as an essential part of what defines us as human beings.

6. We also put different emphases on "thinking" and "feeling" as ways of understanding or decision-making. Some reason their way through to the conclusions they reach. They draw upon logic and deductive reasoning, and use Scripture and tradition as objective data in that process. For others it is how someone feels subjectively which is the important consideration. Does it seem fair, just, helpful, loving, constructive, faithful? They proceed inductively and draw upon Scripture and tradition for the themes and experiences which they articulate.

All of the above differences are not only differences between us; they are also different tendencies within each of us. For example, we all use both logic and sensitivity and recognize the importance of both sexual expression and self-discipline. However, each of us may emphasize one more than the other, and that emphasis then becomes part of the different ways by which we reach different conclusions.

Thus, as we have sought to understand our differences on this Task Force, we have come to appreciate that there are real differences among us such as those described. They are of a different order than whether we agree or not on a particular specific issue. They are "uncollapsible" unless one or the other of us were to change in some of these very basic understandings.

At their deepest level, the issues which we face in questions of human sexuality are thus fundamental:

—different assessments about how much freedom and how much structure is needed in human relationships and society. Some view as primary the freedom to become, to change and grow as a person. Others see structure and order to be primary, providing the necessary context for community.

—different perceptions of what is part of the God-given natural order which we are to be preserve and enhance, and to change and correct. Some believe that they could accept behavior which they now believe to be wrong if scientific information indicated that the God-created nature of human sexuality is different than they now understand it to be. For others, evidence from Scripture and/or experience of the hurtfulness of some behavior would lead them to change their assessment that such behavior is right.

We believe it is crucial for us in the United Church of Christ to continue discussion of human sexuality issues in such a way that there is a mutual invitation for persons to speak out of their deepest values and differing perspectives. We cannot resolve issues as long as they are being addressed by persons who disdain each other or who romantically expect that the "other" can be cajoled into becoming more like oneself.

Identifying and struggling with these differences is not enough. We must act to address issues of oppression and human dignity. Action is a crucial part of the theological task, a deepening of our relationship to and understanding of God and neighbor. Despite periodic lack of consensus, the United Church of Christ at all levels must continue to make its voice heard on issues of public policy. This voice should be determined by careful study and discussion, democratic debate, and majority vote. It should be expressed through letters and public witness by church officials as well as individual members. Acknowledging diversity does not absolve us from action where a majority feel an urgency to address issues of public policy.

Identifying and struggling with these differences has led us to the conclusion that the discussion of human sexuality in the UCC must be done within a framework that seeks to educate all of us theologically, and facilitates action on deeply held convictions, expecting pluralism in method and result. We offer our experience as a small part of that educational process, affirming that we have discovered common theological ground and through our differences we have developed some new understandings of how to be a united and a uniting church.

Appendix I

Vote of the Twelfth General Synod Establishing the Task Force

The Twelfth General Synod:

A. Continues the study of human sexuality.

B. Directs the Executive Council to continue its monitoring of implementation of General Synod XI sexuality actions by the assigned instrumentalities and agencies.

C. Establishes a National Task Force to make an interim report to the Thirteenth General Synod and a final report to the Fourteenth General Synod, each report to be mailed to the delegates three months before the General Synod convenes.

The task force will:

1. Encourage and facilitate the continuing study of human sexuality by all congregations, associations, conferences, and other groups within the church.

2. Identify, test, and publicize various models of study undertaken by conferences, associations, congregations, and other groups within the church.

3. Observe, evaluate, and monitor processes which continue the study of human sexuality in the United Church of Christ, and in other denominations struggling with comparable issues.

4. Seek reports about such studies and circulate to the conferences information about these reports.

5. Report recommendations to the Fourteenth General Synod.

D. Refers to the National Task Force for continuing study, clarification, and possible recommendations for policy development:

1. Actions 2-18, (77-GS-64), and "A Minority Resolution on Recommendations in Regard to Human Sexuality."

2. *Human Sexuality: A Preliminary Study* and encourages, among other material, the study of additional resources, including *Issues in Sexual Ethics,* published by the United Church People for Biblical Witness.

3. Overtures and resolutions to the Twelfth General Synod in the area of human sexuality.

E. Directs the Executive Council, upon nomination by the President, to elect a Task Force of ten members for the Study of Human Sexuality. The Task Force will represent the diverse perspectives found within the United Church of Christ. An inter-staff team for contributed staff services under the direction of the Executive Council will provide staff assistance to the Task Force.

F. Directs the Task Force to present a framework of Biblical and theological understanding, reflecting the diversity within the United Church of Christ and seeking comments from United Church of Christ theologians.

Notes: *In 1983, the Task Force for the Study of Human Sexuality presented this report to the Fourteenth General Assembly of the United Church of Christ. This report, which also contains recommendations for its implementation, calls for a continuation of the debate over the correctness of homosexual activities even after the task force disbands.*

One of the most important features of this report is the fact that it represents one of the strongest statements issued in support of ordination for homosexual ministerial candidates. It suggests that the fact a person is homosexual should not be grounds for denying ordination. However, by the time this report was issued, most church members agreed that celibate homosexuals should be allowed to be ordained—the new debate involved whether or not practicing homosexuals should be allowed to be ordained, a question the report does not attempt to answer. Because the task force knew that a recommendation to approve ordination for practicing homosexuals would be defeated, it chose to not address the topic and allow the issue to remain open.

UNITED CHURCH OF CHRIST

RECOMMENDATIONS OF THE TASK FORCE FOR THE STUDY OF HUMAN SEXUALITY (1983)

As members of the Universal Body of Christ and claimed by the Gospel, claimed for mission, claimed to be stewards of God's creation, the Fourteenth General Synod calls for full implementation of the following:

1. The Fourteenth General Synod receives the report of the Task Force for the Study of Human Sexuality. It directs the Executive Council to forward the report to Associations, Conferences, Instrumentalities, and other national bodies of the United Church of Christ for consideration as they develop plans and programs. The General Synod finds that the overture and resolutions referred to the Task Force have been reviewed and dealt with and therefore dismisses the Task Force with thanks and appreciation for its work.
2. The Fourteenth General Synod urges that attention and support be given to the development of proposals and programs to end sexual violence against men, women and children, regardless of their sexual orientation.
3. The Fourteenth General Synod recognizes that our present knowledge about the bases of sexual orientation and behavior is incomplete, and that psycho-social and ethical issues surrounding the rightfulness or wrongfulness of various forms of sexual expression and embodiment are still being debated within the United Church of Christ.

   It is our hope that all persons will be drawn into the life and ministry of the Church. The Fourteenth General Synod recommends that:

   A. The Board for Homeland Ministries collect and continue to update information about the nature of human sexuality, including variations in sexual orientation and behavior seeking to provide material appropriate for use with all age groups and making this information available for study by churches.

   B. The Board for Homeland Ministries develop resources on human sexuality for use in local churches, Associations and Conferences to facilitate ministry to and with gay/lesbian people (whether they choose to affirm their sexual feelings or attempt to change them), to their families, friends and to all people struggling with issues of sexual identity.
4. The Fourteenth General Synod recognizes that a person's sexual orientation is not a moral issue, but that sexual behavior does have moral significance.

   A. The Fourteenth General Synod acknowledges that Associations have the responsibility for ordination and ministerial standing. It therefore recommends to Associations that in considering a candidate's qualifications for ministry, the candidate's sexual orientation should not be grounds for denying the request for ordination.

   B. It also advocates that sexual orientation not be a basis for discrimination within the United Church of Christ in the employment of staff or use of volunteers.

Notes: *The debate in the United Church of Christ over homosexuality which had been begun some twenty years earlier culminated in 1983. By this time a consensus had been reached, at least on the national level where the more liberal and educated elite had their strongest voice. The views of this elite were held in check by the presence of a large percentage of lay people (and some ministers) who vocally opposed the liberal stance of the denomination and adhered to more traditional approaches to the question of homosexuality. A report issued by the task force summarized the majority (liberal) opinion within the denomination.*

The report took a positive view of human sexuality and an understanding of homosexuality as a state in which many individuals found themselves without any conscious choice. Homosexuality is morally neutral and hence should not be a factor in determining a person's worth or stance within the church. Given the negative situation in which homosexuals are placed by society, the church should actively work to change that situation, including a thorough change of attitude toward homosexuals in the church. Homosexuals should be welcome at all levels, including employment in church jobs. Four resolutions passed by the church in 1983 grew directly out of this report.

By 1983, however, the crucial and still undecided question for the church had become approval of the ordination of practicing homosexuals. In 1982, for example, the Potamac Association of the church's Central Atlantic Conference had approved the ordination of Anne Howard, a lesbian. In this carefully worded statement, and in a subsequent resolution passed at the time of its reception, the church assumes that homosexuality itself is no barrier to ordination. It leaves open the question of approving homosexuality and of the ordination of a sexually active homosexual person. It would appear that, for the time being, the church is unwilling to make that additional step, but one could assume from the assertive and positive tone of all of the church's resolutions on homosexuality (though it is never stated) that the church understands that most of the homosexuals they welcome to the church will not be celibate.

UNITED CHURCH OF CHRIST

RESOLUTION CALLING ON UNITED CHURCH OF CHRIST CONGREGATIONS TO DECLARE THEMSELVES OPEN AND AFFIRMING (1985)

WHEREAS, the Apostle Paul said that, as Christians, we are many members, but we are one body in Christ (Rom. 12:4), and Jesus calls us to love our neighbors as ourselves (Mk. 12:31) without being judgmental (Mt. 7:1-2) nor disparaging of others (Lk. 18:9-14); and

WHEREAS, recognizing that many persons of lesbian, gay and bisexual orientation are already members of the church through baptism and confirmation and that these people have talents and gifts to offer the United Church of Christ, and that the UCC has historically affirmed a rich diversity in its theological and biblical perspectives; and

WHEREAS, the Tenth through Fourteenth General Synods have adopted resolutions encouraging the inclusion, and affirming the human rights, of lesbian, gay and bisexual people within the UCC; and

WHEREAS, the Executive Council of the United Church of Christ adopted in 1980 "a program of Equal Employment Opportunity which does not discriminate against any employee or applicant because of . . . sexual orientation"; and

WHEREAS, many parts of the church have remained conspicuously silent despite the continuing injustice of institutionalized discrimination, instances of senseless violence and setbacks in civil rights protection by the Supreme Court; and

WHEREAS, the church has often perpetuated discriminatory practices and has been unwilling to affirm the full humanness of clergy, laity and staff with lesbian, gay and bisexual orientation, who experience isolation, ostracism and fear of (or actual) loss of employment; and

WHEREAS, we are called by Christ's example, to proclaim release to the captives and set at liberty the oppressed (Lk. 4:18); and

WHEREAS, examples of covenant of Openness and Affirmation and Non-discrimination Policy may be found in the following:

Example 1: Covenant of Openness and Affirmation

We know, with Paul, that as Christians, we are many members, but are one body in Christ—members of one another, and that we all have different gifts. With Jesus, we affirm that we are called to love our neighbors as ourselves, that we are called to act as agents of reconciliation and wholeness within the world and within the church itself.

We know that lesbian, gay and bisexual people are often scorned by the church, and devalued and discriminated against both in the church and in society. We commit ourselves to caring and concern for lesbian, gay and bisexual sisters and brothers by affirming that:

—we believe that lesbian, gay and bisexual people share with all others the worth that comes from being unique individuals;

—we welcome lesbian, gay and bisexual people to join our congregation in the same spirit and manner used in the acceptance of any new members;

—we recognize the presence of ignorance, fear and hatred in the church and in our culture, and covenant to not discriminate on the basis of sexual orientation, nor any other irrelevant factor, and we seek to include and support those who, because of this fear and prejudice, find themselves in exile from a spiritual community;

—we seek to address the needs and advocate the concerns of lesbian, gay and bisexual people in our church and in society by actively encouraging church instrumentalities and secular governmental bodies to adopt and implement policies of non-discrimination; and,

—we join together as a covenantal community, to celebrate and share our common communion and the reassurance that we are indeed created by God, reconciled by Christ and empowered by the grace of the Holy Spirit.

Example 2: Inclusive Non-Discrimination Policy

We do not discriminate against any person, group or organization in hiring, promotion, membership, appointment, use of facility, provision of services or funding on the basis of race, gender, age, sexual orientation, faith, nationality, ethnicity, marital status, or physical disability.

THEREFORE, the Fifteenth General Synod of the United Church of Christ encourages a policy of non-discrimination in employment, volunteer service and membership policies with regard to sexual orientation; encourages associations, Conferences and all related organizations to adopt a similar policy; and encourages the congregations of the United Church of Christ to adopt a non-discrimination policy and a Covenant of Openness and Affirmation of persons of lesbian, gay and bisexual orientation within the community of faith.

Notes: *As the debate over homosexuality drew to a close with the passing of the report of the Task Force for the Study of Human Sexuality at the general synod of the United Church of Christ in 1983, it was obvious that all of the aspirations of homosexuals and their supporters for inclusion in the life of the church (specifically of the church's ordaining practicing homosexuals) would not be realized in the immediate future. Thus, a process of rallying support until a future change in the national situation was adopted. It called for individual congregations to declare themselves open and affirming of homosexual persons in general and homosexual church members in particular.*

The resolution calls upon congregations who accept such a designation, among other responsibilities, to encourage church instrumentalities (referring to the general synod and the associations of the United Church of Christ) to adopt policies of nondiscrimination (i.e., allow ordination of practicing homosexuals). In the years since this resolution, a small number of congregations have adopted such a status.

UNITED METHODIST CHURCH

THE METHODIST SOCIAL CREED (1968)

6. *Sex in Christian Life*.—We believe that sexual intercourse within holy matrimony with fidelity and love is a sacred experience and constitutes a needed expression of affection. We also believe that sexual intercourse outside the bonds of matrimony is contrary to the will of God. The outrageous exploitation of the strong forces underlying sexual experience is a destructive element of our culture. It not only distorts the meaning of sex experience but constitutes a blasphemous disregard of God's purpose for men and women. A case in point is the distribution of hard-core pornographic and other sex-exploitive material. We advocate thorough educational efforts in home, church, and school designed to elevate our whole understanding of the meaning of sexual experience.

Notes: *While not mentioning homosexuality directly, there is an implicit condemnation of it in the condemnation of sexual intercourse outside the bonds of marriage.*

UNITED METHODIST CHURCH

RESOLUTION ON HEALTH, WELFARE, AND HUMAN DEVELOPMENT (1968)

Sexuality

Our society is undergoing a revolution in the area of sex and sexual morality. The prevailing shifting of standards presents both challenge and opportunity to the church.

We bring to this situation openness and encouragement to research in the biological, psycho-social and socio-cultural dimensions of human sexuality. The Christian community must bring also to the situation the theological dimensions, thus casting it into the biblical perspective of Creation. We view our sexuality in the light of the goodness of this creation, believing it to be intended for the fulfillment of personality as well as for procreation, and further affirming that the sex act is never isolated within the separate personalities of participants or within their total relationship as persons. We believe that all dimensions of our sexuality are best satisfied within the marriage covenant.

We recognize that much of our program of sex education is ineffectual, and resolve to bring all resources available to us into study and development of new programs. We recognize that more important than formal sex education is the normal nurture of our children in Christian family environment.

We recognize that many persons who are troubled and broken by sexual problems, such as homosexuality, suffer from discriminatory practices arising from traditional attitudes and from outmoded legal practices. We strongly recommend that wherever possible such persons be brought under the care of our health and human development services rather than under penal and correctional services. We believe that the ministry of the church extends to all human beings troubled and broken by sexual problems and they should find forgiveness and redemption within its fellowship.

Notes: *The United Methodist Church was formed in 1968 by a merger of the Methodist Church (1939-1968) and the Evangelical United Brethren. At its merging general conference, it dealt with homosexuality only in passing as part of its lengthy "Resolution on Health, Welfare and Human Development." It did not take a stand on the issue, apart from an assumed position which limited sexual intercourse to marriage. However, it did call for treatment of problems arising from homosexuality through counseling rather than through criminal prosecution.*

UNITED METHODIST CHURCH

SOCIAL PRINCIPLES (1972)

C. *Human Sexuality.*—We recognize that sexuality is a good gift of God, and we believe persons may be fully human only when that gift is acknowledged and affirmed by themselves, the church, and society. We call all persons to disciplines that lead to the fulfillment of themselves, others, and society in the stewardship of this gift. Medical, theological, and humanistic disciplines should combine in a determined effort to understand human sexuality more completely.

Although men and women are sexual beings whether or not they are married, sex between a man and a woman is to be clearly affirmed only in the marriage bond. Sex may become exploitive within as well as outside marriage. We reject all sexual expressions which damage or destroy the humanity God has given us as birthright, and we affirm only that sexual expression which enhances that same humanity, in the midst of diverse opinion as to what constitutes that enhancement. Homosexuals no less than heterosexuals are persons of sacred worth, who need the ministry and guidance of the church in their struggles for human fulfillment, as well as the spiritual and emotional care of a fellowship which enables reconciling relationships with God, with others, and with self. Further we insist that all persons are entitled to have their human and civil rights ensured, though we do not condone the practice of homosexuality and consider this practice incompatible with Christian teaching.

Notes: *In 1972, the debate on homosexuality was brought to the floor of the United Methodist Church's general conference in full force. The Board of Christian Social Concern wrote a very positive affirming statement which it hoped would become part of the church's "Social Principles." The board's effort was rejected and in a stormy session, the document was rewritten by the conference delegates. Though the debate has continued through the 1980s and into the 1990s, no proposal which attempts to alter the basic position articulated in 1972 has survived.*

The crux of the statement affirmed the general condemnation of any sex outside of marriage and specifically condemned the practice of homosexuality. While everyone can be a church member because the church believes all people have sinned, committing the sin of homosexuality does not prevent a person from joining the church. The condemnation of homosexuality, however, means that no practicing homosexual can be ordained. As worked out in later legislation and rulings by the church's judicial council, funds were to be withdrawn from any organization which advocated homosexuality, and the church was not to employ advocates of homosexuality. While the issue was essentially decided in 1972, new approaches were tried and debated at each general conference held in the 1980s.

UNITED METHODIST CHURCH

SOCIAL PRINCIPLES (1988)

F. *Human Sexuality.*—We recognize that sexuality is God's good gift to all persons. We believe persons may be fully human only when that gift is acknowledged and affirmed by themselves, the church, and society. We call all persons to the disciplined, responsible fulfillment of themselves, others, and society in the stewardship of this gift. We also recognize our limited understanding of this complex gift and encourage the medical, theological, and social science disciplines to combine in a determined effort to understand human sexuality more completely. We call the church to take the leadership role in bringing together these disciplines to address this most complex issue. Further, within the context of our understanding of this gift of God, we recognize that God challenges us to find responsible, committed, and loving forms of expression.

Although all persons are sexual beings whether or not they are married, sexual relations are only clearly affirmed in the marriage bond. Sex may become exploitative within as well as outside marriage. We reject all sexual expressions which damage or destroy the humanity God has given us as birthright, and we affirm only that sexual expression which enhances that same humanity, in the midst of diverse opinion as to what constitutes that enhancement.

We deplore all forms of the commercialization and exploitation of sex with their consequent cheapening and degradation of human personality. We call for strict enforcement of laws prohibiting the sexual exploitation or use of children by adults. We call for the establishment of adequate protective services, guidance, and counseling opportunities for children thus abused. We insist that all persons, regardless of age, gender, marital status, or sexual orientation are entitled to have their human and civil rights ensured.

We recognize the continuing need for full, positive, and factual sex education opportunities for children, youth, and adults. The church offers a unique opportunity to give quality guidance/education in this area.

Homosexual persons no less than heterosexual persons are individuals of sacred worth. All persons need the ministry and guidance of the Church in their struggles for human fulfillment, as well as the spiritual and emotional care of a fellowship which enables reconciling relationships with God, with others, and with self. Although we do not condone the practice of homosexuality and consider this practice incompatible with Christian teaching, we affirm that God's grace is available to all. We commit ourselves to be in ministry for and with all persons.

Notes: *By 1988 the statement on sexuality had evolved into the above-printed text. On the issue of homosexuality it retains all the substance and most of the wording of the decisive 1972 statement.*

UNITED METHODIST CHURCH

STUDY PROCESS ON HOMOSEXUALITY (1988)

WHEREAS, human sexuality is affirmed by the United Methodist Church as a good gift from the God of love, but a gift that can contribute both to fulfillment and to brokenness among imperfect people; and

WHEREAS, the interpretation of homosexuality has proved to be particularly troubling to conscientious Christians of differing opinion; and

WHEREAS, important biblical, theological, and scientific questions related to homosexuality remain in dispute among persons of good will; and

WHEREAS, the church possesses the resources of mind and spirit to resolve such issues reasonably and in faithfulness to the gospel it proclaims;

Therefore, be it resolved, that the General Council on Ministries be directed to conduct a study and report to the 1992 General Conference, using consultants as it deems appropriate, including persons representative of the major existing points of view on homosexuality within the church and persons well-versed in scientific and theological method. The council shall:

a. Study homosexuality as a subject for theological and ethical analysis, noting where there is consensus among biblical scholars, theologians, and ethicists and where there is not.

b. Seek the best biological, psychological, and sociological information and opinion on the nature of homosexuality, noting points at which there is a consensus among informed scientists and where there is not.

c. Explore the implications of its study for the Social Principles.

Be it further resolved, that this action become effective immediately upon the adjournment of the 1988 General Conference.

Notes: *It has been the experience of people in favor of a more positive approach to homosexuality that the church often follows studies of sexuality and homosexuality by church appointed committees with a discussion of the issues that tends to highlight the complex nature of the problem and the impossibility of simple solutions. In 1988, unable to move the United Methodist Church to any other positive action, a plan for a study of homosexuality at the general conference level was submitted and passed. That report will be issued in 1992.*

UNITED REFORMED CHURCH

TOWARDS A CHRISTIAN UNDERSTANDING OF HUMAN SEXUALITY (1984)

A great deal of your response to this section will depend on how you view the Bible. Some will take it as the ultimate authority, no detail of the teaching of which is to be questioned. If it says 'don't', it means 'don't', and that's it, for ever. Others will find its approach to sexuality narrow and unhelpful, and give it only a grudging place in their discussions. Most of us will fall between these extremes, knowing that we must take very seriously what it teaches, yet often finding this hard to interpret, and sometimes quite out of keeping with the understanding of sexuality we have reached in the late twentieth century.

So it will be no good looking for complete agreement on the meaning of a passage in the Bible from a group which contains such varying attitudes. We must also remember that some of our reactions to a subject like sexuality reveal our own fear and insecurity and have little to do with the Bible. We must learn to accept these things, no matter how strongly we hold our own point of view. We shall discover this in the Old Testament, which can seem both embarrassingly frank and explicit, and also primitive and crude. We shall discover this in specific issues raised or touched on in the whole Bible, like divorce and homosexuality.

But a good place to begin, whatever our views, is with the recognition that the Bible is asking us questions, questions about our own assumptions and values, and our attitudes towards those who hold different ones from ours. Even if we do not agree on the 'answers' it gives, we can begin by opening ourselves out to what it is asking.

There's no need to go into the passages quoted in great detail. Some are there to provide examples, others are more important, and these are in bold type. The questions are intended to provide discussion, but you may wish to ask others or pass some over.

Sexuality in the Old Testament

Begin by reading *Genesis 1:26-3:24*. Here we have two different accounts of the creation of the human race by God, and the story of Eden and the Fall. Human sexuality is part of the created nature of man and woman (*1:26-28 and 2:20b-25*).

Compare the first creation story (*1:1-2:4a, especially 1:26-28*) with the second (*2:4b-25, especially 2:20b-25*).

What differences of attitude do you note in the two stories towards the origins of sexuality? Both agree that the division of mankind into two sexes was part of God's purpose; but they give different reasons for this division. Do you respond more to the reasons given in the first or second story? Do you think sexuality is for procreation or for companionship, and do you think attitudes have changed? If you're not sure, compare the reasons given for marriage in the 1662 Book of Common Prayer with those in the *URC Book of Services* (1980) or the *Alternative Service Book* (1980).

Next, look at the roles of man and woman in the two stories. Are they different in both? Who comes first? Do you respond better to the first or second story? (*1:27; 2:21-22*).

You'll find that the idea of *nakedness* symbolizes attitudes towards sexuality in the opening chapters of Genesis: nakedness which is natural and innocent before the Fall (*2:25*) and the cause of guilt, shame and concealment after it (*3:7, 10-11*).

Look now at chapter *3*. The sin of Adam and Eve is traditionally thought of as one of disobedience, but the consequence of their sin is first the opening of their eyes so that they know that they are naked. The first act of fallen humanity is to cover its genitalia! Sexuality has become shameful, childbirth painful (*3:16*), the woman subservient to the man (same verse). At the same time, there is enmity between man and nature, and work becomes a burden (*3:14-15; 17-19*).

You may find it more helpful to approach the story of Eden and the Fall not as a tale about remote times and people, but as an imaginative recreation of a human experience still very much to the fore: a longing for a world of ease, harmony, and peace, and puzzlement at why we seem unable to reach this, and especially at why sexuality can be so wonderfully creative and so powerfully destructive at the same time.

It is hardly surprising that there are so many laws governing sexual behaviour in the Old Testament law books. The Ten Commandments have remained fundamental (*Exod. 20:1-17*): though in fact there is only one which deals explicitly with sexual behaviour (*20:14*). Otherwise, they are concerned with worship, the Sabbath, and social relationships. Do you think the seventh commandment remains valid? And is it to be interpreted in the narrow sense or a wider sense (*see Matthew 5:27-28)?*

You may like to look briefly at some of the more detailed laws, to get their 'flavour' and ask how relevant they still are—for example, Leviticus *15*:16-33; *18*:6-23; *20*:10-21; Numbers *5*:11-31.

But it is through the *people* of the Old Testament that we have our fullest picture. Here we see in flesh and blood rather than abstract laws how they behaved and how the writers understood their behaviour. We may take David and Solomon as the best examples—as they are shown in I-II Samuel and I Kings, rather than in I Chronicles, where they have been whitewashed (if you've a lot of time and enthusiasm, compare the versions of some of the stories, and see what Chronicles omits).

Read the following stories:

David and Jonathan (*1 Sam. 20, II Sam. 1:23-26*).

David and Bathsheba (*II Sam. 11-12:25*).

Solomon and his wives (*I Kings 11: 1-13*).

And think about some of these questions:

1. How can David and Solomon be such heroes of Israel when they broke the Law so consistently?
2. Some have seen a homosexual love in the relationship between David and Jonathan. Does that offend you? Why?
3. How do you react to David's behaviour in his efforts to get Bathsheba? Is the punishment in keeping with the crime?
4. Why is the writer so critical of Solomon for taking *foreign* wives? (Remember Ahab and Jezebel, I Kings 16: 29-33.)

The Old Testament seems particularly interested in the relationship between sexuality and idolatry, and often uses words like 'harlotry' or 'fornication' as a metaphor for national apostasy (*e.g. Hosea 1:2-3; 3: Ezekiel 23*).

But it is also important to see that the Old Testament contains a very positive approach to human sexuality. Nowhere is this more evident than in the Song of Solomon, a poem of great beauty and mystery celebrating the physical love of man and woman. It contains some of the most delicately erotic poetry ever written. For many centuries it has been interpreted on a spiritual level, as the lovesong of God and Israel or Christ and his Church (or Christ and the soul). It has been a source book for mystics and its influence is still present in some of the hymns we sing (e.g. *Jesu, Lover of my soul*). But it is first of all a celebration of physical beauty and love, described in a torrent of images from the natural creation. All created beauty is from God, and that includes our sexuality. We need this voice from the Old Testament to balance the rest.

At first sight, this may seem an unpromising subject. Jesus is very reticent on the subject; we have no evidence as to whether or not he was married, and Christians have tended to react with horror to suggestions that he may have had women lovers or been homosexually inclined. Yet Christian belief insists on the full humanity of Jesus Christ, which includes sexuality. You can test your own attitudes by looking at these questions:

1. Do the birth stories about Jesus (*Matt. 1:18-25, Luke 1: 5-80, especially 26-38*) show any underlying attitudes towards sexuality?
2. Does the traditional doctrine of the Virgin birth suggest a devaluing of normal sexual processes?
3. Would you agree with John Robinson (*The Human Face of God, p. 52*), when he writes: 'It seems to be questionable whether today belief in a physical virgin birth can be stated in a way that does not throw doubt on the genuineness of Jesus' humanity'?
4. If Jesus was fully human, then he must have been a sexual being and have known the power of sexual attraction. Does this idea trouble you?

Questions like these are meant to provoke reactions rather than give answers! But don't spend too long on them.

Jesus seems to have preferred the company of 'tax collectors and sinners' (*Mark 2:15-17*), and he certainly attracted a following of women, among them Mary Magdalene, traditionally thought to have been a prostitute (*Luke 8:2-3*). His sympathy with and understanding of women is seen in the encounter with the woman of Samaria (*John 4*), though his disciples express surprise at this. He also made very close relationships with men—'the disciple whom Jesus loved' features prominently in John's Gospel (*e.g. John 13:23-25; 21:20*).

A few passages in the Gospels deal directly with sexual matters, but we must not isolate these from the many passages in which Jesus speaks more generally about human behaviour and relationships, in terms of forgiveness, healing and love, as well as sinfulness and judgement.

First, look at the more obvious passages:

Matt. 5:27-31 (note that this comes in a series of teachings contrasting the old Law with the interpretation of Jesus).

Matt. 19:3-12 (parallels in *Mark 10:2-12; Luke 16:18;* and bear in mind this teaching on divorce when we look at Paul).

The sorts of questions you might like to discuss are these:

1. Do you accept this teaching?
2. What problems does accepting a 'no divorce' attitude bring, and what problems does permitting divorce bring?

3. Do you find Jesus' distinction between an inward and an outward adultery helpful? What do you think he is trying to get across?
4. Could teaching like this—or should it—be enshrined in law, either by the State or in the Church?
5. How do you interpret *Matt. 19:10-12?*

Now look at *John 7:53-8:11*, the famous story of the woman taken in adultery, a practical example of the earlier teaching. It is sometimes printed in small type or as a footnote in recent Bibles, because there is some doubt as to whether it was originally part of the Gospel. It reveals the attitude of Jesus towards the letter and the spirit of the Law. He does not refuse to carry out its strict penalty, but rather throws the responsibility for deciding what to do on the woman's accusers, and especially in the light of their knowledge of their own sexuality. The story has many nice touches—Jesus writing on the ground, the eldest accuser slinking off first. We need to focus on the dialogue Jesus has with the woman when all have left. What does the story teach us, about the attitude of Jesus, and about our own motivation?

You may want to spend some time on this, and you may find it illuminating to read *Luke 18:9-14* alongside it. The parable of the prodigal son (*Luke 15:11-32*) is also relevant, since it gives a deep insight into the Christian understanding of repentance, forgiveness, and the love of God (*verse 20*). Compare the attitude of the elder son (*verses 20-30*).

Can we draw any conclusions about Jesus' attitude towards sexuality and its expression? On most issues which concern us he said nothing directly. Perhaps that is why St. Paul had such a lot to say on the subject!

With Paul we have more of a problem. On the one hand, so much of his theology is profound and sublime; on the other hand, so many of the moral precepts he seems to derive from it as far as social behaviour (e.g. masters and slaves, men and women) and personal relationships are concerned seem to many people negative and even repressive. His attitude to sex comes over as 'don't do it unless you're married, and don't get married unless you can't contain yourselves'. Can we truthfully accept Paul's understanding of the Gospel and at the same time regard many of his ethical precepts as too conditioned by his own hang-ups and the society in which he lived? Paul would certainly not want us to divorce theology and ethics: believing and acting influence each other all the time.

So we have to ask ourselves whether we're looking at Paul for general principles with universal application, or specific cases, which in other circumstances might be dealt with differently. It is often said, for example, that Paul's attitude towards marriage is affected by his belief in the imminence of the End. Marriage will only bring more 'earthly' responsibilities and ties, when the whole earthly order is about to be swept away at the Second Coming. *I Cor. 7:26, 29* lends support to this, though its meaning is not clear.

There are two other difficulties. Sometimes Paul, because he is replying to a letter, will quote from it and then give his answers. The original manuscripts do not have our system of punctuation, and careful interpretation is need to avoid ascribing to Paul statements which may be quotations from a letter sent to him. *I Cor. 7:1* shows that this is a reply, and in some passages in some translations quotation marks are used to show where the translator thinks these statements occur (e.g. *RSV 1 Cor. 6)*. Second, we must recall that 'fornication' or similar words ('unchastity', 'immorality') can be a metaphor for idolatry. The context of *Acts 15:28-29* suggests this—'unchastity' seems to belong with eating food sacrificed to idols.

Perhaps the three most difficult areas are where Paul deals with the place of women, the issues of marriage and divorce, and homosexuality. We shall look at these in turn:

The Place of Women

I Cor, 11:2-16; Eph. 5;21-33; I Tim. 2:8-15 see also 1 Peter 3:1-7.

These passages will certainly arouse strong feelings! Some will feel that Paul is basically right—'woman's place is in the home', and the husband should make the decisions. But many more will feel that it is because of teaching like this that women have had so rough a deal.

After you've exchanged a few reactions, as honestly as you can, men as well as women, you must face up to the question 'Is this all that needs to be said about women in relation to men?' In other words, is not Paul speaking from the limitations of his culture, rather than from the essence of the Gospel, and may we not also bring our own culture's insights to this problem, notably the revaluation of women and the search for sexual equality?

Elsewhere in this study you will have a chance to think about 'the community of women and men' in the world and in the Church. But the specific teaching of Paul on the subject needs its fuller context. What, for example, do the following passages reveal?

Rom. 16:1-16; 2 Tim. 1:5; Gal. 3:27-28.

It has also often been said that Paul gave women a higher place in the Church than they had in Greek or Jewish society. If that is true, then the details of his teaching may be less important than his searching for a more adequate participation by them in the life of the Christian community.

Marriage and Divorce

Read 1 Cor. 7.

Remember what was said in the introduction to this section, and look again at the 'purpose of marriage' statement in the URC Service Book (cf. *Marriage Today,* page 17). Is our understanding of marriage the same as Paul's here?

- What elements do we stress which he does not?
- What elements does he stress which we do not?

If it helps, ask one member of the group to play Paul's part and try to persuade him that ours is a better understanding of marriage. But don't try to avoid the issues Paul raises.

On divorce, compare Paul's teaching in verses *10-16* with that of Jesus, which we have already looked at. Paul seems much less certain that divorce is wrong. The Church has tended to give greater authority to the teaching of Jesus, thus implying that some parts of the New Testament are more important than others. What factors from contemporary experience would you want to bring to Paul's attention, to persuade him to take a different line on divorce? But first make sure you understand what he is saying!

You may note an interesting distinction Paul himself makes, between teaching which carried Christ's authority and teaching Paul is giving: verse 10, *I give charge, not I, but the Lord;* verse 12, *I say, not the Lord . . . ;* verse 25, *I have no command of the Lord but I give my opinion . . . ;* and verses 39-40. He permits divorce in certain circumstances, even though the Lord does not, and he deals with issues, like the unmarried and remarriage of widows, which do not appear in the teachings of the Lord directly. The New Testament itself interprets, develops and sometimes goes against teaching given in other parts of the New Testament. The implications of this for our understanding of the Bible's authority need to be considered. Do we have the same freedom to interpret or even change, or is it restricted to within the Bible?

Finally, do you find Paul satisfactory on sex and the unmarried?

Homosexuality

This issue raises most sharply the kinds of problem we find when we turn to the Bible for specific guidance. Human sexuality is perceived as a much more complex phenomenon by those who have studied it in the twentieth century than the polarised approach the Bible usually suggests. We have come to recognise that 'masculine' and 'feminine' characteristics (as our culture sees them) are both present in a male or female person. We have been told that our sexuality is like a spectrum of responses, ranging from completely heterosexual to completely homosexual, rather than a choice between either extreme, one natural, the other unnatural. Most heterosexual people have an element of homosexuality in them, and vice versa. This is deeply disturbing to some people, and it exposes a very vulnerable area in others.

Again, you will have a chance to explore this area elsewhere. But since the Bible is always appealed to, it will be important to discuss the main texts people use to resolve the question, and these are mostly (but not wholly) in Paul.

You may have been surprised that no mention was made of the story of Sodom in the section on the Old Testament *(Gen. 12:1-29, especially verses 4-9)*. This is because whenever the story is alluded to elsewhere in the Bible, it has much more to do with the sin of inhospitality than with the sin of Sodom (*compare Judges 19:22-30*). You can check that out for yourselves by looking up 'Sodom' in a concordance. 'Sodom and Gomorrah' become symbols for wickedness in general, rather than of a very specific sin. The text in Lev. *18:22* comes in a long series of ordinances and prohibitions, and in any case raises the whole problem of how far Christians are bound by the details of the Levitical code. Can you pick out those which still seem relevant and ignore the rest? Is that a proper use of Scripture?

In fact, there is hardly anything at all about homosexuality in the Bible, and this needs to be borne in mind, to give us a sense of proportion. There is a great deal more about idolatry, hypocrisy and forgiveness. The word 'homosexual' does not actually occur in the Bible, which is hardly surprising, since it was not used at all until the last century. Even the older word 'sodomy' was used in English to describe 'unnatural' sexual acts (e.g. anal intercourse) between men and women as well as men.

The texts usually mentioned today are *Rom. 1:26-27, 1 Cor. 6:9-10,* and *I Tim. 1:10*. The first of these is the most developed and important; the Greek words used in the other texts are of a more disputed meaning. You will find a full discussion of these texts in the Anglican report (*The Church and Homosexuality*) and chapter 4 of John Boswell's scholarly *Christianity, Social Tolerance and Homosexuality*. But you needn't get stuck on detailed textual criticism unless you want to! You *will* need, though, to look at some of these questions and issues:

Each of these issues we've looked at in Paul—women in Church and society, marriage and divorce, homosexuality—raises the fundamental question of how far we allow a twentieth-century understanding to affect our approach to the Bible. That is a theological question of great practical consequence, for it asks how much the knowledge science has uncovered in the last hundred or so years about the whole range of things, from the cosmos to the tiniest particle, and including all the human sciences, has itself been a revelation of truths about God's creation. Do we interpret the world and ourselves according to every detail in the Bible, or according to what we may call its general principles? What might these 'principles' be, and how would we establish them? And are we free to interpret some of the details in the Bible by what we know about the world and ourselves which the Biblical writers did not? The next section tries to look at some of these questions.

Where does theology come from? Theologians and philosophers? God? Ourselves?

Theology is the study of the truth about God, and Christian theology of the truth about God as revealed in Jesus Christ. It's not something ready made; it needs to be worked at. But the raw materials are there, and they are, in roughly descending order of importance: the Bible; the interpretation of the Bible from the first century till our own by Christian men and women (often called Tradition: 'the Church teaches that. . . .'); human knowledge (philosophy, the sciences) and human experience (including one's own).

To look at the theology of sexuality means to try to work out what the Christian understanding of God leads us to say about the nature and purpose of our lives as sexual beings. It is not a job for experts; the very nature of the subject means we can all share in it. But neither is it a matter of personal opinion and purely subjective feelings. We need to put ourselves under the discipline of Scripture, listen to how it has been interpreted through the ages, and to what our own world and our experience of it is telling us. And at the end of all this, we have to decide, as faithfully and as honestly as we can, where it all points.

Rather than asking a lot of questions to provoke discussion, we shall outline what the possible bases are for a theology of sexuality and how these may relate to what we have been dealing with.

Christian theology is woven around three central truths, which we can summarize as Creation, Fall and Redemption. God created the universe and everything it contains, great and small, seen and unseen; and he created it good. His creating work continues. But human experience recognizes that something has gone amiss with this good creation, and that 'something' is powerfully and imaginatively explored in the story of Eden. The cause of this estrangement and exile from Paradise is mysterious, but it is to do with our knowledge and our moral responsibility. We know we are in exile from our true home because we long for a world of peace and justice and for a perfection in our relationships with one another and with nature which we can dream of but never enter. 'Redemption' gathers up all that Christ, the second Adam, the new humanity, has done for us to restore what has been lost in our Fall; to bring us back to our true home; the kingdom of God, and to bring our lives into harmony with our inmost selves, with one another and with God.

If we begin with the doctrine of creation, we learn at once that sexuality is good. Genesis contains unequivocal statements that our sexuality is both the divinely ordained means of reproducing our species, and of enriching and blessing human relationships (*1:26-31; 2:18*). To regard our sexuality as a *created gift,* not merely as a brute instinct, is to say something Christians find important and to imply that sexual behaviour is more than a bodily function. It comes to us with ethical choices to be made in our use of it.

But because 'fallenness' is part of the human condition, we are always being led into misuse of created gifts: we fill the earth and subdue it, but we also pollute it and destroy nature's balance; we harvest the good gifts of the earth, but we do not share them; we delve into the mysteries of the atom and create great sources of power but also the awesome destructiveness of the Bomb. This is true of our individual selves too. This is the territory of Christian ethics—the use of created gifts in a fallen world, by individuals and societies which share in that fallenness.

Complete acceptance and unrestrained indulgence of our sexual appetites cannot be supported, but neither can complete negation of them, as though they were so incurably evil they were best left alone. The dangers of both extremes are well known in Christian tradition, but the negative attitude has been a powerful and pervasive one. We need to see that the 'Fall' is not only evident in sexual licence but also in sexual repression and the damage this can do to the development of mature personality. The experience of our redemption in Christ means that we should be looking towards the redemption of our sexuality: a moving away from a self-centred use of it simply to gratify our instincts, or from fearing it; and a moving towards its use as a means of deepening loving relationships based on trust and commitment.

We must be careful not to use the Bible to establish the theology of sexuality in a way we would not use it to establish the doctrine of creation. We must not just look at isolated texts, but at the witness of the whole. Can we be content to say 'the Bible says pre-marital sex/ homosexuality is wrong' when we have moved beyond saying 'The Bible says the world was created in six days'? The details need to be tested against the major principles of Biblical teaching.

From the Bible we learn that the Christian Gospel is characterized by mercy, compassion, forgiveness, acceptance of all kinds of people and especially the outcast, by love; but also by judgement, outspokenness against evil (especially self-righteousness and hypocrisy). It is a Gospel of liberation from whatever is preventing our growth into mature, free and fulfilled people, and it brings us the 'measure of the stature of Christ' as our new vision of what it means to be human. Involved in this must be a process of liberation from all in our sexuality which distorts or damages us as people, and the entering into an experience of sexuality as part of our whole nature, which helps us to grow towards personal wholeness. That may mean that instead of setting up a 'normal' or 'natural' pattern of sexual attraction we must accept that each individual's sexuality works in a different way, and individuals are called to a responsible use of the sexuality which is theirs (heterosexual, bisexual, homosexual) so that their sexuality is integrated with their whole selves.

Such an approach would mean that the 'hard-line' texts we have encountered need to be understood within the broad context of Gospel principles. The argument is not about *whether* you use the Bible, but *how* you use it: do the hard-line texts on homosexuality fit the Jesus who was happier in the company of outcasts than of conformists? The Gospel stands against judging others from a position of moral superiority, and to dismiss anyone as inherently depraved is to deny the image of God in which they are created, and the redemption of a fallen humanity.

But the liberation offered by the Gospel is not separate from responsibility. It is not a permission to do what you feel like, but to act responsibly towards the rest of the created order. Especially we need in a fallen world to be constantly inspired and corrected by the vision of love we see in Jesus Christ, which moves in the direction of fulfillment, commitment and permanence, and away from selfish gratification and exploitation of others for our own pleasure. We are dealing with divine gifts, not amoral instincts.

We need to examine more closely the relationship between sexuality and its practice. Many Christian writings seem obsessed with the genital expression of our sexuality, whereas sexuality is a far wider matter than this and affects large areas of our lives without necessarily being expressed in so direct a way. We should try following Matt. 5:27-28, not to make a split between personality and actions. To begin a theology of sexuality, or any sexual ethic, by concentrating on actions which are wrong, instead of on the total meaning of sexuality in the human personality, is disastrous. It is, in theological terms, to give the Fall precedence over Creation and Redemption.

Christians are called to stand alongside those who feel they are rejected by society, and this has implications for the Church's approach to sexual minorities and to those who feel they are discriminated against. They are also called to witness to the characteristics of Christian love—trust, acceptance, fidelity, mutuality, permanence, self-giving. The love which Christ incarnates does not draw people by fear or repression, but by its own inborn attraction. We need to recover that witness to Christian love which does not first condemn and demand conformity, but which makes us want to live in a more Christlike way, and grow into fuller and maturer people, sexual beings and children of God.

Notes: *In 1984, the United Reformed Church (located in the United Kingdom) issued a lengthy study guide on human sexuality that included serious reflection on homosexuality. The guide primarily follows the lead of recent Christian thinking on the issue of sex, but does attempt to separate itself from one perception popular in recent years when it offers a very positive view of sexuality rather than the traditional negative one.*

In reality, the study does not establish a distinct perspective on homosexuality, but rather offers a perspective on sexuality from which decisions about homosexual behavior can be made. For example, it discourages prooftexting (stating a text as if its truth was self-evident) as a means of arriving at biblical opinions. It does not approve of complete sexual license. It asks Christians to support social outcasts. Without approving homosexual activity, the study guide offers a very positive approach to homosexual persons.

UNIVERSAL FELLOWSHIP OF METROPOLITAN COMMUNITY CHURCHES

HOMOSEXUALITY: WHAT THE BIBLE DOES AND DOES NOT SAY (1984)

How great is our need as individuals for a personal relationship with Christ through the church? We all face challenges of growing as a human being. Gay men and Lesbians face problems peculiar to them because of the attitudes of the society they live in, often including the churches they turn to. For all of us, a firm faith and trust in Christ can be the difference in our total adjustment to life—or lack of it.

If you look for bad things in a person or in an organization, you will probably find them. There undoubtedly are many things wrong with most of the church bodies listed in your Yellow Pages, but there are more things right than wrong. It would be well to remember that the wrong things are not a reflection on Christ or the way Christ wants the church to be, but are the products of the fallible and imperfect human beings who guide these churches. A Christian's personal faith should not depend upon a particular church or clergyperson, but rather it should be solidly based on Jesus Christ.

There may be hypocrites in the churches; that is true. You may have been deeply hurt by a particular priest's or minister's attitude toward homosexuality, but do not judge. Any time you let a hypocrite stand between you and God, the hypocrite is then closer to God than you are.

In addition to the attitude of certain ministers, the Scriptures seem to present a stumbling block for some persons who perceive themselves to be both homosexual and Christian.

Genesis 19:1-28

The Story of the Destruction of Sodom and Gomorrah

This is the Old Testament passage most often used to show that God is displeased with homosexuals. According to many people and churches, these cities were destroyed because people in these cities committed the "sin of homosexuality." But the Prophet Ezekiel in another inspired book of the Bible tells us that God was displeased with Sodom for a very different reason.

> *Behold, this was the guilt of your sister Sodom: she and her daughters had pride, surfeit of food, and prosperous ease, but did not aid the poor and needy. They were haughty, and did abominable things before me (King James: committed idolatry); therefore I removed them, when I saw it. . . . (Ezekiel 16:49-50).*

To say that Sodom and Gomorrah were destroyed for homosexuality is to misinterpret the Scriptures. The Bible says God destroyed Sodom because ten righteous people could not be found (Genesis 18:32). The use of the expression "bring these men out to us, that we may *know* them" is the basis for most of the misinterpretation; yet the Hebrew verb (to know) used here is found 943 times in the Old Testament and in only ten places does it mean sexual intercourse—and each time it refers to heterosexual relations. The people of Sodom broke the law of hospitality to strangers which was so religiously observed in their culture. In every other reference in the Bible (and there are several) the sins condemned are such things as pride and inhospitality. If homosexual behavior was involved in the destruction of Sodom, why didn't the writer use the Hebrew word *ahakabh,* which actually means homosexuality or bestiality, instead of *yadha* which means "to know?" Even if the folk of Sodom did make a "homosexual" attack upon the angels, the passage could only serve as a condemnation of rape (certainly an extreme form of inhospitality),and rape is sin under any condition, be it heterosexual or homosexual.

Another Scripture verse that is used to show that the Bible condemns the gay lifestyle is found in the Old Testament Book of Leviticus, 18:22, 'Thou shalt not lie with a man as thou would with a woman.'' Anyone who is concerned about this prohibition should read the whole chapter or the whole Book of Leviticus: No pork, no lobster, no shrimp, no oysters, no intercourse during the menstrual period, no rare meats, no eating blood, no inter-breeding of cattle, and a whole host of other laws, including the law to kill all divorced people who remarry.

As Christians, our law is from Christ. St. Paul clearly taught that Christians are no longer under the Old Law (for example in Galatians 3:23-25); that the Old Law is brought to an end in Christ (Romans 10:4); and its fulfillment is in love (Romans 13:8-10, Galatians 5:14).

The New Law of Christ is the Law of Love. Neither Jesus, nor Paul, nor any of the New Testament Scriptures implies that Christians are held to the cultic or ethical laws of the Mosaic Law. It can further be said that the Bible does not record one work spoken by Jesus about homosexuality. Jesus did affirm what it means to be male and what it means to be female. He did deal with human sexuality in an open and non-threatened manner. And He did affirm on the one hand the goodness of marriage, but He also declared marriage (between male and female) is not for all. (Matthew 19:3-12).

As Christians, we believe that the Old Testament is a divinely inspired revelation of God's Old Covenant with God's Chosen People, a relevant study of Hebrew history, and above all the story of the continuing promise of redemption, showing in all ages and in all places God's never ending love for all people.

But when you read the Bible, you must always take into consideration who is speaking, to whom it is addressed, and the purpose for which it was recorded. In order to understand any writing—whether it is the Gettysburg Address or the Bible—it is necessary to understand its context, the circumstances that brought it about, the situation to which it was applied, and the whole cultural background that it came from and was written for. For example, when the Bible says, ''increase and multiply,'' we need to remember, among other things, that this was addressed to Israel, a very small nation surrounded by enemies, and they needed to ''multiply'' just to survive. Looking at it today, we must not fail to recognize that we are under the New Covenant of Jesus Christ with its cornerstone being the two-fold commandment: *Love God, love your neighbor.*

Secondly, we must keep in mind that the Bible was written in another language (primarily Hebrew in the Old Testament and Greek in the New Testament) and was copied and recopied in the original languages, translated and perhaps interpreted by translators and copyists who were quite capable of human error.

The words used by your personal Bible will depend upon which version or translation you happen to have. There are many English translations of the Bible and each of them uses different English words to translate the passages of the New Testament that people quote to show the sinfulness of homosexuality.

For example, there are two Greek words used in the oft-quoted passages. They are *malakos* and *arsenokoitai*. These words are used in several passages by St. Paul. Neither word meant ''homosexual'' anywhere that Greek was used in the age when Paul wrote. Yet the translators have attached various ''homosexual'' meanings to these words. Scholars are still trying to agree on just what these words meant to the people Paul wrote them to. There were words in Greek for ''homosexual'' and for homosexual activity, but Paul did not select these words. (Several books and pamphlets are available which study this more extensively.)

Compare the following three translations of Romans 1:26-27.

King James:

> *For this cause God gave them up unto vile affections: for even their women did change the natural use into that which is against nature; And likewise also the men, leaving the natural use of women, burned in their lust one toward another.*

Good News for Modern Man:

Because of what men do, God has given them over to shameful passions. Even the women pervert the natural use of their sex by unnatural acts. In the same way men give up natural sexual relations with women and burn with passion for each other.

J. B. Phillips:

God therefore handed them over to disgraceful passions. Their women exchanged the normal practices of sexual intercourse for something which is abnormal and unnatural. Similarly the men, turning from natural intercourse with women, were swept into lustful passions for one another.

Which one is the closest to what was originally written? Does this passage actually condemn people who are "naturally" or "constitutionally" homosexual? It says you should not indulge in sexual behavior that is unnatural for you. It says heterosexuals should not try to become homosexuals. It says homosexuals should not try to become heterosexuals. It condemns lust, which we know is wrong for heterosexuals and homosexuals.

Father John McNeil, the Catholic scholar, says there is ample evidence that the Biblical authors probably had in mind what we would call perversion, namely, the indulgence in homosexual activity on the part of those who were by nature heterosexually inclined. It is unlikely that the Bible makes any reference at all to the genuine condition of homosexual love. True homosexuals as we know them today were seemingly quite unknown by the writers of the Bible.

Dr. Norman Pittenger, the Anglican scholar says, "For a man or woman whose sexual desire and drive is inevitably towards the same gender, acting in homosexual physical expression is in fact a way of glorifying God and opening the self to the working of the divine love in human affairs."

In Timothy 1:10, the King James version uses the word *defile*, Good News For Modern Man uses the words *sexual perverts* and the J. B. Phillips version says *sexually uncontrolled or perverted.* There are, of course, perversions of a sexual nature, but *love* certainly is not one of them, whether it is heterosexual or homosexual love.

In Corinthians 6:9, the King James version uses the words *abusers of themselves,* while Good News for Modern Man uses *homosexual perverts* and J. B. Phillips uses *the pervert.* Again, how can this be a condemnation of homosexuality per se? We will agree that there is homosexual perversion just as there is some heterosexual perversion.

In making these observations, we are not attempting to downgrade the Bible, deny its inspiration or its importance in the life of the Christian. On the contrary, we affirm that the Bible does have a lot to say to us, but that we should hear and learn what it *does* say, not what people say it says, people who have translated it, people who have interpreted it, people who are capable of making mistakes and building doctrines that the Bible *does not* teach, but which are believed by others.

Can we actually believe that a Christ who preached love, lived love (with sinners, foreigners, women, outcasts), who gave His life on a cross to show God's love for all people—can we believe a Christ of such love, who recognizes the human need for human love and its physical fulfillment, would require that legions of homosexuals either live a life of celibacy (denying their natural need for intimacy) or face damnation? Not the Christ who died for each of us!

I know, and am persuaded by the Lord Jesus, that there is nothing unclean of itself: but to the one that esteemeth any thing to be unclean, to that person it is unclean. (Romans 14:14).

Jesus Christ died for our sins, not for our sexuality, to liberate us to a new life of love in God. Neither heterosexual love nor homosexual love is sinful in itself. Sex acts only become sinful when we act in lust or in abuse of another person, abandoning the ways of love. The relationship of two women or two men can be just as loving as a relationship between a woman and a man. Christ died for the sins of both homosexual and heterosexual. Therefore, Gays and Lesbians can come to the saving grace of Jesus Christ and yet still retain their identity and the rightful expression of their sexuality.

How great is our need as individuals for a personal relationship with Christ through the church. The Universal Fellowship of Metropolitan Community Churches (UFMCC) was founded as an outreach to the Gay and Lesbian community. It has worshipping congregations across the United States and in many nations around the world. If you would like more information about the Universal Fellowship or about the subject matter of this leaflet, write to: Universal Fellowship Press, 5300 Santa Monica Blvd., Suite 304, Los Angeles, California 90029.

Notes: *The Universal Fellowship of Metropolitan Community Churches was founded in 1968 with the intention of providing a Christian church in which homosexuals would be loved and accepted. In order to exist, the church had to develop a theology which provided a positive view of homosexuality while dealing with the anti-homosexual statements in Christian scriptures and the general rejection of homosexuality in the Christian tradition. Many words have been written in pursuit of these goals, but the brief statement quoted above, published as a tract by the church, succinctly summarizes the result of its biblical work. The church reached the position that the Bible does not condemn homosexuality, merely the perversion of human relations in a homosexual context. In condemns promiscuity, inhospitality, and the misuse of sexuality (both heterosexual and homosexual).*

The Metropolitan Community Church has drawn upon a significant amount of modern biblical exegesis and other contemporary studies by scholars within the mainline Christian denominations. Many individual scholars agree with much if not all of the church's position, but the church has experienced great difficulty in finding acceptance among other Christians and its application for membership in the National Council of Churches has regularly been turned down.

WESLEYAN CHURCH

HUMAN SEXUALITY (1984)

5. *Human Sexuality.* The Wesleyan Church abhors the trend to ignore God's laws of chastity and purity, and vigorously opposes public acceptance of sexual promiscuity and all factors and practices which promote it. The Wesleyan Church maintains a biblical view of human sexuality which makes the sexual experience, within the framework of marriage, a gift of God to be enjoyed as communion of a man and woman, as well as for the purpose of procreation. Sexual relationships outside of marriage and sexual relationships between persons of the same sex are immoral and sinful. The depth of the sinfulness of homosexual practice is recognized, and yet we believe the grace of God sufficient to overcome both the practice of such activity and the perversion leading to its practice.

Notes: *This statement passed by the 1984 general conference of the Wesleyan Church follows the traditional Christian teaching on the subject.*

Jewish Groups

The traditional Jewish aversion to homosexuality is, if anything, stronger than that within Christianity. While the penalties called for in the biblical injunction (Leviticus 20:13) were reduced in the ancient Talmudic writings from death to whipping, it remained a practice which gave extreme offense. The strong prohibitions had all but driven the practice from the community, though there is every reason to believe that homosexuality continued to appear and was not acted upon.

Given the absence of any visible homosexual behavior by individuals living in the Jewish communities through most of the twentieth century, many Jewish leaders were stunned in the 1970s when Jewish homosexuals suddenly became prominent in the gay liberation movement and gay synagogues appeared in most American cities with significant Jewish population. While Orthodox and Conservative rabbis quickly reasserted their traditional beliefs about homosexual behavior, the issue presented a significant problem for Reform Jews. Reform Judaism is distinguished by its denial of Divine authority to the halakhah, *the Jewish law as codified, and subjects all expressions of the law to contemporary judgment in an attempt to distinguish its eternal expressions from its more limited temporary ones.*

In raising the question of homosexuality among Reform Jews, homosexual Jews suggested that the prohibitions against homosexuality did not bind Reform Jews, since these were part of the halakhah not currently relevant. This argument then opened the debate to consideration of all works of contemporary biblical criticism on the relevant passages from the Hebrew Bible (i.e., the Christian old Testament). In the end, the Reform Jewish organizations accepted the arguments and have admitted gay synagogues to full membership in the Union of American Hebrew Congregations and have ordained gay rabbis.

UNION OF AMERICAN HEBREW CONGREGATIONS

STATEMENT ON HOMOSEXUALITY (1969)

Homosexuality

An inevitable corollary of the sexual revolution is a questioning of the right of society to intrude upon the private behavior of consenting adults. The harsh treatment of homosexuals has recently emerged as a primary test of the morality and propriety of the law. In many parts of the world, reformers have pleaded for a more humane and modern approach to the problem of homosexuality. England has recently shifted from a legal to a medical approach, deeming homosexuality an emotional problem rather than a legal crime against society. Homosexuality is still a crime on the books of United States law, but this problem too is receiving serious study from religious leaders, social workers, psychologists, and criminologists. When a man in North Carolina was sentenced to twenty years for homosexuality, a federal judge ordered a new trial and declared: "Is it not time to redraft a criminal statute first enacted in 1533?"[10] Indeed, the homosexuals themselves have organized a pressure group, the Mattachine Society, to fight for equal rights and humane treatment, putting an end to what they regard as harassment, primitive persecution, and unjust discrimination in employment and other phases of American life.[11] They deny that their sexual lives constitute either crimes or disease; they contend that their private lives are not the business of society. To them, homosexuality is a matter of personal taste within the broad spectrum of normality.

Most psychologists, on the other hand, regard homosexuality as a profound emotional disturbance, resulting from deep psychological distortion in early childhood. Psychiatric treatment sometimes brings the patient to a normal heterosexual life; more often, perhaps, the problem is too deep, and the doctor must content himself with helping the patient to live comfortably with his own aberration. But what should be society's attitude toward such a person? Should he be condemned as a pariah, punished for his "sins", and treated as a "criminal"? Should he, for example, be precluded from sensitive employment—say, government work or teaching? Or is a punitive attitude on the part of society likely to further damage and embitter an already vulnerable human being? What is to be done? Should the laws which proscribe homosexuality as a crime be wiped off the books and relegated to the ash-heap of history along with such barbarities as heresy and witchcraft? But, if that is done, will not society be putting its approval on a long-repressed paganism and sexual license? These are tough questions; the answers are being slowly hammered out on the anvil of frank and serious public discussion.

There is no doubt where traditional Judaism stood on this issue. Judaism condemned homosexuality as an abomination. The Torah prescribed harsh legislation for sexual vices such as adultery, incest, and bestiality; homosexuality belonged in that context. The Bible declares: "If a man lie with a man as with a woman, both have committed an abomination; they shall be put to death; their blood shall be upon them."[12]

But it is doubtful that most modern Jews, including rabbis, will be content to accept so harsh an approach to so vexing a human problem. Rabbi Everett Gendler, for example, regards the Bible's insistence on regulating even the private details of a man's life as contrary to modern views of man. He has said:

> It is general categorical approach to men in general which most troubles the modern conscience, and which provokes the greatest inner resistance. The unique development in modern life has been individual liberty broadly conceived; large areas of life not regulated by any authority, areas to be determined solely by individual preference. The constant expanding of such areas which the individual must determine on the basis of his own daemon, genius, temperament, constitution or inclination; the conception that the individual must himself find the way which suits him, that path which will yield him the greatest satisfaction from life: this is uniquely modern, and is highly respected and esteemed by many as a mark of substantial human progress.[13]

An Orthodox Jewish scholar, Rabbi Norman Lamm, Professor of Philosophy at Yeshiva University, on the other hand, condemned the statement of ninety Episcopalian priests from New York that homosexual acts, like all sexual behavior, cannot be classified as right or wrong as such. He took strong exception to their statement that, "a homosexual relationship between two consenting adults should be judged by the same criteria as a heterosexual marriage—that is, whether it is intended to foster a permanent relationship of love."[14] Deploring the growing trend toward such permissive thinking in various Christian groups, Rabbi Norman Lamm wrote: "While I do not believe that homosexuality between two consenting adults should be treated as a criminal offense, to declare homosexual acts as 'morally neutral' and at times as 'a good thing' is scandalous."[15]

Rabbi Lamm continued:

> What bothers me in reading the reports in the press on the recent Episcopal conference as well as earlier papers by Swedish and British churches, is the readiness to condone and even approve, although not encourage, homosexuality on the basis of "genuine love," "fulfillment," and "happiness."
>
> . . . the exaggerated importance Christians have traditionally accorded to the term "love" and the hedonistic ethic of the contemporary Western World, have joined together to kick away whatever is left of social and religious restraint in a progressively amoral society. To aver that a homosexual relationship should be judged by the same criteria as a heterosexual one—"whether it is intended to foster a permanent relationship of love"—is to abandon the last claim of representing the Judaeo-Christian tradition.
>
> . . . Are we not justified to use a reductio ad absurdum, in using the same reasoning to sanction an adulterous relationship? Love, fulfillment, and happiness can be attained in incestuous contacts, too—and certainly in polygamous relationships. Is there nothing at all left that is "sinful," "unnatural," or "immoral" if it is practiced between "two consenting adults?"
>
> . . . Judaism began its career as the standard bearer of morality in a world which mocked it. Apparently, it is destined to carry on in the twentieth century in the same sense of isolation and—I pray—with the same sense of dedication.[16]

Rabbi Steven B. Jacobs of Miami sent a message to his congregation, urging parents who recognize symptoms of unusual behavior in their children not to shy away from contacting their doctor or clergyman. The rabbi said it is the responsibility of the church and the synagogue to bring to light the prevailing myths about the homosexual world. Two such myths, he said, are that all homosexuals are a danger to small boys and that they are all effeminate. He pointed out that many homosexuals lead effective lives and many are married. He urged a distinction in the law between behavior that is harmful to society in general or to another person in particular and behavior which harms no one. The rabbi pleaded for extending the basic protection of our laws, guaranteed in our Bill of Rights, to the minority of people who are homosexuals. He declared:

> They want to be protected against search and seizure which is unreasonable. They want protection against crimes of violence.
>
> They do not want to be put up to blackmail or held to regular shakedowns by police who may themselves be latent homosexuals. They want to be treated as citizens—and they should be.
>
> Our responsibility in the religious community is to accept every human being and enrich his life. In saving one soul, it is as if we saved the whole world.
>
> Ours is not to control and not to legislate, but to understand.[17]

What do you think? Which rabbi seems closest to Jewish teaching? Which is more humane? Whichever view one agrees with, there is no doubt that enlightened people more and more appreciate that homosexuality may be a symptom of emotional disturbance which requires sympathetic understanding and psychiatric help rather than repression.

Endnotes

10. *Newsday,* May 27, 1965
11. Mattachine Society, 1133 Broadway, New York, New York
12. Leviticus 20:13
13. *National Jewish Post and Opinion,* January 12, 1968

14. *The New York Times,* Nov. 29, 1967

15. *Jewish Life,* publication of Union of Orthodox Jewish Congregations, January, 1968

16. *Ibid.*

17. *National Post and Opinion,* May 3, 1968

Notes: *In 1968 the Union of American Hebrew Congregations, the major organization of Reform Judaism in the United States, issued a book by Albert Vorspan called* Jewish Values and Social Crisis *which sought to engage readers in the discussion of those ideas. Homosexuality was one of several issues discussed under the broad perspective of "The Family, Sex, and Law." The traditional anti-homosexual position of the Jewish community is acknowledged but other perspectives are quickly introduced. The author seems to support the decriminalization and end of repression of homosexual behavior, but also views such behavior as a matter of emotional disturbance in need of treatment.*

UNION OF AMERICAN HEBREW CONGREGATIONS

HUMAN RIGHTS OF HOMOSEXUALS (1977)

WHEREAS the UAHC has consistently supported civil rights and civil liberties for all persons, and

WHEREAS the Constitution guarantees civil rights to all individuals,

BE IT, THEREFORE, RESOLVED that homosexual persons are entitled to equal protection under the law. We oppose discrimination against homosexuals in areas of opportunity, including employment and housing. We call upon our society to see that such protection is provided in actuality.

BE IT FURTHER RESOLVED that we affirm our belief that private sexual acts between consenting adults are not the proper province of government and law enforcement agencies.

BE IT FURTHER RESOLVED that we urge congregations to conduct appropriate educational programming for youth and adults so as to provide greater understanding of the relation of Jewish values to the range of human sexuality.

Notes: *By 1977, the Union of American Hebrew Congregations had taken a major step in endorsing civil rights for homosexuals. Their position grew out of a growing conviction that private sexual acts between consenting adults should be decriminalized.*

UNION OF AMERICAN HEBREW CONGREGATIONS

SUPPORT FOR INCLUSION OF LESBIAN AND GAY JEWS (1987)

Background:

God calls upon us to love our neighbors as ourselves. The prophet Isaiah charges us further: "Let my house be called a house of prayer, for all people. . . ." (Isaiah 56:7). And, armed with the other teachings of our faith, we Jews are asked to create a society based on righteousness, the goal being *tikkun olam,* the perfection of our world. Each of us, created in God's image, has a unique talent which can contribute to that high moral purpose; and to exclude any Jew from the community of Israel lessens our chances of achieving that goal.

In consonance with these teachings, in 1977 the Union of American Hebrew Congregations resolved to support and defend the civil and human rights of homosexuals, and we have welcomed into the UAHC congregations with special outreach to lesbian and gay Jews. But we must do more.

Sexual orientation should not be a criterion for membership of or participation in an activity of any synagogue. Thus, all Jews should be welcome, however they may define themselves.

Service of lesbian and gay Jews as Rabbis is currently under consideration by the Central Conference of American Rabbis. It has appointed a Committee on Homosexuality in the Rabbinate to consider all aspects of the subject. The committee is directed to present a final report at the 1989 CCAR convention. Representatives of the UAHC and Hebrew Union College-Jewish Institute of Religion are serving on the committee.

THEREFORE, BE IT RESOLVED that the Union of American Hebrew Congregations:

1. Urge its congregations and affiliates to:
   A. Encourage lesbian and gay Jews to share and participate in the worship, leadership, and general congregational life of all synagogues.
   B. Continue to develop educational programs in the synagogue and community which promote understanding and respect for lesbians and gays.
   C. Employ people without regard to sexual orientation.
2. Urge the Commission on Social Action to bring its recommendations to the next General Assembly after considering the report of the CCAR committee and any action of the CCAR pursuant to it.
3. Recommend to the CCAR Committee on Liturgy that it develop language that is liturgically inclusive.

Notes: *In the decade following their support for civil rights for homosexuals, the Union of American Hebrew Congregations witnessed the growth of numerous "gay" Jewish synagogues and began to accept the presence of homosexual Jews. A new level of acceptance occurred in 1987 with a resolution calling male homosexual and lesbian Jews into full congregational life in the synagogues of the Union. It also urged the Central Conference of American Rabbis, the Reform Jewish rabbinical association, to follow its lead.*

UNION OF AMERICAN HEBREW CONGREGATIONS

GAY AND LESBIAN JEWS (1989)

In North America today, it is estimated that 100,000 Reform Jews and 500,000 members of the larger Jewish community—are gay or lesbians.

Over the last fifteen years, the UAHC has admitted to membership four synagogues with an outreach to gay and lesbian Jews. Hundreds of men and women who once felt themselves alienated from Judaism and unwelcome in mainstream congregations have joined these synagogues, adding their strength and commitment to our religious community.

In 1977, the UAHC General Assembly called for an end to discrimination against homosexuals, and expanded upon this in 1987 by calling for the full inclusion of gay and lesbian Jews in all aspects of synagogue life.

While that resolution urged that congregations not discriminate in employment, it did not address rabbinic employment, pending the report of the CCAR *ad hoc* Committee on Homosexuality and the Rabbinate. The CCAR committee continues its work, and we eagerly await its report.

Within the larger context of UAHC congregational life, however, we have yet to shed the destructive anti-gay and anti-lesbian prejudices and stereotypes that preclude a genuine embrace of the heart.

Our union of congregations must be a place where loneliness and suffering and exile end, where gay and lesbian Jews can know that they are accepted on terms of visibility, not invisibility; that we place no limits on their communal or spiritual aspirations.

BE IT RESOLVED THAT:

1. The Union of American Hebrew Congregations reaffirm its 1987 resolution and call upon all departments of the UAHC and our member congregations to fully implement its provisions.
2. The Union of American Hebrew Congregations embark upon a movement-wide program of heightened awareness and education, to achieve the fuller acceptance of gay and lesbian Jews in our midst.
3. We urge our member congregations to welcome gay and lesbian Jews to membership, as singles, couples, and families.
4. The Union of American Hebrew Congregations commend the CCAR for its sensitive and thorough efforts to raise the consciousness of the rabbinate regarding homosexuality. We urge the CCAR to pursue its own mandate with vigor and complete its tasks as soon as possible in order to respond to the communal and spiritual aspirations of gay and lesbian Jews.

Notes: *By 1989, the Union of American Hebrew Congregations moved to implement its 1987 resolution welcoming homosexuals into its life. There were several predominantly homosexual synagogues and homosexual rabbis that had already been ordained. This resolution aimed to keep the issue alive so that traditional anti-homosexual attitudes, still prominent in the union's membership, would not stop the process of integrating homosexual Jews into the total life of the union.*

Other Religious Bodies

Outside of the mainstream Christian and Jewish groups, the response to the emerging gay community has varied tremendously. The Church of Jesus Christ of Latter-day Saints has an extremely strong emphasis upon the family based on its earlier practice of polygamy, and thus homosexuality has no place in officially sanctioned Latter-day life. On the other extreme, the very liberal and socially active Unitarian Universalist Association has taken up the cause of the gay community and actively supported it at all levels of church life. In the middle, but leaning toward the conservative side, Islam generally prohibits homosexual behavior, but the American community has written little on the topic except to include it in lists of practices indicative of the decay of western society. Buddhists and Humanists tend to be in the more liberal camp. The Humanist Manifesto does not mention homosexuality, but calls for individuals to be able "to express their sexual proclivities and pursue their life-styles as they desire."

Possibly the most radical group of all is the Gay and Lesbian Atheists, who not only attack and attempt to change traditional religious prohibitions against homosexual behavior, but oppose all organized religion as the primary source of social hostility against gays and lesbians.

AMERICAN HUMANIST ASSOCIATION

HUMANIST MANIFESTO II (1973)

Sixth: In the area of sexuality, we believe that intolerant attitudes, often cultivated by orthodox religions and puritanical cultures, unduly repress sexual conduct. The right to birth control, abortion, and divorce should be recognized. While we do not approve of exploitive, denigrating forms of sexual expression, neither do we wish to prohibit, by law or social sanction, sexual behavior between consenting adults. The many varieties of sexual exploration should not in themselves be considered "evil." Without countenancing mindless permissiveness or unbridled promiscuity, a civilized society should be a *tolerant* one. Short of harming others or compelling them to do likewise, individuals should be permitted to express their sexual proclivities and pursue their life-styles as they desire. We wish to cultivate the development of a responsible attitude toward sexuality, in which humans are not exploited as sexual objects, and in which intimacy, sensitivity, respect, and honesty in interpersonal relations are encouraged. Moral education for children and adults is an important way of developing awareness and sexual maturity.

Eleventh: The principle of moral equality must be furthered through elimination of all discrimination based upon race, religion, sex, age, or national origin. This means equality of opportunity and recognition of talent and merit. Individuals should be encouraged to contribute to their own betterment. If unable, then society should provide means to satisfy their basic economic, health, and cultural needs, including, wherever resources make possible, a minimum guaranteed annual income. We are concerned for the welfare of the aged, the infirm, the disadvantaged, and also for the outcasts—the mentally retarded, abandoned or abused children, the handicapped, prisoners, and addicts—for *all* who are neglected or ignored by society. Practicing humanists should make it their vocation to humanize personal relations.

Notes: *The second Humanist Manifesto, issued in 1973, does not mention homosexuality directly. However, in paragraphs six and eleven quoted above, the group places itself squarely behind the rights of homosexuals to express their sexual preferences as long as it does not harm anyone. The Humanists are against what is termed ''unbridled promiscuity,'' which would seemingly set them against one popular expression of homosexuality as it has developed in the bar and bath house subculture.*

CHURCH OF JESUS CHRIST OF LATTER-DAY SAINTS

STATEMENT ON HOMOSEXUALITY (1982)

Standing High Council Statement on Homosexuality

Since the adoption by the Standing High Council of the memorandum entitled, ''Homosexuality and Other Sexual Perversions,'' (October 18, 1962), there has been a profusion of social, psychological, and medical studies pertaining to the issue of homosexuality, and with it has come debate, reflection, and confrontation, both within and outside the church. Other denominational bodies, through special task forces and in their legislative assemblies, have in recent years attempted to address this pressing problem which exists among many of their members, families, and friends. The church feels under obligation today to restate its position on homosexuality for the guidance of administrative officials, and out of a genuine concern that a responsible, reconciling ministry be developed in relation to this difficult problem.

In June 1978, the First Presidency appointed a Human Sexuality Committee composed of representatives of professional disciplines and World Church divisions and quorums. This committee was charged with the task of exploring the area of human sexuality and recommending to the First Presidency ways in which the church can be ministerially responsible and responsive in this aspect of human life. Two years later the Human Sexuality Committee forwarded its final comprehensive report to the First Presidency. It contained formal papers which explored a wide range of issues and problems in the vital area of human sexuality, and concluded with affirmations and recommendations which it hoped would aid the church in developing an ethical and theological framework to strengthen the teaching of the church in matters of sexual behavior.[1] Subsequently, the church convened a task force to continue the process of developing and sharing insights in this area.

One of the aspects of human sexuality which the task force studied with a view to making recommendations to the church was the subject of homosexuality. The concern of the church is to provide ministries and develop the kinds of values that will lead to better understanding concerning homosexuality and encourage a regard for justice and a respect for dignity which both the church and society owe to all human beings.

While we seek always to keep faith with the moral perceptions of the restored gospel, we recognize that theology is dynamic and needs to be interpreted in light of changing cultures and times. Nevertheless, a position statement on this issue will likely produce tension and controversy on several bases—strongly held traditional attitudes, varying interpretations of scripture, insufficiency of our present knowledge, and the present inadequacies of the church's ministries in helping members understand the meaning of sexuality in human relationships. These, among others, are reasons why judgments about homosexuality are, of necessity, open to further review.

We call attention to the statement on homosexuality as printed in the *Leader's Handbook*, copyright 1980, 1981. "The church leadership continues to explore ways and means of ministering to homosexuals. The emphasis should be placed upon Christian values in all sexual behavior. An attitude of love and understanding should affirm the worth of every person."

The purpose of the present document is to update our understanding of current scientific data, address ethical implications, and make recommendations which will be helpful in assisting church administrators in dealing with the condition and activity of homosexuality.

Current Scientific Data

Although there are many theories, there is still little agreement as to the roles which genetic, glandular, cultural, or psychological factors play in the cause or origin of sexual orientation. In regard to homosexual orientation, all available evidence points to this being an extremely complicated phenomenon for which there seem to be multiple causitive factors. Among these may be an inherited predisposition, or an inappropriate identification with the parent of the opposite sex. Cultural overemphasis on the stereotypes of "masculinity" and "femininity" producing feelings of inadequacy in those not able to fulfill these expectations, and a rigid dichotomy of male and female social roles with no allowance for any variation in personality development also are cited as possible contributing factors.[2]

Scriptural and Ethical Considerations

While the sacred writings of the scriptures provide us with insights into the pattern of God's redemptive and reconciling activity in all ages, they rarely provide final or complete answers. Effective preaching and teaching must always include interpretation relative to changing times and cultures. While the basic witness of scripture holds true for all time, virtually all aspects of humankind's relationship with God, including sexuality, are related to the cultural norms and traditions of the times. For example, it is not possible to interpret correctly the Leviticus Holiness Code without taking into account its historically conditioned context; many scholars suggest that the specific sexual prohibitions are related more to idolatry and other practices of the pagan populations around the Hebrews, rather than to intrinsic deviations.

Any adequate Christian position on homosexuality must regard the authority of scripture. The biblical passages primarily cited in relation to this issue are Genesis 19, Leviticus 18:22, and 20:13, Romans 1:18-32, I Corinthians 6:9, and I Timothy 1:10. All of these indicate that heterosexual relationships are part of God's plan for humankind. Nowhere do any scriptures offer support for or condone homosexual relationships. Our understanding of scriptures affirms that heterosexual marriage is God's will for men and for women. The teachings of Jesus also are clear with respect to marriage—he affirmed heterosexual marriage to be God's original and enduring will for men and women. Specific references to homosexuality are lacking in either the *Book of Mormon* or the *Doctrine and Covenants*.

The principles of the gospel apply equally to heterosexuals and homosexuals. Repentance implies the act of being personally responsible for choices; Christian freedom never allows one to live as he or she selfishly pleases. The love of God and the evidence of Christ's earthly ministry always make a distinction between the sin and the sinner. The power of the Holy Spirit constantly seeks to free each individual from acts of disobedience and alienation.

In summary, the issue of homosexuality is demanding increased attention in Western society today. Though the church is faced with changing attitudes about the existence and expression of homosexuality, it continues to hold to the norm of heterosexuality and exclusively sanctions heterosexual marriage. In doing so, the church recognizes that homosexual Christians and heterosexual Christians are all brothers and sisters and share in common the love and grace of God. In addition, the church is aware that anti-homosexual bias has long existed in Western cultures in general, and that homosexuals have been and still are denied social justice.

In light of the preceding, the following guidelines should be noted by administrative officials in carrying out the teachings of the church and performing ministry involving cases of homosexuality.

1. The church recognizes that there is a difference between homosexual orientation and homosexual activity (defined as sexual acts between persons of the same sex). The former is accepted as a condition over which a person may have little or no control; the latter is considered immoral and cannot be condoned by the church.
2. The church affirms that Christian marriage is a sacred covenant relationship, ordained of God between a man and a woman. The sacrament of marriage has a long theological and ecclesiastical history, and the symbolism is exclusively heterosexual. Homosexual unions are not and should not be considered marriages in the sacramental sense.
3. The church affirms the worth of all persons. Homosexuals as well as heterosexuals are children of God and have full claim upon the acceptance and reconciling ministry and care of the church. That is, individuals with a homosexual orientation who refrain from homosexual acts should be fully accepted into the ongoing life of the congregation. Those persons who engage in homosexual acts should be dealt with in terms of redemptive ministry and/or church law procedures in the same way as those who engage in heterosexual acts outside of marriage.
4. In the critical matter of ordination, the church should not admit a practicing homosexual to the priesthood. It cannot sanction homosexual acts as morally acceptable behavior any more than it can endorse heterosexual promiscuity. If a member of the priesthood admits to, or is found to be engaged in homosexual behavior, the administrative officer having jurisdiction should institute procedures for silencing according to church law.
5. There will be instances in which those in leadership positions will become aware of individuals who are non-practicing homosexuals and who are seeking help in the area of sublimating their sexual impulses. For such persons, the possibility and opportunity for ordination should be kept open.

Endnotes

[1] These affirmations were published in the *Saints Herald* for March 1, 1981 in the first of six articles dealing with a review of the work of the Human Sexuality Committee.

[2] The label of homosexuality is often misunderstood. The word ''homosexuality'' denotes a condition, a state of affairs; it does not denote a course of conduct. A distinction must, therefore, always be made between homosexual orientation and homosexual activity, between the categories of ''being'' and ''doing.''

Notes: *The Church of Jesus Christ of Latter-day Saints has been known for its very conservative view of sex outside of marriage, a view which at one time served as the foundation for its advocacy of polygamy. Having abandoned polygamy in this century, the church has continued a strong program built around the family. Practicing homosexuals fall under the same general category of others who engage in sex outside of marriage. They are people to be loved and engaged in a redemptive ministry. Practicing homosexuals are not to be admitted to the priesthood, a major step in the life of every male member of the church.*

GAY AND LESBIAN ATHEISTS

PREAMBLE TO THE CONSTITUTION (1978)

Because Atheism recognizes the supremacy of reason, and bases its ethics on the experience of living, independent of any arbitrary authority, creed, dogma or ritual; and

Because the primary source of hostility against Lesbians and Gay males has been organized religion, resulting in:

—an irrational hatred and suppression of same-sex affectional and sexual preferences, which, when unfettered by dogma, are natural, beautiful and healthy expressions of love, which should be encouraged rather than discouraged; and

—the harassment and incarceration by governments of Lesbians and Gay males; and

—denial to Lesbians and Gay males of the right to equal access to government programs, which they are compelled to support; and

—discrimination against Lesbians and Gay males in jobs, housing, and public accommodations; and

Because, in spite of religion's longstanding practice of suppressing same-sex affectional and sexual preference, many Lesbians and Gay males, reluctant to interpret the world rationally, have felt compelled by the pervasive and irrational forces of religion to form their own religious groups, loosely based upon the established religious organizations, but which change the religious dogma so that ancient myths and teachings, which are clearly anti-Lesbian and anti-Gay male, are ignored, while the remainder of the myths and teachings are adhered to;

We hereby adopt this constitution of the GAY ATHEISTS LEAGUE OF AMERICA with the following purposes:

1. To provide a forum where Lesbian and Gay male Atheists can meet, and can exchange and disseminate ideas;
2. To counterbalance the predominance, within the Lesbian and Gay male movement, of religiously-oriented organizations;
3. To work toward the complete separation of church and state, and, in particular, to oppose the influence of religious conditioning, and the tax-free institutions which support such conditioning, on legislators, judges, and law enforcement agents when they pass, interpret and enforce the laws that affect the lives of Lesbians and Gay males;
4. To promote a positive image of Lesbians and Gay males, and of the virtues of Atheism as a philosophical stance of freedom from the mind-control of religion, a stance that holds that women and men can be ethical without the influence and intervention of superstition.

Notes: *Gay and Lesbian Atheists (previously the Gay Atheist League of America) was organized in San Francisco in the late 1970s. It shares a hostility to organized religion, especially Christianity, with the larger atheist community, but specifically champions the cause of gay and lesbian people (who it feels are negatively affected by the mind control policies of traditional religious institutions). It opposes the ability of religious organizations to influence the government with what it sees as superstitious religious dogma.*

UNITARIAN UNIVERSALIST ASSOCIATION

DISCRIMINATION AGAINST HOMOSEXUALS AND BISEXUALS (1970)

RECOGNIZING THAT:

1. A significant minority in this country are either homosexual or bisexual in their feelings and/or behavior;

2. Homosexuality has been the target of severe discrimination by society and in particular by the police and other arms of government;
3. A growing number of authorities on the subject now see homosexuality as an inevitable sociological phenomenon and not as a mental illness;
4. There are Unitarian Universalists, clergy and laity, who are homosexuals or bisexuals;

THEREFORE BE IT RESOLVED: That the 1970 General Assembly of the Unitarian Universalist Association:

1. Urges all people immediately to bring an end to all discrimination against homosexuals, homosexuality, bisexuals, and bisexuality, with specific immediate attention to the following issues:
   a. private consensual behavior between persons over the age of consent shall be the business only of those persons and not subject to legal regulations;
   b. a person's sexual orientation of practice shall not be a factor in the granting or renewing of federal security clearance, visas, and the granting of citizenship or employment;
2. Calls upon the UUA and its member churches, fellowships, and organizations immediately to end all discrimination against homosexuals in employment practices, expending special effort to assist homosexuals to find employment in our midst consistent with their abilities and desires;
3. Urges all churches and fellowships, in keeping with our changing social patterns, to initiate meaningful programs of sex education aimed at providing a more open and healthier understanding of sexuality in all parts of the United States and Canada, and with the particular aim to end all discrimination against homosexuals and bisexuals.

Notes: *The Unitarian Universalist Association, having distanced itself from the Christian tradition, had neither biblical injunctions nor tradition to prevent the reworking of its stance on homosexuality once the issue was raised in the late 1960s. This statement is one of the first of several actions it would take to support both complete decriminalization of homosexual behavior between consenting adults and opening the church's fellowship to homosexuals at all levels.*

UNITARIAN UNIVERSALIST ASSOCIATION

CREATION OF AN OFFICE OF GAY AFFAIRS (1973)

WHEREAS, it is among the purposes of the Unitarian Universalist Association to affirm, defend and promote the supreme worth of every human personality; and

WHEREAS, the 1970 General Assembly passed a resolution urging all peoples immediately to bring an end to all discrimination against homosexuals, homosexuality, bisexuals and bisexuality; and

WHEREAS, the Association since then has established no mechanism by which this resolution might be implemented within our churches, fellowships and denominationally related organizations; and

WHEREAS, second class status keeps all oppressed minorities disabled and robs everyone of their potential contributions;

NOW THEREFORE BE IT RESOLVED: That the 1973 General Assembly urges the Board of Trustees of the UUA to create at the denominational headquarters an Office on Gay Affairs. The Office shall be staffed by Gay people and it shall have the full benefit of the experience, talent and status of the UUA in developing sources of funding outside the denominational budget. Should such sources be unavailable, the UUA will not be further responsible for funding the Office.

BE IT FURTHER RESOLVED: That the functions of the Office be a resource to the denomination at all levels in all matters pertaining to Gay people and the Gay community. The office shall initially make a 30-day study of the immediate needs of Gay Unitarian Universalists and ways of developing an outreach into the Gay community. Results of the study shall be distributed to all churches, fellowships and denominationally-related bodies with recommendations for implementation.

Notes: *In 1973, due to the continuance of both a public and church concern with homosexuality, the association moved to establish an office to provide resources and guidance on issues of homosexuality.*

UNITARIAN UNIVERSALIST ASSOCIATION

OFFICE OF GAY CONCERNS (1974)

WHEREAS, the General Assembly 1973 voted as a business resolution to urge the UUA Board of Trustees to create at the denominational headquarters an Office of Gay Concerns; and

WHEREAS, money was not available for the Office and the full benefit of the experience, talent, and status of the UUA to seek sources of funding outside the then denominational budget was urged by the General Assembly and in its resolution; and

WHEREAS, a $600,000 grant of which $300,000 is in unrestricted program funds has since come to the denomination above the basic budget approved by the 1973 General Assembly and yet the Office has not been included in the items approved for funding from that grant;

THEREFORE BE IT RESOLVED: That the UUA Board be urged to include in the Grants Section of the 1974-75 UUA Budget an item for $38,500 to establish the Office of Gay Concerns, such funds to take precedence over two items presently listed in the Grants Section: $24,000 from the Research Program and $14,500 from the Publicity and Television/Radio item; and

FURTHER RESOLVED: That such Office be established in accordance with the proposal developed by the UUA Board and Administration in consultation with the UUA Gay Caucus' Advisory Committee and as revised by the UUA Board at its meeting on June 24, 1974.

Notes: *In 1974 the Unitarian Universalist Association funded its Office of Gay Concerns which had been established the previous year (when it was called the Office of Gay Affairs).*

UNITARIAN UNIVERSALIST ASSOCIATION

OFFICE OF GAY CONCERNS (1975)

WHEREAS, the 1973 and 1974 General Assemblies have voted to establish the Office of Gay Concerns as an integral part of the UUA to serve the needs of our churches and fellowships for education and help on gay concerns; and

WHEREAS, the Office of Gay Concerns is funded from special grant funds outside the regular operating budget of the UUA; and

WHEREAS, the Office staff has had less than one-half year to function and cannot be fairly evaluated in terms of articulating a program based on the approval model of the Office;

BE IT RESOLVED: That the 1975 General Assembly:

1. Commends the Board of Trustees for its action of October 12, 1974 in implementing the General Assembly's resolution to fund the Office of Gay Concerns; and
2. Endorses the action of the Board of Trustees in including continued funding for the Office of Gay Concerns in the grants section of the proposed UUA budget for 1975-76.

Notes: *In 1975, the Unitarian Universalist Association voted to support and encourage its fledgling office of Gay Concerns.*

UNITARIAN UNIVERSALIST ASSOCIATION

GAY HUMAN RIGHTS (1977)

WHEREAS, the bigotry and misinformation presented by the forces of the "Save Our Children" movement led by Anita Bryant encourage violations of the civil rights of gay people; and

WHEREAS, human rights are not an issue on which there should be a vote by which the majority can deny rights to a minority; and

WHEREAS, the false propaganda using a religious basis for persecution strikes at the very foundation of the basic tenet of the Unitarian Universalist Association, to seek the truth and support the worth of all humans;

THEREFORE BE IT RESOLVED: That the General Assembly of the Unitarian Universalist Association calls on all Unitarian Universalists to use their efforts in stopping such biased persecution and intolerance for the gay minority.

Notes: *In response to the anti-homosexual crusade led by singer Anita Bryant and supported primarily by conservative Christians, the association restated its position for full civil rights for homosexuals. Due to this statement and previous mandates, the association's Office of Gay Concerns continued to encourage full acceptance of homosexuals in the association and to make members aware of civil rights issues in the public sphere.*

UNITARIAN UNIVERSALIST ASSOCIATION

MINISTERIAL EMPLOYMENT OPPORTUNITIES (1980)

WHEREAS, the General Assembly of the Unitarian Universalist Association in 1970 passed a resolution calling on the UUA and its member churches, fellowships, and organizations to end discrimination against gay, lesbian, and bisexual persons in employment; and

WHEREAS, the UUA has distinguished itself by its repeated support of the employment rights of minority groups; and

WHEREAS, many of the UUA member societies which have considered openly gay, lesbian, and bisexual candidates have been unwilling to accept the candidates because of their sexual orientations; and

WHEREAS, the hiring of religious leaders by Unitarian Universalist member societies is a matter of local conscience;

BE IT RESOLVED: That the 1980 General Assembly of the Unitarian Universalist Association urge the UUA and its member churches, fellowships and organizations to renew their commitment to end discrimination against gay, lesbian, and bisexual persons through educational programs at the local, district, and continental levels and calls upon the Unitarian Universalist Ministers Association and the UUA Department of Ministerial and Congregational Services to lend full assistance in the settlement of qualified openly gay, lesbian, and bisexual religious leaders.

Notes: *Like women, homosexuals have found it difficult to find employment in church groups which have approved their ordination to the ministry. This resolution raises that issue and calls upon congregations to provide pastoral positions in which homosexuals will be welcome.*

UNITARIAN UNIVERSALIST ASSOCIATION

GAY AND LESBIAN SERVICES OF UNION (1984)

WHEREAS, the Unitarian Universalist Association has repeatedly taken stands to affirm the rights of gay and lesbian persons over the past decade; and

WHEREAS, legal marriages are currently denied gay and lesbian couples by state and provincial governments of North America; and

WHEREAS, freedom of the pulpit is an historic tradition in Unitarian Universalist societies;

BE IT RESOLVED: That the 1984 General Assembly of the Unitarian Universalist Association:

1. Affirms the growing practice of some of its ministers of conducting services of union of gay and lesbian couples and urges member societies to support their ministers in this important aspect of our movement's ministry to the gay and lesbian community; and
2. Requests that the Department of Ministerial and Congregational Services:
   a. distribute this information to Unitarian Universalist religious professionals and member societies;
   b. develop printed material for ministers to assist them in planning and conducting services of union for gay and lesbian couples;
   c. develop a pamphlet intended for laypersons which describes services of union for gay and lesbian couples and is distributed to member societies.

Notes: *In the United States, marriage is regulated by the state; a legal marriage cannot be instituted without a marriage certificate. Because no state issues marriage certificates for homosexual couples, homosexual marriages are not possible. However, in an attempt to bless "marriage-like" relationships between male homosexual and lesbian couples, some churches offer a service of recognition in which vows similar to wedding vows are made in a public setting. The Unitarian Universalist Association gave official approval to such services of union in 1984.*

Acknowledgments

"Homosexuality: What the Bible Does and Does Not Say." Reprinted with permission of the Universal Fellowship Press; Los Angeles, CA.

"Principles to Guide Confessors in Questions of Homosexuality." Reprinted with permission of the U.S. Catholic Conference. (copyright © 1973 by the United States Catholic Conference; Washington, D.C.).

"Statement on Homosexuality." Reprinted with permission of the author, from *Jewish Values and Social Crisis*, pp. 217-221.

"Your View of Sex—What Difference Does it Make?" Reprinted with permission of the Watchtower Bible and Tract Society of New York, Inc., from *True Peace and Security—From What Source?*

Index to Organizations, Statements, and Subjects

Citations in this index refer to page numbers; page numbers rendered in boldface after an organization name indicate the location of that organization's statement(s) within the main text.